A PEOPLE'S HISTORY OF CHRISTIANITY
MEDIEVAL CHRISTIANITY

A PEOPLE'S HISTORY OF CHRISTIANITY

Denis R. Janz
General Editor

Volume 1
CHRISTIAN ORIGINS
Richard Horsley, editor

Volume 2
LATE ANCIENT CHRISTIANITY
Virginia Burrus, editor

Volume 3
BYZANTINE CHRISTIANITY
Derek Krueger, editor

Volume 4
MEDIEVAL CHRISTIANITY
Daniel E. Bornstein, editor

Volume 5
REFORMATION CHRISTIANITY
Peter Matheson, editor

Volume 6
MODERN CHRISTIANITY TO 1900
Amanda Porterfield, editor

Volume 7
TWENTIETH-CENTURY GLOBAL CHRISTIANITY
Mary Farrell Bednarowski, editor

A PEOPLE'S HISTORY OF CHRISTIANITY

Volume 4

MEDIEVAL CHRISTIANITY

DANIEL E. BORNSTEIN

Editor

FORTRESS PRESS

Minneapolis

MEDIEVAL CHRISTIANITY
A People's History of Christianity, Volume 4

Cover image: *Portrait of an Elderly Woman*, Hans Memling (1425/40–1494).
    Photo: © Erich Lessing / Art Resource, N.Y.
Cover design: Laurie Ingram
Book design: James Korsmo
Editorial and typesetting services: Trio Bookworks

Further materials on this volume and the entire series can be found online at www.peopleshistoryofchristianity.com.

ISBN 978-0-8006-9722-8

The Library of Congress cataloged the hardcover edition as follows:

Library of Congress Cataloging-in-Publication Data

Medieval Christianity / edited by Daniel E. Bornstein.
    p. cm. — (People's history of Christianity ; v. 4)
  Includes bibliographical references and index.
  ISBN 978–0–8006–3414–8 (alk. paper)
  1. Church history—Middle Ages, 600–1500. I. Bornstein, Daniel Ethan, 1950–
BR162.3.M43 2009
270.3—dc22
2008039744

The paper used in this publication meets the minimum requirements of American National Standard for Information Sciences—Permanence of Paper for Printed Library Materials, ANSI Z329.48-1984.

Manufactured in Canada
14   13   12   11   10   1   2   3   4   5   6   7   8   9   10

CONTENTS

CONTRIBUTORS

Daniel E. Bornstein is Professor of History and Religious Studies at Washington University in St. Louis, where he holds the Stella K. Darrow Chair in Catholic Studies. A specialist in the religious culture of medieval Italy, he is the author of *The Bianchi of 1399: Popular Devotion in Late Medieval Italy* and a score of articles on female sanctity, parish priests, lay confraternities, and other topics. He edited and translated *Dino Compagni's Chronicle of Florence* and Bartolomea Riccoboni's *Life and Death in a Venetian Convent: The Chronicle and Necrology of Corpus Domini, 1395–1436*, and coedited (with Roberto Rusconi) *Women and Religion in Medieval and Renaissance Italy*.

Gary Dickson is an Honorary Fellow in the School of History, Classics, and Archaeology, University of Edinburgh, where he was Reader in History until his recent retirement. Some of his many essays on medieval religious movements and popular devotion have been collected in the volume *Religious Enthusiasm in the Medieval West: Revivals, Crusades, Saints*. His most recent contribution is "Revivalism and Populism in the Franciscan Observance of the Late Quattrocento," *Studies in Church History* 44 (2008). His latest book, *The Children's Crusade: Medieval History, Modern Mythistory*, clarifies the history of the Children's Crusade of 1212 and explores the way that dramatic event has been reimagined by writers from the thirteenth century to the late twentieth.

Bonnie Effros is Professor of History at Binghamton University, State University of New York. Her publications on the religious and cultural history of Merovingian Gaul include *Merovingian Mortuary Archaeology and the Making of the Early Middle Ages; Caring for Body and Soul: Burial and the Afterlife in the Merovingian World;* and *Creating Community with Food and Drink in Merovingian Gaul.* In 2005–2006 she was named the Archaeological Institute of America's Forsyth Lecturer.

Katherine L. French is Professor of History at the State University of New York at New Paltz. She is the author of two books, *The People of the Parish: Community Life in a Late Medieval English Diocese* and *The Good Women of the Parish: Gender and Religion after the Black Death.* She is coeditor (with Allyson M. Poska) of the *The Parish in English Life: 1400–1600,* and coauthor of *Women and Gender in the Western Past,* a two-volume survey of the history of women from prehistoric times to the present.

Yitzhak Hen is Professor of History at Ben-Gurion University of the Negev. A specialist in the social, cultural, and religious history of early medieval Europe, and in particular early medieval liturgy, he is the author of *Culture and Religion in Merovingian Gaul, A.D. 481–751; The Sacramentary of Echternach; The Royal Patronage of Liturgy in Frankish Gaul to the Death of Charles the Bald (877);* and *Roman Barbarians: The Royal Court and Culture in the Early Medieval West.* He coedited (with Matthew Innes) *The Uses of the Past in the Early Middle Ages* and (with Rob Meens) *The Bobbio Missal: Liturgy and Religious Culture in Merovingian Gaul* and is the general editor of the series Cultural Encounters in Late Antiquity and the Middle Ages (Brepols).

Richard Kieckhefer is Professor of Religion and History at Northwestern University. His research focuses on late medieval religious culture, including mystical theology, magic, witchcraft, and church architecture in relationship to parish religion. A Fellow of the Medieval Academy of America and former president of the American Society of Church History, he is the author of *European Witch Trials: Their*

Foundations in Popular and Learned Culture, 1300–1500; Repression of Heresy in Medieval Germany; Unquiet Souls: Fourteenth-Century Saints and Their Religious Milieu; Magic in the Middle Ages; Forbidden Rites: A Necromancer's Manual of the Fifteenth Century; and Theology in Stone: Church Architecture from Byzantium to Berkeley.

Grado G. Merlo is Professor of the History of the Medieval Church and of Heretical Movements at the Università degli studi di Milano, as well as president of the Società internazionale di studi francescani. His books on orthodox and heterodox medieval religion include *Eretici e inquisitori nella società piemontese del Trecento; Valdesi e valdismi medievali; Tra eremo e città: Studi su Francesco d'Assisi e sul francescanesimo medievale; Intorno a frate Francesco; Eretici ed eresie medievali; Contro gli eretici; and Nel nome di san Francesco: Storia dei frati minori e del francescanesimo sino agli inizi del XVI secolo.*

Teofilo F. Ruiz is Professor of History at the University of California at Los Angeles. His many publications on medieval Spain include *Sociedad y poder real en Castilla; The City and the Realm: Burgos and Castile in the Late Middle Ages; Spanish Society, 1400–1600; From Heaven to Earth: The Reordering of Castilian Society, 1150–1350; and Spain's Centuries of Crisis: 1300–1474.* His *Crisis and Continuity: Land and Town in Late Medieval Castile* won the 1995 Premio del Rey, the American Historical Association's biennial award for the best book on Spanish history. In 1994, the Carnegie Foundation named him Outstanding Master's Universities and Colleges Professor of the Year. He was also awarded a Guggenheim Fellowship in 2007–2008.

Roberto Rusconi is Professor of Church History in the Dipartimento di Studi Storici Geografici Antropologici at the Università degli studi di Roma-Tre. A specialist in late medieval preaching, confession, sanctity, prophecy, and apocalyptic thought, he is the author of *L'attesa della fine: Crisi della società, profezia ed Apocalisse in Italia al tempo del grande scisma d'Occidente (1378–1417); Profezia e profeti alla fine del Medioevo; L'ordine dei peccati: La confessione tra Medioevo ed età moderna;* and *Francesco d'Assisi nelle fonti e negli scritti.* He edited *Predicazione e vita religiosa nella società italiana: Da Carlo Magno* *alla Controriforma*; *Il movimento religioso femminile in Umbia nei secoli XIII–XIV*; and Christopher Columbus's *Libro de las profecías*. He coedited (with Enrico Menestò) *La strada delle sante medievali* and (with Daniel Bornstein) *Mistiche e devote nell'Italia tardomedievale*.

R. N. Swanson is Professor of Medieval History at the University of Birmingham. His research interests lie in the social aspect of church history and in the history of medieval spirituality. He is the author of *Universities, Academics and the Great Schism; Church and Society in Late Medieval England; Religion and Devotion in Europe, c. 1215–c. 1515; The Twelfth-Century Renaissance;* and *Indulgences in Late Medieval England: Passports to Paradise?*; and is the editor of *Catholic England: Faith, Religion and Observance before the Reformation* and *Promissory Notes on the Treasury of Merits: Indulgences in Late Medieval Europe*. He was president of the Ecclesiastical History Society for 2007–2008.

André Vauchez was Professor of History at the Université de Paris X–Nanterre and director of the École Française de Rome until his recent retirement. An expert in the history of medieval sanctity and spirituality, he is the author or editor of more than a dozen books, several of which have appeared in English: *The Laity in the Middle Ages: Religious Beliefs and Devotional Practices; The Spirituality of the Medieval West; Sainthood in the Later Middle Ages;* and (with Joanna Cannon) *Margherita of Cortona and the Lorenzetti: Sienese Art and the Cult of a Holy Woman in Medieval Tuscany*.

Diana Webb retired in 2006 from her position as Senior Lecturer in the Department of History at King's College London. She is editor of *Pilgrims and Pilgrimage in the Medieval West* and author of *Patrons and Defenders: The Saints in the Italian City-States; Pilgrimage in Medieval England;* and *Medieval European Pilgrimage*. Her most recent books are *Saints and Cities in Medieval Italy* and *Privacy and Solitude in the Middle Ages*, both published in 2007.

ILLUSTRATIONS

Figures

Color Plates (following page 204)

FOREWORD

This seven-volume series breaks new ground by looking at Christianity's past from the vantage point of a people's history. It is church history, yes, but church history with a difference: "church," we insist, is not to be understood first and foremost as the hierarchical-institutional-bureaucratic corporation; rather, above all, it is the laity, the ordinary faithful, the people. Their religious lives, their pious practices, their self-understandings as Christians, and the way all of this grew and changed over the last two millennia—*this* is the unexplored territory in which we are here setting foot.

To be sure, the undertaking known as people's history, as it is applied to secular themes, is hardly a new one among academic historians. Referred to sometimes as history from below, or grassroots history, or popular history, it was born about a century ago, in conscious opposition to the elitism of conventional (some call it Rankean) historical investigation, fixated as this was on the "great" deeds of "great" men, and little else. What had always been left out of the story, of course, was the vast majority of human beings: almost all women, obviously, but then too all those who could be counted among the socially inferior, the economically distressed, the politically marginalized, the educationally deprived, or the culturally unrefined. Had not various elites always despised "the people"? Cicero, in first-century BCE Rome, referred to them as "urban filth and dung"; Edmund Burke, in eighteenth-century London, called them "the swinish multitude"; and in between, this loathing of "the meaner sort" was almost universal among the privileged. When the discipline called "history" was professionalized in the nineteenth century, traditional gentlemen historians perpetuated this contempt, if not by outright vilification, then at least by keeping the masses invisible. Thus when people's history came on the scene, it was not only a means for uncovering an unknown dimension of the past but also in some sense an instrument for righting an injustice. Today its cumulative contribution is enormous, and its home in the academic world is assured.

Only quite recently has the discipline formerly called "church history" and now more often "the history of Christianity" begun to open itself up to this approach. Its agenda over the last two centuries has been dominated by other facets of this religion's past, such as theology, dogma, institutions, and ecclesio-political relations. Each of these has in fact long since evolved into its own subdiscipline. Thus the history of theology has concentrated on the self-understandings of Christian intellectuals. Historians of dogma have examined the way in which church leaders came to formulate teachings that they then pronounced normative for all Christians. Experts on institutional history have researched the formation, growth, and functioning of leadership offices, bureaucratic structures, official decision-making processes, and so forth. And specialists in the history of church-state relations have worked to fathom the complexities of the institution's interface with its sociopolitical context, above all by studying leaders on both sides.

Collectively, these conventional kinds of church history have yielded enough specialized literature to fill a very large library, and those who read in this library will readily testify to its amazing treasures. Erudite as it is, however, the Achilles' heel of this scholarship, taken as a whole, is that it has told the history of Christianity as the story of one small segment of those who have claimed the name "Christian." What has been studied almost exclusively until now is the religion of various elites, whether spiritual elites, or intellectual elites, or power elites. Without a doubt, mystics and theologians, pastors, priests, bishops, and popes are worth studying. But at best they altogether constitute perhaps 5 percent of all Christians over two millennia. What about the rest? Does not a balanced history of Christianity, not to mention our sense of historical justice, require that attention be paid to them?

Around the mid-twentieth century, a handful of scholars began, hesitantly and yet insistently, to press this question on the international guild of church historians. Since that time, the study of the other 95 percent has gained momentum: ever more ambitious research projects have been launched; innovative scholarly methods have been developed, critiqued, and refined; and a growing public interest has greeted the results. Academics and nonacademics alike want to know about this aspect of Christianity's past. Who were these people—the voiceless, the ordinary faithful who wrote no theological treatises, whose statues adorn no basilicas, who negotiated no concordats, whose very names themselves are largely lost to historical memory? What can we know about their religious consciousness; their devotional practice; their understanding of the faith; their values, beliefs, feelings, habits, and attitudes; their deepest fears, hopes, loves, and hatreds; and so forth? And what about the troublemakers, the excluded, the heretics, those defined by conventional history as the losers? Can a face be put on any of them?

Today, even after half a century of study, answers are still in short supply. It must be conceded that the field is in its infancy, both methodologically and in terms of what remains to be investigated. Very often historians now find themselves no longer interrogating literary texts but rather artifacts, the remains of material culture, court records, wills, popular art, graffiti, and so forth. What is already clear is that many traditional assumptions, timeworn clichés, and well-loved nuggets of conventional wisdom about Christianity's past will have to be abandoned. When the Christian masses are made the leading protagonists of the story, we begin to glimpse a plot with dramatically new contours. In fact, a rewriting of this history is now getting under way, and this may well be the discipline's larger task for the twenty-first century.

A People's History of Christianity is our contribution to this enterprise. In it we gather up the early harvest of this new approach, showcase the current state of the discipline, and plot a trajectory into the future. Essentially what we offer here is a preliminary attempt at a new and more adequate version of the Christian story—one that features the people. Is it comprehensive? Impossible. Definitive? Hardly. A responsible, suggestive, interesting base to build on? We are confident that it is.

Close to a hundred historians of Christianity have generously applied their various types of expertise to this project, whether as advisers or editors or contributors. They have in common no universally agreed-on methodology, nor do they even concur on how precisely to define problematic terms such as "popular religion." What they do share is a conviction that rescuing the Christian people from their historic anonymity is important; that reworking the story's plot with lay piety as the central narrative will be a contribution of lasting value; and that reversing the condescension, not to say contempt, that all too often has marred elite views of the people is long overdue. If progress is made on these fronts, we believe, the groundwork for a new history of Christianity will have been prepared.

Chronologically speaking, the present volume covers fully half of the Christian story—the millennium between the fall of Rome and the Protestant Reformation. Conventional church historians have long studied these "Middle Ages" by focusing on great events, great personalities, great books, and so forth. Here we sideline these, at least for the moment, and let "ordinary" people come to the fore. Consequently, the scope of our subject is very wide indeed, covering the religious lives of the vast majority of human beings in Western Europe over a thousand-year period. The fainthearted could well despair, were it not for the remarkable roster of accomplished experts featured in this book. Under the talented leadership of Daniel Bornstein, they not only facilitate the complex shift from the great to the ordinary, but they also orient our entree into the labyrinth of data. Step by step these scholars bring into focus a picture of a somewhat independent piety of the people, with its own authentic insight, richness, and power. I am happy to express my gratitude to all of them.

Denis R. Janz, General Editor

CHRISTIANITY AND PAGANISM IN WESTERN EUROPE c. 350–750
Iona
PICTS 563
COLUMBA
NINIAN
Old Melrose
Lindisfarne Aiden c. 635
Armagh
Bangor
Withorn
Monkwearmouth/Jarrow Cuthbert c. 664
Ripon
SCOTTI C. 450
Hexham
York 735
WILFRID
PAULINUS
ANGLO-SAXONS 597-686
WILLIBRORD
Utrecht 695
SAXONS 788
Canterbury
Atlantic Ocean
ANGLIBERT
AUGUSTINE
FRISIANS C. 700
BONIFACE
THURINGIANS
Fulda 744
Early 8th Century
Rouen
Echternach 698
Mainz 743
BAVARIANS
Reims
COLUMBANUS
CORBINIAN
FRANKS C. 500
Eichstatt 742
Tours
Sens
Luxeuil 590
ALEMANS 7TH C.
Freising 730
0 200 Miles
Salzburg 798
Bourges
Besançon
Reichenau 724
PIRMIN
GALL
St. Gall c. 673
BURGUNDIANS C. 540
Bordeaux
Lyon
Vienne
Milan
Aquileia
Toulouse
Bobbio c. 610
Ravenna
Braga
Arles
Narbonne
VISIGOTHS 587
LOMBARDS 679
Salona
Tarragon
Toledo
Rome
Merida
Seville
Cagliari
Mediterranean Sea
Carthage
Syracuse
FRANKS C. 500 Germanic people with date of conversion to Catholicism
Archiepiscopal or primal see c. 600 AD (date given for later foundations)
Major monastic center involved in missions
Activities of Anglo-Saxon missionaries
Activities of Frankish missionaries
Activities of Irish missionaries
Activities of Roman missionaries
VANDALS
Converted to Arian Christianity c. 410, defeated by Catholic Byzantines 534
LUCIDITY INFORMATION DESIGN, LLC

Fig. 0.1. Christianity and paganism in Western Europe, ca. 350–750

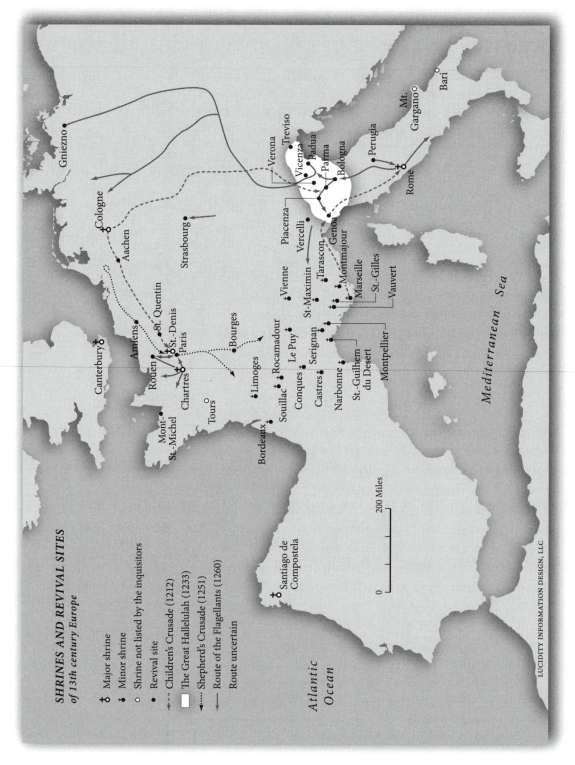

Fig. 0.2. Shrines and revival sites of thirteenth-century Europe

LIVING CHRISTIANITY

DANIEL E. BORNSTEIN

Caesarius, head of the great Cistercian abbey of Heisterbach, recalled with some amusement how his predecessor as abbot once dealt with an audience of inattentive monks. Noting their flagging attention, the abbot interrupted his sermon to say, "There once was a king named Arthur." Suddenly the monks were all ears, eager to hear about the knights of the Round Table and their chivalric adventures.

This story neatly encapsulates some of the most basic problems faced by anyone who seeks to write a people's history of medieval Christianity. I don't mean the obvious problem, shared by all preachers (and all authors), of keeping their audience alert and engaged—though I know that all the contributors to this volume have striven mightily to avoid being soporific. Rather, this little episode calls attention to the vast complexities of topic, terms, and sources. We note that monks, a religious elite set apart from ordinary Christians by their vows of poverty, chastity, and obedience and by their life in a cloistered community dedicated to the work of God, shared an interest in secular literature with their cousins outside the monastery. Indeed, these men, whose whole lives were given to worship and prayer, apparently found stories of a legendary ruler more interesting than a religious sermon.

Moreover, sermon and story alike came to them orally. The sermon may have been written out, and certainly was derived from and referred to written texts, but it was meant to be spoken and heard, not read, and we know that there were many monks and priests who were barely (if at all) literate—to say nothing of ordinary believers in an overwhelmingly rural world. The stories of King Arthur, too, circulated orally, though some of them were eventually written down, and have survived, in sophisticated literary texts. In this case, however, the abbot of Heisterbach clearly invokes the formulaic language of the folktale with his "There once was a king named Arthur."

Here, in what was built to be a bastion of prayer, in lives framed by the most formally explicit rules and committed to the most regular practice of the most official religion, we observe the participation of monks in a larger culture. Monks offered hospitality to weary travelers and listened eagerly to the news and tales they carried with them. Monks built water mills and sponsored fairs, stimulating industry and trade. The seventh-century monk Benedict Biscop brought to England skilled stonemasons to build his church and glaziers to provide it with glass windows; he filled that church with paintings of Old and New Testament subjects to instruct the illiterate; he imported from Rome relics to sanctify the church and singers to fill it with song, in the style that has come to be known as Gregorian chant.

By the same token, representatives of that larger world outside the cloister shared in the monastic life in one way or another. They assembled in monastic churches to hear the singing of the monastic hours and watch the monks worship on their behalf. They donated land and money to monasteries and in return had their names inscribed on monastic prayer lists. They sent their children to monasteries to be raised and educated. They gave their own bodies to monasteries—often their dead bodies, left to await the resurrection in a monastic cemetery, but sometimes their living bodies. Thus the protagonist of the popular thirteenth-century tale "The Tumbler of Our Lady," after a long career as a wandering acrobat, entered the monastery of Clairvaux and there, frustrated by his inability to reverence the Virgin Mary properly in liturgical song and prayer as the other monks did, honored her as best he could by performing somersaults and handsprings in front of her statue.

Monks bored by a sermon perking up at the promise of a rousing chivalric romance; a tumbler turned monk offering an acrobatic routine as worship: clearly, monastic and popular culture mingled more closely than we might have guessed.

THE QUEST FOR THE CHRISTIAN PEOPLE

Anyone setting out to write a people's history of Christianity, or the history of Christianity as a living part of people's lives, faces the fundamental problem of defining what is meant by "the people." This problem is especially acute for the European Middle Ages, that long span of a thousand years stretching from the breakup of the Roman Empire in the fifth century to the discovery of new worlds in the fifteenth century. To be sure, there were tremendous changes—social, cultural, political, economic, and religious—over the course of that millennium, just as there were striking variations from place to place on the European continent. One abiding constant, however, was that learning remained the special preserve of a privileged minority, albeit a minority that grew somewhat larger starting in the eleventh century. These learned men (and a very few exceptional women) wrote about theology and philosophy, medicine and law, love and commerce, in Latin, which remained the language of learning, literature, governance, and worship long after it ceased to be used in everyday speech. Literacy meant knowledge of Latin letters; a person able to read and write only his or her native vernacular could be termed illiterate. And mastery of this arcane skill was associated so closely with the priesthood that the term *clericus*, which gave us the linguistic root of both "clerk" and "cleric," meant both a learned man and a man who had taken holy orders.

One way of identifying the Christian people, then, would be to invoke this contrast between the priesthood—set apart from ordinary folk by the sacred rite of ordination, by their mastery of the sacred Latin of the liturgy, and by their commitment to a life apart from the corrupting trammels of sexual and commercial relations—and the laity. Such a distinction, however, is fraught with problems. For one thing, the clergy did not form a single compact body. The ranks of the priesthood included everything from great ecclesiastical lords to simple parish priests, with all the variation in culture and education that one would expect of such differences in wealth and status. For another, at every level, the church was thoroughly embroiled in society at large, which it came to closely resemble. In the early Middle Ages, right down to the eleventh century, appointment to church office rested in the hands of secular authorities. Rulers and other powerful men built churches and monasteries and endowed them with land: it was only reasonable that they look after the churches they had established or enriched. The king or emperor named the bishops of royal cities and the abbots of royal monasteries. Great nobles similarly named the abbots of monasteries they founded and patronized. As a result, the bishops and abbots who controlled ecclesiastical estates were powerful lords, resembling in every way the secular lords who endowed their churches—to whom they were generally related. They followed the same manner of life and indulged in the same amusements: hunting, drinking, feasting, fighting.

Chronicles of the eighth, ninth, and tenth centuries are full of warrior bishops, men every bit as rough and rude (and, needless to add, illiterate) as their secular counterparts. This one had his ear lopped off in combat; that one was left for dead on the battlefield, buried under a heap of corpses, but managed to struggle out from under that deadweight and make his way home, his armor reddened with other men's blood; still another was struck by lightning while leading his army against the rival city of Lyons. The ninth-century writer Notker the Stammerer delighted in repeating stories that stripped bishops of any sacred dignity. When one bishop made a rude remark about the singing of a young man who happened to be related to Charlemagne, the emperor punched him on the spot; Notker—a monk—was clearly of the opinion that anyone who could deck a bishop with a single blow can't be all bad. On another occasion Notker recalled how a bishop received Charlemagne and his entourage, who had arrived without warning. Since it was a day on which good churchmen were expected to abstain from meat and a place where fish were not readily available, the bishop served the great emperor an excellent cheese, evidently something like a ripe Brie or Camembert. Noting that Charlemagne was eating the creamy interior but discarding the skin, the bishop informed his guest that he was throwing away the best part. Charlemagne tried it, discovered that the bishop was absolutely correct, and ordered the bishop to supply him with two cartloads of these cheeses every year—causing panic in the poor prelate, who feared that he would lose his see if he failed to come up with enough first-rate cheese.

The same pattern pertained at the level of village church. Local lords built churches on their estates, in the villages inhabited by their peasants, and exercised the right of appointing the priests who would officiate at these churches—*their* churches. It was by this system of proprietary churches that Christianity gradually penetrated the countryside, where the vast bulk of Europe's people lived. In that rural world, the village priests were barely distinguishable from their parishioners in their manner of life, cultural formation, and religious beliefs. Minimally literate, they often had only a rote mastery of the liturgy it was their responsibility to celebrate. That sacred function aside, they were relatively well-to-do peasants, village big shots, who worked their lands, drank their beer or wine, and gambled and swore like any other peasant. And like their fellow villagers, they were domestically settled: with legal wives right through the tenth century (and beyond, in some corners of Europe) and then, when monastic-minded reformers banned clerical marriage in the eleventh century, with unofficial domestic partners. The new norm of clerical celibacy met prolonged resistance not simply because of human weakness in the face of sexual desire but because it set the priest apart from his flock in a new and often unwelcome way. As André Vauchez demonstrates in his contribution to this volume, the practice of clerical celibacy, like the canonical norm that called for it, has a complex and revealing history.

If the Christian people cannot be defined as the laity, as distinct from the clergy, neither can they be defined as the masses of the faithful, as distinct from social and political elites. The warrior elites who dominated early medieval Europe were every bit as unschooled as any of their followers and fully shared their cultural outlook. When the Frankish ruler Clovis—the first of the Germanic kings to accept Catholic Christianity—converted around 497, he did so because he was impressed by demonstrations of divine power, displayed both in the healing miracles at the shrine of St. Martin of Tours and, even more dramatically, in the sudden reversal of the tides of battle that gave him a critical victory over his foes. When Clovis converted, so too did his followers, who received baptism en masse in a church adorned with white hangings, perfumed tapers, and clouds of incense. With this act, the Franks officially became Catholic, the first of the Germanic peoples to do so. Their conversion indicates the character of their religion: formal, public, gestural, perhaps superficial—a religion defined by actions and objects rather than by doctrine and belief. Indeed, what belief was involved, beyond the conviction that God was powerful and acted for the Franks? The notion of spirituality, the interior dimension of the religious life that is so vitally important to believers today, seems utterly foreign to such a religion.

The missionary-monks who first spread Christianity to the European countryside encountered a religion localized in holy springs, numinous rocks, sacred trees, and statues of the gods. Often they attacked these objects: St. Martin of Tours (d. 397/400) induced some pagans to chop down their sacred tree by promising that he would let it fall on him; St. Gall (d. ca. 627) smashed statues and threw the pieces into Lake Constance, and later heard the demons of the lake and the mountaintop complaining about their discomfiture. But they also followed the guidelines proposed by Pope Gregory the Great in 601 when he sent missionaries to bring the new religion to England: the idols should be destroyed, but the temples themselves purified with holy water and converted to Christian use; pagan sacrifices should be replaced by Christian festivities. In short, existing holy places and times were to be Christianized, and so could remain holy. Gradually, Christian notions of time and space, the good life and the proper death, came to shape the mental landscape of medieval Europe, in processes elucidated here by Yitzhak Hen and Bonnie Effros.

But this was a cultural and religious reordering that applied alike to the great emperor Charlemagne and the peasants who worked his estates. And though Charlemagne was a man of wide curiosity, broad experience, and great vision, and a ruler who encouraged learning and promoted the copying of ancient texts, he himself was as unskilled with the written word as any peasant. He took in works of literature or history or theology by having them read aloud to him while he dined, and struggled painfully, and unsuccessfully, to learn to write: "With this object in view he used to keep writing-tablets and notebooks under the pillow on his bed, so that he could try his hand at forming letters during his leisure moments; but, although he tried very hard, he had begun late in life and he made little progress."[1] In this respect, as in so many others—such as his devotion to the relics of the saints, his delight in hearing the liturgy performed well, and his inability to observe religious fasts without grumbling—the greatest ruler in medieval Europe was entirely a man of the people.

In attempting this people's history of Christianity, our first precept had to be that the religion of the people is *additive*, not subtractive. It is not Christianity minus monks, minus priests, minus bishops and popes, theologians and saints, kings and emperors. Those social and religious elites (of one sort or another, by one standard or another) can't be left out of the picture, although they are no longer its focus. They appear in the contributions to this volume, but so do many more people: peasants, artisans, warriors, women, children, the dead and those they have left behind. This social inclusiveness grows out of the recognition that religious conviction and heartfelt devotion were not limited to monastic and clerical elites, the authors of the texts traditionally associated with the history of spirituality. When spirituality is defined more broadly as the manner in which people express and live their faith in a given historical and cultural setting, it is easy to see that the illiterate and inarticulate might have religious feelings every bit as strong as the most devout monk and a spiritual life as rich and complex as the most intense mystic. Getting at those religious feelings and that spiritual life—recovering a spirituality often written on bodies rather than in books and uncovering the ideas implicit in devotional actions—has proven to be a daunting task, and an enormously exciting one.

THE PROBLEM OF SOURCES

All medieval historians face the problem of sources. The problem is particularly acute for the early Middle Ages, when few books and documents were produced and fewer still survived. But even for the period from the eleventh century onward, when the growth of government, revival of commerce, and spread of literacy led to the production and preservation of written records in unprecedented quantities, the documentation is unevenly distributed and far from exhaustive. For the historian of religious life, the problem is compounded in several ways. For one thing, most of the surviving documents are administrative records, and even when these come from ecclesiastical institutions, such as Ramsey Abbey in England, the diocese of Vic in Catalonia, or the papal curia in Rome, they tell us a great deal about estate management or the progress of litigation, but precious little about the more properly religious concerns of the monks, priests, and prelates who populated those institutions.

To be sure, some of those ecclesiastical personages—monks, in particular—also produced ascetic and mystical writings, as well as theological treatises, lives of the saints, and commentaries on Scripture. These texts have served as the essential sources for a long and distinguished tradition of scholarship on monastic spirituality, including such masterpieces as Jean Leclercq's *The Love of Learning and the Desire for God* (first published in French in 1957 and translated into English four years later) and Giles Constable's *The Reformation of the Twelfth Century* (1996). These texts continue to furnish rich materials for historians interested in pushing the history of spirituality in new directions, who have posed new questions of often familiar sources and have come up with exciting new answers. One of the most brilliant of these historians, Caroline Walker Bynum, has vigorously maintained the value and relevance of these classic sources. As she says:

> Broadening the history of spirituality from a history of mystical theology to a history of religious attitudes need not involve abandoning the spiritual treatises, saints' lives, and collections of visions that medieval people produced in such relative abundance.... For such treatises take us into the complexities of a few hearts, and in these complexities we find reflected, if we read with sensitivity, the ways in which larger groups of people were burdened or healed, oppressed or encouraged, by the structures of the church and by society.[2]

Bynum, Barbara Newman, and others have done a dazzling job of illuminating medieval religious culture through the close reading of ascetic and mystical writings. Still, getting from the writings of a monastic or clerical elite to the beliefs of a broader public does take a certain leap of faith—or, to bridge that gap, the deployment of other kinds of sources, each with its own possibilities and limitations.

One solution has been to examine sources that were created precisely in order to bridge that gap. The Soviet historian Aron Gurevich, for one, has used this method to good effect. As Peter Burke observed in his preface to Gurevich's *Medieval Popular Culture*, Gurevich took on the challenge "of discovering the attitudes of the lay majority in a period when the sources were produced by a clerical élite, and of excavating oral culture, vernacular culture, from literary texts in Latin."[3] He did this by reading the works of missionaries, proselytizers, popularizers, and preachers—beneficiaries of a scholastic education who labored to bring the ideas and attitudes of that learned culture to a broader audience. In order to do so successfully, they had to become effectively bicultural, able to communicate in terms intelligible to the general public. This process of acculturation moved in more than one direction: these popularizers of elite ideas had to open themselves to, and become fluent in, the culture they sought to transform. The "popular" devotion of the Christian masses and the elite culture of the ecclesiastical leadership developed in a continuous dialogue.

These handbooks, manuals, model sermons, and advice books were aimed not at the general public (who had no professional use for such texts, even if they could read the Latin in which they were written), but at that cultural mediator par excellence, the parish priest. Unlike wandering preachers, who drew crowds and stirred imaginations when they passed through, parish priests resided in a community. They lived with their flock. They spoke its language. They knew its concerns, its needs, its fears and hopes, and their calling—their function in the moral economy of the community— was to minister to those needs and speak to those concerns. The priest made God present to his parishioners: as St. Francis of Assisi said in his *Testament*, dictated shortly before his death in October 1226, "In this world I cannot see the most high Son of God with my own eyes, except for his most holy Body and Blood which they receive and they alone administer to others."[4] At the same time, he presented them to God, offering worship and prayers on their behalf and imploring divine mercy for their sins. As part of his pastoral duties, particularly after the Fourth Lateran Council in 1215, he heard them confess their sins, absolved them, and imposed on them the healing salve of penance. Handbooks for confessors—one distinctive genre of those Latin works of advice—thus reached, through the priest, into the most intimate recesses of every Christian soul in Europe.

In his contribution to this volume, Roberto Rusconi makes great use of such sources as he discusses the peculiar intimacies of the practice of confession and the perils to which this sacrament exposed both confessor and penitent. The intimacy of confession, like every other aspect of the relation between priest and parishioners, was complicated by the normative expectation of clerical celibacy, once that came to be the norm in the eleventh century. Baring one's soul, warned manuals for confessors, could all too easily lead to baring one's body, and the spiritual salves applied as a remedy for sin carried the risk of all sorts of unwanted side effects.

In the later Middle Ages, religious writers also produced devotional guidebooks in the vernacular, aimed directly at a lay audience, rather than mediating their advice through priests. Italy, with its bustling cities and educated urban elites, offered a particularly large market for such texts. A bevy of best-selling authors, including the Dominican friars Domenico Cavalca, Jacopo Passavanti, and a host of others, eagerly fed that market with texts translated from Latin or written directly in the vernacular: lives of the saints, meditations on the passion of the Christ, sermons, letters of spiritual counsel, guides to confession, exhortations to charity and penitence, and instruction in the basics of the faith. Cavalca's *Lo Specchio della Croce* (The Mirror of the Cross), written in the early fourteenth century, survives in countless manuscripts from the fourteenth and fifteenth century and went into print as soon as printing from movable type was introduced, going through at least fourteen editions before the end of the fifteenth century—and that is just one among many such works.

Little pamphlets—their plain format and small size making them cheap to produce and easy to carry in one's sleeve or purse—taught anyone who cared to learn the essentials of Christian doctrine: the Ten Commandments, twelve articles of faith, seven sacraments, seven deadly sins, seven gifts of the Holy Spirit, seven works of mercy, eight beatitudes, three theological and four cardinal virtues, and so on. At times, these booklets could slip into easily memorized lists, with minimal explanation—not the most exciting reading, certainly for historians and (we may easily imagine) for their original intended audience. More often, they took care to explain in the Italian vernacular, and in easily understood terms, the meaning of the Creed and of the most common prayers, such as the Ave Maria and Pater Noster, which people recited in Latin. They touched on intimate and personal concerns, offering guidance on how to live well, how to confess well, and how to die well. Of course, such works are prescriptive and didactic in nature, and it can be hard to tell how people received their instructions and responded to their injunctions. Hard, but not impossible: Eamon Duffy has recently provided an elegant (and beautifully illustrated) discussion of how English people used the prayer book known as the Book of Hours, whose ability to help people give voice to their religious feelings made it the most widely used book of the later Middle Ages.

Rather than prescribing what people ought to do, chronicles, diaries, and letters described what they actually did do, and very often what they did included actions that were religious in character. Chroniclers recorded the spectacular outbursts of popular enthusiasm and public flagellation that Gary Dickson describes in his essay on medieval revivalism, as well as the more ordinary expressions of public piety such as Lenten sermons, devotional processions, performances of sacred dramas based on biblical stories or the lives of the saints, and collective invocations of divine mercy in times of plague or famine. Diarists recalled their own participation in these events and described their experiences while on pilgrimage to Rome, Santiago de Compostela, or Jerusalem. Entire books were devoted to chronicling the crusades, in which the knightly classes of Europe claimed for themselves a sacral identity as warriors of God, fighting to recapture the Holy Land from its Muslim rulers.

To be sure, most of these accounts describe actions and events, leaving it to the reader to guess at the motives that inspired the actors' behavior. Occasionally, however, it is possible to find passages reflecting or voicing religious sentiments that go well beyond a perfunctory "May God bless and keep him." Consider, for instance, the diary entry in which the Florentine merchant Gregorio Dati recorded the death of his third wife:

After that it was God's will to recall to Himself the blessed soul of my wife Ginevra. She died in childbirth after lengthy suffering, which she bore with remarkable strength and patience. She was perfectly lucid at the time of her death when she received all the sacraments: confession, communion, extreme unction, and a papal indulgence granting absolution for all her sins, which she received from Master Lionardo [Gregorio's brother, the master general of the Dominican order], who had been granted it by the Pope. It comforted her greatly, and she returned her soul to her Creator on 7 September, the Eve of the Feast of Our Lady, at *nones*: the hour when Our Blessed Lord Jesus Christ expired on the cross and yielded up his spirit to our Heavenly Father. On Friday the 8th she was honorably buried and on the 9th, masses were said for her soul. Her body lies in our plot at Santo Spirito and her soul has gone to eternal life. God bless her and grant us fortitude. Her loss has sorely tried me. May He help me to bring up the unruly family which is left to me in the best way for their souls and bodies.[5]

In this moving passage, we can see with perfect clarity, as if the passage of six centuries meant absolutely nothing, how deep personal faith, the sacraments of the church, and the happy availability of a papal indulgence comforted both the dying Ginevra and her bereaved family.

In addition to texts that describe actions, we have documents that record them. Perhaps the most studied have been last wills and testaments. In their wills, people stipulated in which church they wished to be buried and designated pious bequests for the benefit of their souls. A close reading of individual wills can thus reveal the testator's spiritual orientations and attachments: she might show a special fondness for her parish church or for one of the religious orders, or encourage Christ's poor to pray for her soul by distributing alms among them; he might adorn God's church (and preserve his memory) by endowing a chapel in it or, heeding Christ's call to care for his least brethren, leave money to support a foundling hospital or furnish dowries for poor girls. Since last wills and testaments survive by the tens of thousands, they can be used to create statistical profiles of patterns in charitable giving and pious bequests, revealing both regional variations and changes over time.

In the late Middle Ages, and in particular after the terrifying devastation wrought by the Black Death of 1348 and subsequent epidemics, testators requested the recitation of masses in ever increasing numbers and on ever more frequent occasions. Masses would be said on the day of the funeral (celebrated with ever more flamboyant pomp) and over the course of the following month or year; they would be sung on the anniversary of the day of death or spread out over ten or twenty years. In much the same way that prayers to the Virgin were multiplied to the point that rosaries had to be used to keep track of them, this investment in the afterlife could lead to an obsessive multiplication of masses: in the region of Bordeaux, Bernard d'Escoussans, lord of Langoiran, stipulated in 1338 that 25,000 masses be said for the repose of his soul, while some thirty years later another nobleman, Jean de Grailly, endowed 50,000. To fulfill the terms of such bequests, church aisles filled with side chapels, where squadrons of chantry priests—a sort of clerical proletariat without pastoral responsibilities or secure incomes— celebrated private masses without pause. As R. N. Swanson points out in his contribution, such charitable concern for the souls in purgatory—both one's own soul and the souls of those near and dear to one—could weigh heavily on devout Christians.

Other records of everyday life, records every bit as pragmatic as wills but far less systematically studied, offer similar insights into the social dimensions of spiritual life (or the spiritual dimensions of social life). The account books kept by parish vestry councils and devotional confraternities show where they derived and directed their resources. Jesus had something very different in mind when he warned that it is impossible to serve both God and mammon and observed, "Where your treasure is, there your heart will be also" (Matt. 6:21). Nonetheless, following the money trail in these records of income and expenditure has proved a useful way of tracking what mattered most to these associations of devout laymen: extending a helping hand to a neighbor in need; adorning the house of God with a new painting or window; aiding in the celebration of the liturgy with new vestments, altar furnishings, or liturgical books; and adding a bit of joy to the village (and, hopefully, money to their coffers) by sponsoring a dance or church ale on the feast day of the local saint or some other festival. Shrine records offer further insights into the spiritual economy, as they note miraculous cures and other assistance given to desperate petitioners and the beneficiaries' grateful testimonials, both in words

of praise for the healing powers of God and his saints and in the reciprocal gifts offered in thanks for grace received: candles, coins, wax or
silver images of the formerly afflicted body part, and crude paintings
depicting the intervening hand of a beneficent God.

These ex-voto offerings bring us to the material remains of medieval religious culture. Material culture has attracted much interest in
recent years as scholars have turned to archaeological remains, works
of art, and objects from everyday life for clues to the religious experience of those who left no written traces of their beliefs. The evidence
offered by such material remains has been especially important for
understanding the early Middle Ages, for which written sources are
fragmentary and rare. Thus Bonnie Effros draws on excavations of
early medieval burial sites from England and France to explore attitudes toward death and the afterlife. Juxtaposing written descriptions
with the material evidence of the grave goods that accompanied the
dead, she traces the gradual Christianization of funerary practices and
subtle shifts in a community of believers that extended beyond the
grave. The churches themselves in which that community of believers gathered to worship offer evidence about the character of that
community, its divisions and aspirations. In an essay that ranges over
several centuries and much of northern Europe, Richard Kieckhefer
shows how much can be learned from careful observation of church
buildings, from simple parish churches to the great preaching halls
of the mendicant orders, and from the familiar cathedral where the
whole city assembled to worship on major feasts to distant shrines
that attracted pilgrims from all over Europe.

Even when written sources become more abundant in the later
Middle Ages, much of what they have to say still refers to material culture. Church inventories from Cortona, in central Italy, reveal the spare
simplicity, if not abject poverty, of rural parish churches and the recto-
ries in which their priests lived. Most priests disposed of only the bare
minimum of essential liturgical books and altar furnishings, and their
vestments were described as poor and shabby, dirty and worn, old and
sad. The quantity, variety, and quality of the rectory's kitchen equipment and bedding matched that of the vestments and altar furnishings. The spiritual consequences of the grim material circumstances in
which most country priests lived can easily be imagined.

Urban elites disposed of far greater material resources, which sustained a far richer spiritual and devotional life. At the very same time that those Cortonese churches were being inventoried, the Dominican friar Giovanni Dominici (1356–1419) offered a well-born Florentine woman advice on household management and child rearing. In his handbook on caring for the family, Dominici urges his reader to surround her children with pictures of the saints, so that little girls can grow up with a love of virginity, a longing for Jesus, and a hatred of sin. A boy should be given a little toy altar, where he and his friends can play at being priests: dressing as acolytes, lighting candles, delivering sermons, and singing Mass in imitation of what they have seen in church. In a striking convergence of patrician household and cloistered nunneries, we can observe professed nuns in pious play with doll-like images of the baby Jesus. By reverently swaddling the infant Jesus and tending him in a cradle carved to resemble a church, these holy virgins—some of whom were barely more than infants themselves when they entered the convent—expressed their identification with the Virgin Mary and developed a deep love for their Savior, their Spouse, the Christ child.

THE VARIETY OF BELIEF AND PRACTICE

As soon as we leave behind normative texts, with their inherent tendency to generalize and standardize, we are immediately struck by the enormous variety of Christian beliefs and practices. Indeed, this volume, like the series of which it is a part, takes to heart Jesus' comment that his father's house has many dwelling places (John 14:2), as it celebrates the capaciousness of that house and the diversity of its dwelling places. The Christianity in this people's history of Christianity is as varied as the people who practiced it, and most if not all of the essays in this volume address those variations, under one rubric or another.

Some of the most significant variations can be ascribed to the variety of persons who comprise the Christian people. We have already touched on many of these categories—lay and clerical, lettered and illiterate, warriors and workers, peasants and city dwellers—and noted both their usefulness and their limitations. None of these

categories was fixed: widows came to the convent after long lives dedicated to domestic cares; bishops took up arms to defend their flocks;
a cloth merchant's son renounced his father's fortune to become a
saintly exemplar of apostolic poverty. None of them was watertight:
even the most carefully maintained cloister wall remained a porous
membrane, allowing communication between monks and nuns
engaged in the work of God and the world outside the monastery,
including most immediately the peasants who worked their fields and
came to worship in their church. The religious concerns of monks
and peasants differed, as did the circumstances in which they lived
their daily lives, and it is important to recognize what is characteristic,
distinctive, even unique to the religious life of certain social groups.
To that end, we must be constantly alert to exactly who is profess-
ing a certain belief or engaging in a particular devotion. At the same
time, we must remember that social interaction was as constant and
pervasive as social identity and look for the shared values that both
enabled and emerged from ongoing conversations between members
of different social groups. Some of the most significant conversations
took place between those who were professionally religious and those
who were not, the clergy and the laity, and several contributors to this
volume (notably Roberto Rusconi and André Vauchez) focus their
attention on those encounters and interactions.

The devotional life of clergy and laity alike unfolded in a variety
of settings, of which the most important were the church and the
home. Richard Kieckhefer describes how churches looked and felt to
the laypeople who gathered there to hear Mass, to worship, to see and
be seen. Katherine L. French shows how the community of worshipers who assembled in the parish church shaped itself, organized itself,
and sustained itself through reciprocal acts of charity. Diana Webb
explores what those parishioners did when at home, performing private devotions in a more private space. In this domestic setting, the
religion of hearth and home enveloped the family with its sense of
comfort, closeness, and easy familiarity. Again, each setting encouraged a certain form of piety; each person carried those characteristic
modes of churchly or domestic devotion with her as she moved from
one setting to another. Young girls who were entrusted to convents for
their early education absorbed monastic models and brought monas-

tic habits of bearing and behavior into their households when they married. But the movement of religious attitudes and objects went in both directions, as when those young girls brought their dolls of the infant Jesus with them into the convent. And by the end of the Middle Ages, domestic altars had become such a commonplace furnishing in patrician homes that laywomen would donate their household altars to convents, as Margarita, the widow of Bartolomeo Luciani, did in 1396 when she bequeathed to the Venetian convent of Corpus Domini "a decorated altar of mine that I have at home."[6]

The Middle Ages used to be described (perhaps optimistically and certainly misleadingly, insofar as it implied a uniformity of belief) as an "age of faith." Not all Christians in the "Christian Middle Ages" were equally intent on, or intense at, being Christian; and the contributors to this volume are all acutely aware of the variations of devotional intensity that come with rote and routine, reflexive habit and conscious choice. Levels of engagement and commitment vary not only from person to person but from moment to moment in a person's life, depending on one's circumstances and one's mood. Everyone's attention flags at some point, after all, and we shouldn't assume that the flagging attention of those monks at Heisterbach with whom I opened this essay was anything more than a momentary response to a dull sermon, a hot afternoon, or a large meal. So while many of the essays in this volume address the "normal" practice of everyday religion, they recognize that every day is different. The banal fact of mortality, for instance, is anything but routine for those who must deal with loss. Words often fail us in the face of grief, yet a simple embrace can speak volumes. Unfortunately for the historian, however, such gestures speak silently, leaving little trace in the documentary record—a record that, in any case, is frustratingly sparse for the earlier Middle Ages.

To overcome that problem, and to try nonetheless to recover some idea of how early medieval people managed death and how survivors coped with loss, Bonnie Effros draws on burial practices, mourning rituals, and the material evidence of grave goods as indices of bereavement, consolation, and hope for a future life beyond the grave. In the later Middle Ages, written and pictorial sources become much richer, allowing R. N. Swanson to invoke a wide range of texts, from devotional handbooks on the art of dying to testaments providing for charitable bequests, as he ponders (perhaps with an eye to the next volume in the People's History series, on the Reformation) the burdens of purgatory, weighing on people as they struggled to hurry themselves and their loved ones along on the difficult road to Paradise.

Some people, I suppose, might manage to be enthusiastically religious all their lives, though even saints complain of spiritual dryness and suffer the dark night of the soul. But everyone is enthusiastic about something, at some time, and those outbursts of enthusiasm, in their very drama and intensity, are a normal (though not everyday) part of religious experience. With an enthusiasm that matches his subject, Gary Dickson evokes the clamorous responses to revivalist preachers, the public processions of nearly naked flagellants, the individual and collective pilgrimages to shrines near and far, and those armed pilgrimages known as the crusades, all of which, at one time or another, engaged the energies of tens of thousands of medieval Christians—and captured the imagination of medieval chroniclers. Sustaining such enthusiasm was never easy; sooner or later, the soaring enthusiasm of a religious revival gave way to the gravitational pull of routine. Even the most successful of mass revivals must be content with a partial transformation, some greater or lesser adjustment of the fabric of society that remains after the initial enthusiasm has evaporated.

In some sense, the most rule-bound of Christian institutions, from the monastic and mendicant orders to lay confraternities, originated—as Christianity itself did, for that matter—as partially successful attempts to capture and preserve enthusiasm. In filling institutions with fresh vigor and setting them on new courses, these religious revivals were pouring new wine into old flasks, whose cracked leather somehow still retained enough flexibility to keep from bursting from the effervescent enthusiasm they captured and contained—and preserved. Religious enthusiasm not only *was* sustained, sometimes to a quite astonishing degree, by zealous individuals and groups. It also sustained and invigorated religious institutions, endowing them with the life and meaning they needed to give meaning and sustenance back in turn to the individuals who lived in and through them.

Some of the most intensely devoted of medieval Christians, to the point of being ready to sacrifice their lives for their religious convictions, were those whose beliefs differed fundamentally from those of the dominant religious culture. Throughout the European Middle Ages, in most times, places, and circumstances, the exponents of Christian orthodoxy were sufficiently confident of their established preeminence that they could be relatively accepting of variations in belief and practice. People might perform one devotion rather than another, revere one saint above another, take communion frequently or receive it only the obligatory minimum of once a year, and offer different explanations of (or simply be befuddled by) how God could be present, in his undivided entirety, in so many Eucharists consecrated by so many priests, but they were all felt to be good Christians at heart. Throughout the early Middle Ages, heresy—the public and adamant profession of beliefs contrary to the orthodox doctrine of the church—remained limited to a few individual intellectuals. That began to change in the eleventh century, when groups like the Patarines in Milan refused to receive the sacraments from clergy tainted by sexual relations. By the twelfth century, as Grado G. Merlo points out in his contribution, for the first time since the conversion of the Franks, heresy could be seen to evoke a broad popular response, as groups of people claiming the title of "Good Christians," or "True Christians," challenged the hegemony of the church. Some of them reacted violently to what they saw as an excessive materialization of worship. But for the most part, heterodox spirituality was informed by the same apostolic and ascetic ideals that inspired orthodox movements of reform and religious revival.

The one doctrinal heresy that drew mass support was that of the Cathars or Albigensians, whose dualist theology opposed spirit, goodness, and light to matter, evil, and darkness, and replaced the Catholic version of sacred history with an elaborate mythology of cosmic struggle between the forces of good and evil. It may be that the Cathar heresy owed its success less to the inherent drama of its theology than to the heroic asceticism of its leaders, who renounced sex and all products of sexual reproduction (meat, milk, cheese, eggs) and undertook regular and extensive fasts on bread and water. Whatever the reason, the Cathar heresy attracted many adherents in southern France and northern Italy and even developed an ecclesiastical structure that rivaled the Catholic Church in regions such as Languedoc, until it was smashed by crusaders and inquisitors.

From the twelfth century on, discussions, arguments, even violent clashes over what constituted true Christianity involved many people, in areas widely scattered across the face of Europe. Few people, on the other hand, lived in close proximity with neighbors who were not Christian at all, and those non-Christians were concentrated in very few parts of Europe. Jewish communities had existed in Mediterranean Europe since before the time of Jesus, but as Teofilo F. Ruiz reminds us, these communities came under increasing pressure in the later Middle Ages. In the course of the thirteenth century, Jews were expelled from England and southern Italy; in the early fourteenth century, they had to leave much of France as well. Throughout Europe, wherever Jews were still allowed to reside, they were subjected to legal restrictions and social ostracism. Muslims could be found in even fewer areas: chiefly the Iberian peninsula, Sicily, and Hungary. Iberia in particular was home to large numbers of Jews and Muslims, and it has often been pointed to as an example of harmonious coexistence between adherents of the three great monotheistic religions. In his essay, Ruiz follows the vicissitudes and tests the limits of this *convivencia* between Iberian Christians, Jews, and Muslims, disclosing in the process how intimately Christian identity could be bound up with anxiety over how to interact with neighbors who were culturally so close yet, in religious terms, irreducibly different.

A PEOPLE'S HISTORY OF CHRISTIANITY

So how, in the end, has the history of Christianity changed as a result of bringing into consideration these new sources, these different protagonists, and this greater variety of religious expressions? What has happened to our understanding of the history of Christianity as the center of attention shifts from the saintly and ascetic athletes of God to their admiring fans, and from prelates and princes to the Christian people?

For one thing, we become acutely conscious of the complex layering of devotions, as later developments were added to earlier ones. When Christianity first spread through Western Europe, the holiest objects at these new Christian shrines were the relics of people like St. Martin of Tours, who may have been universal saints but were nonetheless held to be particularly present, and especially effective, at the sepulchers that contained their physical remains. Crowds flocked to their tombs to ask these friends of God to intercede on their behalf at the heavenly court, and the keepers of their shrines recorded and proclaimed the miracles that ensued. Oaths sworn on relics became a normal part of judicial procedure, and at the beginning of the ninth century, relics were declared an essential element of all churches in the Frankish realm: all altars lacking relics were to be destroyed, and any newly consecrated churches had to contain relics.

In the eleventh century, this religion of formal reverence for sacred objects and rites became suffused with an evangelical tint. A renewed interest in the lives of Jesus and his apostles redirected devotion and inspired new forms of piety. Pilgrims continued to frequent local shrines to local saints, but increasingly they plied the routes that led across France to the apostles Peter and Paul in Rome or to St. James at Compostela in northwestern Spain. Others, not content with honoring Jesus' kin or close associates, set off for the Holy Land, where they could follow the footsteps of Jesus himself, from his birthplace in Bethlehem to his holy sepulcher in Jerusalem. Thousands of people, from lords and knights to peasants and children, took the sign of the cross and marched off to wrest the Holy Land from the Muslim enemies of the faith, pausing en route to eliminate more domestic enemies of the faith—the Jews—from the heart of Christendom. Returning crusaders brought back to Western Europe a fresh harvest of relics of the saints and above all of Jesus: a lumberyard's worth of fragments of the true cross and the crown of thorns for which Louis IX, the saintly king of France (1226–1270), built that great glass reliquary known as the Sainte Chapelle. Renewed interest in the apostolic life also encouraged reverence for those living holy men who best embodied the evangelical ideal, an ideal that was increasingly defined in terms of apostolic poverty.

The triumph of orthodoxy over popular heresy in the thirteenth century owed something to the elaboration of ecclesiastical structures and the calculated application of force, but even more to the proliferation of opportunities for the faithful to take an active part in religious life. The spread of the mendicant orders meant more, better, and longer sermons for the laity to hear. Prolonged or repeated elevation of the host during the Mass, the use of monstrances to display the consecrated Eucharist, and the introduction of Corpus Christi processions all served to satisfy the laity's fervent desire to see the body of Christ, made present by the priest's words and the miracle of transubstantiation. Urban parishes paraded the relics of their saints in annual processions; villagers followed their priests each spring as they blessed the fields. In times of trouble, the faithful invoked the most powerful force at their command: the orthodox magic of the church. When swarms of locusts threatened the crops, the village priest was asked to excommunicate the insects. When floods threatened Paris in the summer of 1426, parish processions wended their way through the city and converged on the cathedral of Notre Dame, imploring the rains to cease and the waters to recede.

In addition to more or less passive attendance at Mass, sermons, and processions, the laity formed religious guilds or confraternities, thousands of which were founded in the late Middle Ages. Every village had its confraternity, and each city had several; there were thirteen confraternities in Aix-en-Provence by 1400, and thirty in Dijon by the end of the fifteenth century. These pious associations were an important source of charity: they fed the hungry, clothed the poor, dowered young women, visited the sick, and buried the dead. This assistance aimed to knit up the social fabric by extending Christian brotherhood; the confraternity of St. Paul in Paris did not merely distribute food to the poor but invited them to its annual feast, seated them in the best places, and gave them the choicest morsels. Confraternities staged religious processions or performances on major festivals and met more often for private devotions. At their weekly or monthly meetings, the members heard Mass or listened to sermons: that is, they duplicated what they normally experienced in church, but on their own terms and often with the participation of lay preachers. They also performed devotional exercises—prayer, the singing of hymns, flagellation—according to the specific bent of the confraternity. Confraternities thus provided an institutional framework within which laymen and laywomen could appropriate for their own use such monastic practices as penitential flagellation and meditative prayer.

It must be stressed, however, that these later developments were added to earlier ones without replacing them. What we see is an overlay of devotions, in which the early dedication to objects such as relics and shrines was supplemented first by reverence for those living holy men and women who best embodied the evangelical ideal and then by an effort to sanctify one's own self through the assiduous performance of charitable and pious acts. Those acts were often directed toward the most traditional of sacred objects; the cult of relics, for instance, was as important at the end of the Middle Ages as it was at the start.

The rhythms of the history of Christianity also look somewhat different when it is conceived as a history of the Christian people rather than the history of ecclesiastical institutions. To be sure, no one would dream of denying that monasticism was central to Christian devotion (not to mention European society, economy, and culture) throughout the thousand years of the European Middle Ages. Nor would one want to downplay the significance of the Gregorian reform as a historical watershed. From the middle of the eleventh century, the Gregorian reform movement transformed the structure and amplified the ambitions of the Catholic Church. Gregory VII and his fellow reformers called for a church freed from secular interference, a clergy purified of the twin taints of sexuality and simony, a priesthood dedicated to pastoral care and the performance of the sacraments. The Catholic Church emerged from the long travail of reform in the institutional form it has maintained to the present day: a centralized hierarchical organization headed by the bishop of Rome, the pope. Over the course of the twelfth and thirteenth centuries, it steadily refined its organization until a network of parishes covered the face of Europe. It consolidated a system of canon law that governed the workings of the ecclesiastical machinery and guided the application of religious principles in everyday life. And it elaborated a systematic theology that explained and justified Christian beliefs, from the most universal precepts to the most abstruse details.

For all that, various contributions to this volume come together in identifying another, and rather different, key transformation in medieval Christianity: what we might call the pastoral revolution of the thirteenth and fourteenth centuries. Up to this point, the territorial organization of the church had consisted of relatively large districts, with numerous chapels and their officiating clergy subordinated to a head church held by the district's archpriest. Individuals heard Mass at their local chapel, but only the head church had a baptismal font. Even a city the size of Florence, which counted a hundred thousand inhabitants around 1300, still had only one baptistery, Dante's beloved San Giovanni, where all Florentines received baptism. Over the course of the thirteenth and fourteenth centuries, these large ecclesiastical districts were broken up into smaller units. Subordinate chapel-churches won the right to provide a fuller range of religious services: now the people who were accustomed to gathering there for Mass could bring their infants there to be baptized and their dead to be buried. The resulting parish system, in city and countryside alike, was a far finer web of ecclesiastical institutions, with often quite tiny churches, capable of holding perhaps fifty to a hundred families, providing cradle-to-grave pastoral care to close communities of the faithful in which everyone was intimately known to his or her parish priest.

An increasingly literate laity demanded more of their priests, and got it. Parishioners, as well as the ecclesiastical hierarchy, expected their priests to perform the ritual sacrifice of the Mass more frequently, more proficiently, and more elaborately. They expected their priests to preach well and often and to hear confession. Perhaps especially in cities, they began to expect their priests to live a life of greater holiness, in closer conformity to their clerical vows. And as the clergy grew more conscious of its distinctive social and religious identity, so too did the laity. By the end of the Middle Ages, laymen and laywomen had laid claim to their way of life—a life of labor and commerce, of marriage and sexuality, of sociable entanglements with family, friends, and neighbors—as a fully Christian life.

FOR FURTHER READING

Brooke, Rosalind, and Christopher Brooke. *Popular Religion in the Middle Ages: Western Europe, 1000–1300*. London: Thames & Hudson, 1984.
Bynum, Caroline Walker. *Jesus as Mother: Studies in the Spirituality of the High Middle Ages*. Berkeley: University of California Press, 1982.

Duffy, Eamon. *Marking the Hours: English People and Their Prayers, 1240–1570.* New Haven: Yale University Press, 2006.

Gurevich, Aron. *Medieval Popular Culture: Problems of Belief and Perception.* Translated by János M. Bak and Paul A. Hollingsworth. Cambridge: Cambridge University Press, 1988.

McGinn, Bernard, and John Meyendorff, with Jean Leclercq, eds. *Christian Spirituality: Origins to the Twelfth Century.* World Spirituality 16. New York: Crossroad, 1985.

Raitt, Jill, with Bernard McGinn and John Meyendorff, eds. *Christian Spirituality: High Middle Ages and Reformation.* World Spirituality 17. New York: Crossroad, 1987.

Swanson, R. N. *Religion and Devotion in Europe, c. 1215–c. 1515.* Cambridge: Cambridge University Press, 1995.

Vauchez, André. *The Laity in the Middle Ages: Religious Beliefs and Devotional Practices.* Translated by Margery J. Schneider. Notre Dame, Ind.: Notre Dame University Press, 1993.

———. *Spirituality of the Medieval West: From the Eighth to the Twelfth Century.* Translated by Colette Friedlander. Cistercian Studies. Kalamazoo, Mich.: Cistercian Publications, 1993.

CHRISTIANIZING
THE PEOPLE

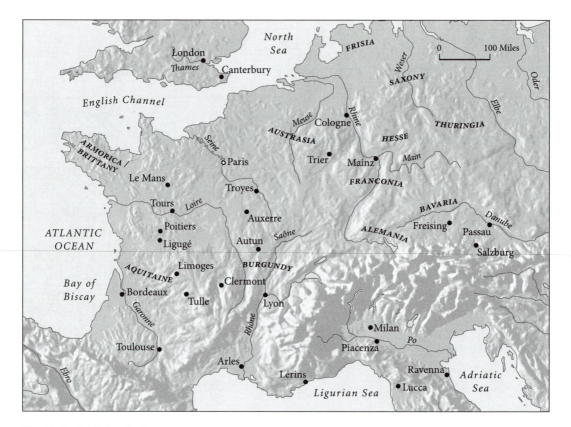

Fig. 1.1. The Frankish territories

CONVERTING THE BARBARIAN WEST

YITZHAK HEN

Go therefore and make disciples of all nations, baptizing them in the name of the Father and of the Son and of the Holy Spirit, and teaching them to obey everything that I have commanded you" (Matt. 28:19-20). This simple mandate to spread the Word, which concludes the Gospel according to Matthew, represents a significant turning point in the history of ancient religions. As demonstrated by Martin Goodman, missionary activity was not an inherent feature of ancient religions, and in the Roman Empire it was found only sporadically among both Jews and pagans.[1] Christianity, however, was different. Whether the Christian notion of mission was triggered by Jesus himself (whose preaching, one must constantly bear in mind, was directed almost exclusively at Jews) or whether it was a later innovation is still an open question. Nevertheless, it appears that from a fairly early stage Christianity adopted a missionary stance. The Acts of the Apostles relates how Jesus' disciples and followers gradually assumed the missionary vocation, and the history of Christianity from then onward is, to a large extent, the history of mission and evangelization (even though in some periods evangelization has been relatively insignificant).

During the first four centuries of its existence, Christianity made a considerable attempt to Christianize the Roman world. From a persecuted minority, Christianity grew to be the most influential religious faction in Late Antiquity. From a religion of the wretched and the poor, Christianity became the religion of aristocrats and emperors. From an underground cult, Christianity's monuments became the most dominant feature both in the urban landscape and in the countryside. Within less than four centuries, Christianity gained an unrivaled position among the various religions of the Roman Empire, and in 391 Emperor Theodosius I (d. 395) issued two edicts against pagan sacrifices and pagan cults that established Christianity's leading position among the religions of the empire.[2] At least from that time, if not much earlier, the Roman Empire was perceived as a Christian empire, and consequently Christianity became part and parcel of what may be termed "late-antique *Romanitas*." The rise of Christianity to prominence was, no doubt, a long and slow process, but its success in the long term was rather impressive and long lasting.

Unfortunately, very few sources refer to the Christianization process before the fourth century, and in many cases we are ignorant of the first steps made by Christians to propagate their faith. If we take, for example, the region of Gaul, we only know that by the end of the second century, Christianity had managed to secure a stronghold in a small area of southeastern Gaul, mainly in and around the cities of Vienne and Lyons, where Bishop Photinus and his companions were persecuted in 177. However, from the beginning of the fourth century onward, there is plenty of evidence (written and archaeological) for the expansion of Christianity throughout the Rhone valley, most parts of the Auvergne, southern Aquitaine, and along the Seine and the Loire. No fewer than eight church councils were convened in Gaul during the fourth century, and many more were held under Merovingian rule. These councils provide the clearest and most obvious proof for the progress Christianity made in the West. For example, representatives of forty-five episcopal sees, from Carthage in North Africa to Lincoln in Britain, and from Mérida in Spain to Syracuse in Sicily, were present at the first provincial council convened by Emperor Constantine in Arles (314),[3] and their presence at the council reflects quite accurately the spread of Christianity into every corner of the western Roman Empire.

The fourth century was also marked by the activity of individuals who embarked on a mission to promote Christian ideas. From the start, evangelization was the work of devoted individuals who wandered throughout the Roman Empire preaching the Christian message. Christ's own disciples—the Apostles (Greek: messenger)—were the first, but many more followed suit. An excellent case in point is Martin of Tours (d. 397), who, after being discharged from the Roman army, dedicated his life to the conversion of the rural areas of Gaul; ultimately he became the bishop of Tours and the patron saint of the Frankish kingdom. Consequently, the conversion of Europe is a story of individual missionaries who, like Martin of Tours, took upon themselves the burden of spreading the Christian message. Ulfilas (d. 383), Patrick (d. mid or late fifth century), Pirmin of Reichenau (d. 753), Willibrord (d. 739), Boniface (d. 754), Anskar (d. 865), Cyril (d. 869), and Methodius (d. 885) are just a few of the most prominent missionary figures of the early Middle Ages. They were all devoted Christians whose personal decision to embark on a missionary life contributed to the spread of Christianity throughout the empire. Moreover, from the end of the fourth century, following the example of Sulpicius Severus's *Vita Martini* (published in 396), the activities of such individuals were recorded by Christian authors, and hence we are better informed of the missionary zeal and activity of later generations.

After Constantine's victory at the Milvian Bridge (312) and the publication of the Edicts of Milan (313), which turned Christianity into a *religio licita* (Latin: permitted religion, that is, a religion whose cult is permitted), new forces joined the attempts of individual Christians to evangelize the Roman Empire—the emperors themselves (and later the rulers of Barbarian Europe) and the Roman army. While the emperors backed the missionary activity with both political support and lavish financial resources, the Roman army became one of the most important agents of Christianity, and its actual presence all over the empire facilitated the spread of Christianity throughout the Roman world. Once again the example of Martin of Tours is instructive. Before embarking on his missionary career, Martin served as a soldier in the Roman legion that was stationed in Gaul.

It is precisely against this background of missionary activity that the conversion of the Barbarians should be understood. The initial impetus was given, so it seems, by a single devoted Christian—Ulfilas (or "Ulphilas," ca. 311–383), the so-called apostle of the Goths. After being consecrated (ca. 341) as a bishop by Eusebius of Constantinople (previously of Nicomedia), Ulfilas dedicated his life to the

Ulphilas and the Conversion of the Goths

In the reigns of Valerian and Galienus, a large number of Scythians from beyond the Ister crossed into Roman territory and overran much of Europe. Crossing also into Asia, they reached as far as Galatia and Cappadocia. They took many prisoners, including some who were members of the clergy, and went home with a great quantity of booty. Now the pious band of prisoners, living as they did among the Barbarians, converted many of them to the way of piety and persuaded them to adopt the Christian faith instead of the pagan. Among these prisoners were the ancestors of Ulphilas; they were Cappadocians by nationality, from a village near the city of Parnasus called Sadagolthina. It was this Ulphilas who led the exodus of the pious ones, being the first bishop appointed among them. He was appointed in the following circumstances: sent with others by the ruler of the race of the Goths on an embassy in the time of Constantine (the barbarian people in those parts owed allegiance to the emperor), Ulphilas was elected by Eusebius and the bishops of his party as bishop of the Christians in the Getic land. Among the matters which he attended to among them, he was the inventor for them of their own letters, and translated all the Scriptures into their language—with the exception, that is, of Kings. This was because these books contain the history of wars, while the Gothic people, being lovers of war, were in need of something to restrain their passion for fighting rather than to incite them to it—which those books have the power to do, for all that they are held in the highest honor, and are well fitted to lead believers to the worship of God. The emperor established this mass of refugees in the territories of Moesia, where each man chose to live; and he held Ulphilas in the highest esteem, so as often to refer to him as the "Moses of our time."

—Philostorgius, *Church History* 2.5, in Peter Heather and John Matthews, *The Goths in the Fourth Century*, Translated Texts for Historians 11 (Liverpool: Liverpool University Press, 1991), 143–45

conversion of his fellow countrymen. He received the support of two Roman emperors—Constantius II (d. 361) and Valens (d. 378)—and despite some disruption during the Gothic anti-Christian persecutions in the late 340s, he had probably completed his mission among the Goths before they crossed the Danube in 375. It may well be that conversion to Christianity was one of the conditions put forward by Valens before he allowed the Goths to cross the border and settle on Roman soil.

When Ulfilas embarked on his mission to convert the Goths, at first within the borders of the Roman Empire and later in the province of Moesia II, Arianism was the dominant Christian faction in Constantinople. Consequently, the Goths embraced the Arian doctrine that stressed the human nature of Christ, and their crucial role in the conversion of other Germanic peoples turned Arianism into one of the most prominent Christian doctrines among the Barbarians. Most, if not all, of the Barbarian peoples who "invaded" the western provinces of the Roman Empire adopted Christianity (albeit in its Arian form) before they crossed the border into

Roman territory, and it seems that their settlement in the regions of Gaul, Spain, Italy, and North Africa during the fifth and early sixth centuries left minor imprints on the state of Christianity.

Although the Arian rulers of the Barbarian West were often depicted as heretics who took up the persecution of Catholics, reality was most probably different. To understand the Arian attitude toward other Christian doctrines and sects, one can cite the words of the Arian Visigoth Agila, who once admonished Bishop Gregory of Tours (d. 594):

> You must not blaspheme against a faith which you yourself do not accept. You notice that we who do not believe the things which you believe nevertheless do not blaspheme against them. It is no crime for one set of people to believe in one doctrine and another set of people to believe in another. Indeed, it is a proverbial saying with us that no harm is done when a man whose affairs take him past the altars of the Gentiles and the Church of God pays respect to both.[4]

Toleration, rather than ruthless persecutions, characterized the Arian attitude toward Catholics in the West. Apart from Vandal North Africa, where a savage persecution of Catholics was conducted by the Arian Vandal kings Geiseric (d. 477) and Huneric (d. 484), there is no evidence whatsoever that the Arian rulers of the post-Roman West ever tried to impose their beliefs on the indigenous inhabitants of their kingdoms. This, of course, must not be taken to imply that Arian kings did not depose Catholic bishops or confiscate Catholic churches from time to time. After all, religious allegiance was part and parcel of politics throughout the early Middle Ages. Nevertheless, these sporadic and rather local affairs should not be confused with intolerance.

The anomaly in which the ruling Barbarians were Arians while the indigenous population adhered to so-called Catholic Christianity did not last for long. The Franks were the first from among the Barbarians to adopt Catholic Christianity. The personal conversion of the Frankish king Clovis (d. 511) in either 496 or 507/8 paved the way for the conversion of the entire Frankish population of his kingdom. In 516, the Burgundians abandoned Arianism in favor of Catholicism. In 533, Vandal North Africa was conquered by Belisarius, Emperor Justinian's chief in command, and in 552/3, the Arian Ostrogothic kingdom of Italy was finally subdued by the Byzantine army, with the result that in both kingdoms Arianism ceased to exist as a significant religious faction. In 589, the Visigoths of Spain converted to Catholicism, following the conversion of their king Reccared (d. 601), and only the Lombards in Italy wavered between Arianism and Catholicism until the mid-seventh century.

Obviously, the triumph of Catholicism in the West did not happen universally and at the same time, but it seems that by the end of the sixth century, Western Europe was, to a large extent, Catholic. Consequently, missionaries could either promote and consolidate the Christian belief in an already Christianized territory or direct their missionary effort at territories beyond the former border of the Roman Empire, such as Frisia and Saxony, where there were still many pagans to be converted.

MAKING A DIFFERENCE

The huge amount of scholarly literature about mission and conversion in Late Antiquity and the early Middle Ages has mostly been concerned with the nature and course of missionary activity as well as with issues of doctrine and theology, rather than the effects it had on the converted population. Therefore, in what follows, I should like to concentrate on what difference conversion actually made during the early Middle Ages. Needless to say, such a short survey can hardly be exhaustive. Not only are local variations abundant and the time span enormous, but also the subject matter is extremely vast and highly complicated. Any scholar who embarks on such a mission has to make many choices of issues, sources, and interpretations, with the inevitable result of a highly personal, even (in some respects) impressionistic view of early medieval Christianity. Nevertheless, the following selection of topics and issues may give us a rather fair indication of what was going on and provide a stimulus for further discussions.

Although most scholars today agree that by the end of the sixth century the vast majority of the inhabitants of Western Europe were in fact baptized Christians, there is little consensus regarding the degree to which they had adopted Christianity. On the one hand, the minimalists would argue that conversion to Christianity includes very little apart from two obvious things: baptism and the renunciation of all pagan gods and worship rituals. According to these criteria, Western Europe of the early Middle Ages was indeed an utterly Christian society. On the other hand, it has been argued that true conversion entails a change in every aspect of the individual's life. Arthur Darby Nock wrote in his 1933 vanguard study of conversion: "By conversion we mean the reorientation of the soul of an individual, his deliberate turning from indifference or from an earlier form of piety to another, a turning which implies a consciousness that a great change is involved, that the old was wrong and the new is right."[5] Subsequently, Ramsey MacMullen wrote that "so disturbing and difficult must be conversion, or so incomplete."[6] According to this view, early medieval Europe was, no doubt, Christian by name but still pagan by practice and spirit. However, to understand conversion as "the reorientation of the soul of the individual" and "the adhesion of the will to a theology"[7] is to impose modern perceptions on the past. It further assumes deep knowledge and understanding of Christianity's theology and doctrine on the part of the people. Yet very few Christians have ever attained deep and thorough theological understanding like St. Augustine (d. 430), and to judge the conversion of a society according to this Augustinian yardstick is, to my mind, misleading. The Christianity of "ordinary" men and women, which is based mainly on acts and participation in ceremonies, was not the Christianity of theologians, and it is unreasonable to expect of the former a total reorientation of the soul and a complete adhesion to a theology.

Hence, the two extreme views of conversion adduced above leave much to be desired. Neither is sufficient on its own to describe the complicated and most colorful situation of early medieval Europe. I tend toward a middle view: conversion, although not altering completely the lives of the people, had some impact on the individual's life and on society as a whole. True, this was not a total "reorientation of the soul" accompanied by deep and thorough theological understanding as envisaged by Nock, but certainly it entailed much more than just baptism and official renunciation of past beliefs. Let us, then, take a few case studies from the public domain as well as from everyday life in order to demonstrate what difference Christianity made in actuality.

CHRISTIAN TIME

In his famous letter to Abbot Mellitus (d. 624), Pope Gregory the Great (d. 604) offered some guidance on various matters pertaining to the conversion of pagans:

> I have decided after long deliberation about the English people, namely that the idol temples of that race should by no means be destroyed, but only the idols in them. Take holy water and sprinkle it in these shrines, build altars and place relics in them. For if the shrines are well built, it is essential that they should be changed from the worship of devils to the service of the true God. When this people see that their shrines are not destroyed they will be able to banish error from their hearts and be more ready to come to the places they are familiar with, but now recognizing and worshiping the true God. And because they are in the habit of slaughtering much cattle as sacrifices to devils, some solemnity ought to be given them in exchange for this. So on the day of the dedication or the festivals of the holy martyrs, whose relics are deposited there, let them make themselves huts from the branches of trees around the churches which have been converted out of shrines, and let them celebrate the solemnity with religious feasts.[8]

Gregory's instructions to Mellitus, which constitute a dramatic change in papal missionary strategy, were aimed at bolstering the missionary activity in England.[9] After scolding the English king for not doing enough to promote Christianity, Gregory realized that the slow progress in the Christianization of the English was not because of insufficient zeal and motivation on the king's part. The whole concept of conversion as a ruthless confrontational process suddenly seemed to him unsuitable for the conversion of pagans; he considered that maybe a lenient flexible approach would do the job more effectively.

Hence, according to Gregory's new approach, Christianization should entail as little disruption as possible to everyday life. By avoiding any confrontation and brutal interference in the life of the people, Gregory set up a papal scheme to Christianize time. Slowly and inadvertently, Christian feasts would be introduced as a proper replacement to the pagan ones, and subsequently the entire pagan calendar, according to which the English lived, would be replaced by an utterly Christian one.

Gregory the Great was not the first pope to realize the importance of Christian time to the conversion of the masses. In fifth-century Rome, Pope Leo the Great (d. 461) made a noteworthy attempt to shape the lives of Rome's inhabitants by public liturgical worship. As Robert Markus has pointed out, "What Leo's preaching to his Roman congregations reveals is an overriding concern to draw them into the rhythm of the Church's public worship. Time and again he is trying to awaken in his audience a sense of the moment in the sacred time-scheme whose deep rhythms he wishes to reverberate in the hearts and the minds of his hearers."[10] Hence the Christianization of time became an integral part of the evangelization process. It was perceived as a crucial prerequisite for the success of any mission, and both missionaries and clergymen made a constant effort to formulate a Christian calendar for their communities. This was done by the introduction of the so-called Christian temporal cycle (the feasts associated with Christmas and Easter) and more so by the introduction of the sanctoral cycle, which was local in nature and changed through time.

Let us take, for example, the sanctoral cycle of Auxerre in Burgundy. Very few saints were venerated in Auxerre before the fifth century, and none of them can be identified as a local saint. This situation, however, was changed dramatically by Bishop Germanus (d. 437/448), whose dynamic personality manifested itself not only in building churches, collecting relics, and instituting new saints' feasts in the city but also in the fact that he was the first saint from Auxerre in a long line of local saints. After Germanus's episcopacy, the number of saints venerated in Auxerre continuously multiplied, and by

Willibrord and Radbod, King of the Frisians

The king was roused to intense fury and had a mind to avenge on the priest of the living God the insults that had been offered to his deities. For three whole days he cast lots three times every day to find out who should die; but as the true God protected his own servants, the lots of death never fell upon Willibrord nor upon any of his company, except in the case of one of the party, who thus won the martyr's crown. The holy man [i.e., Willibrord] was then summoned before the king and severely upbraided for having violated the king's sanctuary and offered insult to his god. With unruffled calmness the preacher of the Gospel replied: "The object of your worship, O King, is not a god but a devil, and he holds you ensnared in rank falsehood in order that he may deliver your soul to eternal fire. For there is no God but one, who created heaven and earth, the seas and all that is in them; and those who worship him in true faith will possess eternal life. As his servant I call upon you this day to renounce the empty and inveterate errors to which your forebears have given their assent and to believe in the one Almighty God, our Lord Jesus Christ. Be baptized in the fountain of life and wash away all your sins, so that, forsaking all wickedness and unrighteousness, you may henceforth live as a new man in temperance, justice, and holiness. If you do this you will enjoy everlasting glory with God and His saints; but if you spurn me, who set before you the way of life, be assured that with the devil whom you obey you will suffer unending punishment and the flame of hell." At this the king was astonished and replied: "It is clear to me that my threats leave you unmoved and that your words are as uncompromising as your deeds." But although he would not believe the preaching of the truth, he sent back Willibrord with all honor to Pippin, leader of the Franks.

—Alcuin, *Life of Willibrord*, ch. 11 in *Soldiers of Christ: Saints and Saints' Lives from Late Antiquity and the Early Middle Ages,* ed. Thomas F. X. Noble and Thomas Head (University Park: Pennsylvania State University Press, 1995), 199–200

the time of Bishop Aunarius (d. 605), the sanctoral cycle of Auxerre was composed of feasts in honor of more than thirty saints, the vast majority of whom were bishops, clerics, abbots, and monks in and around the city.[11] There is no way to gauge how many of these feasts were solemnly celebrated. But even if not all the saints' days that are mentioned in our sources were celebrated in Auxerre with great pomp, it seems only fair to conclude that the annual cycle of Auxerre was punctuated with various local liturgical festivities.[12]

Yet the sanctoral cycle of Auxerre is extremely revealing in another aspect as well. The exact date of a saint's death was not always known. However, the day of the relics' translation and deposition in the church, which eventually became the day on which the saint was venerated, could have been planned carefully, and the sanctoral cycle of Auxerre seems to have been a well-planned case. Twelve feasts in honor of local saints were assigned in Auxerre to the month of May, and this attempt to turn the month of May into a prolonged period of liturgical celebrations is enough to demonstrate how the Christian authorities used and manipulated the various saints' feasts in order to Christianize time. This is exactly what Gregory the Great had in mind when he advised Mellitus to encourage the celebration of Christian feasts at the recently converted pagan shrines. No wonder, then, that missionaries were equipped with long lists of potential saints' feasts. The so-called Calendar of St. Willibrord, for example, lists more than a hundred saints' feasts.[13] At any given moment a Christian feast could be found in order to replace a pagan celebration or a celebration thought to be pagan by the church and its representatives.

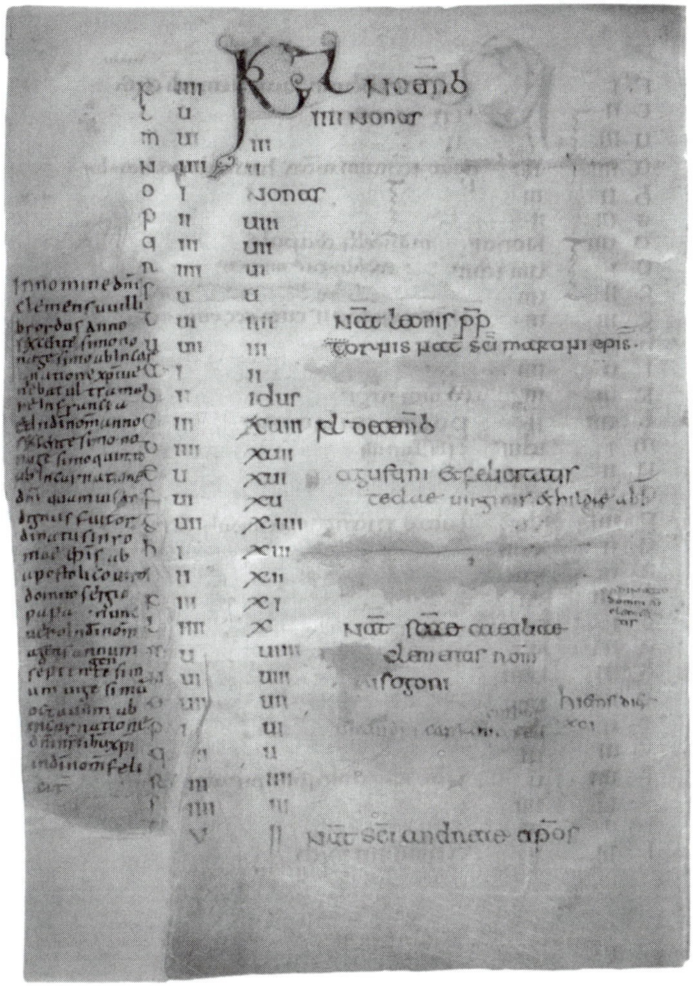

Early medieval Europe, one should stress, was by and large an agrarian society, which lived according to the seasonal cycle long after the introduction of Christianity. Nevertheless, the Christian liturgical cycle became an important factor in everyday life, and local churches throughout Europe strove to create an essentially Christian rhythm that was to replace the pagan sequence of festivals. The agrarian cycle was never abolished, but coexisted alongside the Christian cycle with some points of connection, such as Easter, which often coincided with the spring harvest. But from the moment that a Christian rhythm was established, the pace of life even in those agrarian societies was clearly measured against a Christian scale.

Fig. 1.2. Willibrord's calendar with his so-called autobiography scribbled in the left-hand margin. Paris, Bibliothèque nationale de France, MS Lat. 10837, fol. 39v.

CHRISTIANIZING KINGSHIP

One of the most prevailing idiosyncratic notions in modern historiography is the idea of sacred Germanic kingship. According to this notion, Germanic kingship combined both religious and political functions, and the king, being the arbiter between his people and the gods, was perceived as the charismatic embodiment of his people's "luck."[14] There is growing agreement in recent years, however, that such a notion of Germanic kingship gains no convincing evidentiary support. Whenever our sources are carefully examined, the form of Germanic kingship that emerges from them is overwhelmingly Roman in character.

The lack of any reliable source, untouched by Roman and Christian perceptions, did not confuse modern scholars, who happily embraced the notion of sacral kingship and savagely forced it upon their sources. An excellent case in point is the legendary origins of the Franks. A small passage in the seventh-century chronicle of Fredegar reports that "when Clodio was staying with his wife on the sea shore in the summer, his wife went to the water to bathe at noon, and a beast of Neptune resembling the Quinotaur [= Minotaur] sought her out. As she conceived right away, either by the beast or by her husband, she afterwards gave birth to a son called Merovech, after whom the kings of the Franks were later called Merovingians."[15] This account of Merovech's birth was interpreted in the past as an informative Frankish "foundation myth." According to this interpretation, the Merovingians believed themselves to be descended from a supernatural ancestor—a mythical sea monster. Such an interpretation of Fredegar's account, however, is based on extremely shaky ground. Both Alexander Callander Murray and Ian Wood have demonstrated quite persuasively that this version of Merovech's birth tells us more about seventh-century politics than about perceptions of kingship among the early Franks.[16] Moreover, such a notion of kingship runs contrary to the prevailing Roman character of rulership, which emerges from other Merovingian sources.

The early Merovingians inherited the Roman imperial tradition of political thought, and subsequently rulers were described in traditional imperial nomenclature and addressed in the reverential language that had customarily been employed to address the emperor.

At the same time, Roman imperial ideals gradually infiltrated the various statements on the virtues that a good king should display. As we have already noted, in the later Roman period and more so in the sixth and seventh centuries, the Roman tradition was inherently Christian. Hence, when Merovingian authors addressed the Frankish kings in traditional Roman imperial language, they automatically defined their status—or, rather, their political ideology—in Christian terms. Piety and justice, for example, were indeed two of the Roman attributes of a good ruler, but they were gradually Christianized and thus became a structural Christian piety and justice, and qualities that a king, as king, was supposed to possess. After all, it is only to be expected that kings and queens who, in personal terms, were Christian would conceive their royal office in this way.

Thus, already by the sixth century, Christian ideas and notions were an integral part of the so-called Frankish perception of kingship. As clearly pointed out by Janet Nelson, "If Merovingian sacrality ever existed, it is very unlikely to have survived the powerful impact of Christianity on Frankish royal ideology and practice in the sixth and seventh centuries."[17] Moreover, it is impossible to isolate reliably any sacral elements within the Merovingian perception of kingship, since any element that might qualify as sacral can be understood in a purely Christian sense.

In his survey of Germanic kingship in England and on the Continent, John Michael Wallace-Hadrill noted that "a change in emphasis comes over western kingship in the seventh century; kings move into an ecclesiastical atmosphere; they are required to consider their duties in a fresh light, and many actually have done so."[18] There was nothing new in this trend, which had already started in the sixth century, if not earlier. Nevertheless, it is obvious that there was a change in tone in the seventh century, and therefore we hear more about kings in ecclesiastical terms. First steps in that direction can be identified in King Guthramn's edict of 585, in which the image of the Frankish king as God's minister was first outlined.[19] Thereafter, and throughout the early Middle Ages, Christian themes came to dominate ideas of rulership and government in Frankish Gaul.

One significant effect of this shift of emphasis was the frequent recourse to biblical examples and citations, which denote the

Christian complexion of the newly formed political thought. It was not to Byzantium that Merovingian authors looked for a royal model but to the Bible—and more particularly to the historical books of the Old Testament. Obviously, this also had some sixth-century antecedents, but during the seventh century, biblical comparisons became more frequent and the Christian message still more direct.[20] Consequently, wisdom in judgment, defense of the church, and aid for the poor became the principal components of the late Merovingian views on the duties of a king.

Another manifestation of the Christianization of rulership in Merovingian Gaul was the emergence of the royal patronage of liturgy. Merovingian kings and queens bestowed large amounts of landed property, precious objects, and various immunities upon monasteries and religious communities in order to secure their spiritual support. It is thus no mere coincidence that several of the liturgical books from late Merovingian Gaul contain prayers for the king. These prayers—the most eloquent witness to the Christianization of rulership—beseech God to protect the kingdom's peace, to secure its stability, and to grant victory to the ruler. Not only were these prayers an emotional appeal for God's protection; they also disseminate what appears to be an utterly Christian political ideology.

For example, the Old Gelasian Sacramentary, which was copied at the mid-eighth century in either Chelles or Jouarre (both closely connected with Queen Balthild's activities), includes a Mass urging God to "let your servants N., our kings, adorn the triumph of your virtue skillfully, so that they, who are *principes* [Latin: leaders] by your command, may always be powerful in their duty." Later on in the same Mass, God is asked to give the guidance of his wisdom to the rulers, "so that drinking from your fountain for their assemblies they may please you and may rise above all the kingdoms." Similarly, another prayer of the very same Mass beseeches God to accept the oblation: "just as you regarded it worthy to bestow upon him the power of ruling, gracious and generous [as you are], receive [him under your protection]; and implored grant our entreaty, so that confident in the protection of your majesty, he may be blessed with age and kingdom." Finally, the Mass concludes with a wish for peace: "O God, who prepared the eternal Roman empire by evangelical predicting, present the celestial arms to your servants N., our *principes*, so that the peace of the churches may not be troubled by the storm of wars."[21] Although the formula *rex Dei gratia* (Latin: king by the grace of God) was not yet used by the Merovingian kings and their advisors, its notion was already embedded in the Mass for the kings.

In 751, when Pippin III (d. 768) assumed power over the Frankish kingdom, he simply continued the religious policy of his Merovingian predecessors and propagated the very same Christian ideology of rulership. But as they did in so many matters, the Carolingians operated on a much more grandiose scale. It will suffice to mention here the immense effort taken by the Carolingians to organize coronations, large-scale liturgical processions in times of crisis, lavish acts of patronage, and, of course, the *laudes regiae*. Carolingian politics from the time of Pippin III onward was accompanied by a massive downpour of rhetoric that highlighted, among other things, a Christian theocratic concept of rulership. Biblical examples, once again, offered an attractive general model, and as early as 775, Charlemagne (d. 814) was addressed as both David and Solomon.[22] Subsequently, this rhetoric gave rise to one of the standard tropes of Frankish

---

A Mass for a King

O God, protector of all the kingdoms and of the greatest Roman empire, let your servants N., our kings, adorn the triumph of your virtue skillfully, so that they, who are *principes* by your command, may always be powerful in their duty.

O God, in whose hand lay the hearts of the kingdoms, lend the ears of your compassion to our humble prayers and give the guidance of your wisdom to our *principes*, your servants, so that drinking from your fountain for their assemblies they may please you and may rise above all the kingdoms.

SECRET: Accept, O Lord, the supplicant prayers and sacrifice of your Church for the safety of N., your servant, and work the old miracles of your arm for the protection of the faith of the people, so that after the enemies of peace are surpassed, the secure Roman freedom may serve you.

DURING THE ACT: Thus, O Lord, accept this oblation of your servant N., which we offer you by the ministry of the sacerdotal office, just as you regarded it worthy to bestow upon him the power of ruling, gracious and generous [as you are], receive [him under your protection]; and implored grant our entreaty, so that confident in the protection of your majesty, he may be blessed with age and kingdom.

AFTER COMMUNION: O God, who prepared the eternal Roman empire by evangelical predicting, present the celestial arms to your servants N., our *princeps*, so that the peace of the churches may not be troubled by the storm of wars.

—From the Old Gelasian Sacramentary
III.62.1505–9, in Y. Hen, *The Royal Patronage of Liturgy in Frankish Gaul to the Death of Charles the Bald*, Subsidia (Henry Bradshaw Society) 3 (London: Boydell, 2001), 40

political ideology under the Carolingians: the equation of the Franks with the chosen people of the Old Testament—the New Israel. The Christianization of rulership was over, and the sacralization of kingship had begun.

THE PERSONAL LIFE CYCLE

The individual life cycle, from birth to death, is punctuated by various events that mark significant social, religious, and personal changes in life. It could only be expected that Christianity, which only recently got a stronghold in society, would strive to gain control over these crucial junctions in the personal life cycle and to provide them with a Christian religious context, if not a proper Christian meaning. This process, one should stress again, did not happen instantly or uniformly throughout Western Europe. Each region had its own pace and intensity, and no uniformity ever existed. But the overall impression from combing through the sources is that throughout the formative period of the early medieval West (roughly from the fourth until the eighth century), the individual life experience witnessed a dramatic Christian makeover. Let us take for example the rite of passage commonly known as *barbatoria*, which was the most important event in the life of the early medieval man.

Rites of passage are significant events in the life of the individual and the society in which he or she lives. They usually mark a transition in the social status of the person who experiences them, and hence they reflect society's own views of its structure and function. As the anthropologist Arnold Van Gennep pointed out in his pioneering work on the subject, many societies have such a mandatory public rite for young men, one that symbolizes their separation from the world of childhood.[23] The Jewish Bar Mitzvah, circumcision in certain Muslim and African societies, and the grant of the toga in Republican Rome are all ritualized turning points that distinguish a man from a boy, and the barbatoria had exactly the same function in several post-Roman Barbarian kingdoms.

According to Tacitus, the ceremonial arming of the young man was the most common rite of passage among the Germans.[24] It seems,

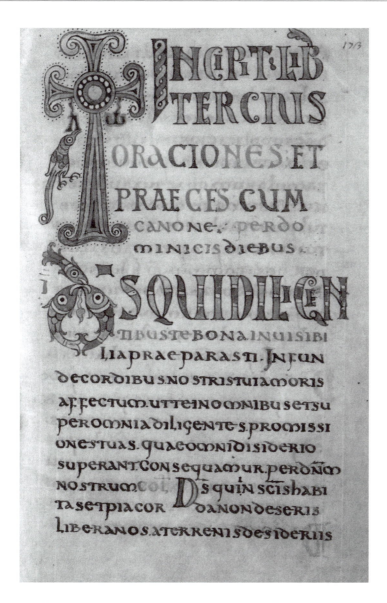

Fig. 1.3. Opening of the third book of the Old Gelasian Sacramentary. BAV Reg. Lat. 316, f. 173r. Copyright © Biblioteca Apostolica Vaticana.

however, that the inhabitants of early medieval Europe favored a different, arguably Greco-Roman rite of passage for the young male—the barbatoria—which was celebrated when the beard (*barba* in Latin) of the young adult was shaved for the first time. Given the scanty evidence at our disposal, it is impossible to determine whether the Barbarians had ever celebrated barbatoria before they first encountered Roman civilization. But it appears that by the time they settled in Western Europe (late fifth and early sixth centuries), most of the Barbarian peoples had already adopted the barbatoria as the most significant rite of passage for young men.

How exactly the barbatoria was celebrated is very difficult to ascertain, since no detailed description of it survives. From the little we know, one may conclude that the ceremony was performed by the boy's father or, in the case of an orphan, by the closest male relative and in front of family members and close friends. It is highly probable that no actual shaving of the beard took place during the ceremony, not only because shaving in the Middle Ages was a long and rather painful process but also because of the fact that in order to shave the beard one needs to have one. Since barbatoria was performed when the young boy was around twelve or thirteen years old, it is doubtful whether he had grown a beard by that age. Hence, a symbolic gesture of patting or touching the cheek was performed during the solemn ceremony itself.

The classical origins of the barbatoria are well known. The poet Callimachus (d. ca. 240 BCE) mentions a similar ceremony that was performed in Delos, and several later sources describe how the Romans celebrated such events with feasts. The Barbarians followed this classical tradition and made it their own. During the early Middle Ages, the ceremony of barbatoria did not remain stagnant and completely detached from cultural and religious developments, and following the conversion of the West, it was also Christianized. A first allusion to this process comes from a poem by Paulinus of Nola (d. 431), in which he describes how the first hairs of his beard were shaved and offered at a tomb of a saint.[25]

The best evidence for the Christianization of the barbatoria comes from a series of sacramentaries that were composed in Frankish Gaul, Visigothic Spain, and Byzantium. The following prayer, for example, was included in the so-called Gelone Sacramentary (dated roughly 790 to 800):

O God, through whose providence every adult creature rejoices in growth, be gracious to this servant of yours, flourishing in youthful blush of age and shaving his bloom for the first time. May he be strengthened in every respect through the support of your protection; may he live to old age and may he rejoice in your protection in this life and in eternity. Through our Lord.[26]

This and similar prayers from the various sacramentaries clearly indicate that a valiant effort was made to adapt the barbatoria to a Christian context, and it may well be that the ceremony moved altogether to the church and that an entire Mass was sung in honor of the occasion.

We do not know whether the impetus behind the Christianization of the barbatoria came from the people themselves or from the ecclesiastical authorities. Nevertheless, there is little room to doubt that the early medieval barbatoria was gradually Christianized, and this reflects a larger process that went over many aspects of the individual's life cycle. For example, the concept of marriage was gradually Christianized in the early Middle Ages. Although the decree *Tametsi* of the council of Trent (1563) was the first to recognize the rite of marriage as a sacrament, this was the result of a long process that started with the Christianization of everyday life in Late Antiquity and the early Middle Ages. The works of Christian scholars, such as Tertullian (d. ca. 230) and especially Augustine (d. 430), paved the way for such a change, and already by the ninth century, marriage was perceived as a sacrament by Hincmar of Rheims (d. 882). This conceptual change had a dramatic effect on the ceremony that was celebrated, as the various matrimonial prayers and masses in early medieval sacramentaries clearly suggest. Although we cannot be sure that a Christian ceremony was performed every time a couple was married in the early Middle Ages, the fact that a Christian rite already existed is significant in itself.

Other prayers in various sacramentaries tell a similar story. The Old Gelasian Sacramentary, for example, contains numerous prayers for domestic affairs, such as a Mass to encourage rain, an oration to be said after a storm, or benedictions to ensure good crops. Other prayers were dedicated to medical problems, such as women's sterility, and a few were meant to ensure the health of all family members. Prayers to be said on the occasion of visiting a new house, as well as masses to secure the well-being and safe return of travelers, were also included in early medieval prayer books. All these prayers and masses indicate that Christianity became a crucial component in shaping society's practices and attitudes, and hence the Christianization of the individual's life cycle (or at least some parts of it) provides the clearest evidence for the penetration of Christianity into the Barbarian West.

PAGAN SURVIVALS

When E. A. Judge asked A. H. M. Jones what difference Christianity made to Rome, Jones answered briefly and bluntly: "None."[27] Several years later, Ramsey MacMullen asked the same question and concluded that in many respects very little had changed, while in others Christianity made "an absolutely remarkable impact . . . that was to shape the whole millennium to come."[28] The few examples adduced above are enough, I hope, to convince that even if its impact was not felt everywhere, Christianity did indeed make a lot of difference. But as MacMullen clearly pointed out, in some areas very little had changed *because of* Christianity, and various changes that did take place during the formative period of the early medieval West could be attributed to other factors. For example, the slow but consistent disappearance of slavery came about for some practical reasons, such as a shortage of supply and changes in land distribution, rather than the introduction of Christian moral standards. In other domains, it appears that non-Christian moral attitudes run parallel to Christian ones. Sexual promiscuity, to give just one example, was unacceptable by both pagan/Roman and Christian standards. Hence, when Augustine, Gregory the Great, or even the penitentials refer to this issue, they simply rehearse (in a Christian guise) moral attitudes that could also be found in the writings of Cicero (d. 43 BCE), Pliny (d. ca. 114), and even the second-century satirist Apuleius. These examples clearly demonstrate how complex and multilayered the question of conversion is. To make things even more complicated, there is the issue of "pagan survivals."

Early medieval society has traditionally been described as Christian by name but pagan by nature, in which non-Christian practices and superstitions were rife. This derogatory view was partly conditioned by Nock and his followers' definition of conversion, but it also derives from our sources, which mention numerous "non-Christian" practices and classify them as "pagan." But are we to understand these descriptions at face value? Could it be that the sources' crusade against pagan practices and superstitions tells us more about the authors' worries and anxieties than about the actual survival of pagan religions among the newly converted inhabitants of Western Europe?

Let us take for example the celebration of the Calends of January, evidently a reminiscence from the Roman pagan past. These celebrations were condemned by Ambrose of Milan (d. 397) and Jerome (d. 420) in the fourth century, by Maxim of Turin (d. ca. 423) and Peter Chrysologus (d. 450) in the fifth century, and by Caesarius of Arles (d. 542) in the late fifth and early sixth century. Sub-

Fig. 1.4. Boniface baptizing the Frisians and his martyrdom, from the Sacramentary of Fulda. Bamberg, Staatsbibliothek, Msc. Lit. 1, fol. 126.

sequently, similar condemnations were repeated with minor changes and variations by Martin of Braga (d. 579), Pirmin of Reichenau, Halitgar of Cambrai (d. ca. 830), Hrabanus Maurus (d. 856), Regino of Prüm (d. 915), and Burchard of Worms (d. 1025).[29] In 742, Boniface even scolded Pope Zacharaias that such events were still celebrated at Rome:

> They [visitors to Rome] say that on the first of January year after year, in the city of Rome and in the neighborhood of St. Peter's church by day or night, they have seen bands of singers parading the streets in pagan fashion, shouting and chanting sacrilegious songs and loading tables with food day and night, while no one in his house is willing to lend his neighbor fire or tools or any other convenience.... If your Paternity would prohibit these heathen

practices at Rome, it would bring rewards to you and the greatest advantage to us in our teaching.[30]

All the Christian authors who condemned the celebration of the Calends of January classified them as "pagan survival." Modern historians followed suit and, taking these condemnations at face value, argued for the persistence of pagan religious practices among the newly converted Christians.

In doing this, they failed to take into account "the sheer vitality of non-religious, secular institutions and traditions and their power to resist change."[31] True, celebrating the Calends of January had some pagan religious meanings in the Roman past. But when celebrated in eighth-century Rome, the Calends of January was a social celebration, completely detached from its original pagan connotations. Even Caesarius of Arles was aware of the fact that many of the practices he condemned as "pagan" were often detached from their original pagan meaning, and therefore scholars should be extremely cautious when attributing the label "pagan" to social customs practiced by people converted to Christianity. Not everything that survives from the pagan past or described in our sources as "pagan" retains its pagan religious meaning.

But the issue of pagan survivals is even more complicated than that. It raises a whole series of problems concerning the artificiality,

---

The Preaching of Caesarius of Arles

He delivered sermons suited to particular feasts and spiritual passages, and also against the evil of drunkenness and lust, against discord and hatred, against anger and pride, against the sacrilegious and fortune-tellers, against the utterly pagan rites of the Kalends [of January], and against augurs, worshipers of trees and springs, and vices of different kinds. He prepared these sermons in such a way that if any visitor requested them, he did not refuse to share them. Even if his visitor did not suggest that he ought to take any of them, Caesarius nonetheless offered them to him to read and brought them to him. To clerics located far away in the Frankish lands, Gaul, Italy, Spain, and other provinces, he sent through their bishops sermons they could preach in their own churches, so that when they had cast aside frivolous and perishable things, they might become, according to the apostle, "followers of good deeds" [Titus 2:14]. In this way he diffused the fragrance of Christ far and wide. Through his accomplishments he burned brightly, [even] where he himself never appeared. He touched the hearts of those he never met in person.

—*The Life of Caesarius* I.58 in *Caesarius of Arles: Life, Testament, Letters*, trans. and ed. William E. Klingshirn (Liverpool: Liverpool University Press, 1994), 37–38

in a sense, of written models and traditions. Combing through the various beliefs and practices that were condemned in the early Middle Ages as "pagan" or "superstitious," one may ask what relationship the resurfacing of such practices bears to changing realities. Moreover, the late seventh and early eighth centuries in Western Europe were a turning point in the references made to pagans and paganism. From that period onward, the written sources are obsessed with pagan practices and superstitious observances. There is a sharp contrast between, on the one hand, the general terms with which practices are condemned in the sixth century and, on the other hand, the specific, detailed, and wide-ranging prohibitions in later sources.

It has been suggested in the past that the preoccupation with paganism and superstitions in the late seventh and early eighth centuries was influenced by insular missionaries who operated on the Continent.[32] Moreover, it may well be that missionary activity in remote regions, such as Frisia and Saxony, where pagan religions were still alive and active, helped to kindle interest in pagan practices closer to home. But are we to understand these preoccupations and repetitive condemnations as a reflection of the reality the authors seem to describe? No doubt, the repetition of various unauthorized observances, such as the Calends of January, and their classification as "pagan" are, in a sense, the result of some well-rooted literary conventions. At the same time, the preoccupation with pagan practices and superstitions in our sources reflects a certain reality. This reality was a mental reality rather than a practical one, and therefore these texts and condemnations should be regarded as evidence for what the people who wrote them thought ought to be prohibited. They should be regarded as evidence for norms, not facts.

From the fourth century onward, various practices that the Christian authorities could not abolish, transform, or control were defined by Christian authors as "pagan." Hence, a certain image of what is "pagan" emerged in the writings of Christians such as Ambrose of Milan, Jerome, and Augustine, and this image was later used and recycled by preachers, theologians, missionaries, and legislators. Needless to say, the image that emerges from these writings was far from being an accurate description of reality. But it helped Christianity to set up clear-cut boundaries by defining what is permitted from a Christian point of view and what is not. More often than not, the past practices that survived the conversion of the West no longer had religious meaning, and yet they were a crucial part of Christianity's view of paganism and consequently of itself. As Robert Markus put it, the condemnation of pre-Christian patterns of behavior "functioned, rather, to define the identity of the group, the Christian community united with its bishop under a shared loyalty and a shared value system."[33] This, I would submit, is the ultimate proof that Christianity had indeed struck deep roots in the early medieval West, infiltrating into many corners of the individual's life and into society as a whole. The fact that in the second half of the eighth century and throughout the ninth century the Carolingians manipulated the issue of paganism for propaganda purposes in order to justify their coup and defame their Merovingian predecessors leaves little room for doubt that Christianity did indeed make a huge difference. Conversion was much more than a mere acceptance of Christianity by baptism and the renunciation of old pagan beliefs.

FOR FURTHER READING

Brown, Peter. *The Rise of Western Christendom: Triumph and Diversity, A.D. 200–1000.* 2nd ed. Oxford: Blackwell, 2003.

Carver, Martin, ed. *The Cross Goes North: Processes of Conversion in Northern Europe.* Woodbridge: Boydell & Brewer, 2002.

Fletcher, Richard. *The Conversion of Europe: From Paganism to Christianity, 371–1386 AD.* London: HarperCollins, 1997.

Hen, Yitzhak. *Culture and Religion in Merovingian Gaul, A.D. 481–751.* Leiden: Brill, 1995.

Levison, Wilhelm. *England and the Continent in the Eighth Century.* Oxford: Clarendon, 1946.

MacMullen, Ramsey. *Christianity and Paganism in the Fourth to Eighth Centuries.* New Haven: Yale University Press, 1997.

Markus, R. A. *The End of Ancient Christianity.* Cambridge: Cambridge University Press, 1990.

Mayr-Harting, Henry. *The Coming of Christianity to Anglo-Saxon England.* 3rd ed. London: B. T. Batsford, 1991.

Wallace-Hadrill, J. M. *Early Germanic Kingship in England and on the Continent.* Ford Lectures. Oxford: Clarendon, 1971.

Wood, Ian N. *The Missionary Life: Saints and the Evangelisation of Europe, 400–1050.* London: Longman, 2001.

DEATH AND BURIAL

BONNIE EFFROS

CHAPTER TWO

Traces of burial rites are not hard to find in the historical and archaeological record of early medieval Europe. Of all types of ritual, it is one of the few in which we may assume the majority of the population participated. Although the evidence is undeniably biased toward the social constituencies that could create the most lavish or permanent monuments, which were more likely to be preserved, cemeteries and the human and archaeological vestiges they contain have the potential, ideally in conjunction with written evidence, to shed light on many aspects of early medieval society. Mortuary archaeology offers a unique window into the daily lives of the large majority, including the structure of complex social hierarchies, the production of luxury goods, and the expression of gender ideology, ethnic identity, and religious belief. Undoubtedly archaeological finds associated with mortuary practices will also allow scholars to further unmask the subjective or contradictory nature of the written sources on which historians up until now have depended almost exclusively.

Promising as it is, this kind of multidisciplinary work requires the exercise of great caution: each genre of evidence has its peculiarities and unique problems. Thus, for instance, artifacts from funerals do not represent random or chance survivals, as is the case of finds at most settlement sites. Rather, they were in most cases consciously deposited with the dead. This in itself calls for the employment of interpretive strategies from a variety of disciplines—above all, anthropology. Interdisciplinary and multidisciplinary approaches stand the greatest chance of gleaning information from highly fragmentary remains.

TOMBS OF THE SAINTS

For a discussion of early medieval burial and mourning rites, the most logical starting place from the perspective of the written evidence is at the tombs of the saints. The deaths of exemplary Christians were highly celebrated events, since the souls of martyrs and confessors were believed to rise directly to heaven regardless of the state of their human remains. Saints' funerals theoretically represented occasions of great joy for their followers, even if the most devout Christians sometimes had difficulty expressing their elation at the loss of one of their own.[1] Emphasis was placed on the belief that the beneficial presence of the holy did not end with their decease but rather continued through the safekeeping of their relics, which became a direct conduit to the heavenly sphere for those Christians left behind.

The veneration of such figures meant that priests, monks, and nuns, who were often members of the religious communities out of which these figures emerged, had great incentive to compose hagiographical works that recalled not only their virtues and accomplishments during their lifetimes but also the miracles performed in their names after their deaths. These biographical accounts differed widely in factual accuracy. Together with decorated tombs or funerary inscriptions, such as in the eighth-century carved stone sarcophagus of Chrodoara or Ode of Amay (d. before 634) in modern Belgium,[2] they allowed contemporary Christians glimpses into holy lives. These images were reinforced by processions that escorted the deceased to the grave as well as the liturgy performed at that time and on annual commemorations. Modern scholars have supplemented these sources with art historical and archaeological evidence of the iconography and architecture that graced the churches in which early medieval saints' cults flourished.

Despite such a welcome wealth of evidence, scholars have been notably cautious about how to proceed with studies of saints' burials. After all, hagiographical accounts were often composed long after the events they commemorated, and the longer the time that passed, the greater the leeway their authors had in the manner in which they chose to describe the lives of their subjects. Moreover, these writers aimed primarily at convincing the faithful of the unstained reputation of the deceased and of God's reward for extraordinary feats of asceticism. Such concerns could directly affect the sections of the lives (that is, biographies) dedicated to the deaths and funerals of the saints. The anonymous author of the *Life* of Gertrude of Nivelles (d. 659), in modern-day Belgium, for instance, focused on the humble petition by the holy abbess to be buried simply with a penitential hair shirt and a veil left behind by a female pilgrim to her monastic house. Neither of these garments was perceived by contemporaries as befitting of her noble status.[3] Such a claim nonetheless satisfied the purposes of the hagiographer, who sought to contrast Gertrude's veneration of relics and desire for heavenly reward with the worldly aims of the powerful Pippinid family to which she belonged.

Hagiographers also frequently accompanied their idealized picture of saints' deaths with descriptions of the wondrous events that signaled God's immediate recognition of the merits of the holy. Among the most common miracles recorded in such cases were the sweet fragrances that were said to have emanated from the bodies of the deceased. For example, the monk Jonas of Bobbio alleged this with respect to a seventh-century nun, Gibitrude, in the monastery of Faremoutiers to the east of Paris.[4] This passage

---

Augustine of Hippo on Burial near to the Remains of the Saints

And if this is true, a place provided for burying bodies among the memorials of the saints is surely a matter of good human affection in attending to the funeral of one's own relatives. Indeed, if there is some religious requirement that they be buried, there can be some when the question is considered as to where they shall be buried. But, when such comforts are sought for the living by which their pious intentions toward their own loved ones are evident, I do not see what aids there are for the dead except for this purpose, that, while the living are worshiping in the place where the bodies of those whom they love are buried, they may commend to the same saints, as if to patrons, those whom they have undertaken before the Lord to aid by prayer. Actually, they could do this even if they had not been able to bury them in such places. For no other reason are those things which plainly become sepulchers of the dead said to be memorials or monuments, unless it is because of this: Memorials admonish us to think of and to recall to our memory those who have been taken away by death from the eyes of the living, lest by forgetfulness they be removed from our hearts also.

—Augustine of Hippo, "The Care to Be Taken for the Dead," trans. John A. Lacy, in *Augustine of Hippo, Treatises on Marriage and Other Subjects*, ed. Roy J. Deferrari, Writings of Saint Augustine 15 (=The Fathers of the Church 27) (Washington, DC: Catholic University of America Press, 1955), 358

was intended in part as propaganda encouraging pilgrims to visit the burial site of the nun in question.

Another factor that should make us skeptical about the reliability of accounts of the funeral rites performed for the special dead is the content and focus of saints' *Lives*. These works often evolved over time in response to the changing predilections and customs of the faithful. The anonymous account composed circa 699, eleven years after the death of Cuthbert, the holy bishop of Lindisfarne in the north of England, gave significant attention to the priestly garments, shoes, and shroud that accompanied the saint into his grave. When the congregation opened Cuthbert's sepulcher at Lindisfarne eleven years later with the permission of Bishop Eadbehrt, the author noted that the saint was found lying so entirely untouched by decay that he appeared to be sleeping.[5] The narrative glorified the deceased saint by confirming that God's favor had prevented the ordinary putrefaction of human flesh. While Cuthbert's soul had already reached Heaven, his body, the site of miraculous events and healings, became the locus of devotion for untold numbers of Anglo-Saxon and Irish monks and pilgrims who visited the church in which he had been buried.

By contrast, when the Venerable Bede authored a new work in honor of Cuthbert in the 720s, he augmented these passages considerably to include a request by the abbot that he be buried humbly with a shroud in a sarcophagus interred on the north side of his private oratory on a remote island. Although the alleged petition was not respected by the disciples of Cuthbert, who carried his remains to a stone sarcophagus to the right of the altar in the church of St. Peter on the semi-island of Lindisfarne,[6] these scenes secured Lindisfarne's claims to Cuthbert's bodily relics and allowed Bede to promote the saint's cult. Importantly, too, in this same work, Bede gave attention to the fact that Cuthbert had received the viaticum prior to his passing. Although this detail had been mentioned briefly by the anonymous author of the earlier *Life*, the custom of giving communion to a person at the point of death had grown increasingly common on the Continent following strong recommendations by church leaders such as Pope Gregory the Great (d. 604) in his *Dialogues*. Worried about the purgatorial suffering that might afflict Christian souls in the time preceding the Last Judgment, Bede used this description of Cuthbert's humble preparations for death to reinforce the beneficial nature of the Eucharist even for the holy in achieving salvation. In the north of England where Bede wrote, the advice of this influential pope was especially important following the decision made by clerics at the Council of Whitby (664) to prefer Roman over Irish liturgical traditions. Bede's prominent reference to Cuthbert's taking of the wafer thus offered him the opportunity to assert that in the Irish-founded stronghold of Lindisfarne, too, Cuthbert and his followers were loyal to papal precepts.

In ways like this, descriptions of the events surrounding the death and burial of saints were often ideologically loaded. These works presented rosy models of what a good Christian death should be: a soul joyously embraced by the company of angels and wondrous signs of divine favor to reassure survivors that the soul of the deceased had risen safely upward. For historians, such miracle accounts shed light on the clerical understanding of the topography of the afterlife. Clerics surely conveyed to their congregations what they considered requisite for heavenly reward, although it is nearly impossible to measure the popular reception of these ideas. Hagiographical and visionary accounts also offered descriptions of the fates that awaited those who led less than exemplary lifestyles. One need only peruse the visions of the Irish monk Fursey (d. ca. 649–650), who had exiled himself to the continent with the intent of doing missionary work, to find cautionary tales of a shadowy valley filled with burning fires.[7] Following a near-death experience in the last quarter of the seventh century, a Frankish monk named Barontus recounted to his brethren his horrifying encounter with airborne demons that ravaged the souls of unrepentant sinners with talons and long teeth.

Hagiographical recollections and visionary warnings, undoubtedly conveyed by clerics to their congregations, thus provided vivid lessons for the faithful in the rites, behavior, and belief essential to achieving the grace of eternal salvation. Formal rites and bodily actions thus opened the way to a salvation conceived in corporeal terms, just as sinful acts led to the intensely physical sufferings of the damned.

CHRISTIAN LITURGY FOR THE DEAD

Yet, as might be expected, hagiographical descriptions of the events surrounding the last days of the saints were hardly representative of the early medieval mortuary practices of the more general population. Although regional church councils such as the one held in Arles (442–506) declared that clerics were to administer penance to those who requested it at the time of their final confession, little is known about how frequently such petitions were made or honored. The Council of Agde (506) likewise forbade priests from depriving the dying of the Eucharist, but it is difficult to substantiate the frequency with which rural or poor Christians had regular access to a priest or deacon or might be able to find their way to a local church for last rites. Although contemporary clerical sources claimed that the priest's role as intermediary between the ordinary Christian and God was steadily growing, the survival of very few sacramentaries predating the eighth century makes it impossible to measure the clergy's involvement with the dying beyond the members of religious communities or the elite constituencies of private churches.

As in late antiquity, funerals were largely the responsibility of families. It appears that clerics neither dictated the place of burial nor imposed a particular liturgy upon the graveside services.[8] Their attention was mainly directed at regulating commemoration of the deceased after the funeral. While psalms and masses for the dead had been declared beneficial for all but impenitent sinners since at least the time of Augustine of Hippo, it was certainly not obligatory for Christians to request such arrangements. One of the earliest extant services in the medieval West for commemorating the dead was appended to the early sixth-century *Rule* of Caesarius of Arles for his sister Caesaria's monastic house of Saint-Jean in Arles, but its impact on lay Christians of the region is uncertain.

What is clear from the late seventh-century penitential attributed to Theodore of Canterbury is that Anglo-Saxon and probably continental laypeople were expected to wait three days for masses to be recited for their deceased family members, whereas clerics were entitled to such privileges on the day of their interment. Even in the latter case, it seems that the service was not necessarily performed in the cemetery.[9] Many scholars surmise that ordinary Christians in Western Europe typically lacked access to a priest who could perform the Mass either on the day of their funeral or on anniversaries of their death. Agreements made in Frankish synods at Attigny in Champagne (762) and Dingolfing in Bavaria (770) similarly privileged the recitation of masses in commemoration of the deceased among the predominantly clerical membership of large prayer confraternities. These rites probably remained beyond the reach of most of the laity, who did not have connections to the clerical hierarchy or the means to make requisite donations. At least in the case of Francia, there is no evidence for the existence of a formal office for the dead earlier than the ninth century.

GRAVES AND CEMETERIES

Besides describing the ritual activities linked to the saints' last days and funerals, accounts of the lives of saints emphasized the importance of burial *ad sanctos* (next to the saints) for early medieval Christians. These accounts reinforced the idea that graves in close proximity to the tombs or reliquaries of the saints were beneficial to the welfare of Christian souls. Beyond such exclusive resting places, however, the early medieval church does not appear to have regulated the graves of Christians particularly carefully. For much of the period, the majority of the population, both pagan and Christian, were interred in rural cemeteries, while only a minority of Christians were buried in or near churches.

In northeastern Gaul as early as the fifth century and spreading to Brabant, Limburg, the Alps, and farther afield during the sixth century and afterward, the predominant form of burial was in row grave cemeteries (*Reihengräberfelder*) that likely included individuals of different religious persuasions. These necropolises might contain anywhere from some dozens to a few thousand interments, and they seem to have been used by the inhabitants of communities in the general vicinity. Other cemeteries in these regions were of smaller size and might be situated near ruins or prominent features in the landscape. Most appear to have had no documented link to local church or secular authorities.

Some fashions in the arrangement of burial places arose in particular geographical locations. During late antiquity and the early Middle Ages, the topography of cemeteries was often shaped by the specific needs or the physical or political environment of the communities they served. These adaptations took a variety of forms according to the needs of inhabitants, as may be seen in the development of the Christian catacombs in late antique Rome. In the region of Paris, we may observe that sarcophagi fashioned from local plaster grew popular in the sixth and seventh centuries due to its greater accessibility. The difficulty of importing large pieces of cut stone to this region in this period probably made the option of locally produced decorated tombs increasingly desirable to those seeking to honor their dead.[10]

In eastern England, on the other hand, the practice of cremation persisted for some time after it had disappeared elsewhere in Western Europe. Cemeteries here were typically larger than those reserved exclusively for inhumation of bodies. Such sites, dating from the mid-fifth to the mid-seventh centuries, could contain as many as several thousand burials. Many of these cremation burials typically contained artifacts. Such cemeteries seem to have served not just immediately adjacent settlements but communities at a greater distance, since ashes were more easily transported than bodies.[11]

Another example of inhabitants opting for relatively unusual cemeterial configuration is the revival of the prehistoric rite of mound burial in northern England between the seventh and the ninth centuries. Some presumably high-status families in these areas chose to bury their dead in already standing or newly erected barrows accompanied by elaborate assemblages of grave goods. While scholars traditionally interpreted this form of inhumation as an expression of pagan

Fig. 2.1. Sixth-century sarcophagus fashioned from an oak log and decorated with a two-headed dragon. Found in an Alemannic cemetery in Oberflacht, Baden-Württemberg, in Germany (O.37363). Reproduced by permission of the Römisch-Germanisches Zentralmuseum Mainz.

defiance toward the spread of Christianity among the Anglo-Saxons, the adoption of this ancient rite may have been motivated instead by its powerful symbolism and the impression it made on contemporaries. The attractiveness of the practice likely involved few religious considerations, but instead focused on the prominence of the site or its implied link to the ancient inhabitants of the region. This monumental form of burial evidently affected the landscape in a manner that families hoped would highlight their resources and influence.

An unusual precedent, then, in terms of official intervention in the organization of cemeteries by lay authorities, was Carolingian legislation directed against the Saxons, who had been forcibly converted to Christianity following their defeat by the Franks. A series of measures passed in the late eighth century forbade them from interring their dead in pagan cemeteries and represented an innovative manner of preventing a hostile population from maintaining a separate identity.[12] Largely the product of political rather than religious

---

On Despoiling Dead Bodies

1. He who furtively despoils the body of a dead man before it is placed in the ground and it is proved against him (called *chreomosido* in the Malberg gloss) shall be liable to pay twenty-five hundred denarii (i.e., sixty-two and one-half solidi).

2. He who despoils or destroys the tomb covering a dead man (called *tornechale* in the Malberg gloss) shall be liable to pay fifteen solidi.

3. If a man destroys the enclosure (*charistatone*) over a dead man (called *manduale* in the Malberg gloss), or if he destroys the *lave* which is the burial mound over a dead man (called *chreoburgio* in the Malberg gloss), for each of these things he should be liable to pay six hundred denarii (i.e., fifteen solidi).

4. In an old law: he who digs up and despoils a body already buried and it is proved against him (called *muther* in the Malberg gloss) shall be outlawed (*wargus*) until that day when it is agreeable to the relatives of the dead person and they ask on his behalf that he be permitted to come among men again. And that one who, before compensation has been paid to the relatives, gives him [who was outlawed] bread or hospitality, whether it be his parents or his wife or other near relative who does it, shall be liable to pay six hundred denarii (i.e., fifteen solidi). The perpetrator of the crime who is proved to have committed it or dug it up (called *tornechale* in the Malberg gloss) shall be liable to pay eight thousand denarii (i.e., two hundred solidi).

5. He who in evil or stealth places a dead body on top of another one in a wood (*nauco*) or stone sarcophagus and it is proved against him (called *chaminis* in the Malberg gloss) shall be liable to pay eighteen hundred denarii (i.e., forty-five solidi).

—*The Laws of the Salian Franks*, trans. Katherine Fischer Drew (Philadelphia: University of Pennsylvania Press, 1991), 118 (Pactus Legis Salicae, chap. LV)

considerations, the restrictions placed on the Saxons thus cannot be seen as representative of efforts to regulate Christian burial among the rest of the population. Aside from sermons meant to discourage drunkenness and other inappropriate behavior in graveyards, few efforts were made by either lay or clerical authorities to control or regulate cemeteries. Scholars therefore believe that burial in consecrated cemeteries did not become standard prior to the tenth or eleventh centuries.[13]

PERFORMANCE OF FUNERARY RITES

As we have seen, hagiographical accounts of the deaths and burial of the saints were not as influential in the shaping of contemporary practices as their authors hoped they would be. Nonetheless, they did share some important underlying similarities with less exceptional funerals. To varying degrees, all forms of mortuary ritual, whether in pagan or Christian households, were "sacred fictions"[14] and required the temporary suspension of critical memories of the dead. Like the descriptions of the merits or deeds of the deceased to be found on funerary inscriptions and in saints' *Lives*, the configuration of a funerary ceremony, the objects deemed appropriate additions to a grave, and the location and housing chosen for the deceased's resting place each represented part of a deliberate strategy by competing families to renegotiate the memory of the dead in their communities. The burial rite thus had performative elements in its structuring with respect to an anticipated target audience. All aspects of the undertaking contributed to the end product: an idealization of the achievements (or potential achievements in the case of children) of the deceased. These symbolic qualities became part of the personality of the dead, a multilayered composite that was constructed through the funerary ceremony and various features of the burial place. Commemorative events held on anniversaries of the individual's death, either at the gravesite or elsewhere, in the right conditions could sustain the memory of the deceased for years to come.

The theatrical potential of funerals is most easily demonstrated by the elaborate burials for kings and other powerful elites. For the main ship burial in Mound One at Sutton Hoo in East Anglia, for example, not only were a large number of individuals required to deposit the sailing vessel and its precious contents on land and cover the part above ground level with earth, but these activities themselves represented part of the ritual process. Moreover, the objects—for example, feasting vessels, baptismal spoons, and coins—that likely accompanied the deceased, whose skeletal remains did not survive, came from a wide range of places both near and far. A number of unusual burials deposited nearby, including possible executions or human sacrifices, suggest that the site was used on multiple occasions for a variety of ritual purposes. Although the precise symbolic significance of individual artifacts to participants is largely lost to modern observers, scholars have suggested viewing the combined features of Sutton Hoo as a deliberate statement by local magnates intent

Mourning for the Blessed Radegund of Poitiers

The blessed Radegund, whom I mentioned in the beginning of my book about martyrs, migrated from this world after completing the labors of her life. After receiving the news of her death I went to the convent at Poitiers that she had founded. I found her lying on a bier; her holy face was so bright that it surpassed the beauty of lilies and roses. Standing around the bier was a large crowd of nuns, about two hundred of them, who had converted because of Radegund's preaching and adopted the holy life. According to the status of this world not only were they [descended] from senators, but some were [descended] from the royal family; now they blossomed according to the rule of their piety. They stood there weeping and saying: "Holy mother, to whom will you leave us orphans? To whom do you entrust us who have been abandoned? We have left our parents, our possessions, and our homeland, and we have followed you. What will you leave us except perpetual tears and endless grief? Behold, until now this convent was more important for us than were the open spaces of villas or of cities. Wherever we went, when we saw your glorious face we found there gold and silver; there we saw blossoming vineyards, waving cornfields, and meadows blooming with a variety of different flowers. From you we picked violets; for us, you were a glowing red rose and a brilliant lily. Your words shone for us like the sun; like the moon they illuminated a clear lamp of truth for the darkness of our conscience. Now, however, our entire world has been darkened and the sea of this place has been constricted, since we do not deserve to see your face. Alas for us, who have been abandoned by our holy mother! Happy were those who migrated from this world while you were alive! We know that you have been admitted to the chorus of holy virgins and to the Paradise of God. Although we are consoled by that, the fact that we cannot see you with the eyes of our bodies is a reason for us to weep."

—Gregory of Tours, *Glory of the Confessors*, trans. Raymond Van Dam (Liverpool: Liverpool University Press, 1988), 105–6

on resisting the spread of Christianity and political might issuing from the south of England in the early decades of the seventh century. Evidence points to the idea that a large group, one that identified itself as independent, pagan, and allied closely to Scandinavian mortuary traditions, used the funeral of the powerful individual whom current consensus identifies as Raedwald, king of East Anglia (d. 624), as an opportunity to express its politics in a radical and meaningful fashion.[15]

Fig. 2.2. Sixth-century garnet brooch found in Worms-Abenheim, Rheinland Pfalz, in Germany (0.15137). Reproduced by permission of the Römisch-Germanisches Zentralmuseum Mainz.

The lavish grave of the pagan Frankish king Childeric I (d. 482), found at Tournai in southern Belgium in 1653, likewise shows the great potential of funerals to convey the symbolism of continuity and power. Containing richly decorated weaponry, objects related to personal dress, as well as a collection of other artifacts including a crystal globe, golden bees, and a signet ring, the sepulcher was probably marked by an enormous mound with a diameter of between twenty and forty meters (about twenty-two to forty-four yards). In the 1980s, on the periphery of this zone, archaeologists found the remains of twenty-one horses deposited in three pits.[16] Although they cannot be dated precisely enough by means of carbon 14 to be linked for certain to the funeral of Childeric, and the three zones do not appear to be contemporaneous to one another, the location of the horses' sacrifice or execution suggests the likelihood of their having some relationship to his grave. The interment of the horses, like the funeral of Childeric himself, may have served as an opportunity for possibly generations of supporters to commemorate the king and display their loyalty to his successor and son, Clovis I.

Fig. 2.3. Full reconstruction of a sixth-century bucket found in grave 61 (female) of the cemetery of Bonn-Schwarzrheindorf in Germany (0.2711). Reproduced by permission of the Römisch-Germanisches Zentralmuseum Mainz.

In the absence of mandatory funerary rites or circumscribed burial places for early medieval pagans and Christians, families thus had significant latitude in determining how and with what to bury their dead. The status or visibility of the deceased within the community played a determining role, since the more prominent or notorious an individual, the larger the group that participated in funeral arrangements and attended the ceremonies that accompanied burial. The main constraints on their range of ritual choices appear to have been largely self-imposed and fell within a parameter of factors such as the wishes of the deceased, prevailing local customs, and economic considerations. Therefore, families that used the same cemeteries, especially smaller graveyards belonging to single communities, tended to share the traditions by which they laid their dead to rest. Although kin might still opt for funerary practices that were not taken up by their neighbors, their choices were not entirely arbitrary.

> ### Burial in Holy Ground Will Not Help a Sinner
>
> My witnesses for the story of an incident that took place in Genoa are the saintly Venantius, at present Bishop of Luni, and Liberius, a man of high rank and honest character. They know the circumstances of this incident from their servants who were present when it happened. According to them, Valentine, the defender of the Church at Milan, was an extremely dissolute man given over to every kind of frivolity. When he died, he was buried in the Church of St. Syrus the Confessor. At midnight, a commotion was heard in the church as though someone was being forcibly cast out. The sacristans came running to see what was wrong and found that two vile-looking spirits had bound Valentine's feet and were dragging him out of the church, while he kept shouting and railing at them. Terrified at the sight, the sacristans returned to their beds. In the morning, on opening the tomb where Valentine had been laid, they found it empty. Looking around the church to see what might have happened to the body, they found it lying in another grave, the feet bound as they had seen them during the night.
>
> Learn from this, Peter, that if one dies in the state of mortal sin and arranges to have himself buried in church, he is sure to be condemned for his presumption. The holy place will not win him forgiveness, but will add to his guilt the sin of rashness.
>
> —Gregory the Great, *Dialogues*, trans. Odo John Zimmerman, O.S.B., Fathers of the Church 39 (New York: Fathers of the Church, Inc., 1959), 264–65

Contemporaries modified this shared ritual vocabulary in conjunction with a constellation of elements that included but was not limited to the gender, age, status, and achievements of the deceased, along with the circumstances of his or her death. Whereas in some cases the rites remained relatively static over generations, in other cemeteries abrupt changes in usages could occur without a clear stimulus. An important example of the latter development is the European-wide transition in the late fourth century of the orientation of graves from facing north-south to pointing west-east, with the head in the former direction and feet in the latter. This development cannot be attributed exclusively to the spread of Christianity because of the speed and range of its adoption, and thus it is still not well understood.[17]

BURIAL INSCRIPTIONS

One prominent feature of many late antique and early medieval cemeteries in and sometimes beyond the territories occupied by the Roman government was the presence of burial inscriptions. Among Christians the use of epitaphs was far less common than had been the case among Roman pagans, who had employed inscribed markers not only as a form of commemoration but also in fulfillment of legal obligations and traditions related to inheritance and the rights of citizenship. While many of their practical functions had disappeared by the fourth century, some pagan and Christian families evidently continued to believe that epitaphs were an effective way to mark the graves of the deceased and preserve their memories of close relations.

Despite many similarities to its pagan predecessor, Christian epigraphy concentrated more heavily on matters related to the afterlife. Aside from naming the deceased and often the family member or members responsible for commissioning the inscription, compositions of more substantial length might draw attention to the piety of the deceased, express hope for his or her imminent salvation, and ask those passing by to pray for the departed soul.

In practice, the use of Latin burial inscriptions was a predominantly urban phenomenon, since it was in cities that literacy was more widespread. In the case of Christian epigraphy, local workshops across Western Europe appear to have reached their peak of production in the last quarter of the fourth century. By far the largest number of inscriptions from late antiquity and the early Middle Ages, currently around 35,000, has been found in the city of Rome. By contrast, the number of extant inscriptions, including pilgrim graffiti, for a comparable period in Spain is 1,257, with the largest concentration of them located in the cities of Tarragona and Mérida. In Gaul it is estimated that more than 2,941 inscriptions, among them a few hundred pilgrim graffiti, survive for this period, but their distribution is uneven, with 887 discovered to date in just the imperial city of Trier.

For purposes of comparison, however, it is useful to note that epigraphy was not an exclusively urban tradition. Approximately four hundred inscriptions in Primitive Irish composed in the indigenous ogham script have been found in Ireland from the period before 700 CE, whereas no more than one mentioned by the Venerable Bede has been identified as having been composed among the Anglo-Saxons before the mid-seventh century.[18] In early medieval Wales, burial inscriptions could incorporate a combination of Latin and ogham and fulfilled a variety of functions beyond commemorating the dead, including identifying kinship relations and marking territorial boundaries. Unfortunately for scholars studying early medieval mortuary practice, however, very few epitaphs are found in situ. A large number of those extant today were collected in the eighteenth and nineteenth centuries by antiquaries interested in local history, and it is therefore a very rare occasion that graves and their contents may be identified as belonging to the specific individuals named in burial inscriptions.

GRAVE GOODS

Regardless of location and the religion of the deceased, grave goods were one of the most widespread burial customs practiced in Western Europe during the early Middle Ages. Both pagans and Christians often cremated or, after inhumation became the dominant rite in most parts of Western Europe in the late third century, buried their dead clothed and accompanied by a range of other objects, including, in a few cases, those related to the activities of specific professions like blacksmiths and surgeons. Frequently, coins were placed in the hand or mouth of the deceased, a custom that originated from pagan belief that a penny (Charon's obol) was required to pay the ferryman to cross the river Styx. Interestingly, this rite was not limited to pagans but survived long after Christian conversion.

In late antiquity and the early Middle Ages, another common practice in many parts of the former Roman Empire was to include food and drink deposits in the graves of the dead, along with the detritus of feasting rituals such as ashes. Feasts of this sort constituted a sign of respect for the dead and had once commemorated the pagan *Manes*, or general community of spirits of the dead; they were originally held after the period of mourning, on anniversaries of the deceased's passing, and at special holidays such as the annual *Parentalia* in February. Among both pagan and Christian families well into the sixth century, grave depositions might include an assortment of earthenware and glass vessels containing food and drink offerings for the dead. Christian rites thus showed considerable continuity with their pagan antecedents.

By the fourth century, however, the range and quantity of grave goods deposited with the dead broadened on both sides of the Roman frontier to include a larger range of possibilities. In addition to items associated with garments, such as belt buckles, jewelry, and toiletry items, the deceased were often laid to rest with weaponry, purses filled with small miscellaneous objects, and even furniture in exceptional circumstances. Historians and archaeologists have long debated the reasons for the evolution of the rite into one in which weapons played a prominent role: for decades the transition was attributed to the emergence of a Germanic warrior elite in the Roman army

Fig. 2.4. Grave assemblage including, among other items, reconstructed weaponry, a bronze liturgical pitcher, a glass bowl, and a purse fitting from the fifth-century grave 319 (male) of the cemetery of Lavoye (Meuse) in France. Reproduced by permission of the Musée d'archéologie nationale de Saint-Germain-en-Laye.

who buried their dead with the items that they had received as pay for their service. Yet there are great difficulties in making a definitive link between archaeological remains and specific ethnic populations, since one of the most notable differences between these customs and those of provincial Romans was an increased emphasis on brooches and armament, most of which were of Roman manufacture. Moreover, from the small number of interments that included swords, we must conclude that most of those who possessed swords were not buried with them.[19]

For example, although the outfitting of elite graves with horse-riding equipment and sometimes entire horses in the Carpathian basin may be attributed generally to the Avar population that occupied the region from the seventh century, we must keep in mind that such rites also may have been adopted by other wealthy inhabitants of the region. Weapon graves—or for that matter any sort of lavish burial rite—are more likely to have represented a means of expressing political legitimacy rather than constituting a passive reflection of the ethnic identity of those interred in these locations.

Mourning the Death of Beowulf

The Geat race then reared up for him
a funeral pyre. It was not a petty mound,
but shining mail-coats and shields of war
and helmets hung upon it, as he had desired.
Then the heroes, lamenting, laid out in the middle
their great chief, their cherished lord.
On top of the mound the men then kindled
the biggest of funeral-fires. Black wood-smoke
arose from the blaze, and the roaring of flames
mingled with weeping. The winds lay still
as the heat at the fire's heart consumed
the house of bone. And in heavy mood
they uttered their sorrow at the slaughter of their lord.

A woman of the Geats in grief sang out
the lament for his death. Loudly she sang,
her hair bound up, the burden of her fear
that evil days were destined her
—troops cut down, terror of armies,
bondage, humiliation. Heaven swallowed the smoke. . . .

They placed in the tomb both the torques and the jewels,
all the magnificence that the men had earlier
taken from the hoard in hostile mood. . . .

Then the warriors rode around the barrow,
twelve of them in all, athelings' sons.
They recited a dirge to declare their grief,
spoke of the man, mourned their King.
They praised his manhood and the prowess of his hands,
they raised his name; it is right a man
should be lavish in honouring his lord and friend,
should love him in his heart when the leading-forth
from the house of flesh befalls him at last.
—*Beowulf*, trans. Michael Alexander
(Harmondsworth, U.K.: Penguin, 1973), 150–51

Fig. 2.5. Assortment of jewelry excavated from the seventh-century grave 2 (female) of the cemetery of Keszthely in Hungary (0.6573–0.6578, 0.6581). Reproduced by permission of the Römisch-Germanisches Zentralmuseum Mainz.

Many interconnected identities—including age, gender, status, ethnicity, religious affiliation, and kinship—played into decisions made by families regarding what goods to deposit with the deceased at the time of the burial. Although ethnicity has long been privileged in the archaeological discussion of such artifacts, greater attention has recently been given to factors such as gender and age that were once judged by means of grave goods but can now be identified more accurately using the most recent techniques for osteological analysis and DNA testing. In the mid-fifth- to early seventh-century cemetery of Sewerby in East Yorkshire, for instance, new studies demonstrate that some discrepancies exist between biological sex and modern gender associations of archaeological artifacts. The finding that 15 percent of the graves identified osteologically as possibly male contained jewelry may be used to challenge traditional assumptions about early medieval social mores.[20] In the region of Metz, close study of the distribution of artifacts with strong gender associations reveals that during the sixth century, males of fighting age and females of childbearing age tended to receive the most extensive and high-quality grave assemblages. By contrast, those of more advanced age were typically buried with fewer goods. These trends, which broke down to a large degree in the course of the seventh century, mirror priorities established in contemporary law codes. Such practices suggest the kinds of contributions contemporaries valued most highly.

Along with gender, some features of the early medieval custom of depositing grave goods appear to have been more directly linked to religious customs or concerns related to the physical safety of the remains of the deceased or his or her soul in the afterlife. In the Jura, Savoy, and Burgundy (areas of southeastern France and Switzerland), for instance, numerous finds have been made of sixth- and seventh-century decorated buckles, most frequently inscribed with a depiction of Daniel in the lions' den. Not only did these often include inscriptions of the owner's or artisan's name, but some seem to have been fashioned to hold relics. Besides their practical function in early medieval dress customs, the buckles seem to have been understood to have protective or amuletic powers.[21] Likewise, in some Alemannic and Bavarian regions, as well as in parts of Italy and the Balkans, sixth- and seventh-century families occasionally deposited gold-leaf crosses on the foreheads of the dead or sewed these votive objects onto their clothing prior to interment.[22] Unfortunately, the precise significance of this rite and the reasons for the custom's spread to certain regions and not others remain unknown. Nonetheless, we may propose that like gravestones and tombs carved with crosses, the deposition of gold-leaf crosses reveals some Christians' desire to protect the dead from harm or identify them as members of the faithful in anticipation of the Final Resurrection.

Although the deposit of grave goods with the dead was customary in all regions of Western Europe, many individuals do not appear to have been buried accompanied by such goods. The lack of artifacts in individual sepulchers cannot be attributed confidently to the economic means or religious beliefs of the dead. In some cases, poorly appointed graves may have simply been the consequence of the decay in largely unprotected graves of organic goods such as clothing or flowers accompanying the dead.[23] As with the study of the historical sources,

Fig. 2.6. Pectoral cross dated to the seventh or eighth century found in the vicinity of Liège, Belgium (0.17901). Reproduced by permission of the Römisch-Germanisches Zentralmuseum Mainz.

Fig. 2.7. Seventh-century belt buckle decorated with the figure of a griffin found in the south of Spain (O.40950). Reproduced by permission of the Römisch-Germanisches Zentralmuseum Mainz.

archaeological research on the early medieval burial rite has been shaped in large part by the extant sources. The material record is heavily biased toward the elite, who could afford to erect or deposit in their graves items produced from stone, iron, and precious metals that were more likely to survive the test of centuries.

While the custom of grave goods was never formally banned or denounced by clerics, the quantity and quality of such objects seem to have declined steadily over time. It is uncertain what motivated this trend, but it generally appears that by the seventh century in Gaul and the eighth century in large parts of Germany, the custom of grave goods grew less fashionable or effective in communicating families' concerns with regard to the dead. The decreasing quality and quantity of grave goods chosen to accompany the dead into their graves were matched by growing disorganization in the arrangement of cemeteries and a significant increase in the incidence of grave robbery, which sometimes affected as much as two-thirds of the burials in a given cemetery.[24]

The eventual abandonment of the rite of grave goods nonetheless cannot be attributed to the spread of Christianity or the adoption of a more "Christian" form of burial, since early medieval clerics never denounced the deposition of artifacts in sepulchers as pagan and many were themselves laid to rest with such goods. It is more accurate to propose instead that Christian families in the seventh and eighth centuries found more effective ways to use their resources to commemorate their dead. The redistribution of funerary expenditure increasingly took the form of exclusive or aboveground burial places in churches or church cemeteries, and it could also include the donation of lands to churches for the performance of masses on behalf of the deceased. Instead of resting upon the efforts of family members or supporters, the performative aspects of these rites fell increasingly to clerical representatives, who were the only individuals authorized to engage in the liturgical aspects of such undertakings.

THE IMPORTANCE OF FUNERALS

Early medieval burial customs were more complex and varied than it has been possible to convey in this brief essay: they differed regionally and locally and underwent significant change over time according to the contemporary needs of the individuals who used them to commemorate their dead. Nonetheless, it is important to recognize that what the inhabitants of Western Europe shared in making decisions about funerals on behalf of their kin was the common understanding that funerals constituted important opportunities for the remembrance and idealization of the deceased through the display of their physical remains. Whether they involved cremation or inhumation, such ceremonies represented momentous occasions at which to commemorate and actively build upon the worldly and otherworldly relationships of the deceased as envisioned by their families and, in the case of elites, their religious communities or lay followers.

FOR FURTHER READING

Brown, Peter. *The Cult of the Saints: Its Rise and Function in Latin Christianity*. Haskell Lectures on History of Religions, new series, 2. Chicago: University of Chicago Press, 1981.

Bullough, Donald A. "Burial, Community, and Belief in the Early Medieval West." In *Ideal and Reality in Frankish and Anglo-Saxon Society: Studies Presented to J. M. Wallace-Hadrill*, ed. Patrick Wormald with Donald Bullough and Roger Collins, 177–201. Oxford: Basil Blackwell, 1983.

Effros, Bonnie. *Caring for Body and Soul: Burial and the Afterlife in the Merovingian World*. University Park: Pennsylvania State University Press, 2002.

———. *Merovingian Mortuary Archaeology and the Making of the Early Middle Ages*. The Transformation of the Classical Heritage 35. Berkeley: University of California Press, 2003.

Geary, Patrick J. *Living with the Dead in the Middle Ages*. Ithaca, N.Y.: Cornell University Press, 1994.

Hadley, D. M. *Death in Medieval England: An Archaeology*. Stroud: Tempus, 2001.

Halsall, Guy. *Settlement and Social Organization: The Merovingian Region of Metz*. Cambridge: Cambridge University Press, 1995.

James, Edward. "Burial and Status in the Early Medieval West." In *Transactions of the Royal Historical Society,* 5th series, 39 (1989): 23–40.

Moreira, Isabel. *Dreams, Visions, and Spiritual Authority in Merovingian Gaul*. Ithaca, N.Y.: Cornell University Press, 2000.

Morris, Ian. *Death Ritual and Social Structure in Classical Antiquity*. Cambridge: Cambridge University Press, 1992.

Paxton, Frederick S. *Christianizing Death: The Creation of a Ritual Process in Early Medieval Europe*. Ithaca, N.Y.: Cornell University Press, 1990.

RELICS, ASCETICS, LIVING SAINTS

DANIEL E. BORNSTEIN

CHAPTER THREE

Christianity can be defined by a number of distinctive claims about the body and the flesh. Its central doctrines—the incarnation, the crucifixion, the resurrection—and its essential rituals—baptism and communion—are all theological assertions in corporeal form. Christian creeds hold that God took flesh in the incarnation; that he offered his flesh for the sins of all humankind; that he suffered in the flesh and died on the cross; that he rose in the flesh; that at the end of time, his followers will share in this resurrection of the flesh; and that while awaiting the promised resurrection, they should commemorate his saving sacrifice by ritually consuming his body and blood. At the same time, Christianity often views bodily desires with profound distrust, sees the flesh as opposed to the spirit, and calls for a renunciation of the material world. The body is a site of sin and source of temptation, and yielding to its lure will lead to damnation, but ascetic self-discipline can turn the body into a vehicle of sanctification, reaping heavenly rewards in the resurrected flesh. This sharp ambivalence about the body marked Christianity from the very start and set it apart from its classical and Judaic cultural heritage.

From the classical Greek and Roman world, Christianity inherited a rather mild soul/body dualism. The body was viewed as inferior to the soul, an awkward and unreliable partner that all too often inconvenienced the soul. For the patrician male, it was something to be governed tolerantly but never indulged. With regard to women, the attitude was rather less tolerant—certainly because of the lower status and social subordination of women, but also perhaps because

Gregory, Bishop of Tours (573–594/595), Recalls the Relics His Father Owned

I will now narrate what happened with the relics that my father once carried with him. At the time when Theudebert ordered the sons of Clermont to be sent off as hostages, my father had been recently married. Because he wished himself to be protected by relics of saints, he asked a cleric to grant him something from these relics, so that with their protection he might be kept safe as he set out on this long journey. He put the sacred ashes in a gold medallion and carried it with him. Although he did not even know the names of the blessed men, he was accustomed to recount that he had been rescued from many dangers. He claimed that often, because of the power of these relics, he had avoided the violence of bandits, the dangers of floods, the threats of turbulent men, and attacks from swords.

I will not be silent about what I witnessed regarding these relics. After the death of my father my mother carried these relics with her. It was the time for harvesting the crops, and huge piles of grain had been collected on the threshing floors. Just like the Limoges, which is clothed with crops but stripped of its trees, so during those days when the seeds were already threshed there was no place to light a fire when a frost appeared. So the threshers kindled fires for themselves from the straw. Then everyone retired to eat. And behold, the fire gradually began to be spread through the straw bit by bit. Quickly, fanned by the wind, the fire spread to the piles of grain. The fire became a huge blaze and was accompanied by the shouts of men, the wails of women, and the crying of children. This happened in our field. When my mother, who was wearing these relics around her neck, learned of this, she rushed from the meal and held the sacred relics in front of the balls of flames. In a moment the entire fire so died down that no sparks were found among the piles of burned straw and the seeds. The grain the fire had touched had suffered no harm.

—"Gregory of Tours: The Power of Relics," in *Medieval Saints: A Reader*, ed. Mary-Ann Stouck (Peterborough, Ont.: Broadview, 1999), 362

in a society that offered them fewer intellectual, cultural, and political options, women were viewed as more purely bodily. In Judaism, women were more starkly subordinated and more rigorously defined in terms of their bodies. In the law of Moses, bodily fluids were considered ritually polluting, and women emitted more fluids than men.

Menstruation rendered a woman impure, as did blood shed in childbirth. As a consequence, women were rigorously excluded from religious life. According to one notorious rabbinical saying, it was better to burn the Torah than to allow a woman to handle it. In life, women's bodies were more bodily, but after death, all bodies were the same. They became pure bodies, bereft of soul—and hence unclean. On this, there was complete agreement between Judaism and Roman polytheism. This was the point of Jesus' biting denunciation of the Pharisees as being like whitewashed tombs, clean and pure on the outside but full of death and filth and corruption within (Matt. 23:27). Romans, too, excluded the dead from the habitat of the living, burying them outside of the city, away from the altars.

Christianity transformed attitudes to the body and its relation to the holy, in some cases exaggerating its classical and Judaic inheritance; in others, reversing earlier norms. The readiness to see the body as a tangible point of contact with the divine—a view expressed most dramatically in the honor paid to relics, those venerated remains of venerated persons—was peculiarly Christian. So too was its emphasis on sexual renunciation, which treated the body as something that had to be conquered to accede to the divine. These two attitudes toward the body, equally strongly held, pulled Christians in different directions, for they are obviously and fundamentally contradictory. This essential ambivalence is the topic I shall address as I explore its articulation in popular belief and everyday practice and follow its shifting expressions over the thousand years of the European Middle Ages.

THE WITNESS OF THE FLESH: MARTYRS AND ASCETICS

In the beginning, it was easy to tell who was truly holy. The saints were those Christians who had borne witness to their beliefs by giving up their lives rather than their convictions. Jesus had called on his disciples to pick up their crosses and follow him, and in the early centuries of the church, when it was subject to occasional spasms of persecution, there were indeed those who did just that. Christian writers celebrated the sufferings of those who died for their faith, and theologians declared that the church grew precisely because it was watered with the blood of these martyrs—encouraging the enduring misapprehension that large numbers of Christians suffered martyrdom under pagan persecution. In fact, Roman persecution of the early Christians was rarely general and never sustained for very long. To be sure, these intermittent attacks could, on occasion, be quite intense, as they were in the last years of the reign of Diocletian (284–305), but Christian worship was never banned outright, and any Christian unfortunate enough to be caught up in one of these bouts of persecution could escape punishment merely by going through the motions of paying respect to the traditional gods. As a result, in the nearly three hundred years between the resurrection of Jesus and the conversion of Constantine, only about a thousand Christians were martyred in the entire Roman Empire. A far greater number were martyred in the fourth century alone, by Christian emperors who strove to crush competing forms of Christianity.

As Christianity became an accepted religion, an ordinary part of the fabric of everyday life, it inevitably lost something of the fervor of its earliest days, and there were those who were troubled by this lack, who wanted something more than the routine devotion of a settled Christian life. Anthony the Egyptian is exemplary in this regard. In the mid to late third century, this relatively prosperous peasant lived in a Christian village in the Nile valley, where at the age of eighteen or twenty, on the death of his parents, he inherited the family farm and along with it responsibility for his sister. One day he heard the priest reading the passage in the Gospel according to Matthew in which Jesus tells a would-be disciple to sell all he has, give it to the poor, and follow him. The rest of the congregation heard these same words but did not take them as Anthony did, literally and personally. He sold all he had, made arrangements for his sister to live with a group of devout women, and embarked on a life of rigorous asceticism. He was obviously not the first to do so: his biographer, Athanasius, describes how Anthony sought out other hermits and learned from each, and some of these individual ascetics had evidently begun to group together into something resembling monastic communities, if Anthony could place his sister in a community of pious women. But the intensity with which Anthony sustained his commitment to the ascetic life (and he did sustain it for decades, until he finally passed away at the age of 105), along with the literary success of his biography, made Anthony an influential model.

Athanasius recounts in gripping detail Anthony's struggle with temptation and the brutal beatings he endured at the hands of demons. Anthony emerged from these battles with the devil dead to the world. He aspired to a literal death: when he heard of persecution raging in the city, Anthony eagerly cleaned his tattered robe and headed off to perform his prayers by the roadside in the hope of attracting the authorities' ire. But such martyrdom was relatively rare; the Roman authorities saw nothing to be gained by bringing charges against a person of no standing in society or his church. Ignored by the authorities, Anthony had to remain content with a sort of self-inflicted martyrdom, subjecting his own body to the harshest of disciplines. He renounced property, sex and marriage, food, sleep, and other basic creature comforts and retreated into the desert. Others, inspired by his example, followed him, and the desert filled with ascetics pursuing their various regimens.

Martyrs triumphed over the body in one moment of glorious self-immolation. Those who dedicated themselves to a life of continence embarked on relentless campaigns against the body and its urges, a program of abstinence and sexual renunciation. The dead heroes of Christ were joined by a living elite marked off from normal society by their distinctive way of life, resolutely maintained despite the constant assaults of temptation, lust, and bodily desire. The body was no longer a mere inconvenience, an inferior companion to the soul that made its presence felt through weakness, illness, and the need for food and sleep; it was an obstacle on the road to salvation. The body was no longer something that ought to be governed tolerantly, if strictly; it was now an enemy to be ravaged. Monks gave up all worldly belongings and renounced all weaknesses of the flesh, which they starved and scourged.

It would be wrong, however, to see the rise of ascetic Christianity only in terms of the enmity between spirit and flesh. The doctrines of the incarnation, the crucifixion, and the resurrection make it impossible to see the flesh in purely negative terms, for it is through the flesh that humanity is redeemed. Because of the incarnation, in orthodox eyes the flesh could not be (as it was for Manichaean dualists in the third and fourth centuries and for Cathar dualists in the twelfth) in absolute opposition to spirit, a carnal cage in which the spark of divine light was imprisoned as part of the eternal conflict between good and evil. Insofar as it tended to draw people away from God, the flesh needed to be chastised and subdued, but the flesh remained nonetheless part of God's creation, and hence inherently good. Just as God had opened the road to salvation by assuming flesh, so the faithful could—indeed, *had to*—work through and on the flesh in their hope for salvation.

THE TREASURE OF THE FLESH: RELICS

When he felt the time of his death approaching, Anthony went off into the mountains with two close disciples who had sworn to bury his body and reveal its location to no one. Anthony had long resisted the trend to preserve and display the remains of martyrs, objecting that this practice was neither holy nor even proper, and he sought in this way to see that his body would not be treasured after his death. His companions complied with his instructions. They "wrapped him up and buried him, hiding his body underground," writes Athanasius, "and no one knows to this day where it was buried, save those two only." But Anthony's attempt to frustrate the growing cult of relics met

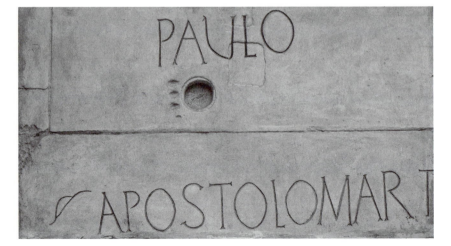

Fig. 3.1. PAULO APOSTOLO MARTYRI inscribed on the presumed tomb of the apostle Paul, probably made during the reign of Constantine (280–334); San Paolo fuori le Mura, Rome. The round opening in the stone allowed worshipers to touch the relic and light incense. Photo: © Erich Lessing / Art Resource, N.Y.

with only partial success. His body may have been lost to those who wished to honor it, but (adds Athanasius) his clothing was not: "Each of those who received the sheepskin of the blessed Anthony and the garment worn by him guards it as a precious treasure."[1]

Other Christians, far more educated and urbane than Anthony, shared his visceral distrust of the cult of relics. St. Jerome had to respond to the accusations of Vigilantius, who charged that the cult of the saints was a form of paganism in Christian guise. "What need is there," lamented Vigilantius, "for you not only to pay such honor, not to say adoration, to the thing, whatever it may be, which you carry about in a little vessel and worship? . . . Under the cloak of religion we see what is all but a heathen ceremony introduced into the churches: while the sun is still shining, heaps of tapers are lighted, and everywhere a paltry bit of powder, wrapped up in a costly cloth, is kissed and worshipped."[2] Vigilantius was wrong, of course, about the pagan character of reverence for the saints. As Peter Brown has pointed out, the Christian practice of treasuring the physical remains of martyrs and saints,

Fig. 3.2. Reliquary arm of St. Luke (c. 1337–1338); Louvre, Paris, France. This reliquary in the shape of a forearm and hand holding a quill pen, once part of the royal treasury of Medina del Campo, was crafted of silver, crystal, gold, and enamel to encase a bone from the arm of the evangelist Luke. It was made for Queen Sancia of Majorca and bears her coat-of-arms. Photo: © Réunion des Musées Nationaux / Art Resource, N.Y.

of keeping them with them in their homes, and of depositing them in places of worship ran directly contrary to pagan custom, which located burial sites outside of the city, away from human habitation, and held that the presence of unburied remnants of the dead rendered a place unfit for worship.

Eunapius of Sardis gave voice to the profound revulsion that pious Greeks and Romans felt about the way Christians handled the lacerated, mutilated, dismembered, and charred remnants of their martyrs: "For they collected the bones and skulls of criminals who had been put to death for numerous crimes . . . made them out to be gods, and thought that they became better by defiling themselves at their graves. 'Martyrs' the dead men were called, and ministers of a sort, and ambassadors with the gods to carry men's prayers."[3] But Jerome did not answer his critic by pointing out that it was Vigilantius, and not those Christians who treasured and adored the relics of the saints, who truly embraced a pagan point of view. Instead, he tried to distinguish the inner essence of Christian worship from pagan. For Jerome, the saints were living beings, while pagan idols were lifeless, and the honor Christians paid to the saints was an expression of reverence, not worship. But from the outside, in the eyes of someone observing the gestures expressing this reverence, did they really look any different from worship? To the troubled Vigilantius (as to Protestant reformers twelve hundred years later), evidently not.

Vigilantius lost this argument. Christians continued to do as they had been doing, collecting, treasuring, and revering the physical remains of those who had borne witness to their faith with their bodies. With the waning of persecution, Christians came to treasure the relics of ascetics like Anthony alongside those of the martyrs, honoring those who had made of their lives a continuous sacrifice as well as those who had borne witness with their deaths. The tombs of the martyrs became shrines, where local bishops promoted annual celebrations on the anniversaries of their deaths—or, in the paradoxical expression universally employed to describe gruesome martyrdom, their birth to new life in God. The holiest objects at these new Christian shrines were the relics of people like St. Martin of Tours, who may have been universal saints but were nonetheless held to be particularly present, and especially effective, at the sepulchers that contained their physical remains. Crowds flocked to their tombs to ask these friends of God to intercede on their behalf at the heavenly court, and the keepers of their shrines recorded and proclaimed the miracles by which the lame were made straight, the blind given sight, demons put to flight, lepers made clean, and other diseases cured. The tangible evidence of miraculous healing, visible everywhere that sacred power

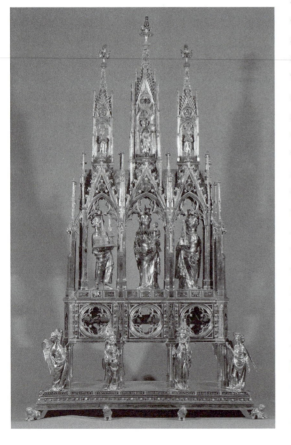

Fig. 3.3. Reliquary in the form of three gothic spires, 1370–1390. Cathedral Treasury, Cathedral (Palatine Chapel), Aachen, Germany. Photo: © Erich Lessing / Art Resource, N.Y.

congealed with the blood of the martyrs, confirmed the reliability of the New Testament accounts of the miracles of Jesus.

Reverence for the relics of martyrs and saints quickly came to be generalized in practice and even mandated by ecclesiastical law, and oaths sworn on relics became a standard part of judicial procedure. Around 400, a church council in Carthage decreed that all altars that did not contain relics of a saint must be destroyed. This local ruling was later revived and adopted as general policy by the Frankish ruler Charlemagne. In 801 (and again in 813), he declared relics an essential element of all churches throughout his vast realm: all existing altars that lacked relics were to be destroyed, and any newly consecrated altars had to contain relics. Since Charlemagne was aggressively expanding the boundaries of his realm (and with it, the reach of Christianity) ever farther to the east at the same time that he was encouraging the establishment of a network of parish churches covering the country-side, this official Carolingian policy created a tremendous demand for relics, which were in short supply north of the Alps. To meet that demand, Charlemagne and his successors turned to the same source from which they derived their models of imperial rule: Rome.

Access to the necessary relics became an important element in the alliance between the Carolingian rulers and the papacy, since Rome was the great repository of the bones of saints and martyrs. Relics of the early martyrs and saints emerged from the catacombs of Rome and other Italian repositories and flowed north to the Carolingian realm. Some went as prized gifts, bestowed by popes and other prelates on favored lords. Others went as merchandise, brokered by specialized merchants, such as Deusdona, a deacon of the Roman church who provided Charlemagne's biographer, Einhard, with such treasures as the bodies of saints Peter and Marcellinus, and other eager Carolingian clerics with prizes nearly as rich. Deusdona and his associates clearly knew where to lay their hands on sought-after relics and astutely traded in these high-value, low-bulk, luxury goods, so well suited to the demands of their clientele and the primitive and hazardous travel conditions of the central Middle Ages. And like any portable item of value, relics could become prized booty of war. During the political turmoil that accompanied the dissolution of the Carolingian Empire, monks hid their relics, like the rest of their treasure, from plundering Vikings and Hungarians, or fled with them to some more secure refuge. Between 836 and 862, the body of St. Philibert journeyed in this manner from its island home at the mouth of the Loire River to a new resting place near Tournus, more than three hundred miles away.

The traffic in relics did not all trend northward across the Alps. Relics flowed into Italy as well, often as objects of pious theft. A host of relics were saved in this way from Muslim hands after conquering Arab armies seized the Middle East and North Africa from Byzantine rule. A tenth-century text describes how Venetian merchants smuggled the body of St. Mark out of Alexandria in Egypt, hiding it under pieces of pork to discourage Muslim inspectors from looking too closely for this sacred contraband. St. Nicholas of Myra became St. Nicholas of Bari when merchants from that southern Italian city managed, for once, to pull a fast one on the Venetians and make off with his body before their commercial rivals could lay their hands on it. The greatest single influx of relics came in 1204, when the Fourth Crusade, deflected from its goal of freeing the Holy Land from Muslim rule, instead sacked the Eastern Orthodox city of Constantinople. As part of their portion of the loot, the Venetians laid claim to Constantinople's unparalleled collection of relics, which they carried off to enrich the treasury of St. Mark's basilica in Venice. As always, the perpetrators of these pious thefts justified their actions as being permitted, even desired, by the saints whose remains were thereby removed to a more secure home, where they could receive the reverence that was their due. After all, the argument went, no person so powerful could be carried off against his or her will.

Sometimes relics had to take matters into their own hands rather than wait for human intervention. In 1291, upon the collapse of the last crusader outposts in the Holy Land, the Holy House of Nazareth—the humble abode where the Virgin Mary was born, received the Annunciation, and raised her infant son—took flight from the destruction that threatened it. Borne on the wings of angels, it arrived miraculously at Tersato, in what is now Croatia. Three years later, the angels moved it across the Adriatic to its present home in Loreto, on the eastern coast of Italy. By the fifteenth century, Mary's little house

The Monks of Laon Use Relics to Raise Funds

The monks raised the funds to rebuild their cathedral after it was damaged by riot and fire in 1112.

Meanwhile, in keeping with the customary way, such as it is, of raising money, the monks began carrying around the relics of saints as well as their reliquaries. As a result the great Judge, who chastises with one hand but shows mercy with the other, accomplished miracles everywhere the relics passed. Now they were carrying, along with some box that is barely memorable, a magnificent reliquary containing parts of the robe of the Virgin Mother, of the sponge that was presented to the Savior's lips, and of the Cross. (Whether it really contained some of the hair of Our Lady I don't know.) This reliquary is made of gold and decorated with precious stones; and it has a verse inscription engraved in the gold that praises the wonderful things inside. . . .

The relic bearers made their way safely to England and came to the city of Winchester, where they worked a great number of miracles. The same thing happened at Exeter, which also produced an abundance of gifts. Let us pass over the ordinary healings of the sick and speak of the exceptional cases. For we are not recording their itinerary—they can write that themselves—nor considering each individual fact, but are picking out examples useful for sermons.

They were received almost everywhere with the reverence they deserved; but in one village they were refused admittance by the priest in his church, and by the peasants in their homes. Finding two uninhabited houses they stored all their baggage in one and used it for their lodgings, while the other was used to shelter the holy relics. The loathsome peasants persisted, however, in their obstinate refusal of things divine, and the clerics left the village the very next day. As they were leaving, suddenly, with a terrific clap of thunder, a bolt of lightning burst out of the clouds and struck the village, reducing all of its houses to ashes. And—a sign of God's marvelous sense of discrimination!—those two houses, which were situated in the midst of the others that were on fire, were spared. God wanted to give a very clear sign that if these wretches had been afflicted with fire it was because of their irreverence toward the Mother of God. As for the wicked priest, who had merely increased the cruelty of these barbarians he was supposed to educate, he gathered up household goods that he was delighted to think had escaped heaven's fire, and came to the edge of a river (or of the sea, I'm not sure which) hoping to get across. But there everything he had collected to move elsewhere was annihilated on the spot by lightning. Thus, this savage band of rustics who were uninstructed in the mysteries of God were taught to understand through their sufferings.

—"Fundraising with Relics: The Monks of Laon," *Medieval Saints: A Reader*, ed. Mary-Ann Stouck (Peterborough, Ont.: Broadview, 1999), 398, 400–401

(just 28 by 12.5 feet) had been encased in a grand basilica and become a major object of pilgrimage, which it remains to this day.

Possession of a major relic could make the fortunes of a small town. Doge Enrico Dandolo, the venerable leader of the merchant republic of Venice, took relics as the Venetian share of the booty from the sack of Constantinople because he was acutely aware of their economic value, no longer as articles of trade but as magnets for pilgrims. The religious revival of the eleventh and twelfth centuries coincided with a commercial one, and pilgrims on their way to visit shrines jostled with merchants and trade goods as they plied the network of roads linking the cities and shrines of Western Europe. Since crowds of pilgrims made ready customers, markets were often held in conjunction with major feast days and in the vicinity of major pilgrimage shrines. Pilgrim routes linked the principal shrines of France and Germany—the relics of St. Martin at Tours and of Mary Magdalene at Vézelay, the jewel-encrusted image of St. Foy at Conques, the dramatically situated monastery dedicated to the archangel Michael at Mont-St.-Michel, the Marian shrines of Le Puy and Rocamadour, and countless others—and stretched beyond them to the far corners of Europe. Churches and inns beaded the road leading from France across northern Spain to the basilica of Santiago de Compostela, dedicated to the apostle St. James the Greater—known in Castile as Santiago Matamoros, St. James the Moor-Slayer, and invoked as the powerful patron of Christian armies in the protracted struggle to win back the Iberian peninsula from Muslim rule.

For a time, Santiago de Compostela could claim to be the most famous pilgrim destination in Europe. The scallop shell worn by pilgrims who had made this journey became the classic marker identifying pious wayfarers, and the wealth and status that accrued to the bishop of Santiago encouraged him to style himself, like the pope, the servant of the servants of God. Another web of roads, known as the Via Francigena, carried French pilgrims south to Rome and its peerless collection of relics: the remains of St. Peter and St. Paul, many other early Christian martyrs, and the countless other relics on display in the churches of Rome. Still other pilgrims took sail across the English Channel to the shrines of St. Mary in Walsingham and, after his martyrdom in 1170, of Thomas Becket in Canterbury. Some even pressed on to the ancient cave-shrine known as St. Patrick's Purgatory, located on an island in Lough Derg in Donegal, in the far northwest of Ireland.

As any reader of Chaucer's *Canterbury Tales* will know, social conviviality and simple curiosity about seeing strange lands mingled with more properly religious motives in the minds of pilgrims. In her memoir—the earliest known autobiography in English—Margery Kempe describes how in midlife, after twenty years of marriage, fourteen children, and a couple of failed business ventures, she experienced a religious conversion and set off on a series of pilgrimages: to Aachen, Assisi, Rome, Santiago, and the Holy Land. She found the worldly merriment of her fellow pilgrims deeply disturbing; they, in turn, found her constant weeping and talk of holiness so insufferable that, on more than one occasion, they tried to ditch her on the road. Margery's traveling companions, however unkindly they were to a middle-aged woman who feared she might be robbed of her life, her virtue, and her meager funds in a land whose language she didn't know, were at least devout enough to undertake this pilgrimage of their own volition. However, not all pilgrims took to the road entirely willingly. Ecclesiastical and secular courts sometimes assigned pilgrimages as a form of penance or punishment. As Diana Webb observes:

> A short local pilgrimage was a form of public penance which exposed the offender to the scrutiny of people who knew him; a lengthier pilgrimage preserved something of the character of exile, and might be imposed where the offence was not merely severe but made it desirable to remove the offender from circulation for a prolonged period. In 1283, John Pecham, archbishop of Canterbury, commanded an incorrigibly fornicating priest of the diocese of Chichester to go to Santiago, Rome and Cologne in three successive years.[4]

And when these less than pious pilgrims arrived at the goal of their pilgrimage, they could be skeptical or even derisive of the relics they found there.

Around 1526, in his Latin dialogue "A Pilgrimage for Religion's Sake," which drew on his own experience of visits to the churches of

St. Thomas at Canterbury and Our Lady of Walsingham, the great Dutch humanist Erasmus poked gentle fun at the many relics displayed at those great shrines. At Canterbury, one pilgrim was given an extraordinary opportunity to kiss a relic of the martyred bishop, but offended his clerical guide when he recoiled from the proffered arm with the bloodstained flesh still on it. At Walsingham, another exclaimed, when shown a vial containing the milk of the Blessed Virgin, "O Mother most like her Son! He left us so much of his blood on earth; she left so much of her milk that it's scarcely credible a woman with only one child could have so much, even if the child had drunk none of it." Over a century earlier, the Florentine merchant and storyteller Franco Sacchetti expressed similar views in describing a special viewing of the relics of St. Ugolino of Cortona. The recipient of this signal honor fled the saint's presence, crossing himself in fear and exclaiming that he had never seen a body so black. If the bodies of saints are so repulsive, he asked, what must the bodies of the damned be like? And why, he wondered, should we seek out these new saints whom nobody has ever heard of, when we already have Jesus Christ, his mother, the apostles, and the other great saints of Paradise?[5]

THE WORD MADE FLESH

Of course, as Sacchetti well knew, we do not have Jesus and his mother in the way that Cortona has the bodies of saints Margaret and Ugolino, unattractively darkened, perhaps, but undeniably present. The body of Jesus was resurrected from the grave and then, forty days later, ascended to heaven; Mary's body, according to the doctrine of the corporeal assumption, was taken up to heaven upon her death. This left Christians on earth without any bodily relics of their savior or his mother. For much of the Middle Ages, this lack does not appear to have been particularly troubling. For one thing, they had—in ever-increasing abundance—the relics of the apostles, martyrs, and other saints. For another, they could boast of possessing objects that had touched or articles of clothing that had once adorned the bodies of Jesus or Mary. Thus, Chartres had Mary's sacred tunic, given to the cathedral in 876 by Charlemagne's grandson Charles the Bald. This contact relic proved more powerful than the remains of St Philibert, which had to flee from the Vikings, when it saved Chartres from Norman siege in 911: when the bishop displayed the tunic from the city gate, the Norman warriors fled in panic. The tunic survived unharmed when the church that housed it was destroyed by fire in 1194, along with most of the city of Chartres. Convinced that Mary had permitted the destruction of the old basilica because she wanted a new and more beautiful church to be built in her honor, the people of Chartres proceeded to rebuild their cathedral within less than a generation.

Fig. 3.4. The scene of the relics (detail); fourteenth-century mural in St. Mary's Church, Karlstein Castle, Czech Republic. Emperor Charles IV places a relic of the True Cross in a crucifix on the altar. Photo: © Erich Lessing / Art Resource, N.Y.

Most of all, Christians had the body of Christ immediately to hand, and in limitless quantities, in the form of the Eucharist. The consecrated eucharist was by far the most readily available relic of Jesus, or of any saint, and throughout the early Middle Ages it was treated like a relic: placed in the altar, along with or instead of other relics, and brought out to receive oaths, like other relics, during solemn judicial proceedings. As a condensation of the redemptive self-sacrifice of Jesus, the living flesh that he had offered on the cross, the Eucharist was a relic like no other, for it represented an unequaled sacrifice, suffering, and love. Unequaled, but not, in the end, unrivaled: the evangelical revival of the eleventh and twelfth centuries inspired a fresh interest in the humanity of Jesus, and the unexpected success of the First Crusade opened the way to satisfying that curiosity.

Renewed Christian control of the homeland of the historical Jesus brought to Western Europe a sudden influx of relics of Jesus. Most, inevitably, were objects connected with him, from the crown of thorns (for which the king of France built the Sainte Chapelle) to the wood of the true cross (of which, in Mark Twain's memorable phrase, there were enough pieces to shingle a barn). But there were also those body parts that Jesus had shed in the course of his earthly existence: his baby teeth, his umbilical cord, and his foreskin. This last held special theological significance, for God's covenant with Abraham had been signaled by the ritual of circumcision, which marked the flesh of all male Jews as being part of the people of God. Theologians considered the circumcision of Jesus—the first shedding of his holy blood—a foreshadowing of the final, saving sacrifice on the cross by which he established the new covenant, superseding the old covenant of circumcision. As a result, the holy foreskin of Jesus was a particularly prized relic, one that no fewer than eight churches claimed to possess.

Such untoward multiplication of body parts (like the several heads of John the Baptist conserved in various European churches) offered far too easy a target for the mockery of skeptics. Rather than defend the indefensible or take on the impossible task of distinguishing true claims from false (which, in any case, would end by offending more people than it pleased), ecclesiastical leaders such as Pope Innocent III (1198–1216) preferred to leave the resolution of such mysteries to God. In Innocent's mind, the far more pressing need was to defend the central doctrines and sacraments of the church from the attacks of radical dualists, who saw body and soul as locked in eternal conflict and denied that material things could bring any spiritual benefits. For these Cathar dualists, the orthodox doctrines of the incarnation, crucifixion, and resurrection were delusional: since divine spirit and worldly matter were inherently incompatible, God could not really have taken flesh, suffered on the cross, and risen from the grave. The physical water of baptism could not possibly wash a soul clean of sin. A morsel of mere bread could not contain God, nor could any spiritual benefit ensue from eating that bread. Obviously, such claims struck at the very heart of Christian belief and practice and demanded an urgent response. Skeptics and heretics had to be shown in no uncertain terms that orthodox doctrine was true, orthodox sacraments valid. To that end, Innocent assembled councils of prelates and theologians, launched a crusade against the heretics, and welcomed miracles that confirmed the teachings of the church.

On December 30, 1230, in the Florentine convent church of Sant'Ambrogio, the word became flesh in dramatic and disturbing fashion. An elderly priest named Uguccione failed to wipe the chalice properly clean after celebrating Mass, and when he returned to it a little later, he found it to contain not dregs of wine but warm flesh and blood.[6] Uguccione announced his startling discovery to the Benedictine nuns who resided in Sant'Ambrogio and then carefully transferred the bloody matter into a crystal vial and brought it to the bishop for his inspection. The bishop took his time about it: nearly a year passed before the relic was returned, on the feast of St. Ambrose (December 7), to the convent dedicated to his honor. Soon after its return, however, both the bishop and one of the novices in Sant'Ambrogio reported visions urging them to preserve the miraculous substance in a suitably magnificent reliquary. Beginning in 1257, bishops and popes granted a series of indulgences to those who visited the relic. By 1340, the relic rested in a golden casket, which itself was housed in a series of three chapels, each more magnificent than the last. It was displayed inside the church three times a year, on the Sunday following the feast of Corpus Christi, on the feast of St. Ambrose, and on the anniversary of the miracle, December 30; and by the early fourteenth century, it was paraded through the streets of Florence every year, during the octave of Corpus Christi in June, by a lay confraternity founded to honor this relic and tend to its cult.

The bloody mess in the chalice at Sant'Ambrogio is just one of a number of miracles reported all over Europe in the first half of the thirteenth century, as devout Christians struggled to comprehend the doctrine of transubstantiation. Such is the term that the Fourth Lateran Council, meeting under Innocent III's leadership in 1215, used to describe what happened in the Mass when the priest pronounced the formula of consecration, *Hoc est corpus meum* (This is my body). In this commemoration of the words spoken by Jesus at the Last Supper (Matt. 26:26), declared the fathers at Lateran IV, "the same Jesus Christ is both the priest and the sacrifice, whose body and blood are truly contained in the sacrament of the altar under the species of bread and wine, the bread being transubstantiated into the body and the wine into the blood by the divine power, in order that, to accomplish the mystery of unity, we ourselves may receive of His that which He received of ours."[7] Lateran IV did not exactly define this technical term for what happened to the bread and wine, nor did it explain how this transformation came about; those tasks it left for future generations of scholastic theologians. But the sense of it was clear enough: even though the sensory impressions (the accidents, as they were termed in scholastic theology) of the bread and wine remained unaltered, their essence (or substance) was transformed into the body and blood of the Christ. The Eucharist might still look like bread, feel like bread, smell like bread, sound like bread as the priest broke it, and taste like bread as the believer received it, but once the priest spoke those four simple words, it no longer was bread: it was the body of Christ.

Evidently, good Christians had a hard time accepting as true something that ran so counter to their experience. The story of St. Gregory's Mass, first reported in an eighth-century biography of Pope Gregory the Great, received wide distribution in that thirteenth-century best seller *The Golden Legend*, a hugely popular collection of saints' lives by the Dominican preacher Jacobus of Voragine, and in scores of paintings depicting the miracle. There was a woman, Jacobus tells us, who used to bake altar breads every Sunday and present them to Gregory. "One day, during the celebration of mass, when Gregory held out to her the body of the Lord, with the words 'The body of our Lord Jesus Christ preserve you unto everlasting life,' the woman let out a hoot of laughter." Gregory, shocked at her levity, asked the woman how she could laugh at this holy moment. She replied, "Because you were calling the bread, which I made with my own hands, the 'body of the Lord'!" Gregory prostrated himself and prayed for a sign, and when he arose he found that the particle of bread had turned into raw and bloody flesh in the shape of a finger. The woman's faith was restored, Gregory prayed again, and the flesh turned back into bread. He handed it to the woman, who made her communion—rather nervously, no doubt.[8]

It wasn't only laypeople who harbored doubts about this doctrine. Stories proliferated of doubting or sinful priests who were forcefully reminded that Christ's body was really present in their hands and deserving of all respect. The *Life* of Bishop Hugh of Lincoln (1135–1200) includes the story of a priest who celebrated Mass in a state of mortal sin. When he broke the host in three before consuming it, "immediately blood began to flow copiously through the break, and the middle part of the host which I held in my hand suddenly took on the appearance of flesh and became blood."[9] Even more famous (though perhaps not so well documented) is the miracle of Bolsena, which occurred in 1263 when a German priest, Peter of Prague, stopped to celebrate Mass while on pilgrimage to Rome. Peter was evidently a pious priest, having undertaken this long and arduous pilgrimage, but one who nonetheless had a hard time accepting that God was really present in the consecrated Eucharist. That day, however, he had barely pronounced the formula of consecration when blood began to seep from the host, dripping from his fingers and staining the corporal (the cloth used to hold the Eucharist) and altar cloth. Peter, flustered and dismayed, at first tried to hide the blood but soon gave up this fruitless attempt to conceal a miracle. Instead, he interrupted the Mass and asked to be taken to Orvieto, where Pope Urban IV was residing. The pope absolved the erring priest and opened an inquiry into what had transpired. The bleeding host, altar cloth, and corporal were all brought to Orvieto in reverent procession and placed in the cathedral church. The blood-spotted corporal is still displayed there, encased in an elaborate reliquary.

By the end of the thirteenth century, the characteristic protagonists of stories about bleeding hosts were no longer doubting Christians, lay or priestly, but Jews. In what would be the first of many such accusations over the following

Fig. 3.5. The mass of St. Gregory; colored woodcut by an anonymous fifteenth-century German artist; Kupferstichkabinett, Staatliche Museen zu Berlin, Berlin, Germany. This inexpensive devotional image of the instruments used to crucify Jesus was intended to help focus prayerful meditations on the passion of the Christ. Photo: © Bildarchiv Preussischer Kulturbesitz / Art Resource, N.Y.

Bishop Hugh of Lincoln's Devotion to Relics Shocks Some Monks

When he was at the celebrated monastery of Fécamp, he extracted by biting two small fragments of the bone of the most blessed lover of Christ, Mary Magdalen. This bone had never been seen divested of its wrappings by the abbot or any of the monks who were present on that occasion, for it was sewn very tightly into three cloths, two of silk and one of ordinary linen.

They did not dare to accede even to the bishop's prayer to be allowed to see it. He, however, taking a small knife from one of his notaries, hurriedly cut the thread and undid the wrappings. After reverently examining and kissing the much venerated bone, he tried unsuccessfully to break it with his fingers, and then bit it first with his incisors and finally with his molars. By this means he broke off the two fragments, which he handed immediately to the writer, with the words, "Take charge of this for me with especial care."

When the abbot and the monks saw what had happened, they were first overcome with horror, and then became exceedingly enraged. They cried out, "What terrible profanity! We thought that the bishop had asked to see this holy and venerable relic for reasons of devotion, and he has stuck his teeth into it and gnawed it as if he were a dog." He mollified their anger with soothing words. Part of his speech is worth recording. "If, a little while ago I handled the most sacred body of the Lord of all the saints with my fingers, in spite of my unworthiness, and when I partook of it, touched it with my lips and teeth, why should I not venture to treat in the same way the bones of the saints for my protection, and by this commemoration of them increase my reverence for them, and without profanity acquire them when I have the opportunity?"

—"Bishop Hugh of Lincoln's Devotion to Relics (1186–1200)," in *Medieval Popular Religion, 1000–1500: A Reader*, ed. John Shinners, 2nd ed. (Peterborough, Ont.: Broadview, 2007), 182–83

---

two centuries, reports spread that a Jew in Paris, scornful of these nonsensical doctrines that Christians taught, had desecrated the host during holy week of 1290. Explanations of how he obtained a consecrated host varied: in some versions, the woman who provided it was a servant, in others a debtor who in this way hoped to satisfy his financial demands. Once the host was in his hands, the Jew began to test it, using instruments that often echoed those of Christ's passion. He cut the host with a knife, but it remained whole and started to bleed. He proceeded to drive a nail into it and stab it with a lance, with the same results. Finally, he threw it into a cauldron of boiling water; the whole pot turned blood red, and then the crucifix (or, in some versions, the Christ child) rose from the seething cauldron. Unable to conceal this wondrous and indestructible host, the sacrilegious Jew was discovered, tried, and executed; his wife and children, convinced by the miracle they had witnessed (or terrified of the alternative), converted to Christianity.[10]

The fame of this miracle in Paris quickly spread in Latin sermons and vernacular histories. It was recorded in Florence, in Giovanni Villani's popular chronicle of the events of his time, and depicted in paintings from Catalonia (where it was the subject of some crude, almost amateurish altar frontals) to Urbino (where Paolo Uccello told the story in six painted scenes in the predella of an altarpiece commissioned for the patrician confraternity of the Corpo di Cristo). It inspired numerous similar accusations, from Barcelona to Passau to Poznan, a number of which led to legal condemnations or extralegal massacres of local Jewish communities, testifying to the brutal power of a compelling narrative—and, just possibly, to Christians' need to exorcise their own lingering doubts about the doctrine of transubstantiation, which they projected onto a despised Other.

LIVING SAINTS: THE TESTIMONY OF THE FLESH

The late medieval proliferation of bleeding hosts coincided with an intense fascination with, and identification with, the human, suffering Jesus, the Man of Sorrows, Christ in his passion. At the same time, renewed interest in the apostolic life also encouraged reverence for those living holy men who best embodied the evangelical ideal, an ideal that was increasingly defined in terms of apostolic poverty. Making a striking contrast to the gold and jewels that adorned the relics of the saints, popular preachers like Robert of Arbrissel, Bernard of Tiron, and Vitalis of Savigny abandoned secure clerical livelihoods, dressed in rags, and withdrew to the wilderness. But paradoxically, those who most resolutely renounced the world found that an awestruck world pursued and enfolded them. Throngs of admirers gathered around hermits like Éon de l'Étoile in Brittany or followed Peter the Hermit to disaster on the People's Crusade. Occasionally these unstable groupings achieved a more regular and enduring structure, as when St. Norbert of Xanten (d. 1134) and his followers gave rise to the Premonstratensian order. But far more often these holy hermits left no trace in the historical record, beyond a brief and disapproving notice from some ecclesiastical chronicler.

To be sure, the impulse to "follow naked the naked Christ" was nothing new. Anthony the Egyptian had answered that call when he heard the Gospel call to sell all he had, give it to the poor, and follow Jesus. But Anthony's gesture did not entail a new vision of Jesus himself, as did Francis of Assisi's similar response, nearly a millennium later, to the same passage in the Gospel according to Matthew. Francis

Fig. 3.6. A cassock that belonged to St. Francis of Assisi; sacristy of Santa Croce, Florence, Italy. The coarse undyed wool of St. Francis's robe, patched and belted with the simple cord used by Francis and his order, makes a stark contrast with its ornately carved and gilded frame. Photo: © Scala / Art Resource, N.Y.

stripped himself of all he had—quite literally stripping himself of even the clothes on his back in front of the cathedral of Assisi—and set about an equally literal pursuit of the apostolic life, as he found it described in the Gospels. He became a wandering preacher, with no place to lay his head. He wore a simple tunic, patched and mended; he took no staff, nor bag, nor bread, nor money for his journey, instead begging his daily bread. He not only embraced the life of apostolic poverty: he embraced the actual poor and lepers and other outcasts. Such was the impression he made, with his simplicity and devotion, that others soon joined him in this evangelical life. And so complete was his imitation of the poor Christ that his own body came to resemble that of his model and inspiration. Two years before his death, at the hermitage of La Verna, Francis received the imprint of the stigmata, the wounds in his hands and feet and side that Jesus had received on the cross; Francis bore these as the miraculous seal confirming how perfectly he had shaped his life to that of Jesus.

Francis's followers, in a familiar and controversial phrase, called him an *alter Christus*, a second Christ, who had conformed himself in every way to the original. What is less often noted is the corresponding implication that, if Francis resembled Jesus in every essential detail, Jesus must, by the same token, have been equally like Francis. Francis made memorably visible a different God-Man: not the ruler magnificently seated in judgment, as he was carved in so many church portals—portals beneath which bishops pointedly imitated Christ by sitting in judgment over their

Fig. 3.7. St. Francis of Assisi, his body showing the stigmata, embraces the crucified Christ. Anonymous thirteenth-century crucifix with St. Francis (detail). S. Francesco, Arezzo, Italy. Photo: © Scala / Art Resource, N.Y.

flocks—nor the preacher carved on the pulpits from which priests and friars preached, but the poorest of the poor, emaciated, shivering, lice-ridden, clothed in the meanest of rags and wracked with illness.

The stigmata of St. Francis proved enormously controversial. This novel miracle and new manifestation of sanctity provoked such widespread and enduring skepticism—much of it coming from priests and members of other religious orders, who felt that Francis's stigmata somehow infringed on the uniqueness of Jesus—that a whole series of popes had to issue bulls attesting to its authenticity. But the miracle of Francis's stigmata also proved enormously influential. In the three centuries following this first confirmed appearance of the stigmata, a number of other cases were reported. Remarkably, between Francis of Assisi at the start of the thirteenth century and Padre Pio in the middle of the twentieth, nearly all of those whose bodies displayed miraculous

Francis of Assisi's Veneration of the Eucharist

During his last illness, St. Francis explained his reverence for churches, priests, and the Eucharist (1226).

And God inspired me with such faith in his churches that I used to pray with all simplicity, saying, "We adore you, Lord Jesus Christ, here and in all your churches in the whole world, and we bless you, because by your holy cross you have redeemed the world."

God inspired me, too, and still inspires me with such great faith in priests who live according to the laws of the holy Church of Rome, because of their dignity, that if they persecuted me, I should still be ready to turn to them for aid. And if I were as wise as Solomon and met the poorest priests of the world, I would still refuse to preach against their will in the parishes in which they live. I am determined to reverence, love, and honor priests and all others as my superiors. I refuse to consider their sins, because I can see the Son of God in them and they are better than I. I do this because in this world I cannot see the most high Son of God with my own eyes, except for his most holy Body and Blood which they receive and they alone administer to others.

Above everything else, I want this most holy Sacrament to be honored and venerated and reserved in places which are richly ornamented. Whenever I find his most holy name or writings containing his words in an improper place, I make a point of picking them up, and I ask that they be picked up and put aside in a suitable place. We should honor and venerate theologians, too, and the ministers of God's word, because it is they who give us spirit and life.

—"The Testament of St. Francis," in *St. Francis of Assisi's Writings and Early Biographies: English Omnibus of the Sources for the Life of St. Francis*, ed. Marion A. Habig, (Chicago: Franciscan Herald, 1983), 67–68

stigmata were women: Christina of Stommeln, Lukardis of Oberweimar, Catherine of Siena (who, out of modesty, asked to receive the visible wounds in invisible form), Osanna Andreasi of Mantua, Lucia of Narni, Caterina Racconigi, and others.

Perhaps it is not so surprising that women received the stigmata far more often than men did. In a deeply rooted cultural tradition reaching back at least to late antiquity, women were viewed as more bodily than men. If they were saints, then, their bodies would give visible and tangible signs of sanctity. They were also more given to bodily austerities. By the late Middle Ages, the most flamboyant ascetics were women like Christina the Amazing, Catherine of Siena, and innumerable others. These holy women threw themselves into ovens, fell into fireplaces, starved themselves, bound themselves with chains, macerated their flesh with hair shirts, and lacerated it with whips. In return, they were rewarded with equally bodily manifestations of sanctity. Their bodies levitated and lactated, gave off heavenly perfumes, and oozed miracle-working oils. With an appalling literalness, their bodies demonstrated the simple truth of religious metaphors, images that to others had become mere clichés.

When Clare of Montefalco died in 1308, some of the sisters in her Augustinian convent recalled that she had always spoken of holding Christ's passion in her heart. Curious about what she had meant, four of them performed an autopsy—an early and entirely unofficial instance of this medical-juridical procedure. In her heart they found a tiny crucifix and the three nails that fixed Christ to the cross, along with a miniature whip and pillar, crown of thorns, lance, and the rod with the sponge. In addition, her gall bladder yielded three stones of perfectly equal size and weight, which the amazed sisters took to be a symbol of the Trinity. When Margaret of Città di Castello died a few years later, in 1320, her heart was found to contain

> ## Catherine of Siena Writes to Queen Joanna of Naples (August 4, 1375)
>
> Your unworthy servant and the slave of God's servants is writing to you in the precious blood of God's Son. I long to see you a true daughter and spouse consecrated to our dear God. You are called daughter by First Truth because we were created by God and came forth from him. This is what he said: "Let us make humankind in our image and likeness." And his creature was made his spouse when God assumed our human nature. *Oh Jesus, gentlest love, as a sign that you had espoused us you gave us the ring of your most holy and tender flesh at the time of your holy circumcision on the eighth day.* You know, my reverend mother, that on the eighth day just enough flesh was taken from him to make a circlet of a ring; to give us a sure hope of payment in full he began by paying this pledge. And we received the full payment on the wood of the most holy cross, when this Bridegroom, the spotless Lamb, poured out his blood freely from every member and with it washed away the filth of humankind his spouse.
>
> Notice that the fire of divine charity gave us a ring not of gold but of his own purest flesh. This gentlest of fathers celebrated his wedding with us in a feast not of animal flesh but of his own precious body. This food is Lamb, roasted over the fire of charity on the wood of the sweet cross. So I beg you most courteously in Christ Jesus to lift up your heart and soul with all your affection, energy, and caring, to love and serve so gentle and dear a Father and Spouse as God, high eternal Truth, who tenderly loved us without being loved.
>
> —*The Letters of St. Catherine of Siena*, vol. 1, trans. Suzanne Noffke, O.P. (Binghamton: Medieval and Renaissance Texts and Studies, 1988), 128–29

three small stones, each of which bore a different image: the Virgin Mary with her golden crown; the baby Jesus in his cradle, surrounded by flocks of sheep; and Joseph, bearded and bald, with a woman in a Dominican habit—presumably Margaret herself—kneeling by his side. Margaret, a blind cripple who as a child had been abandoned by

A Laywoman Attempts Ascetic Devotions

A young Venetian laywoman imitates the ascetic devotions of Dominican nuns and of St. Catherine of Siena (ca. 1400).

With admirable fervor, this woman beloved of God longed to act upon what she heard in holy sermons, and not only (as just said) by busying and occupying herself with hearing and saying the Divine Office, but also concerning austerity of corporal life. She strove to observe not just the life of the Preaching Friars of Santi Giovanni e Paolo or their nuns of Corpus Domini in Venice; she even sought to follow, to the best of her abilities, the austerities of life of the blessed Catherine of Siena, Sister of Penance of St. Dominic. Thus, she never ate meat so long as she was healthy; and even when she was ill, she would not eat it except by special command. By the same token, she never wore fur in any season and observed the greatest fasts; and she always slept (when she slept) dressed and almost on her knees and out of bed, on some planks—except when she happened to be sick with some serious illness, and then on account of holy obedience. She also covered her flesh day and night not simply with clothing of wool or ordinary haircloth, but rather with especially coarse haircloth.

Sometimes I questioned her, saying: "Tell me, how can you wear such rough hair shirts so constantly?" With a face all happy and smiling, in her dovelike simplicity she answered me humbly and sweetly, saying: "Dear father, I tell you truthfully that I don't feel it at all, as if I were wearing none of these things." And indeed great things seemed very tiny to her, because of the superabundance of her fervor. Thus, when one of her and my sisters in Christ among these nuns secretly gave her a whip with bits of metal and a good thick brass chain, she often beat herself with that whip and bound herself with that chain, girding her flesh to the very end of her life. These objects—that is, hair shirts, chain, and whip—are preserved to this very day by the Sisters of Penance of St. Dominic in Venice, out of reverence for her.

Here it should be particularly noted that the penitence and austere life of this beloved woman were all the more marvelous and commendable in that she was of youthful age and always nourished on and accustomed to sensual pleasures and delicacies. Moreover, she resided in the home of her parents, who led a particularly delightful life, and by whom she was especially loved and coddled. Nonetheless, with admirable joy and admirable energy and the agreement of the entire household, she supported these hardships and used them to mortify her sensuality.

—Thomas of Siena, "The Legend of Maria of Venice,"
trans. Daniel E. Bornstein, in *Dominican Penitent Women,*
ed. Maiju Lehmijoki-Gardner with Daniel E. Bornstein
and E. Ann Matter (New York:
Paulist, 2005), 123–24

her own parents, meditated so intensely on the persons of the Holy Family that they miraculously materialized in her heart.

At times of more general crisis, living saints could move out of the cloister and find a place at princely courts and in the public eye. During the Hundred Years' War between England and France (1337–1453), the long exile of the papacy from Rome (1305–1377), and the ensuing Great Schism (1378–1417), when Europe was divided between two (after 1409, three) contending popes, visionaries, seers, and political prophets proliferated. Many of them were women. With political and ecclesiastical institutions in terrible disarray and their male leaders obviously incapable of restoring order, princes and people alike turned to other sources of inspiration and guidance. Joan of Arc was just the most famous of the holy women—including Constance of Rabastens, Jeanne-Marie of Maillé, Marie Robine, and Piéronne the Breton—who announced encouraging and menacing visions, addressed rulers and church councils, and even took up arms, lending their sacred charisma to the cause of French victory and ecclesiastical unity. In Italy, Birgitta of Sweden and Catherine of Siena dictated accounts of their revelations, called for humble submission to papal authority, and addressed a steady stream of appeals to the pope

Fig. 3.8. Supplicants approach the body of Margaret of Cortona; a scribe records the ensuing cures. Canonization dossier for Margaret of Cortona; Archivio Storico del Comune di Cortona, H 27, fol. 1035r. Photo: FOTOMASTER di Gaetano Poccetti, Cortona.

in Avignon, in person and through scores of letters, calling on him to restore the papacy to its rightful, Roman seat. If their visions and revelations found a receptive audience among the eagerly credulous or merely curious, it was not simply because things were so bad that anything was worth a try. These particular women deserved to be taken seriously because their austere lives and virginal purity made them appropriate vessels of divine grace and channels of divine revelation.

A LAY CULTURE OF PENANCE

In 1215 the Fourth Lateran Council required all Christians to confess their sins to their priest at least once a year and to do the penance he imposed on them. However, penance was not just something imposed by clerical confessors. For a thousand years, members of the monastic orders—the religious, in the terminology of the time—had functioned as specialists in the worship life and the ascetic life: in the spiritual economy of medieval Europe, monks and nuns had renounced sex, marriage, and personal property and dedicated themselves to the work of God, offering their prayers on behalf of the larger community that in turn supported them with its donations. But now, in the closing centuries of the Middle Ages, laypeople self-consciously adopted penitential practices that had long been the special preserve of the monastic orders, took upon themselves the obligation to live chastely and act charitably, and claimed for themselves a religious identity that remained distinctively lay.

We can catch a rare glimpse of how this culture of penance touched the individual conscience in an entry in the diary of the Florentine merchant Gregorio Dati. Reflecting that he had not always been as good as he ought, Dati resolved to refrain from conducting business on church holidays, abstain from sex on Fridays, and perform some pious or charitable act each and every day, with set penalties in varying amounts if he should fail to keep these resolutions. Dati had not the slightest intention of giving up sex and commerce entirely. On the contrary, his diary documented his assiduous and successful participation in both of these activities throughout his long life, as he meticulously recorded the various business partnerships he formed and the twenty-six children he fathered, by a succession of one slave and four wives. However, Dati clearly believed that by shaping his sexual and commercial relations according to the moral and religious precepts of the church, he could lead a good Christian life without renouncing the activities that distinguished lay existence from the clerical life.

Unlike such private revelations of individual conscience (which are rare enough discoveries at any time), collective participation in penitential activities left its mark everywhere in the late Middle Ages. In 1260, for instance, the rite of self-flagellation—which had been for centuries a standard monastic form of penance—abruptly left the quiet of the cloister and took to the streets and piazzas of central Italy, as laymen paraded through their hometowns and from city to city, whipping their bare torsos in imitation of the beating inflicted on Jesus by Roman soldiers. In the aftermath of this first dramatic

A Florentine Merchant Resolves to Live in a More Christian Manner (January 1, 1404)

I know that in this wretched life our sins expose us to many tribulations of soul and passions of the body, that without God's grace and mercy which strengthens our weakness, enlightens our mind and supports our will, we would perish daily. I also see that since my birth forty years ago, I have given little heed to God's commandments. Distrusting my own power to reform, but hoping to advance by degrees along the path to virtue, I resolve from this day forward to refrain from going to the shop or conducting business on solemn Church holidays, or from permitting others to work for me or seek temporal gain on such days. Whenever I make exceptions in cases of extreme necessity, I promise, on the following day, to distribute alms of one gold florin to God's poor. I have written this down so that I may remember my promise and be ashamed if I should chance to break it.

Also, in memory of the passion of Our Lord Jesus Christ who freed and saved us by His merits, that He may, by His grace and mercy preserve us from guilty passions, I resolve from this very day and in perpetuity to keep Friday as a day of total chastity—with Friday I include the following night—when I must abstain from the enjoyment of all carnal pleasures. God give me grace to keep my promise, yet if I should break it through forgetfulness, I engage to give 20 *soldi* [an amount roughly equal to one quarter of a florin] to the poor for each time, and to say twenty Paternosters and Avemarias.

I resolve this day to do a third thing while I am in health and able to, remembering that each day we need Almighty God to provide for us. Each day I wish to honor God by some giving of alms or by the recitation of prayers or some other pious act. If, by inadvertence, I fail to do so, that day or the next day I must give alms to God's poor of at least 5 *soldi*. These however are not vows but intentions by which I shall do my best to abide.

—*Two Memoirs of Renaissance Florence: The Diaries of Buonaccorso Pitti and Gregorio Dati*, ed. Gene Brucker, trans. Julia Martines (Prospect Heights, Ill.: Waveland, 1991), 124–25

movement of collective public flagellation, hundred—thousands, even—of flagellant confraternities were founded throughout Mediterranean Europe and beyond. By the fifteenth century, Florence had forty-two flagellant confraternities; the little Tuscan town of Cortona, with less than a tenth of the population of Florence, had seven. These lay confraternities, which held regular and frequent meetings in the privacy of their own chapels and sponsored rather less frequent public processions, firmly established the voluntary self-flagellation of devout laymen as the premier form of public penitence, ready to be employed whenever disaster threatened the community or an apocalyptic preacher stirred religious enthusiasm.

Those who did not care for flagellation could join confraternities dedicated to singing vernacular hymns, running hospitals, distributing bread to the poor, providing dowries for needy and deserving girls, or comforting condemned prisoners on the way to execution. Whatever one's devotional bent or charitable concern, there was a confraternity to suit it. Their numbers grew exponentially between the thirteenth century and the fifteenth: in Florence, the number of confraternities of all sorts multiplied from six in the mid thirteenth century to thirty-three in the middle of the fourteenth; it then tripled again, to ninety-six, over the course of the next century. The confraternities became the institutional means par excellence by which laymen participated in religious life—as active sharers in a devotional and penitential life suited to their status, and not just a more or less passive audience for the priestly performance of the Mass. But it was far from the only form such participation took.

As tertiaries affiliated with one or another of the mendicant orders, converts attached to monasteries and hospitals, and members of hymn-singing or blood-letting confraternities; as footsore pilgrims trekking to distant shrines and as anchoresses confined in narrow cells as if in tombs; as fasting saints and housewives reading their Book of Hours while they stirred a simmering stew pot; as devotees of apostolic poverty; and as merchants fining themselves for failing to resist turning a fast buck—in all these ways and more, late medieval men and women shared in a remarkable democratization of penance. This riotous profusion of penitential activities and forms of life bears little resemblance, at heart, to sixteenth-century notions of the

Statutes of a Flagellant Confraternity

The statutes of the Bolognese flagellant confraternity of San Domenico remind the brethren about what they should do every day (September 19, 1443).

Because we are men of the world and have charge of goods and families, we cannot always remain busy in the service of God like monks. Nonetheless, we should call our Lord to mind in the morning and the evening and at mealtime. For Solomon says: "Mane semina semen tuum et vespere non cesset manus tua, quia nescis quid magis oriatur, hoc aut illud, et si utrumque simul melius erit" [Eccles. 11:6]; that is, in the morning when you rise from bed, begin to perform good works, and in the evening do not omit to perform some good works before you go to bed, for you do not know whether what you did in the morning was acceptable to God, and so therefore do good in the evening, and if both the one and the other are received by God, so much the better for your soul.

We desire, therefore, dearest brethren, that when you rise in the morning you raise your mind to God and devoutly make the sign of the holy cross and say a Paternoster and an Ave Maria with the lesser Credo, fixing your mind on not offending God in your neighbor and on wishing to refer to His honor and glory every good thing that may happen to you that day, and pray Him that He may give you that grace. You should also do this same thing in the evening before you go to bed, being sorrowful, beating your breast, and lamenting for every evil thought, evil word, and evil deed done that day against God and your neighbor, asking for His forgiveness and determining to do better from now on than in the past.

The psalmist also says: "Nolite fieri sicut equus et mulus, in quibus non est intellectus" [Ps. 32:9]; that is, do not be like beasts that have neither reason nor understanding and enter their stalls and eat without any respect; for man, to whom God has given understanding, should eat in fear of God and with moderation. Therefore, dearest brethren, when you wish to lunch or dine, make the sign of the holy cross over the table. Whoever does not know the benediction should devoutly say one Paternoster and the Ave Maria and the Benedicite before eating; and after you have eaten, say the Paternoster and Ave Maria, thanking the Lord God for the benefit received. Thus says the apostle St. Paul: "Cibos creavit Deus ad percipiendum cum graciarum actione fidelibus" [1 Tim. 4:3]; that is, God created foods so that faithful Christians may eat them and enjoy them with God's blessing, giving thanks unto him. Therefore, let us bless our tables and render thanks unto God like reasonable men. May God grant us the grace to do so. Amen.

It would also be very praiseworthy to make an effort, if one has the time and opportunity, to try to hear a mass devoutly every day or at least visit the church, which is the house of your heavenly father, recalling to mind that poor artisan who became rich by devoutly hearing a mass every day. But this is a suggestion, not a commandment.

—Gilles Gerard Meersseman with Gian Piero Pacini, *Ordo Fraternitatis: Confraternite e pietà dei laici nel Medioevo* (Rome: Herder, 1977), 671–72

priesthood of all believers or the disciplined sanctification of the lives of the faithful, which democratized salvation in quite other terms. If anything, it represents a return to earlier times, the times of Anthony the Egyptian, when a simple peasant could become the exemplar of the ascetic life.

FOR FURTHER READING

Arnold, John H. *Belief and Unbelief in Medieval Europe*. London: Hodder Arnold, 2005.

Bornstein, Daniel E., and Roberto Rusconi, eds. *Women and Religion in Medieval and Renaissance Italy*. Chicago: University of Chicago Press, 1996.

Brown, Peter. *The Body and Society: Men, Women, and Sexual Renunciation in Early Christianity*. New York: Columbia University Press, 1988.

———. *The Cult of the Saints: Its Rise and Function in Latin Christianity*. Chicago: University of Chicago Press, 1981.

Bynum, Caroline Walker. *Fragmentation and Redemption: Essays on Gender and the Human Body in Medieval Religion*. New York: Zone Books, 1992.

———. *Holy Feast and Holy Fast: The Religious Significance of Food to Medieval Women*. Berkeley and Los Angeles: University of California Press, 1987.

———. *Jesus as Mother: Studies in the Spirituality of the High Middle Ages*. Berkeley and Los Angeles: University of California Press, 1982.

Geary, Patrick J. *Furta Sacra: Thefts of Relics in the Central Middle Ages*. Princeton: Princeton University Press, 1978.

Rubin, Miri. *Corpus Christi: The Eucharist in Late Medieval Culture*. Cambridge: Cambridge University Press, 1991.

———. *Gentile Tales: The Narrative Assault on Late Medieval Jews*. New Haven: Yale University Press, 1999.

Swanson, R. N. *Religion and Devotion in Europe, c. 1215–c. 1515*. Cambridge: Cambridge University Press, 1995.

Webb, Diana. *Medieval European Pilgrimage, c. 700–c. 1500*. New York: Palgrave, 2002.

ORDERING WORSHIP

THE IMPACT
OF ARCHITECTURE

RICHARD KIECKHEFER

CHAPTER FOUR

Viewed romantically, a medieval church was a place where the entire community of the faithful gathered in pious solidarity, laypeople spiritually joined with their clergy in common worship. In this romantic telling, the building of churches was largely a collaborative effort in which the laity participated enthusiastically. Two accounts of the mid-twelfth century are cited to make the case for church-building as a collective endeavor: Archbishop Hugo of Rouen, reporting on the construction of Chartres Cathedral, recounted how the citizens formed devout companies to aid in the transportation of materials, and Abbot Haimon of St.-Pierre-sur-Dives told how even noblemen helped to pull wagonloads of stone, wood, and other supplies for the construction of a church, while a thousand or more individuals joined the procession in pious silence.

But an alternative telling of the story is possible: a more critical perspective deemphasizes such stories of pious harmony and represents medieval churches as sites of division between clerical and lay culture. This version of the story sees laypeople as detached, passive spectators at the clerical celebration of liturgy. This critical account points to the screens erected in medieval churches separating the clergy in their chancels from the laypeople in their naves, so that people in the congregation could barely even see what was transpiring in what one historian calls the "alienated liturgy of the altar." This viewpoint suggests that laypeople comprehended the Mass only faintly and experienced it only fleetingly. They might be persuaded to attend, but they paid close attention only at particular moments, especially when the priest had just consecrated the host and held it up in elevation. One medieval writer said that people would rush forward to see the elevated host—God himself present in a wafer of bread—and then immediately dash out, as if they had seen not God but the devil.

Both of these perspectives, of course, are simplifications. The way laypeople would have experienced church buildings and the liturgy celebrated in them depended on many factors. It would make a great deal of difference whether the Mass being celebrated was at the high altar at the far east end of the church or at one of several other altars, usually more accessible to laity. It might matter whether the layperson in question was of higher or lower social status, a woman or a man. An individual's experience of the church would be conditioned also by whether the purpose in coming was to hear Mass, to witness a baptism, to venerate the relics of a saint as the climax of a shorter or longer pilgrimage, to attend a parish meeting, or perhaps even to dispatch some purely secular business. The experience might be quite different in a large urban church, a small rural parish church, a chapel, a cathedral, or a monastic church. Because the design and furnishing of churches developed differently in various parts of Europe, it would make a difference whether the layperson in question lived in Anglo-Saxon England, in late medieval Spain, or in some other time and place.

If one is inquiring about lay use of church buildings, the first and most basic matter to investigate is the establishment of separate spaces within the church. The simplest distinction within a church is between the nave at the west end, in principle meant for the laity, and the chancel at the east end, restricted to the clergy. One might go further and say that the nave is where the laypeople sit in pews, while the chancel is where the priest stands at the altar. But all of these points require qualification. The distinction between clerical care of the chancel and lay responsibility for the nave was clearer in principle than in practice. Laypeople may have occupied the nave more than the chancel, but they would mostly have stood throughout Mass; at least until the late Middle Ages there would have been nothing like what we call pews. And the priest might celebrate Mass at the high altar (in the chancel) or in an altar in a side chapel, in the center of the nave, in an aisle to the north or south of the nave, under one of the arches in the arcade separating the nave from an aisle, or perhaps in a gallery or tower.

If we want to know how laypeople experienced church architecture, we need to distinguish between initiative and accommodation. There were circumstances in which laity might play a major role in the building of churches: local nobility in the early Middle Ages had chapels built for themselves and for local peasants; wealthy burghers in late medieval towns often endowed chapels for themselves and wrested control of church-building from the hands of clergy. But even when churches were not built on the *initiative* of laity, they usually were meant in various ways to *accommodate* laypeople. Even a monastic church built mainly on the initiative of the monks could make elaborate provision for a lay congregation and for laypeople who came as pilgrims.

We need to be clear also about the screens erected in medieval churches. Screens had a long and varied history. There is evidence for them in late antiquity; in some circumstances they were massive, and in the later Middle Ages they could be highly ornate. They could separate clergy from laity and sometimes women from men. But they did not necessarily separate the lay congregations very effectively from the priests celebrating Mass. The paradox here is that the more massive the screen was, the less laity were cut off from the clergy at the masses they were attending. If the screen was a see-through wooden structure, it might indeed serve as a partial barrier to visibility as well as to access, and the congregation in the nave might need to peek through to see masses celebrated at the high altar. But if it was a massive stone structure, its function was rather to separate off one part of the building as in effect a private chapel for the clergy or monks, leaving the larger space as one in which laity could cluster around nave altars and have close experience of the liturgy being celebrated.

Furthermore, we need to be clear about the variety of available worship spaces both within and outside of churches. By the end of the twelfth century, most of Western Europe was divided not only into dioceses but into parishes, and everyone lived in a more or less clearly bounded territory with a parish church to which she or he belonged. But it took centuries for that grid to become established, and even after it did so, there were many alternatives to attending Mass in one's parish church. Chapels of various kinds—public and private, inside and outside of church buildings—might be available.

In the later medieval centuries, pious Christians increasingly identified themselves not simply as members of a parish but as belonging to a confraternity or guild that on more or less frequent occasions would hold separate liturgy.

Moreover, the correlation of parishes with communities was imperfect. Two or more villages might share a single parish church;

Church Decoration as Instruction for the Illiterate
(ca. 1286)

Pictures and ornaments in churches are the lessons and the Scriptures of the laity. Thus [Pope] Gregory [the Great] says: "It is one thing to adore a picture, and another by means of a picture to learn a story that should be adored. For what writing supplies to those who can read, a picture supplies to those who are uneducated and look at it. Since they who are uninstructed thus see what they ought to follow, they 'read' it even though they do not know letters." It is true that the Chaldeans worship fire and force others to do the same, burning other idols. But pagans adore images like icons and idols; Saracens do not, who neither possess nor look on images, grounding themselves on that saying, "Thou shalt not make to thyself any graven image, nor the likeness of anything that is in heaven above, nor in the earth beneath, nor in the waters under the earth" [Exod. 20:4], and drawing on this and other subsequent authorities, they greatly rebuke us about this. But we do not worship images, nor account them to be gods, nor put any hope of salvation in them; for this would be idolatry. Yet we venerate them for the memory and remembrance of things done long ago. Thus the verse,

> Whenever you pass the image of Christ bow humbly,
> Adoring not the image but him whom it represents.
> It makes no sense to ascribe God's being
> To material stone shaped by human hand.
> The image you see here is neither God nor man,
> He is God and man which this holy image represents.

—William Durandus on the symbolism of church art,
in *Medieval Popular Religion, 1000–1500*, ed. John Shinners
(Peterborough, Ont.: Broadview, 1997), pp. 21–22

peasants in larger parishes might need to travel some distance to attend any church and arrive to rub shoulders with people from other communities, whom they might not often see in their everyday lives. Gervase Rosser has suggested that in the parish church of Ludlow during the fifteenth century, as many as eleven subgroups would be clustered around their various nave altars for Mass: members of guilds, or residents of particular vicinities, all worshiping together as theoretically members of the same parish but in fact identifying themselves first with their subgroups and perhaps secondarily as individuals who through these subgroups stood in relationship with the parish church.

On all three points, therefore, broad generalizations are little more than invitations to qualification and nuance. Whether one is speaking of separate spaces, boundaries between those spaces, or communal gatherings, historical realities do not lend themselves to tidy overview. Still, in an effort to bring some order out of the complexities of church-building, we may begin with a historical overview (focusing largely but not entirely on England) and then proceed to discuss some specific themes and issues.[1]

THE MISSIONARY PHASE (SEVENTH THROUGH NINTH CENTURIES)

The chronology of missionary activity varies a great deal from one country to another: in Ireland there were missionaries as early as the fifth century, in Gaul the project of converting the countryside extended from the Gallo-Roman period of late antiquity into that of the Frankish conquest in the fifth century and beyond, while in Italy the churches originally concentrated in cities faced the triple challenge of missionary work not only among indigenous peoples but among Ostrogothic and then Lombard invaders. When Pope Gregory I sent Augustine of Canterbury as missionary to southern England in 596, Irish missionaries were already coming down from the North. Irish monks in the seventh century and English monks in the eighth began missionary journeys on the Continent.

All these missionaries would have preached and even celebrated Mass largely in the open air. If they built churches, they would usually have used wood; a classic example is the chapel that St. Boniface is said to have constructed with timber from the sacred oak that he chopped down at Geismar. Pope Gregory told Augustine that he might sprinkle pagan temples with holy water and use them as churches if they were of sound construction; these too would presumably have been of wood. But the churches from this era that survive are the stone ones, built mainly (apart from metropolitan centers) during the seventh and following centuries.

We may concentrate here on England, which is particularly rich in church buildings surviving from the early Middle Ages, archaeological evidence that is supplemented to some extent by written sources. Thus the Venerable Bede wrote at several points in his *Ecclesiastical History* about church-building in England during the period of the conversion, and his account is supplemented by later writers such as William of Malmesbury. We learn from these sources that a church for the monastery at Lindisfarne was built "after the Irish method, not of stone but of hewn oak, thatching it with reeds," later replaced with lead sheets. A church at York was dilapidated by the late seventh century, serving "only for the nesting-place of birds," so Bishop Wilfrid repaired it, whitewashed the masonry, covered it with sheets of lead, and glazed the windows that had previously been covered only with linen or fretwork. At Ripon, Wilfrid constructed a new church "with marvelous curve of arches, courses of stones, and adornment of porches." He was aided by masons "whom the hope of liberal reward had drawn hither from Rome." Contemporary opinion had it that construction of this sort had never before been done north of the Alps, and even visitors from Rome testified of the church at Hexham that "they could fancy the pride of Rome was here."

Among the oldest surviving churches in England is the one at Escomb in County Durham, probably built in the later seventh century. The nave is long, high, and narrow. A tall arch connects the nave with a small chancel. While the south side has been much altered, the north side with its small, high windows gives a reasonably good sense of what such a church might have looked like in the early Saxon era. The stone used for construction seems to be reused Roman masonry, possibly from a fort that stood nearby during the years Britain was a Roman colony. Several features are characteristic of Saxon building, in particular the use of "long and short work," a configuration of masonry that Saxon builders used at the corners of buildings and beside doorways. Fragments of the sort of colored glass used in Saxon buildings have been found on this site.

Roughly contemporary with the church at Escomb is one at Brixworth in Northamptonshire. But while the relatively remote building at Escomb is fundamentally simple in its design, the one at Brixworth was from the outset more complex. Unlike the church at Escomb, this one is usually taken to be a Saxon reinterpretation of churches the Roman missionaries would have known back in Italy: a series of chapel-like rooms called *porticus* along the north side approximates the aisle of a Roman basilica, and an arcade between the sanctuary and the nave resembles the screen that had begun developing in churches of Mediterranean antiquity. Both churches might well have been built by monks, but the one at Brixworth with its *porticus* would more clearly have served the purposes of a monastic community, particularly if it had multiple priests who needed side altars for liturgical celebration.

During the missionary period, then, the role of the laity vis-à-vis the clergy was inseparable from the conditions of mission. Monastic missionaries were the bearers of a foreign culture represented and perceived as superior to indigenous culture; even if they were themselves from the receiving culture, they had through education become representatives of a tradition imported from abroad. Under these conditions, it is not surprising if whenever possible foreign models of church-building were preferred. When they were used, the point would be visibly clear: natives of the mission territory were on the receiving end of cultural and religious transmission.

A further development was occurring in this early period, having to do with the position of the priest at the altar. While in the very early church it was the norm for the priest to stand facing the people, Josef Jungmann traces a gradual spread of the alternative pattern, in which priest and people faced the same direction (in principle, east). The latter arrangement was the norm in Syria and parts of North Africa already by the fourth century, in other Mediterranean regions soon afterward, in northern Europe by the seventh century, in Italy by the eighth, and everywhere by the turn of the millennium.

THE "MINSTER AND MANOR" PHASE (TENTH AND ELEVENTH CENTURIES)

In the next phase (the later Saxon era in England), regions were served by the clerical communities resident at large "minster" churches, to which people would resort for special occasions: baptisms, feast days, perhaps burials. On ordinary Sundays, rather than trudging several miles to the nearest minster, the peasantry might typically join with the lord of the manor at a private church that he had erected. Minsters and manorial churches were not the only ecclesiastical structures on the landscape; there were also monastery churches and cathedrals. But for ordinary lay experience of worship, minsters and manorial churches played the dominant role.

How a regional church functioned during this period can be illustrated by two examples. The eleventh-century church of San Vincenzo in Galliano, at Cantù in Lombardy, was built on the site of an early Christian church of the fifth century. The original structure had been a simple rectangle with a broad apse at the east end serving as sanctu-

Fig. 4.1. The church at Escomb, among the earliest in England, dates from the later seventh century, although the south side (shown here) has later features. Photo: Richard Kieckhefer.

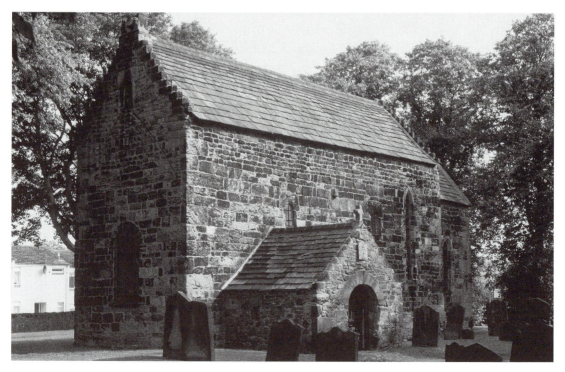

ary. By the early eleventh century, however, a key alteration had been made: the sanctuary in the apse was elevated several feet, and beneath it was a crypt. The attention of a layperson standing in the nave, therefore, would be led visually both upward to the sanctuary and downward toward the crypt. The sanctuary was fully visible from the nave; a simple rood beam extended from the north to the south wall, marking the boundary between nave and sanctuary but not impeding the visibility of the altar. Access from the nave to the sanctuary was by a broad and high stairway leading upward from the nave. The effect was to introduce clear vertical distinction between clerical and lay space and to highlight the dignity of the sanctuary in which the priest stood at the altar.

On each side of this central stairway were portals leading to much narrower stairways that led down into the crypt. By this point side chapels had been added in apses on the east ends of the two aisles.

Fig. 4.2. San Vincenzo in Galliano, at Cantù in Lombardy, eleventh century, with an elevated sanctuary above the crypt. Photo: Richard Kieckhefer.

To the south of the church lies a detached baptistery (like those still found in several Italian cathedrals), which, like the church, is well preserved. The baptistery is a sign of the church's function as a regional *pieve*, or what in other countries would be called a minster: a place where infants born to families living throughout the region would be brought for baptism.

The second example is the church of St. Peter at Barton-on-Humber in Lincolnshire. Much of what stands now is of later construction, but at the west end are two of the three units that made up the late tenth-century church: a small square baptistery at the far west end, and a larger tower (originally about forty-seven feet high) that would originally have served as the nave, to the west of which there once was a small and square chancel. The base of the font, found by excavations, lay in the southwest corner of the baptistery, allowing a modest-sized group of people to gather in the rest of the chamber to witness the sacrament. As a regional church with the sacramental rights associated later with parish churches, St. Peter's had not only a

Fig. 4.3. Odda's chapel, built in 1056, was later incorporated into a farmhouse and rediscovered in 1885. It is an example of the sort of proprietary chapel that might have been found in many places. Photo: Richard Kieckhefer.

baptistery (attached to the church, not detached as at Cantù) but a churchyard, in which many Saxon graves have been excavated.

Alongside the minsters, the countryside during this period was dotted with small chapels built for the local aristocracy and used in the first instance as family chapels, although serfs of the manor would in most cases have gathered here too on most Sundays of the year. These "proprietary" chapels or churches would have been directly controlled by the lay aristocrats who built them, even if in later centuries they were removed from lay ownership and control, turned over to ecclesiastical institutions, and made into parish churches. One example is the chapel built in 1056 at Deerhurst in Gloucestershire by the local earl Odda. There was a priory church very close by, which did come to have parochial functions, perhaps the reason Odda's chapel remained private until at the Reformation it was absorbed into a farmhouse and quickly forgotten.

Crowds Jam the Old Basilica of St. Denis before Its Reconstruction (ca. 1144–1147)

Through a fortunate circumstance attending this singular smallness—the number of the faithful growing and frequently gathering to seek the intercession of the Saints—the aforesaid basilica had come to suffer grave inconveniences. Often on feast days, completely filled, it disgorged through its doors the excess of the crowds as they moved in opposite directions, and the outward pressure of the foremost ones not only prevented those attempting to enter from entering but also expelled those who had already entered. At times you could see, a marvel to behold, that the crowded multitude offered so much resistance to those who strove to flock in to worship and kiss the holy relics, the Nail and Crown of the Lord, that no one among the countless thousands of people because of their very density could move a foot; that no one, because of their very congestion, could [do] anything but stand like a marble statue, stay benumbed or, as a last resort, scream. The distress of the women, however, was so great and so intolerable that you could see with horror how they, squeezed in by the mass of strong men as in a winepress, exhibited bloodless faces as in imagined death; how they cried out horribly as though in labor; how several of them, miserably trodden underfoot [but then] lifted by the pious assistance of men above the heads of the crowds, marched forward as though upon a pavement; and how many others, gasping with their last breath, panted in the cloisters of the brethren to the despair of everyone. Moreover the brethren who were showing the tokens of the Passion of Our Lord to the visitors had to yield to their anger and rioting and many a time, having no place to turn, escaped with the relics through the windows.

—*Abbot Suger on the Abbey Church of St.-Denis and Its Art Treasures*, ed. Erwin Panofsky, 2nd ed. (Princeton: Princeton University Press, 1979), 87–89

These churches were all clearly linked with authority, whether the ecclesiastical hierarchy of the region or the secular lord of the manor. It was with them that initiative lay. But the religious requirements of ordinary laypeople were accommodated in these structures, albeit somewhat differently. The manorial church was built in the first instance for the lord of the manor; if it was no larger than Odda's chapel, it could have accommodated other laity, but not capaciously, and serfs who attended might well have had a sense of being guests in someone else's spiritual home. Nobility did oblige, and churches of this sort were the ordinary places of worship for much of the population, but spacious and gracious accommodation was probably the exception. At a minster, the entire purpose was to serve the needs of the people, and a family gathered for a baptism in a place such as Cantù might have had a sense that for that moment they were being well and hospitably received indeed. But at the church next door, where the high altar was in a very literal sense quite high, the relationship between clergy and laity was increasingly remote, at least when Mass was at the high altar.

CONSOLIDATION AND REFORM (MID-ELEVENTH THROUGH LATE TWELFTH CENTURY)

The mid-eleventh century brought exceptionally important developments in the organization of grassroots Christianity throughout the West. This was the time of the "Gregorian reform," the movement championed by Pope Gregory VII that had as one of its main goals the independence of the church from secular authorities. This goal was pursued at all levels, from that of papal and episcopal elections down to control of local churches and appointment of local clergy. In principle, laypeople were meant now to relinquish the proprietary churches that had been so vitally important in the previous period. When they did so, they usually entrusted them not to the local bishop but rather to some ecclesiastical establishment: a monastery, a community of canons, or perhaps a cathedral chapter, which then would administer the revenues, hire a vicar to serve the church, and at times let the church fabric fall into serious disrepair, perhaps especially when the institution charged with the church's care was at a distance from it.

This was also the period in which parish boundaries became established; by the end of the twelfth century, everyone was supposed to belong to a fixed territorial parish. This process often meant, among other things, deciding which of several liturgical structures in a particular territory would be designated as the parish church, leaving others (as we shall see) to occupy the lowlier status of chapels.

In England this was a period of both secular and ecclesiastical consolidation under the Norman conquerors. Churches were built in the English version of Romanesque style, called "Norman." Soon after 1066, the cathedrals and monastery churches that had been built earlier were quickly replaced by much grander edifices in this Norman style. During the twelfth century, attention turned to parish churches, which had most often been done in wood and now were rebuilt in stone. When rebuilding was done in this period, frequently the entire church was built anew, not just the chancel or the nave.

A small Norman church at Kilpeck in Herefordshire was built near a castle between 1140 and 1180. Typically for the period, the walls have a core of rubble stone with red sandstone facing. The building is best known for its carvings, particularly on the south porch, where dragons and warriors mingle with other themes in a medley that shows no inkling of a boundary between secular and sacred themes, between the numinous and the grotesque. Carvings on the interior are

---

Abbot Haimon Describes How Laypeople Hauled Building Materials to Chartres Cathedral (1145)

Who ever saw, who ever heard, in all the generations past, that kings, princes, mighty men of this world, puffed up with honors and riches, men and women of noble birth, should bind bridles upon their proud and swollen necks and submit them to wagons which, after the fashion of brute beasts, they dragged with their loads of wine, corn, oil, lime, stones, beams, and other things necessary to sustain life or to build churches, even to Christ's abode? Moreover, as they draw the wagons we may see this miracle that, although sometimes a thousand men and women, or even more, are bound in the traces (so vast indeed is the mass, so great is the engine, and so heavy the load laid upon it), yet they go forward in such silence that no voice, no murmur, is heard; and, unless we saw it with our own eyes, no man would dream that so great a multitude is there. When, again, they pause on the way, then no other voice is heard but confession of guilt, with supplication and pure prayer to God that he may vouchsafe pardon for their sins; and, while the priests there preach peace, hatred is soothed, discord is driven away, debts are forgiven, and unity is restored between man and man.

—"Pious Church-Builders at Chartres Cathedral (1145)," in *Medieval Popular Religion, 1000–1500*, ed. John Shinners (Peterborough, Ont.: Broadview, 1997), 391–92

tamer and more consistently sacred, but what is most important about the interior is that it is divided into three units or "cells," and the markers of division are elaborately carved arches between the nave and the choir, and between the choir and the small apsidal (or rounded) sanctuary. Each unit, from west to east, is progressively smaller and lower, as if the sections of the church were like those of a telescope. The visual focus on the interior is clearly the altar at the east end, but it is doubly framed by arches, and it is distanced from the nave by an architecturally distinct choir between nave and sanctuary.

Fig. 4.4. The Norman church in Kilpeck has arches clearly distinguishing the nave from the choir and the choir from the sanctuary. Photo: Richard Kieckhefer.

ELABORATION OF BUILDING AND WORSHIP (LATE TWELFTH AND THIRTEENTH CENTURIES)

The next phase was a time not of institutional organization so much as of liturgical and architectural elaboration. Chancels were often rebuilt on a much larger scale to accommodate increasingly rich and elaborate ritual, with growing numbers of clergy joining in the celebration at the altar and in choir stalls. Naves were less often expanded in this era, except by the addition of aisles; from this period onward, additions to a church such as aisles, porches, or clerestories were often built piecemeal. The increasing complexity of liturgical celebration during this period is epitomized by the liturgical usage of Salisbury Cathedral, where the number of clerics serving at any one Mass multiplied, and processions inside the building became famously grand affairs. Particularly important was the expanded number of singers (including chaplains and young boys) who would occupy the increasingly extensive choir stalls during Mass and other services. The division of the chancel into the sanctuary (with the high altar) and the choir (with its choir stalls) was not new to this period, but increasingly elaborate liturgy meant lengthening of both sanctuary and choir and making clearer distinction between the two units.

While laypeople would not typically worship at a cathedral such as the one at Salisbury, parish churches were built or rebuilt at the time with similarly expanded chancels for grander liturgical celebration. One at Uffington in Oxfordshire resembles Salisbury Cathedral in its style and represents in miniature something approximating the proportions of the cathedral.

Someone needed to pay for this rebuilding and for the inevitably needed maintenance. In England earlier than in other countries, synodal legislation made building and upkeep of the chancel the responsibility of the clergy, while laity were in charge of building and maintaining the nave. But the distinction was rarely absolute, and

Fig. 4.5. The thirteenth-century church at Uffington, in Oxfordshire, has a chancel approximately as long as the nave, allowing for the more elaborate liturgical practice becoming common at the time. Photo: Richard Kieckhefer.

frequently the laity took charge of raising and administering funds for both parts of the church. It was during this period that the office of church warden arose: a layperson designated as administrator of finances for an ever costlier building operation and then entrusted with other responsibilities as well, such as representing the lay community to the clergy and the hierarchy.

This was also a time when *seeing* the sacred became increasingly important for laypeople, and *displaying* the sacred was correspondingly a privilege of clergy. The most important manifestation of the sacred was the elevation of the consecrated host. Synodal legislation from Paris around 1200 marks a turning point in the history of this practice: a statute issued under archbishop Odo of Sully required a priest to elevate the host to the level of his chest before the consecration, and then high enough that the congregation might see it after the words of consecration had been said. By the mid-thirteenth century, the custom was widespread throughout Western Europe. In some places the urge to display the sacred was so strong that priests had to be admonished not to elevate the host several times and not to wave it about. A more discreet way of highlighting the elevation was with a backdrop: at Chartres Cathedral, a bright purple cloth was hung behind the altar so the elevated host might be more sharply visible. Still, it is important to bear in mind that when Mass was being celebrated at the high altar of a church, the newly elongated chancel meant that the elevation involved display at a greater distance than before.

In the thirteenth century, a nave may have been expanded, especially with the construction of north or south aisles, because the population of the parish was growing and more space was needed for parishioners to stand during Mass. Another explanation is that space was needed for chapels, particularly certain types of chapels. From the late twelfth into the early thirteenth century, churches in England were being given new chapels dedicated to Mary, known in English as "Lady chapels," where an office or a Mass in honor of the Virgin might be sung on a weekly or even daily basis, at a time when devotion to the Virgin as the universal patroness was everywhere on the rise in Western Europe.

One more innovation of the period is worth noting, that being the granting of indulgences throughout Western Europe for those who donated to church-building efforts. Indulgences had earlier been given to crusaders, and in the course of the thirteenth century, they came to be assigned for a range of devotional practices. Before the century's end, cathedrals such as the one at Salisbury were the foci of such indulgences. In the following period, the custom spread to parish churches and chapels, and by the fifteenth century, it was very common for ordinary parish churches to be subsidized in this manner.

HEIGHTENED CIVIC PIETY (FOURTEENTH AND FIFTEENTH CENTURIES)

The succeeding phase brought heightened manifestation of civic piety: laypeople not only played a leading role in building, expanding, and furnishing churches but frequently provided their own chapels for use of their families or their guilds. Not infrequently, naves were rebuilt separately from chancels; sometimes this meant catching up with chancels that had been rebuilt in grand style in the thirteenth century. Towers and porches were often added; towers served for the ringing of bells, porches could function for betrothals, and both could provide dignity and ornament that made the church more prominent in the landscape or cityscape.

It would not be an exaggeration to speak of a revolution in wooden furnishings in the later Middle Ages. Furnishings in wood now became more common than before and more ornate. Two forms of furnishing proliferated in large measure because preaching became increasingly popular: pulpits in which preachers could stand and benches (which we now call pews) where congregations could sit. There is documentary reference to English pulpits from the twelfth century, but the earliest surviving wooden pulpits are from the fourteenth century, and very few pulpits in either stone or wood predate the fourteenth century. Wooden benches, too, were an invention of this era. Stone seating along the sides of a nave had been introduced earlier in some churches, but it was in the thirteenth century that crude wooden benches first began to appear and only in the fifteenth century that they proliferated.

Fig. 4.6. Like stalls for clergy in the choir, wooden furnishings provided for laity in the nave were sometimes carved with comic or folkloric scenes. These bench ends from Brent Knoll in Somerset show Reynard the Fox, dressed as a bishop and preaching to birds, then being hanged. Photos: Richard Kieckhefer.

Having furniture for congregational seating made a great difference to the ethos of preaching. As Margaret Aston says, "A seated audience—especially one that is mewed in pews—is more of a captive audience than one that remains on its feet."[2] The building of benches did not come about uniformly, and other forms of seating were certainly possible. There is abundant evidence that women would bring portable stools to church and sit with other women, typically on the north side of the nave. When fixed seats came into use, this was sometimes perceived as an abuse, and we hear of irate parishioners breaking and removing such seating because it interfered with their freedom to move about and stand where they wished. At the end of the Middle Ages, parishioners began to pay for rental of seating in churches, as churchwardens' account books indicate, and typically it was men who paid for the seating of their wives.

The elaborately carved wooden choir stalls still found in many medieval churches—famous especially for the often fancifully carved misericords on which the occupants were to lean—were also products of this revolution in furnishings. We might suppose choir stalls are more relevant to the history of clerical than of lay experience, but laypeople could and often did sit in them alongside clerics. Church legislation of the thirteenth century permitted individuals of high social status, particularly the patrons of churches, to sit in the choir. Aston has cited late medieval evidence of a judge who carpeted and cushioned his own chancel stall to make it more comfortable, a goldsmith who requested burial near his chancel seating, and a schoolmaster who wanted burial near his wife's seat in the chancel. Robert Mannyng complained of "lewd men" who stood in the chancel during Mass, and (even worse) of women who stood beside the clergy during Mass or matins, causing temptation and distraction from proper devotion. Preachers might insist that women not approach the high altar—except at communion. Still, it was proverbially the case that "the worse the whore, the nearer to the choir she stands."

This revolution in furnishings extended to screens—not only the rood screens that separated chancel from nave but also "parclose" screens that could be used for various purposes, especially to close off a portion of the church, often one end of an aisle, for use as a private chapel. Women and men might be separated by screens, as at Santa Croce in Florence. One might expect these partitions to arouse resentment from laypeople who were excluded from the areas thus enclosed, but the chapels created this way were most often for the use of lay families, and even rood screens were largely subsidized by lay donors. Wealthy lay donors who helped finance screens at times had their own coats of arms included in the ornament on screens. Besides, screens could be used for purposes other than separating: they could serve as platforms for preachers and singers, and Mass could be celebrated at an altar placed on top of a screen.

The late Middle Ages witnessed a multiplication of nave altars. These were largely controlled by laity, who endowed them and provided them with altar cloths, altarpieces, and candles. Lay donors might indicate seasons and times when these altars should be used. They could indicate collects and other prayers to be said

Disrespectful Behavior in Church (1373)

In the deeds of Athens there is the story of a holy hermit who led a good and saintly life. In his hermitage he had a chapel dedicated to St. John, and knights, ladies, and maidens from that country went there on pilgrimage, as much to celebrate the saint's feast as for the saintliness of the holy man. As the hermit chanted high mass, he turned to the people after he had said the Gospel and saw the ladies, the maidens, and several of the knights and their esquires chattering and jangling and taking counsel among themselves during the mass. He looked at their foolish faces and next to each of their ears saw dark and horrible demons laughing at their jangling and writing down each word they heard. These demons were leaping on their hair done up like horns, on their rich attire, and on their finery like little birds hopping from branch to branch. The holy man crossed himself and was astonished. From the beginning to the end of the canon of the mass he heard them talking and flattering each other, laughing and jesting. He struck the book to make them be quiet, but none of them stopped talking. Then he said, "Good Lord God, make these people be quiet and realize their folly." At that moment those who had been laughing and jangling started to weep and wail, men and women both, like people possessed and suffering such torment that it was a pitiful thing to hear. And when mass was sung, the holy hermit told them how he had seen the demons of hell with their horrible faces laughing at what they were doing at mass. Then he told them how dangerous and what a fault it was to talk and jest, and how sinful it was to laugh, since no one should come to mass or the divine office except to listen to it humbly and devoutly and to adore and pray to God.

—"Behaving Piously: A Knight's Advice to His Daughters (1373)," in *Medieval Popular Religion, 1000–1500*, ed. John Shinners (Peterborough, Ont.: Broadview, 1997), 324–25

in masses at these altars, and even additional Gospel texts to be read before the "last Gospel" at the end of Mass.

This period also witnessed the building of west towers where they had not previously been erected. They were often added to parish churches in the fifteenth century, for various reasons. First, larger and louder bells were being cast, with elaborate frames on which they could be turned fully 180 degrees, and towers were built to accommodate such bells at an elevation that allowed their sound to travel widely. Second, towers were objects of civic pride; a church near a marketplace in the center of town would be an obvious place for the construction of a particularly grand, imposing tower that provided a clear visual focus for the entire area.

CHURCHES AND CHAPELS

Throughout the Middle Ages, but especially in the last centuries, chapels proliferated. To understand how laypeople experienced worship, it is vitally important to take chapels and their relationship with churches into account. The very definition of a chapel is, however, a complicated matter. It is largely a catch-all category for religious architecture that does not fit into other standard categories: a liturgical structure that is neither a cathedral, nor a monastic church, nor a parish church. A chapel is defined mainly in terms of what it does *not* have. Because it lacks the status of even a parish church, it usually cannot serve for baptisms or burials and therefore cannot (or at least in principle should not) have a font or a churchyard. For our purposes, however, what is perhaps most important is that, standing outside the parochial network, a chapel was usually more under the control of the founders, often laity, who paid for its construction and its upkeep and hired the priests who served in it.

Already in the early Middle Ages it is possible to distinguish two broad categories of chapels: some were built into or annexed onto larger church buildings, while others were separate and independent structures. Chapels incorporated into larger building complexes could serve for veneration of particular saints. In the later Middle Ages they often served for chantries (endowed to ensure that masses were celebrated for the souls of the founders) or for confraternities and guilds. Freestanding chapels served a much wider range of purposes: they could be "chapels of ease" for parishioners living at a distance from the parish church, devotional centers for newly popular saints such as Ann or George, bridge chapels where travelers could pause for prayer and make oblations, field chapels that might serve as stations for Rogationtide processions (celebrating the harvest before Ascension Day), woodland oratories for hermits, urban preaching halls, memorials for prominent men who had been murdered, pious markers on battlefields, or centers for funerary ritual in churchyards. The influence of lay patrons was most obvious when chapels were incorporated not within churches but rather within larger secular structures such as town halls, guild halls, castles, and manor houses. A chapel for a town council, whether in the town hall or nearby, was where Mass would be celebrated before council sessions, and this was typically a private Mass for council members. In the later Middle Ages everyone was expected to belong to a parish,

---

The Lord Mayor of London Tries to Improve Behavior in St. Paul's Cathedral (1554)

Forasmuch as the material Temples of God were first ordained for the lawful and devout Assembly of People, there to lift their Hearts, and to laud and praise Almighty God; and to hear his Divine Service, and most Holy Word and Gospel, sincerely, said, sung, and taught; and not to be used as Markets, or other profane places, or Thorough-fares, with carriage of Things: And for that (now of late years) many of the Inhabitants of the City of London, and other People repairing thither, have, (and yet do) commonly use and accustom themselves very unseemly and unreverently (the more the pity) to make their common Carriage of great Vessels full of Ale and Beer, great Baskets full of Bread, fish, Flesh and Fruit, and such other Things; Fardels of Stuff, and other gross Wares and Things, through the Cathedral Church of St Paul's. And some leading Mules, Horses and other Beasts through the same unreverently; to the great Dishonour and Displeasure of Almighty God, and the great Grief also, and Offence, of all good People; Be it therefore, for remedy and reformation thereof, Ordained, Enacted, and Established, etc. That no Person, either Free or Foreign, of what Estate or Condition soever, do at any time from henceforth, carry or convey, or cause to be carried through the said Cathedral, any manner of great Vessel or Basket, with Bread, Ale, Beer, Fish, Flesh, &c., or any other like Thing or Things, upon pain of forfeiture of losing for every such his or their first Offence, 3s. 4d., for the second 6s. 8d., for the third 10s., and for every other offence, after such third time, to forfeit 10s., and to suffer Two Days' and two Nights' Imprisonment, with Bail or Mainprise.

—J. G. Davies, *The Secular Use of Church Buildings* (London: SCM; New York: Seabury, 1968), 142

and everyone was expected to pay tithes to the local parish church, yet many people attended Mass much of the time not in parish churches but in chapels.

Any altar—the high altar in a church, a side altar, or an altar in a detached chapel—was in the later Middle Ages expected to be dignified by an altarpiece or retable of some sort. But as devotions to specific saints and to particular representations of Christ and the Virgin became more prominent, chapels might be known very largely for the images they housed. A chapel dedicated to St. Ann outside the town of Bristol was founded by the Lord de la Warr. It was fifty-seven feet long and fifteen feet wide, making it small in comparison to a typical parish church yet not tiny.[3] It had an image of the patronal saint, before which candles and possibly incense were burned in veneration. The weavers and cobblers of Bristol committed themselves to donating each year a candle lofty enough to extend up to the vaulting.

A chapel inside a church, like the church itself, might be referred to by the name of the saint to whom it was dedicated—although either

Fig. 4.7. The chapels off the choir of St. Nikolai Church in Stralsund, Germany, show the tendency found in many German churches of the fourteenth and fifteenth centuries to build into the structure series of chapels that could be financed and used by laypeople as chantry chapels or as guild chapels. Photo: Richard Kieckhefer.

a church or a chapel could be dedicated to more than one patron saint, and the patronage could be changed. Even a chapel known for its dedication, however, might also be called by the name of the family that had founded it, and chapels inside churches were very often established, built, and owned by families. Privately founded chapels were typically closed off with locked screens, to which few individuals apart from the owners held keys. It was the wardens who granted permission for building and who sold the land to the founder. Such sales could provide much of the cost for constructing a new church: the external chapel walls served also as external walls of the church, so in effect private individuals were subsidizing what would otherwise have to be built and paid for by the church administrators.

Fig. 4.8. The church at West Tanfield in Yorkshire was rebuilt in the fourteenth century, but the north aisle was reconstructed in the mid-fifteenth century as a burial chapel for the Marmion family, a local aristocratic family that had founded a chantry here much earlier. The iron hearse used in funerals can be seen toward the east end of the north aisle. Photo: Richard Kieckhefer.

Founders paid for the land a chapel was built on, for construction and glazing, and for any wall paintings that were intended. They might need to pay for authorization. They financed all the needed liturgical furnishings: books, vessels, vestments, the altar and its cloths, altarpieces, ambries, stalls or other seating, lamps, and screens. They paid for the consecration ceremony and the feast that followed. And they had to provide a fund to pay the vicar hired to fill the benefice. Antje Grewolls has calculated that a chapel in Lübeck could cost between four hundred and a thousand marks, while in the later fourteenth century a substantial house in the center of that town would cost between five and eight hundred marks. A chapel financed by a family would be passed down through its generations, and if the church was demolished, the wardens were responsible for providing a new chapel in the new construction.

External chapels were more variable in their purpose and in their form. The numbers of chapels varied widely from one place to another, as did the ratio of chapels to parish churches. At the end of the Middle Ages the city of Norwich, which had long been one of the largest cities in England and by the early sixteenth century had a population of roughly ten thousand, had perhaps forty-six parish churches and eight chapels.[4] The nearby coastal city of Lynn, which grew in population relatively late but by the early sixteenth century had roughly six thousand inhabitants, had only one parish church, to which two chapels of ease were attached. In Winchester as well there was a single parish church and many chapels. In the relatively populous Lincolnshire, parish churches were perhaps more than twice as numerous as chapels, while Devonshire had probably three times as many chapels as parish churches. In general, places that were populous before the firming up of parish boundaries tended to be rich in parishes, while in places where population expanded at a later date, it was notoriously difficult to secure elevation of mere chapels to the status of new parish churches.

Among the most elusive of chapels for historical research—but perhaps the most important for our purposes—were those in private homes of wealthy burghers. In Regensburg there were 348 chapels,

Fig. 4.9. The chapel of St. Apollonia, by St. Marien Church in Stralsund, was built in 1416 to expiate the city's offense of burning to death three members of the clergy; it is said to have had three altars. Photo: Richard Kieckhefer.

largely in private residences. These were built mainly by members of the patriciate in the fourteenth and fifteenth centuries, sometimes in towers or over town gateways, often in bays extending outward from an otherwise ordinary residential chamber. If the resident had obtained ecclesiastical permission and had the chapel properly consecrated, Mass could be celebrated there, and we have records of papal or episcopal authorization for such use. But private chapels need not have been meant for liturgical use; some were only for nonliturgical devotions, but even so they might have altarlike tables with pious images on them. With sufficient resources and commitment, a burgher might decorate a private chapel lavishly, with larger or smaller (and sometimes fairly significant) panel paintings, wall paintings, and stained glass. The altar might be supplied with altar cloths, candles, even relics. When a liturgical or devotional altar was established on the side of an otherwise ordinary room, it might be closed off with a curtain, which could be opened when needed to give the entire space a religious character. The parallel to a church is particularly clear in cases where an indulgence was obtained for visitors to a domestic chapel. One chapel built at Straubing in the home of Ludwig Zeller was granted a forty-day indulgence in 1466 by the archbishop of Salzburg: anyone who had made confession, prayed in the chapel, and made a donation on any of various feast days could gain this indulgence.

MONASTERIES AND PARISHES

As we have seen, monastic missionaries were often the ones responsible for building churches in territories converted to Christianity in the early Middle Ages. In subsequent periods, other forms of church became typical: minsters, proprietary churches in manors, parish churches, and chapels. But monasteries retained a role throughout the Middle Ages in service to the laity, and often a monastic church doubled as, in effect, a parish church. Monasteries often became the nuclei for surrounding communities, whose residents might serve as workers for the monks or might be drawn to the place by a market run at the behest of the monastery. When a lay community was established, the monastery church served also as a parish church for that community, and some part of the church building would become designated as the space for the lay parish—perhaps the west end, an aisle, or a chapel attached to the church. At the monastery of St. Albans, in England, there is evidence for lay altars placed under the arches of the nave arcades, but we know also that a chapel attached to the church at the northwest corner served the local laity.

One particularly interesting piece of evidence helps us piece together how monks and a local lay community could be accommodated within a single church: the famous plan of St. Gall. Found at the monastery of St. Gall in Switzerland, this plan was drawn on parchment in the early ninth century, and it seems to represent an ideal conception of how a monastery and its church should be laid out. No church may ever have been built corresponding precisely to this plan, yet in its detail it tells a great deal about what churches of the

Fig. 4.10. St. Albans Cathedral was a monastery church in medieval England that became a cathedral in the nineteenth century. The pillars between the nave and the side aisles have paintings that would have served as altarpieces for altars erected alongside them. Photo: Richard Kieckhefer.

early Middle Ages were expected to provide. Close examination makes clear that the plan is above all else a careful exercise in the coordination of monastic and lay presence in a church where both monks and laypeople worshiped. Toward this end, the interior was elaborately divided and subdivided, with low screens that partitioned numerous different spaces.

The plan shows the church as having many altars: a high altar, one in the east apse and one in a west apse, one for laity in the nave, and others in the aisles, the transepts, the towers, the baptistery, and at the crossing steps. These altars had screens around them defining where the celebrating clergy were to stand and where the congregation was allowed. The main areas for lay participation were the lay altar and the baptistery. The baptistery was situated in the bay of the nave lying farthest to the west, and an altar dedicated to St. John the Baptist and St. John the Evangelist in the adjacent bay served for masses celebrated at the time of baptism. Farther east was the altar "of the Savior at the Cross," at which the tenants and serfs of the monastery—the lay community living outside the walls of the monastery proper—would gather for worship. In short, the liturgical centers of the church were highly scattered, but the nave was given over largely for the use of the laypeople for whom it served in effect as a parish church.

LAY INFLUENCE AND CONTROL

Lay donations in support of church architecture were routine in virtually all periods and places, but the nature and function of these contributions differed. Patronage on a lavish scale was a form of prominent and lasting self-advertisement for the donor and the donor's family, but smaller donations could be made with no intention of memorialization. Thus the early fourteenth-century glass in the east end of Cologne Cathedral has the coats of arms of several patrician families; patronage of glass presupposed considerable wealth and was an opportunity for self-advertisement by the donors, whereas contributions of all sizes were made toward work on the building itself, and what relatively poor people offered was pooled with the oblations of wealthier patrons.

When chapels were built by and for laypeople, there was little to keep these proprietors from exerting their influence on the design of the buildings. This was the case already with the proprietary chapels or churches in the "minster and manor" phase of church-building, and again in the proliferation of chapels in the period of heightened civic piety. What is perhaps less expected is that in the later Middle Ages lay influence extended also to parish churches and in some places even to cathedrals. Lay administrators increasingly controlled the construction and maintenance of church fabric, not necessarily limiting themselves to the nave. And the design of churches, particularly where it had demonstrative function, came under lay influence if not determination.

At Strasbourg, construction of the cathedral was taken into the hands of lay administrators in the late thirteenth century, and despite some opposition in the late fourteenth and early fifteenth centuries, it remained mainly a lay concern for the rest of the Middle Ages. As early as 1261, there was lay involvement in the administration of cathedral-building in this city, with interested and wealthy laymen taking much of the responsibility upon themselves.[5] By the 1280s, the administration was in the hands not just of concerned lay individuals but of the municipal government, which had the right to alienate property donated for construction. For example, a citizen might bequeath a house to the building administration, and the lay administrators would sell the house and use the proceeds to pay for work on the cathedral. A further source of revenue was a Marian altar, designated from the late thirteenth century as the "altar of the [building] fabric," the special place for making donations toward the cost of construction. The system seems to have worked well, judging from the rapid progress on construction made while the city government was administering the work.

Laypeople often took a special interest in construction along the periphery of a church building: the aisles, the porches, and the towers. Klaus Jan Philipp suggests that when side portals of churches were more lavishly decorated than other entrances, this was because laypeople visiting churches were most interested in the direct access these portals gave to aisle chapels in which they had invested their funds, and to altars at which weekday masses and masses for members of their families were celebrated. Construction of massive west towers in particular, added to many churches toward the end of the Middle Ages, was often a matter of special interest to burghers. Sankt Bartholomäus in Frankfurt am Main was historically patronized by the German monarchy and used as a place for royal elections (and later coronations), but the west tower was rebuilt in the fifteenth century as a civic monument for the imperial free city, and it was called the "Parish Tower." At Strasbourg, townspeople showed new enthusiasm for construction of their cathedral in the late fourteenth century, when work began on the upper stages of the northwest tower.

PILGRIMAGE SHRINES

So far we have focused mainly on churches intended to serve a local population, but already we have seen cases of churches and chapels meant chiefly or secondarily for pilgrims. The major pilgrimage sites of antiquity remained pilgrims' goals throughout the Middle Ages: the visit to Rome was all the more important in the late Middle Ages, when popes began to offer special indulgences during Jubilee years. While Jerusalem was not always a safe place to visit, it never lost its allure as the ideal destination for the truly serious pilgrim. To these classical pilgrimage sites new ones were added in the Middle Ages that had strong international appeal: Santiago de Compostela and Canterbury in particular, but also Rocamador, Aachen, Einsiedeln, and other places. Further along the spectrum were shrines that attracted mainly, or perhaps almost exclusively, the short-distance pilgrims from nearby villages or counties.

The institution of pilgrimage was both a blessing and a challenge for church architecture. It was a blessing because pilgrims brought donations, which could be used for building, expanding, and maintenance of churches. The challenge was to accommodate potentially large numbers of pilgrims without their interfering with the other functions of the church, particularly the Eucharistic liturgy. Pilgrimage presupposed first a route and second a destination. The route was a lengthy pattern of roads leading to the city, followed perhaps by a stairway or some other immediate access to the church building, then a pathway and perhaps a corridor within the building. The destination was a sacred object, usually the relics of a saint, but in some cases a miracle-working image or a miraculous host or blood of Christ. Laying out the pathway was relatively easy; most medieval churches were already meant as processional space, and in one way or other, the final goal of the pilgrimage could be simply integrated into the liturgical structure of the building. What required more ingenuity was deciding where and how to position the object that served as the pilgrims' final goal.

We have seen how the plan of St. Gall envisaged a church designed to accommodate both a monastic and a lay community. The further complication in this plan was its provision also for pilgrims coming to venerate the relics of the patron saint. Wealthier pilgrims would approach by one route through the crypt, ordinary pilgrims via another, and monks by yet a third. All three groups might converge on

Fig. 4.11. The relics of St. Alban were venerated in the retrochoir of the monastery church, now St. Albans Cathedral. The watchers' gallery is to the far right. Photo: Richard Kieckhefer.

the tomb from their different directions. Monks and laity, aristocrats and commoners encountered each other at the center point of devotion but without converging.

The "corridor crypt" found in the St. Gall plan was not an innovation. Pope Gregory I had designed a crypt of this sort for St. Peter's basilica in Rome, which gave pilgrims a narrow and deliberately constraining route leading them to the saint's tomb. An alternative was the vaulted "hall crypt," a more open space that usually had two or more aisles separated by arcades, allowing in principle for more fluid movement around the tomb. Whether the crypt had the narrower form of a corridor, the more spacious form of a hall, or some combination of the two options, it provided a devotional focus for the church at the same end as the main liturgical focus, but beneath it.

The parish church of St. James in Rothenburg, built in the fifteenth century, demonstrates the opposite approach. Here again a single dominant relic, the corporal believed to be stained with the blood of Christ, was the center of pilgrimage. The solution adopted in this

Fig. 4.12. Just outside of Görlitz, in Upper Saxony, a complex built in the later fifteenth century includes a Holy Cross Chapel, an Anointing Chapel, and a Holy Sepulchre, allowing a vicarious pilgrimage to the holy sites of Jerusalem. Photo: Richard Kieckhefer.

church, as in many of the period, was to establish an alternative focus at the other end of the church from the high altar. The sacred object, rather than being placed on a lower level, was elevated to a higher one: a chapel in a gallery at the west end of the church, opposite the liturgical focus on the east end.

The monastic church of St. Albans in Hertfordshire illustrates a third approach. There, too, as at the church in the St. Gall plan, a route enabled pilgrims to visit relics at the east end. But the relic was placed on the same level as the high altar, in a retrochoir farther east, behind the monks' worship space in the chancel. Pilgrims made their way to the retrochoir via a path to the side of the nave, the crossing, and the chancel. On one side of this retrochoir is a massive wooden watchers' gallery of the fifteenth century, from which guards could keep surveillance over the pilgrims and the offerings they brought to the church.

But what solution was appropriate if the church held not one major relic but several, all of which were important to pilgrims? Here the classic example is the monastery church of St. Denis at Paris. From the sixth century onward, this was one of the most important churches of France, the place where kings of the Merovingian and succeeding dynasties were buried. It was famed also as the burial place of St. Denis, the "apostle" and patron saint of France, who had long been confused with the Dionysius mentioned in the Acts of the Apostles as a convert brought to the Christian faith by St. Paul. Among the further treasures of St. Denis were relics of Christ's crucifixion (a nail and a portion of the crown of thorns) and a banner associated with Charlemagne. The church had been rebuilt with a crypt in the eighth century, but the structure erected then was inadequate to accommodate the crush of pilgrims who thronged there on feast days and during major markets. And so Abbot Suger had a new "chevet" built (completed in 1144) to make for easier circulation of pilgrims: an east end with an ambulatory around the choir, and chapels radiating outward from the ambulatory for the display of relics. Services could now be held in the choir without direct interference from the crowd's commotion, and the pilgrims could be brought into contact with the relics without having to navigate the stairway and possibly confined quarters of a crypt. This arrangement was not altogether new: it had been introduced in the monastic church of St. Martin at Tours more than two centuries earlier. But in this as in other ways, St. Denis served as a prototype for later church-building.

What would the pilgrims do when they visited the saints' tombs? Obviously they could be expected to pray and to leave oblations. If they were coming in satisfaction of a vow, to offer thanks for a healing or rescue worked through the saint's intercession, they would typically leave behind an ex-voto, or votive, offering, commonly a model of the body part whose affliction had been cured. Physical contact of one sort or other was often important to the pilgrims as well. If the relics were in a hall crypt, pilgrims might spend the night sleeping at the side of the tomb (the practice of "incubation"). Holes in an outer shell might enable them to place their hands on an inner receptacle containing the saint's relics. The relics were the earthly remains of powerful intercessors in heaven, and the bodies left behind—which at the Last Judgment were to be restored to life and rejoined with the now separated souls—shared in the spiritual power of the saints. They were channels through which miracle-working power could be accessed, and this was the chief motive for the effort of pilgrimage. Stories of the miracles worked at the tombs could be dramatic. A cripple who managed to drag himself to the shrine of St. Godric of Finchale crouched beside the saint's tomb, moaning, and with a great crackling sound his legs began to straighten; he spent the night at the tomb, and by dawn he was entirely healed.[6] Cases of this sort could easily be multiplied, with afflictions of all sorts said to be suddenly and often dramatically remitted. But not all pilgrims went in the expectation of special favors: many would present themselves because visiting the saints was a work of piety, and pilgrimage was a form of spiritual tourism at once diverting and devout.

SECULAR USES

Katherine L. French has brought to our attention an inquiry of 1379, in which people of Walton in Lancaster were asked about an event that had occurred in their parish church. They not only recalled the occasion but also explained why it was that they happened to be in church that day. Three of them were there to meet other individuals: "to see John del Hethe," "to see a man from Liverpool," or simply for a meeting about a dispute. One had been there "to hear news from Ireland" and another "to buy corn," while yet another had gone "for a cockfight," presumably held in the nave. Of the nine men questioned, only three said they were at church to hear Mass, and in each of these cases the Mass was expressly preliminary to a journey or some other undertaking: they had gone to church "before going to Kirkdale," "before going to Litherland," or "before going to buy fish."[7]

The point is twofold. First, a church was a public place where secular as well as sacred activities might be performed. Second, and perhaps more interestingly, even the religious activity of attending Mass was a moment integrated into the fabric of everyday life, and a reasonably pious person might wish to sanctify a business trip by stopping in for Mass before leaving town. Indeed, we hear elsewhere of masses being arranged specifically at times that would facilitate attendance of merchants or travelers before they left on journeys.

Churches were public buildings, and in many villages and neighborhoods, they were the only such buildings available. Until the late Middle Ages, there was no equivalent of parish halls. Marketplaces were often adjacent to churches, but sellers could not count on having covered markets for inclement weather. If it was necessary to hold public meetings for administrative or judicial functions, the church might be the only space serving these purposes. And churches were routinely so used. The south portal of Strasbourg Cathedral was a place where conflicts between burghers were resolved, where citizens made public oaths, where the mayor received those freed from banishment, and where kings presented themselves to receive homage.

Church buildings were used for church ales, at which parishioners would gather to eat and drink: "scot-ales" served as fund-raisers, "bid-ales" were held to aid individuals in need, and "bride-ales" and "dirge-ales" were held in conjunction with weddings and memorials, respectively. Critics of such events complained of people sitting at trestle tables in the church naves as if they were gathered in taverns. These ales were often accompanied by music and perhaps by dancing. Nor was a fund-raiser required as an excuse for feasting. As J. G. Davies says, "Few activities took place in connection with a church without their being accompanied by eating and drinking."[8] When bells were hung, a new crucifix was erected, a weathercock was installed on a spire, a patron saint's feast day was celebrated, or the Easter sepulcher was dismantled after the feast—or on countless other occasions—fish and flesh, cheese and bread, wine and ale were dispensed.

At times of popular festivals—such as Christmas, St. John's Day, the Feast of Fools, and the like—clergy might become as rowdy as laity. The theologians of Paris complained in 1445 of clerics wearing grotesque masks, dancing in women's dress, playing dice, and feasting on black pudding not just in the nave but in the choir. The next morning, no doubt after at least a perfunctory cleaning up, the nave or choir of a church might be used for a parish school, if no other space was available for that purpose.

A church might be the best place available for storage of fire-fighting equipment, public weights and

---

A Bequest to Support the Church Fabric and Worship from the 1398 Will of John de Ake

First I give my soul to Almighty God, the blesed virgin Mary, and all the saints in heaven, and my body to be buried in the chapel of the virgin Mary in Beverley.

Item, I give to the fabric of the said chapel 8s 4d. Item, I give to the fabric of the collegiate church of St. John in Beverley 6s 8d. Item, I give to the fabric of St. Peter's church in York 6s 8d. I give to the Friars Minor in Beverley 66s 8d ob. on condition that they pray for the good state of my soul and the souls of all the faithful. Item, I give to the Friars Preachers 66s 8d on the same condition. Item, I give to the Friars Minor in Beverley 5s on condition that they celebrate one trental mass [i.e., daily mass over thirty days] for my soul and the souls of all the faithful deceased. Item, I give to the Friars Preachers of Beverley 5s on the same condition. Item, I give to the friars of the orders of the blessed virgin Mary in Kingston upon Hull 5s on the same condition as before. Item, I give to the Austin friars in Kingston upon Hull 5s on the condition before mentioned. Item, I give to Friar William Grovall 13s 4d. Item, I give to Friar Robert Grovall 13s 4d. Item, I give to the rector for tithes forgotten 40s. Item, I give to Sir William Scardeburgh, perpetual vicar of the aforesaid chapel, 6s 8d. Item, I give all my lands [and] tenements in Beverley to Helen my wife during her life, and after her decease to be applied to the further erecting and endowing a chapel on the Crossbridge in Beverley and for the building and endowing an hospital for 24 poor [people], and as often as any of them shall die the twelve governors of Beverley for the time being (after the death of the said Helen) to appoint their successors as also a chaplain to do divine offices in the aforesaid chapel agreeable to the king's charter in that behalf granted after the decease of Robert Garton and Henry Maupas, the two priests first appointed.

—George Poulson, *Beverlac, of the Antiquities and History of the Town of Beverley in the County of York, and of the Provostry and Collegiate Establishment of St. John's, with a Minute Description of the Present Minster and Church of St. Mary, and Other Ancient and Modern Edifices* (London: Longman, for G. Scaum, Beverley, 1829), 2:785

measures, or other goods used for the community. When there was space between the roof and the vaulting, it might be used for storage of grain; in village churches such as one at Münsingen in Swabia, there are doors in the roofs through which goods could be lifted for storage. Davies cites cases in which the church became a kind of museum of curiosities: meteors (at Sugolia and Enisheim), a stuffed crocodile (St. Bertrand-de-Comminges), and a huge bone said to have belonged to a giant cow that supplied milk for all of Bristol (St. Mary's Redcliffe).

While the gospel of peace and of charity was preached in churches, they were hardly places of escape from the harsher realities of life. Criminals and soldiers had their own reasons for recourse to sacred architecture. Felons taking refuge from secular justice could flee to churches and obtain sanctuary there. The institution of sanctuary for criminals might seem dysfunctional, yet in the long run it could provide for rehabilitation where little other such opportunity was available. In the short run it kept criminals in a place where they could be guarded and kept safe from the sort of private vengeance that led to blood feuds. In England, the custom was regulated by statute in 1285, when Edward I required surveillance of criminals claiming sanctuary until such time as an investigation could take place. There were certain places, such as Durham Cathedral or Westminster Abbey, where charters established extended sanctuary privileges, allowing the criminals to stay for protracted periods, even for life, not just inside the church building but on its grounds or in a surrounding district.

Often churches were built—or, more often, refashioned in time of war—for defensive as well as liturgical use, especially at their upper levels. At ground level a church might have a more conventional appearance, but farther up it could be marked with functioning and not merely decorative battlements. The elevated position of churches made them apt for defense against attackers, and their towers especially could be helpful in defending a town or village. The parish church at Pérouge in France is only one of several churches built along the walls of the town, with archers' slits in the walls of both nave and choir. Elsewhere there were churches built with moats and other defensive works. In the extreme case, such as Albi Cathedral, the entire building was fortified; the fourteenth-century church of Simorre resembles a castle more than a church. In 1429, the pope granted an indulgence for rebuilding the church of Saint-Étienne near Boulogne-sur-Mer, noting that it "is fortified against enemies" and that "parishioners and others of the vicinity have recourse there to safeguard their bodies and their goods," but it had gone to ruin "on account of the incursions of the English, with which that region is often afflicted."

Davies's conclusion is that there was scarcely any secular activity that could not be connected with a medieval church, and yet "there was no conscious irreverence."[9] The sacred and the secular were on the whole comfortably conjoined; excesses might be condemned, and secular functions might be directed by preference to the nave rather than the chancel, but few even among the reformers could hope to purge churches altogether of secular use.

LAY ACCOMMODATION AND LAY INITIATIVE

Neither the romantic nor the critical view of church architecture can be applied to all churches or to all traditions of church-building in medieval Europe. But if we distinguish between lay initiative and accommodation of laity, it is possible to sketch some general trends in development across the centuries. First, almost all churches were meant to *accommodate* lay congregations, including a great many monastic churches. They might do so with greater or lesser effectiveness; a proprietary church of a local nobleman was not necessarily the most inviting place for the serfs who worked his lands, although it surely did accommodate them.

Second, while there was lay *initiative* at more than one point in the medieval history of church-building, it was of different sorts. In the period before the Gregorian reform, lay initiative was essentially aristocratic and proprietary: the nobility built and owned the churches that served them, their families, and their agricultural workforce. In the thirteenth through fifteenth centuries, the dominant form of lay initiative was that of the urban patricians and artisans who ran municipal governments, formed confraternities and guilds, and built many of the chapels inside and outside of churches. The laypeople who took this initiative still represented an elite, but it was a considerably broader elite than the aristocratic classes who had earlier served as church proprietors.

Third, the very end of the Middle Ages—the fourteenth and fifteenth centuries—witnessed a high point in both lay accommodation and lay initiative, a convergence of lay responsibility for the building and maintenance of churches together with a proliferation of parish churches, internal chapels, and numerous different types of external chapels, designed more than anything else to provide for the diverse needs of an increasingly complex and educated laity.

FOR FURTHER READING

Aston, Margaret. "Segregation in Church." In *Women in the Church: Papers Read at the 1989 Summer Meeting and the 1990 Winter Meeting of the Ecclesiastical History Society*, ed. W. J. Sheils and Diana Wood, 237–94. Studies in Church History 27. Oxford: Blackwell, 1990.

Davies, J. G. *The Secular Use of Church Buildings.* New York: Seabury, 1968.

Duffy, Eamon. *The Stripping of the Altars: Traditional Religion in England, c. 1400–c. 1580.* New Haven: Yale University Press, 1992.

Finucane, Ronald C. *Miracles and Pilgrims: Popular Beliefs in Medieval England.* Totowa, N.J.: Rowman & Littlefield, 1977.

French, Katherine L. *The People of the Parish: Community Life in a Late Medieval English Diocese.* Philadelphia: University of Pennsylvania Press, 2001.

Horn, Walter, and Ernest Born. *The Plan of St. Gall: A Study of the Architecture and Economy of, and Life in a Paradigmatic Carolingian Monastery.* Berkeley: University of California Press, 1979.

Jung, Jacqueline. "Beyond the Barrier: The Unifying Role of the Choir Screen in Gothic Churches." *Art Bulletin* 82 (2000): 622–57.

Orme, Nicholas. "Church and Chapel in Medieval England." *Transactions of the Royal Historical Society*, ser. 6, vol. 6 (1996): 75–102.

Rosser, Gervase. "Communities of Parish and Guild in the Later Middle Ages." In *Parish, Church and People: Local Studies in Lay Religion, 1350–1750,* ed. S. J. Wright, 29–55. London: Hutchinson, 1988.

MEDIEVAL REVIVALISM

GARY DICKSON

CHAPTER FIVE

Whether medieval or modern, Catholic or Protestant, revivalism has not always received a good press. The portrait of the professional enthusiast has rarely been flattering. Think of Chaucer's Pardoner, Molière's Tartuffe, and Sinclair Lewis's Elmer Gantry, and one imagines a rogues' gallery of zealots, fanatics, fraudsters, manipulators, blasphemers, and conniving hypocrites. But just as the revivalist has been scorned, revivals—occasions of collective religious enthusiasm—have also been disparaged. Such a reaction has a long history. According to the author of Luke-Acts, the spectators witnessing Christianity's first instance of collective enthusiasm, Pentecost, "were amazed and perplexed, saying to one another, 'What does this mean?'" That same query has echoed down the centuries. Those who witnessed medieval revivals were similarly bewildered. Lack of understanding could find expression in mockery, just as at Pentecost: "Others sneered and said, 'They are filled with new wine'" (Acts 2:12-13).

Unsurprisingly, explanations of this kind, both from eyewitnesses and academics, have been used ostensibly to account for the uncomfortably perplexing behavior of religious enthusiasts—but in reality to dismiss it. Writing in 1905, at a time when scientific-sounding medical or psychological explanations had become fashionable, F. M. Davenport called attention to revivalism's supposedly "primitive traits" left over from humanity's "mental and social evolution." Using medical parlance, he wrote of "the social and religious epidemics of western Europe in the Middle Ages," prompting him to conclude that the "enormous amount of mental and nervous instability in evidence was due not only to special conditions, such as the massing of women in convents, but also to barbaric inheritance."[1] Allegedly hysterical nuns aside, medieval Christian revivalism, in Davenport's scheme of things, was a living link to a centuries-old pagan tribal past. Where, then, does this "evolutionary" approach to medieval revivalism lead us? It leads us nowhere.

Among American intellectuals casting a cold eye on revivalism we may count William James, psychologist and philosopher, who in his *Varieties of Religious Experience* (1902) displayed great sensitivity toward conversionary autobiography. James, however, distanced himself from revivalism, which in his day was enjoying boisterous good health; he regarded it as Wesleyan conversion "codified and stereotyped."[2] For the Harvard professor, the vulgar showmanship and noisy theatrical atmosphere of late-nineteenth-century tent meetings could not have been congenial. Moreover, James was responding to the routinization of revivalism, that is, the calculated arousal of religious excitement on the part of the preacher (and frequently his musical assistants) in order to produce the desired effect, namely, conversion on the spot. But the routinization of revivalism also has a medieval history. The church came to understand the practical uses of popular enthusiasm. Preachers became skilful at raising funds for church-building: well-managed campaigns date from at least the 1050s. Then came the crusades, which during the twelfth and thirteenth centuries demanded both recruitment and revenue.

James, however, neither demonized nor psycho-pathologized collective enthusiasm as others did and continue to do. Until recently, scholars have highlighted the "badness" (violence, social revolt, heresy, anticlericalism) or "madness" (hallucinogenic poisoning, apocalyptic fantasy, "mass hysteria") of medieval collective fervor. Norman Cohn's brilliant, if overdrawn, *Pursuit of the Millennium*, for example, is an ingeniously mixed cocktail of socioreligious "badness" and "madness." Cohn was an outstanding scholar of collective "millenarian movements," which he thought of as appealing especially to the poor and disoriented, swayed by messianic leaders and their end-of-the-world prophecies. Cohn concentrated almost exclusively upon medieval enthusiasms that ended in murderous violence—thus supporting his thesis that "millenarian movements" had as their aim the revolutionary transformation of the social order—while he takes little account of medieval revivalist peace movements and their appeal to a broad section of medieval society. Unfortunately, an unbalanced interpretation detracts from Cohn's scholarship, impressive though it is.

Today medieval revivals that manage to escape allegations of badness risk a descent into madness. A perfect illustration of this is the medieval revival known as the Children's Crusade (1212). An unofficial peasant crusade, it most likely lacked any internal controls. Exceptional for a popular crusade, however, it left no Jewish corpses behind it, butchered no priests, and gave birth to no heresies. So the usual accusations of badness are ruled out, except that the chroniclers adopted the view that the enthusiasts were the real victims of the Children's Crusade. Often ill-informed, the chroniclers relished describing how this unauthorized crusade brought suffering, disillusionment, enslavement, and death to the *pueri* (the youngsters) as well as to others—including elderly people—caught up in it. Because the *pueri* had disobeyed clergy and parents, their foolish enterprise came to grief. God did not will it. As a Victorian bedtime story, the sad outcome of the Children's Crusade served as a dreadful warning to girls and boys tempted to run away. In reality, the many *pueri* who did survive the long trek to the Mediterranean maritime cities remained there as immigrants. One of them, a German ex–child crusader named Otto, most likely stayed on in northern Italy, either as a student or a scholar, and pursued a clerical career.

So if badness appears implausible, then madness beckons. Accordingly, one of its ablest historians interprets the Children's Crusade as a

---

The Children's Crusade (1212)

In the month of June of the same year [1212] a certain boy, by occupation a shepherd, of a village named Cloyes near the town of Vendôme, said that the Lord had appeared to him in the form of a poor pilgrim, had received bread from him, and had delivered letters to him to be taken to the king of the French. When he came, together with his fellow shepherd-boys, nearly thirty thousand people assembled around him from all parts of France. While he stayed at St. Denis, the Lord worked many miracles through him, as many have witnessed. There were also many other boys who were held in great veneration by the common multitude in many places because they were also believed to work miracles, to whom a multitude of boys gathered wishing to proceed to the holy boy Stephen under their guidance. All acknowledged him as master and prince over them. At length the king [Philip II], having consulted the masters of Paris about this gathering of boys, commanded them to return to their homes; and so this childish enthusiasm was as easily ended as it had begun. But it seemed to many that, by means of such innocents gathered of their own accord, the Lord would do something great and new upon the earth, which issued far otherwise.

—Anonymous Chronicler of Laon, in *Medieval Popular Religion, 1000–1500*, ed. John Shinners (Peterborough, Ont.: Broadview, 1997), 395

demented creature: "It was a release to be found, then as now, in the crowd, 'a device for indulging ourselves in a kind of temporary insanity by all going crazy together.'"[3] The study of medieval Christian revivalism surely deserves something better than this. A fresh approach, perhaps, unburdened by past prejudices? Would this allow us to cast new light upon an age-old phenomenon?

TOWARD A DEFINITION

"Medieval" is a tricky term, subject to disputed chronological frontiers. Here it will encompass the half-millennial span between the Peace and Truce of God movement (ca. 975–1038), originating in southern France, and the English Pilgrimage of Grace (1536–1537). Defining "revivalism" is trickier still. The sociologist Emile Durkheim, discussing large-scale social upheavals, observed that "there are periods in history when, under the influence of some great collective shock, social interactions . . . become much more frequent and active. Men . . . assemble together more than ever. That general effervescence results which is characteristic of revolutionary or creative epochs."[4] Durkheim's emphasis on new forms of collective behavior during certain periods of historical discontinuity is helpful, while "general effervescence" is an appropriately sparkling way of characterizing mass enthusiasm, religious or otherwise. If "general effervescence" sounds rather too celebratory, like French champagne, at least it carries no necessarily alarming message of social dysfunction.

Medieval religious enthusiasms of diverse kinds were features of extended and sometimes overlapping periods. Certain types of enthusiasm coincided with particular periods. For example, one can speak of a reformist enthusiasm roughly from circa 1000 through the mid-eleventh-century papal (or Grego-

Fig. 5.1. The Children's Crusade, 1212, J. Kirchhoff from J. Sporschil, *Geschichte der Kreuzzüge* (1843). Photo: © SuperStock.

rian) reform movement to the primarily monastic "Reformation of
the twelfth century." This current of reformist enthusiasm certainly
provoked popular responses, orthodox and heretical. And in the midst
of it, interacting with it, came the long crusading epoch, which generated its own brand of religious enthusiasm, again both popular and
official. Beginning with Pope Urban II's Council of Clermont in 1095,
crusade enthusiasm persisted intermittently right up to Christopher
Columbus's departure on his first voyage in 1492—the crusader's red
cross on his caravels' white sails. Other genres of medieval enthusiasm,
the cult of saints prominent among them, borrowed and absorbed
characteristic features of revivalism—preachers, crowd arousal,
miracles—without becoming fully fledged revivals, that is, without
fully conforming to the revivalist paradigm, which was collective,
conversionary, and dynamic.

Broadly speaking, medieval revivals were relatively short-lived
and intense episodes of public, collective religious enthusiasm, frequently characterized by distinctive three-part structures; unusual
manifestations of collective fervor; and public conversionary experiences—including conversions to monasticism, the crusades, itinerant popular movements, and personal moral regeneration. Medieval
revivals were also often strongly influenced by prophetic ideas. Finally
and crucially, unroutinized medieval revivals carried with them a
scent of the extraordinary, an odor as identifiable as a fingerprint or
DNA sample. Medieval revivals, therefore, generated an atmosphere
of the miraculous at times powerful enough to overturn the routines
of daily life, which, in a customary society, was liable to be disorient-
ing but perhaps also exhilarating, rather like a Durkheimian-style
general effervescence.

Crusaders and Monks

One medieval Latin word came to approximate our modern sense of
"revival." That word was *devotio*, which implied a peculiarly active or
ritual sense of devotion. A survey of twelfth- and thirteenth-century
revivalist movements carrying the label of *devotio* should therefore
illustrate some of the essential features of medieval revivalism. As André
Vauchez notes, however, *devotio* was also used by Italian chroniclers in

connection with popular cults of recently deceased saints,[5] confirming what has already been said—that the characteristic traits of revivalist behavior were not limited to medieval revivals in the strict sense.

At the Council of Clermont in 1095, Pope Urban II called for a new kind of holy war. Urban's army was to be composed of people whose sole prescribed quality was pious intent—devotion alone (*sola devotione*). The product of Clermont, the crusader, came into being as a hybrid creature: a holy warrior who went by the name of pilgrim. Conventionally, the Christian pilgrim was unarmed and vulnerable, but the crusader was a new kind of pilgrim, purpose-built to seize Jerusalem as a Christian prize. The monastic chronicler Robert of Rheims writes, "When [at Clermont] Pope Urban . . . said these things . . . everyone, moved by the same feeling, shouted in unison, 'God wills it! God wills it!'"[6] Their acclamation affirmed God's providential blessing on the new enterprise. The conciliar outcry became the crusaders' war cry.

Fig. 5.2. Flagellants in the Netherlands town of Tournai (Doornik), 1349. Flagellants, known as the Brothers of the Cross, scourged themselves as they walked through the streets in order to free the world from the Black Death (bubonic plague). Ann Ronan Picture Library, London. Photo: © HIP / Art Resource, N.Y.

Vociferousness is audible evidence of revivalist enthusiasm. Time after time, the shouts of medieval revivalist crowds compressed complex ideas into popular slogans. At Clermont, too, taking the cross, becoming one signed with the cross (a *crucesignatus*, or crusader) meant assuming a new spiritual identity. It was a conversionary act.

Crusading experience broadened the use of *devotio*, adding motifs of penance and conversion. The spiritual meaning of the term was also enriched by the charismatic twelfth-century crusade preacher and advocate of Cistercian monasticism, Bernard of Clairvaux. Bernardine spirituality, diffused throughout Christian Europe by the rapid growth of the Cistercian order, saw *devotio* becoming a code word for religious fervor, exhibited, for example, in the gift of tears that was increasingly linked to the cult of the humanity of Christ. Nor can it be forgotten that Cistercian monasticism, along with all the other twelfth- and thirteenth-century monastic orders, was, like the crusades, dependent upon a steady stream of new recruits—in other words, converts.

Together, the crusades and a resurgent monasticism inaugurated a new medieval conversionary age, nothing less than the second conversion of Europe. Old-style missionary activity was still, of course, continuing beyond the expanding frontiers of Christian Europe, but now in Latin Christendom, instead of tribal or ethnic Christianization, the emphasis was beginning to be placed on an interiorized conversion of non-infant, already baptized Christians. For monks, as well as for crusaders, this kind of conversion resulted in a change of legal status, whether temporary (crusaders) or permanent (monks). These Christians were converted to a committed religious life, whether within the world or in flight from it. Highly relevant in this respect is that popular, collective revivalist movements also served as a setting and stimulus for individual conversionary acts. Revivalism, in short, extended the opportunities for the conversion of Christians to new forms of Christian commitment.

Popular Revivalism in the Thirteenth Century

Theorists of *devotio* in the thirteenth century, theologians such as David of Augsburg, Thomas Aquinas, and Bonaventure, were to some extent responding to the mighty waves of popular revivalism that were then sweeping over northern and southern Europe. During the same period, ideas of *devotio* were transmitted to the monastic and mendicant chroniclers who observed and commented upon popular revivalist movements. A few of these chroniclers were imbued with the teachings of the spiritual writers. A good example is the anonymous monastic chronicler of Laon. When he terms the Children's Crusade of 1212 *puerilis illa devocio* (that childish—or, better, since he is well disposed toward it, childlike—revival),[7] he reveals the spiritual imprint of Bernard of Clairvaux.

The Laon Anonymous confines his narrative to a single episode of the Children's Crusade, or *peregrinatio puerorum*, the pilgrimage-crusade of the *pueri*, which most likely began at Chartres before heading to the Paris region, then northeast into the Rhineland, finally crossing the Alps and reaching its Mediterranean terminus. The Laon Anonymous recounts that Stephen of Cloyes, together with his age-mates and fellow shepherd boys, embarked upon a pilgrimage to the king of France at St. Denis, after Stephen was entrusted to deliver letters to the king by Christ, who had appeared to him in the guise of a poor pilgrim. The contents of these letters are never divulged. The same chronicler states that Stephen attracted "nearly 30,000 people" (an exceptionally large following) to St. Denis "from all parts of France." Yet he also makes clear that Stephen's mission was part of a much wider outpouring of collective enthusiasm, for elsewhere, too, there were hordes of children—miracle-workers among them—eager to merge with Stephen's followers. Stephen, the reputed leader of the French *pueri*, was neither a cleric nor a crusader knight. Although as a lowly shepherd boy he could claim no religious authority, nevertheless Stephen emerges as the first charismatic leader of Christian Europe's earliest youth movement.

The Franciscan chronicler Salimbene designates 1233 as the *tempore illius devotionis famosi* (the date of that famous revival). Variously described as the Great Devotion or the Great Hallelujah, this powerful religious awakening swept across the cities of northern Italy, including Parma, Piacenza, and Bologna. Growing up in Parma, the twelve-year-old Salimbene eagerly responded to the thrilling processions and crowd scenes he witnessed in 1233. Vividly chronicling his childhood memories in old age, Salimbene remembers, "This *Alleluja* . . . was a time of peace and quiet, when all weapons of war were laid aside; a time of merriment and gladness, of joy and exultation, of praise and rejoicing."[8] Its initial, purely popular phase was inspired by a lay preacher. Next came the Franciscan and Dominican friars, who fashioned it into an organized peace movement and preaching campaign, for the Great Hallelujah satisfied a widespread craving for peace. Salimbene's north Italian civic milieu was a fractured, violent society, splintered by political faction and ravaged by clan vendettas. In such an environment, civic peace, temporarily achieved by inspired preachers, seemed nothing short of miraculous. But if Lombardy's Great Hallelujah of 1233 counts as one of medieval Europe's most outstanding revivalist peace movements, it was certainly not unique. The fact is that medieval Christendom gave birth to an extended family of revivalist peace movements.

Almost thirty year later, Salimbene took part in, as well as chronicled, another of the thirteenth century's most astonishing popular revivals. This too was a peace movement, although its appeal for civic amnesty and the release of prisoners was only one of its interlocking motifs. Its historical significance was much greater than that of the regional Lombard Hallelujah of 1233, for, like the Children's Crusade of 1212, this was a revival on a European scale. Salimbene calls it the *verberatorum devotio* (the revival of the flagellants).[9] Invited in 1260 to lead processions of these self-lacerating penitents, Salimbene agreed without hesitation. His responsiveness to revivalism's spiritual quickening had become part of his nature.

The penitential performance of these flagellants or *disciplinati* (from *disciplina*, whip) amounted to a new sort of Christomimetic urban theatre, a new kind of Passion play in which the scourging of Christ was not so much reenacted as imaginatively reexperienced. From Perugia in Umbria, central Italy, to Rome, then northward through Italy, Germany, and ultimately as far as Gniezno in Poland, the *disciplinati* marched through town and countryside. In the towns women also undertook the ritual, but privately, apart from men. Female participation in the movement of 1260 was repeated in nearly all the major medieval revivals. Hearing doleful chants and outcries and watching the bloodstained, half-naked penitents slowly process through the streets of the city, many spectators were overcome with awe. Some embraced the new enthusiasm, and these converts brought the *devotio* of the flagellants to new localities. Their revivalist drama was a religious movement in two crucial respects: the flagellants were both ambulatory (processional) and itinerant (peregrinatory).

But not even a thumbnail sketch of the revival of the flagellants can ignore the influence of prophecy in its origins. The year of the coming of the *disciplinati*, 1260, was, after all, the very year in which the Joachites, the adherents of the Calabrian prophet Joachim of Fiore (d. 1202), predicted that there would be an unparalleled crisis-transition in sacral history—a terrible persecution of the faithful, heralding the reign of the Antichrist. Repentance was the required response (and self-flagellation was a long-established penitential exercise, although for monks rather than laypeople). Once the transitional period had passed, however, the glorious Third Status of Christian history, the age of the Holy Spirit, would dawn. Salimbene cites two verses from Revelation, both ominously speaking of "twelve hundred sixty days" (Rev. 11:3; 12:6). Translated into the year 1260, that date became the focus for an impending universal crisis.

Fig. 5.3. *Flagellants at the Time of the Black Death*. Colored woodcut. Photo: © Image Select / Art Resource, N.Y.

Apocalyptic prophecy made the actual social and political crises of the year 1260 comprehensible; it also made them providential signs of what was soon to come. Evidence of a prophetic-Joachite consciousness in Perugia around the time of the flagellant movement can be detected in the iconographic program of a wall painting (ca. 1270) at the Templar church of San Bevignate, which became the home of Perugia's first confraternity of flagellants. The San Bevignate fresco appears to cast the Perugian *disciplinati* in an eschatological role, as men of history's last days. Below the dead rising from their graves in a Last Judgment, there they stand, possibly representing Joachim's *viri spirituales* or new "spiritual men."

Discovering a link between prophetic currents and revivalism in the Middle Ages, as with the *disciplinati* and Joachite thought, helps to clarify the circumstances of collective arousal. Coming forty years after the flagellants, in 1300, the first Roman Jubilee, or *anno santo* (Holy Year), is a case in point. It too arrived amid prophetic expectations, in part occasioned by the approach of the new century. This, of course, was neither the first nor the last medieval revival to appear on the

Fig. 5.4. Pope Boniface VIII (r. 1294–1303) proclaims the First Jubilee (Holy Year) in 1300 from the Benediction Loggia at the Lateran Palace. Late sixteenth-century miniature, copy of a fresco by Giotto. Biblioteca Ambrosiana, Milan. Photo: © Scala / Art Resource, N.Y.

hinge of the fin de siècle. Popularly initiated but papally legitimated, the Roman Jubilee of 1300 was the ancestor of a long line of medieval and postmedieval Holy Years. The Jubilee, the last devotio of the thirteenth century, attracted huge crowds of pilgrims to Rome from all over Christendom, Dante probably among them. Cardinal Lemoine spoke of the Christian people coming to the Roman basilicas to obtain the lavish Jubilee indulgence "with intense fervor and urgent devotion." "Not since ancient days," declaimed the cardinal, "has there been such *devotio*."[10]

The Jubilee of 1300 also highlights another of the defining manifestations of medieval revivalism: the mixed religious crowd. The medieval revivalist crowd

Pope Boniface VIII Announces the Holy Year of Jubilee (February 22, 1300)

The trustworthy tradition of our ancestors affirms that great remissions and Indulgences for sins are granted to those who visit in this city the venerable Basilica of the Prince of the Apostles. Wherefore We who, according to the dignity of our office, desire, and ought to procure, the salvation of each, holding all and each of these remissions and Indulgences to be authentic, do, by our apostolic authority, confirm and approve the same, and even grant afresh and sanction them by this our present writing. In order that the blessed Apostles Peter and Paul may be the more honored as their Basilicas in this city shall be the more devoutly frequented by the faithful, and that the faithful themselves may feel that they have been replenished by an abundance of spiritual favors in approaching their tombs, We, confiding in the mercy of Almighty God, in the merits and power of these His Apostles, in the counsel of our brethren, and in the plenitude of the apostolic authority, grant to all who, being truly penitent, and confessing their sins, shall reverently visit these Basilicas in the present year 1300, which commenced with the festival of the Nativity of our Lord Jesus Christ which has just been celebrated, and to all who being truly penitent, shall confess their sins, and shall approach these Basilicas each succeeding hundredth year, not only a full and copious, but the most full pardon of all their sins. We determine that whatever persons wish to gain these Indulgences granted by us must, if they be inhabitants of Rome, visit these same Basilicas for thirty days, whether successively or at intervals, at least once a day; if they be foreigners or strangers, they must in like manner visit the Basilicas for fifteen days. Nevertheless, each one will merit more, and will the more efficaciously gain the Indulgence as he visits the Basilicas more frequently and more devoutly. Let no man, therefore, dare to infringe or impugn this our rescript of confirmation, approval, renewal, grant, and decree. And if any one presumes to assail it, let him know that he will incur the indignation of Almighty God and of the blessed Apostles Peter and Paul.

—Herbert Thurston, *The Holy Year of Jubilee: An Account of the History and Ceremonial of the Roman Jubilee* (St. Louis: Herder, 1900), 13–14

was an all-encompassing assembly of the faithful, bringing together believers regardless of generation, gender, or social rank. Because medieval society was structured and hierarchical, mixed crowds were out of the ordinary; indeed, in some situations they could appear quasi-miraculous. More than just *popular*, the mixed crowd was *populist*. Although distinctions of social rank were never really abolished in mixed revivalist crowds, such distinctions were often momentarily stripped of religious significance.

The Roman Jubilee, a unique kind of pilgrimage whose guidelines could only be determined by the pope, preserved the populist character of pilgrimage. Thus all pilgrims, whether priests or laypeople, rich or poor, were—*as pilgrims*—of equal status. A fresco attributed to Giotto of the Jubilee pilgrim crowd at the feet of Pope Boniface VIII illustrates this very well. A mixed religious crowd appears in the lower register. The nobles (the knights or *milites*) are mounted on horseback, whereas the commoners or *pedites* appear on foot. Women as well as men are present in the throng. High above them all in the upper register is the pope surrounded by his cardinals, bishops, and priests. They are not pilgrims. Down below, a crowd of Jubilee pilgrims has positioned itself at the pope's feet, ready to catch the papal blessings.

Thus we see that medieval revivals were collective enthusiasms, behaviorally varied yet sharing common features. They were responsive to prophetic impulses; conversionary in nature; and perceived as "extraordinary"—marked, that is, by the miraculous, the charismatic, and the astonishment of observers. More generally, the medieval revivalist trajectory was brief, intense, and public. Medieval revivals could be triggered by political and social crises. Their outcomes were unpredictable, and they came in all shapes and sizes.

VARIETIES OF MEDIEVAL REVIVALISM

At the outset a distinction should be made between programmatic and nonprogrammatic revivals, despite the fact that medieval revivals were overwhelmingly programmatic—that is to say, they were "about" something. But this does not imply that a group of enthusiasts banded together to put forward a coherent set of beliefs, let alone to execute a concrete plan of action. What it does mean is that programmatic outpourings of medieval collective enthusiasm were infused with an identifiable source of spiritual energy. Quickening the pulses of potential converts, animating them, and compelling their adherence were spiritual aspirations usually combining diffuse, unsystematic religious and social ideals. We know that this is true because participants in programmatic revivals were invariably eager to disclose (and so disseminate) the fundamental spiritual ideals that energized their movements.

Programmatic Revivals: Three Modes of Expression

To communicate with the bewildered, curious onlookers who stared at them as they marched in procession through the streets or performed in town squares, medieval enthusiasts had recourse to three expressive modes. The first was behavioral iconography. In much the same way that medieval illiterates could read the language of Christian art because its conventional symbols were everywhere, so too medieval spectators of revivalist movements could easily decode the meanings of the dress, gestures, and rituals of medieval enthusiasts. Like the instantly recognizable papal keys of St. Peter in thousands of church images of that saint, the revivalists' iconographic attributes were culturally legible. And just as in the iconography of Christian art, where the saint's type (apostle, martyr, virgin, or virgin-martyr) was crucial to his or her identification, so it was with the behavioral iconography of medieval enthusiasts.

Pilgrims, for example, both individually and collectively in mass pilgrimage revivals (such as the Jerusalem-bound Great German Pilgrimage of 1064–1065), constituted a distinct type of Christian enthusiast. In art, as well as in life, pilgrims were recognizable from the twelfth century, if not earlier, by their *habitus*, or dress, and the emblems of their special status—their staves and wallets. Crusaders, also visibly distinctive, wore the cross, usually displayed on their outer clothing (frequently on the right shoulder, where Christ had carried it) but sometimes—as we know from the shipwrecked corpses of first-crusaders washed ashore—tattooed on their flesh. Likewise, the Italian flagellants of 1260, barefoot and half-naked, were identifiably penitents.

In contrast, the German flagellants of 1261 wore a kind of uniform like that of monks. Their faces were partially concealed by hoods or cowls, while a long garment covered their lower parts and stretched down to their ankles. This alarmed the clergy. Were these laymen members of some heretical, pseudo-religious order? The revival of the northern Italian *Bianchi* ("the Whites") of 1399, on the other hand, aroused no such suspicions. Indeed, leading clerics enthusiastically joined the processions of this mass movement dedicated to peace and piety. The Bianchi derived their name from "their simple white robes" supposedly enjoined upon them in their foundation legend. During the nine days of their devotional exercises, the Bianchi clothed themselves in them. The color symbolism of pristine innocence is unmistakable. "Their dress is pure," wrote Franco Sacchetti.[11] Behavioral iconography thus conveyed a concentrated message of the essential spirituality of the revival.

Pictorial iconography of the traditional sort was a second means of spiritual shorthand. Every church was an art gallery, but thanks to processional banners embellished with various saints and symbols, Christian art was exhibitable out of doors. A good instance is the peace revival of the *Caputiati* or *Chaperons Blancs* (White Hoods) of late 1182 to circa 1184, so named because of their distinctive white woolen or linen garb. Affixed to a banner or piece of parchment together with an image of the Virgin and Child was the motto that proclaimed their millenarian-pacific ideals: "Lamb of God, who takes away the sins of the world, give us peace." Both the motto of the Caputiati and their image were reputed to have been given to their founder Durand, a carpenter of Le Puy, by Mary or Christ.

The same holds for the *pastores* or Shepherds' Crusade of 1251. By displaying banners of the Lamb and the Cross, traveling bands of armed shepherds asserted both their elect status in the Christian story and their crusading purpose of rescuing the king of France, Louis IX, from Muslim captivity in Egypt. Because the scene of the Annunciation to the Shepherds was regularly sculpted above the portals of Gothic churches, everyone knew that shepherds were uniquely privileged. They were the first to see the Lamb of God, the infant Jesus. The flagellants of 1310, as depicted in a medieval chronicle, show these *disciplinati* marching, lashing their shoulders, exchanging the kiss of peace, all the while gazing at a banner at the head of their procession surmounted by a cross, representing the flagellation of Christ. A more powerful visual encapsulation of the spirituality of their movement cannot be imagined.

Among the most impressive visual displays in medieval revivalism were the immense banners held aloft during the late-fifteenth-century plague processions in the towns and cities of Umbria. Such processional banners or *gonfaloni* were mute prayers to God for forgiveness and pity during times when bubonic plague raged among the helpless citizenry. One of these was the banner or gonfalone painted by Bonfigli in 1464, which shows a large, protective Madonna della Misericordia, Our Lady of Mercy, shielding her city of Perugia from the three arrows of her beardless Son. Under her cloak, as under a fallout shelter, citizens and religious huddle, while in the foreground, through the winding city streets, a *Bianchi* confraternity is solemnly processing. Then at the foot of the gonfalone, amid those fleeing the city and the corpses of plague victims, is as comforting an image as the words of John Donne: "And death shall be no more; death, thou shalt die."[12] Around the Virgin gather the patron saints of the city (including, nearest the viewer, the most recent of them, St. Bernardino of Siena, on the left) and the plague-saint specialist St. Sebastian (pierced by nonfatal arrows representing plague wounds, on the right). The most optimistic sign of all is at the banner's head. One angel (top left) unsheathes his sword: the plague begins. Another angel (top right) sheathes his sword: the plague ceases.

Already remarked upon are the raised voices of medieval enthusiasts as they shouted, cried out, chanted, and sang about their most fervent desires. This was their third expressive mode broadcasting their beliefs. The conciliar outcry of Clermont (1095)—which became the battle cry of the first crusade, *Deus le volt!* ("God wills it!")—has previously been mentioned. But before Clermont came the thunderous acclamations of the late-tenth-, early eleventh-century revival known as the Peace and Truce of God, whose most eloquent chronicler was Rodulfus Glaber (ca. 980–ca. 1046).

In his *Five Books of Histories* (ca. late 1030s) Glaber evokes the intense religious emotions roused by the peace councils—councils of the "great, middling, and poor" people—summoned by "the

Fig. 5.5. Agostino di Duccio (1418–1498). St. Bernardino expels the devil. Oratorio di S. Bernardino, Perugia, Italy. Photo: © Scala / Art Resource, N.Y.

bishops and abbots and other devout men" of Aquitaine and Burgundy following the millennium of Christ's passion in 1033. To these councils, Glaber says, "were borne . . . innumerable caskets of holy relics." Oaths of peace were taken in an atmosphere of miraculous healing. "Such enthusiasm was generated that the bishops raised their crosiers to the heavens, and all cried out with one voice to God, their hands extended: *Pax! pax! pax!* ('Peace! peace! peace!'). This was the sign of their perpetual covenant with God."[13]

Another instance is the earliest processions linked to the start of the Children's Crusade of 1212. Here the clerically directed liturgies held at Chartres to gain divine and human support for the endangered Spanish church passed out of clerical control and into the hands of the laity. Led by the French *pueri*, the massed enthusiasts shouted out, "Lord God, exalt Christendom!" "Lord God, return to us the True Cross!"[14] This plea for God to "exalt Christendom" was especially associated with the crusades, something entirely appropriate in the context of the impending, decisive battle of the Spanish Crusade. Contrariwise,

---

Response to Pope Urban II's Call for the First Crusade, Council of Clermont (1095)

After this speech, those present were very enthusiastic in the cause, and many, thinking that nothing could be more laudable than such an undertaking, at once offered to go and diligently exhort the absent. Among these was the Bishop of Puy, Adhemar by name, who later acting as the Pope's vicegerent prudently and wisely led the whole army of God and vigorously inspired them to accomplish the undertaking. So, when those things which have been mentioned were determined upon in the council and unanimously approved of, and after the papal blessing was given, they withdrew to their homes to make known to those who were not present at the council what had been done. When these tidings were published throughout the provinces, they agreed under oath that the peace which was called the Truce should be kept mutually by all. Finally, then, many persons of every class vowed, after confession, that they were going with a pure intent whither they were ordered to go.

Oh, how fitting and how pleasing to us all to see those crosses, beautiful, whether of silk, or of woven gold, or of any kind of cloth, which these pilgrims, by order of Pope Urban, sewed on the shoulders of their mantles, or cassocks, or tunics, once they had made the vow to go. It was indeed proper that soldiers of God who prepared to fight for His honor should be signed and fortified by this fitting emblem of victory; and, since they thus marked themselves with this symbol under the acknowledgement of faith, finally they very truly obtained the Cross of which they carried the symbol. They adopted the sign that they might follow the reality of the sign.

—Chronicle of Fulcher of Chartres, in *The First Crusade: The Accounts of Eye-Witnesses and Participants*, ed. August C. Krey (Princeton: Princeton University Press, 1921; repr., Gloucester, Mass.: Peter Smith, 1958), 40–41

"Lord God, return to us the True Cross!" suggests another locale altogether: the Holy Land, where the True Cross was lost to the Saracens at the battle of Hattin in 1187. When the two chants are juxtaposed, consequently, the direct connection between "exalt Christendom" and the imminent Spanish clash becomes somewhat doubtful. Was it, perhaps, a more generalized, if equally fervent, crusading outcry, denoting all of Christendom in peril, not only Spain, but also, more important, the Holy Land? If so, it could signify a change of direction for the *pueri*—from the crusader West to the crusader East.

Like the acclamations of the *pueri*, those of the flagellants or *disciplinati* of 1260—"Mercy and peace, Lord, give them to us!" "Mercy, Lord, send us peace!"—were probably more transparent to contemporaries than they are to us. Nonetheless, they articulate the miseries of the time and hint at a socioreligious program. What the *disciplinati* were pleading for was an end to the wars between city-states, clan vendettas, and factional violence within cities, as well as an amnesty for political prisoners. Acclamations alone, however, did not exhaust the vocal repertoire of the flagellants.

Fig. 5.6. Madonna della Misericordia, detail with city of Perugia during the plague by Benedetto Bonfigli (ca. 1420–1496). Cappella Oddi. S. Francesco, Perugia, Italy. Photo: © Scala / Art Resource, N.Y.

A gifted contemporary chronicler heard their voices:

And not only by day, but also by night with lighted candles, during a most bitter winter, by hundreds and thousands and tens of
thousands, they went from city to city and from church to church,
humbly prostrating themselves before the altars, preceded by
priests with crosses and banners. They did the same in the villages
and small towns, so that plains and mountains alike resounded
with their voices crying unto the Lord. Silenced, then, were all
musical instruments and love songs. Only the sorrowful songs of
the penitents could be heard everywhere, as much in the cities as
in the villages, and their doleful rhythms would move hearts of
stone, and the eyes of the most obstinate could not contain their
tears.[15]

So in addition to their acclamations, there were "the sorrowful songs
of the penitents." Other revivalist movements as well—the northern
European *pueri* and the Italian Bianchi among them—are known to
have raised their voices in song. Would that we possessed the lyrics of
all medieval revivals.

In short, what programmatic revivalist crowds give us is an oral
epigraphy. As with written inscriptions, their meaning naturally
requires decoding. Once deciphered and contextualized, however,
acclamations provide the soundtrack for the moving pictures of
revivalist behavioral iconography. In addition to communicating their
spiritual beliefs, they permitted enthusiasts to proclaim their identity
and affirm their solidarity. Shouting together and marching together
gave these noninstitutionalized, informal groupings sufficient social
cohesion to make their deepest aspirations known.

Programmatic Revivals:
Types, Species, Families

When medieval chroniclers began to understand that revivalism was
a recurring phenomenon, they saw it within the framework of specific revivalist families, such as papally authorized crusades, popular
crusades, flagellant movements, peace movements, Jubilees, and so

on. But any modern attempt to classify medieval revivals runs into difficulties, because many categories intersect and overlap, meaning that any single movement could well find a place in more than one revivalist family. For example, there were medieval revivals like the Children's Crusade of 1212, in which young people were a conspicuous or a leading element. It happens that a good number of these movements were also shrine-directed, that is, pilgrimage revivals, such as the astonishing fourteenth- and fifteenth-century youth movements that converged on the abbey of Mont-St.-Michel in Normandy. These drew young people from northern and southern France, the Low Countries, as well as parts of Germany and Switzerland. Hence medieval revivals were more varied than is usually supposed.

This is particularly true when it comes to the localized urban revivals of the later Middle Ages. Among them was a distinctive subspecies: urban revivals led by preachers, whose centerpiece was a flamboyant religious spectacle, "the burning of the vanities." A collective ritual of purgation and purification leading to civic moral regeneration, it involved laymen and laywomen surrendering their morally dubious valuables to feed the flames in a spectacular public conflagration. How freely such items were given up is debatable. Some evidence exists of direct or indirect social pressure having been applied. But to those whose contributions were wholly voluntary, self-dispossession amounted to a conversionary act. Thus purged and purified, individuals and their city were made new.

First and foremost, "the burning of the vanities" is associated with St. Bernardino of Siena (d. 1444, canonized 1450), an Observant Franciscan and one of the supreme urban revivalists of his age. Bernardin came to Perugia in 1425. On September 23, he preached out of doors in the cathedral square (or piazza) before a congregation that a contemporary Perugian chronicler estimates as "more than 3000 persons." "His preaching was of the Holy Scriptures," says the chronicler, "rebuking the women for painting and plastering their faces, for their false and borrowed hair . . . and likewise the men, for their playing cards, dice, and painted faces, for talismans and charms." Within fifteen days, Perugia's luxury-loving womenfolk and menfolk had delivered their "false hair, paints and cosmetics" along with their "dice, playing cards, and backgammon sets" to the convent of San Francesco. Then in the same *piazza* Bernardino had "a castle of wood" constructed on which were placed all of their surrendered items together with assorted expensive baubles. The next day, Sunday, October 30, after he finished his sermon, Bernardino had the entire heap of "vanities" set alight. "And so great was the fire that words cannot describe it; and therein were burned things of passing great price."[16]

Bernardino's example was followed by other fifteenth-century urban revivalists, including the Franciscan Brother Richard in Paris and the Dominican Girolamo Savonarola in Florence. But the burning of the vanities was only one of a number of strategies adopted by the medieval preachers of urban revivals who labored for the moral regeneration of town dwellers. In the early thirteenth century, the itinerant French priest Fulk of Neuilly (d. 1202) tried to convert usurers while also endeavoring to reform prostitutes by establishing convents for them or by raising money for dowries to marry them off. Around the same time, a Norman abbot, Eustace de Flay, toured England (1200–1201), preaching Sabbath observance and threatening Sabbath breakers with God's wrath.

If local or regional urban revivals occupied a surprisingly broad category within medieval revivalism, one must not overlook revivalism in the medieval countryside. Notable in this respect were the vast gatherings of country folk who camped out to hear Berthold of Regensberg, the celebrated thirteenth-century German Franciscan revivalist preacher. In sum, the varieties of medieval programmatic revivals were so extensive as almost to defy categorization.

Nonprogrammatic Revivals:
Ecstatic Enigmas

By their nature, nonprogrammatic revivals are more enigmatic. Indeed, it could be argued that far from being "about" nothing, they may simply have been the incipient stage of what later emerged as a full-blown programmatic revival. Thus what is now looked upon as the initial phase of the Lombard Great Hallelujah of 1233 may have actually been a self-sufficient nonprogrammatic revival before the mendicant friars grafted a socioreligious program onto it.

According to Salimbene, it was inspired by a wandering, horn-blowing, oddly costumed, itinerant lay evangelist called Fra Benedetto de Cornetta (Brother Benedict of the Horn). The name "Benedetto" fit his practice of leading the crowd in threefold benedictions—to God the Father, Son, and Holy Spirit, while "de Cornetta" probably derives from the cornet that was his musical accompaniment. Salimbene praises Fra Benedetto as "a simple and unlettered man, but . . . of pure and honorable life." A "second John the Baptist," he calls him, thereby designating him as the precursor of the friars who were to come. "He would go into the churches and the squares [in Parma], preaching and praising God, followed by great multitudes of children." After his praises and benedictions would come "Hallelujah, Hallelujah, Hallelujah!" Then he would "preach, sounding forth praise to God." Apparently, this was the extent of Fra Benedetto's preaching—blessings, praises, Hallelujahs. Would this, then, be medieval revivalism's "pure" state, that is to say, a simple effusion of religious spirit—ecstatic and joyous—devoid of any agenda, however prayerful? If so, unlike programmatic revivals, it simply *was*, rather than was "about."

More enigmatic and definitely darker in tone than Benedetto's Hallelujah was the revival of the ecstatic dancers (*dansatores, chorisantes*) of 1374. Few revivalist rituals were as extraordinary as theirs. Medieval onlookers were astonished at their spiritual acrobatics. To one clerical chronicler, theirs was a "violent suffering [*passio*] . . . rare and amazing." To another, a "sickness." The group's life span of around five months, from late June to November 1374, was typically brief. Itinerant, hopping (as it were) from shrine to shrine, the chorisantes set off on a pilgrimage that took them through the Rhineland and parts of the Burgundian Low Countries. Their ecstatic performances probably climaxed in and around Liège, where the clergy finally managed to snuff them out. Their dancing was so wild and disorderly that some chroniclers likened it to epilepsy, but the notion of large groups of epileptics having simultaneous ritual seizures is scarcely credible.

With their "loud voices" filling the air, the dancers journeyed from one settlement to another, performing their ecstatic gyrations in front of bemused clergy and laity. They danced and jumped in private houses, in the streets, in the squares of towns, but most notably in churches, where, leaping and dancing before the altars, they aroused the anger of the clergy for disrupting public worship. As with all revivalist rituals, their behavior was imitative. Those who joined the pilgrimage of the chorisantes necessarily were obliged to master intricate behavioral routines before they could perform in public.

To the clergy this was a religious affliction: "many people, men as well as women, irrational folk as well as those oppressed by illness, none of them at peace . . ." Another chronicler affirms: "Usually, between eight and fifteen days they were fully restored to mental and bodily health." Certain that the cause of their illness was demonic possession, the clergy prescribed the traditional cure: exorcism. The chorisantes acquiesced, yet their submission proves nothing, for the clerical explanation was imposed upon them. When asked, they were unable to explain why they did what they did. Whether theirs was a dance of divine affliction or a creative religious performance, the meaning of their ecstatic choreography escapes us.

THE THREE STAGES OF MEDIEVAL REVIVALISM

Quite often there is insufficient historical evidence to reconstruct the beginning, middle, and end of any given medieval revival. Despite this lack of specific evidence, however, to assume that the life cycle of an archetypical or "perfect" revival passed through three distinct phases lets us spot things we might otherwise overlook.

This is particularly true when it comes to the first phase of the model, the mixed religious crowd, already referred to. This initial stage is frequently missing from the chroniclers' reports, which is not surprising. Medieval chroniclers rarely knew anything about a revival's local beginnings, let alone the circumstances of its birth. Large-scale revivals were usually noticed only after they reached their mature, itinerant, second, or "movement" phase, when they had already spread over a wide area. So instead of giving us an account of a revival's historical origins, they supply the foundation legend current among the enthusiasts of the second phase or substitute a picturesque tale of their own invention.

Nevertheless, mixed religious crowds had a formative influence on medieval revivalism. Crowds gathered for a reason; they had a focus (such as a liturgical or popular procession) and a locus (an urban space, a sacred place). Finally, it goes without saying, crowds had to be aroused. Here a preacher's galvanizing rhetoric is the obvious mechanism. The supreme medieval paradigm would seem to be Pope Urban II's powerful speech at Clermont (1095), which summoned the first crusade. This would conform perfectly to the formula—crowd + preacher = religious movement. Nowadays, however, historians prefer to stress the impact of Urban's preaching tour in France, following Clermont—in addition to the cumulative effect of the returning bishops and priests—on subsequent crusade recruitment. Yet there was no doubt on the part of the clerical chroniclers who later reimagined Urban's speech that it was the spark that ignited crusade enthusiasm throughout Latin Christendom. And it is certainly true that revivalistic preaching was conversionary preaching. Such preaching roused crowds, encouraged an atmosphere of the miraculous, opened up a classic route to charismatic leadership, and demanded an immediate response.

The remarkable career of Vitalis of Savigny (d. 1122) is a good illustration of this. Educated cleric, hermit, itinerant preacher of apostolic poverty, and monastic founder, Vitalis, according to a chronicler, "spared neither rich nor poor in his public sermons." "Many multitudes journey[ed] to hear his words.... Every rank was mortified by his true allegations, every crowd trembled before him.... So ... he saved many and brought many to his side."[17] Among the "many [brought] to his side" were numerous converts who habitually followed him on his preaching tours. Revivalist preachers like Vitalis regularly attracted groups of especially devoted followers who behaved more like disciples than members of a mixed religious crowd.

But the leaders of revivalist crowds were not necessarily preachers or clerics. They might be laymen like Durand, a carpenter of Le Puy, of the peace army of Caputiati; the shepherd boy Stephen of Cloyes of the Children's Crusade; or Rainero Fasani, who may have inspired the Perugian *disciplinati*. Hermits, like Vitalis of Savigny, or the better-known Peter the Hermit, popular preacher of the first crusade, even if clerics, occupied a quasi-religious status of their own. Medieval hermits had a love affair with crowds, and by no means was it an unrequited love. Nor did all medieval religious crowds acquire the momentum of revivals and transmute themselves into religious

The Difficulty of Sustaining Enthusiasm:
Responses to the Preaching of Fra Robert of Lecce
(Perugia, 1448)

On March 29, which was Good Friday, Friar Roberto resumed preaching in the piazza every day, and on Holy Thursday he preached about communion and invited the public for Good Friday, and at the end of that sermon about the Passion he put on this performance. . . . When it was time to display the Crucifix, Eliseo di Cristofano, a barber in the Porta Sant'Agnolo neighborhood, came out of San Lorenzo in the guise of the naked Christ with the cross on his shoulders and the crown of thorns on his head, and his flesh looked as if it had been beaten and scourged like when the Christ was beaten. A crowd of soldiers led him to be crucified. . . . In the middle of the platform they were met by a woman done up as the Virgin Mary, dressed all in black, weeping and lamenting about what was happening as a mystical likeness of the passion of Jesus Christ. When they had arrived at Friar Roberto's pulpit, he remained there for a while with the cross on his shoulders, and all the people were pouring tears and crying "mercy." Then they set down that cross, and put on it a crucifix that had been there before and arranged it on the cross; and then the wails of the people grew even louder. At the foot of the cross Our Lady began her lament together with St. John and Mary Magdalene and Mary Salome, who recited several verses of the lament for the passion. Then came Nicodemus and Joseph of Arimathea, who unfastened the body of Jesus Christ and laid it on the lap of Our Lady, and then they placed it in the tomb, with all the people wailing loudly the whole time. Many people said that Perugia had never seen a more beautiful and more devout devotion than this one. And on that morning six people became friars, one of whom was the aforementioned Eliseo, who was a foolish young man. . . . When three or four months had passed, this Eliseo di Cristofano of Porta Sant'Agnolo left the friary and went back to being a barber, and he is known as Mr. Lord God; and he later took a wife, and was a bigger scoundrel than he had been before.

—A. Fabretti, "Cronaca della città di Perugia dal 1309 al 1491, nota come Diario del Graziani," in Roberto Rusconi, *Predicazione e vita religiosa nella società italiana da Carlo Magno alla Controriforma* (Turin: Loescher, 1981), 192–93

movements. Crowd enthusiasms could remain isolated, seemingly spontaneous events; at other times they were carefully stage-managed. Revivalist preachers, who sought to engineer collective enthusiasm as part of fund-raising tours, crusade recruitment campaigns, or moral crusades, became adept practitioners of crowd psychology, a fundamental skill in routinizing revivalism.

After the mixed religious crowd, there appeared the second, itinerant or peregrinatory stage of the revival, the "movement" proper—people in motion. This phase corresponds to the evangelical diffusion of the revival, in which collective enthusiasm gathers pace, makes converts, and sets out to conquer new territory. Most medieval revivals remained local; others gained adherents over a considerable region; only a minority became genuinely European in scope. Following the movement phase, most medieval revivals expired.

But not all. The exceptional revivals that managed to survive went on to achieve relative immortality in a third stage. Institutionalization was the primary route to survival. New religious movements led to the genesis or renewal of religious institutions that in some way preserved—some would say, fossilized—the spiritual impulses originally animating the revival. We have already seen that the hermit and wandering preacher Vitalis of Savigny was accompanied by troops of faithful devotees. Almost like the "groupies" surrounding pop stars, such traveling bands of ardent enthusiasts were by no means unique in the history of medieval revivalism. (For example, the renowned late-fourteenth, early-fifteenth-century Dominican preacher Vincent Ferrer, famous for delivering apocalyptic sermons across half of Christendom, was escorted from town to town by processions of his fervent, self-flagellating supporters.) As for Vitalis, toward the close of his career he founded a monastic house near the village of Savigny. The entourage who joined him on his preaching tours now had a permanent home. Their days of evangelical wandering were over. Apostolic itinerancy was exchanged for monastic stability.

So enthusiasm for the *vita apostolica*, the apostolic life lived in preaching and poverty, resulted in a proliferation of new twelfth-century religious orders. Like Vitalis of Savigny, a number of wandering hermits and apostolic preachers dedicated to the apostolic life, among them Bernard of Tiron, Robert of Arbrissel, and Norbert of Xanten, went on to become monastic founders. All of them came to be venerated as saints. Crusading enthusiasm also laid the foundation for the new military orders, such as the Templars, the Hospitallers, the Teutonic Knights, and a host of Spanish analogues. During the thirteenth century, there was continuity but also change, because conversionary enthusiasm for preaching and poverty gave birth to a radically new kind of monasticism—the mendicant orders or begging monks. The most influential of these mendicants were the Franciscans and Dominicans. Both developed into highly structured religious organizations indispensable to the papacy.

Putting these new mendicant orders in the framework of medieval popular revivalism is not as paradoxical as it may seem, for here too we see institutionalization as the product of revivalism. First, there emerged a charismatic leader, let us say, Francis the *poverello* or little poor man of Assisi. Disciples were drawn to him as if to a magnet. Francis's initial small fraternity of holy beggars in ragged robes then dispersed and began preaching to mixed crowds in villages, towns, and cities. Conversions to the Franciscans multiplied; the fraternity grew prodigiously, a growth spurt that corresponds to the diffusion or movement phase of a revival. Tighter organizational controls became necessary, and Franciscanism went through an institution-building process that at times was painful, although something of the original Franciscan adventure was still preserved.

The Flagellants of 1260:
The Chronicle of Salimbene de Adam

The Flagellants came through the whole world; and all men, both small and great, noble knights and men of the people, scourged themselves naked in procession through the cities, with the Bishops and men of Religion at their head; and peace was made in many places, and men restored what they had unlawfully taken away, and they confessed their sins so earnestly that the priests had scarce leisure to eat. And in their mouths sounded words of God and not of man, and their voice was as the voice of a multitude: and men walked in the way of salvation, and composed godly songs of praise in honour of the Lord and the Blessed Virgin: and these they sang as they went and scourged themselves. And on the Monday, which was the Feast of All Saints, all those men came from Modena to Reggio, and the Podesta and the Bishop with the banners of all the Gilds; and they scourged themselves through the whole city, and the greater part passed on to Parma on the Tuesday following. So on the morrow all the men of Reggio made banners for each quarter of the town, and held processions around the city, and the Podesta went likewise scourging himself. And the men of Sassuolo at the beginning of this blessed time took me away with the leave of the Guardian of the convent of the Friars Minor at Modena, where I dwelt at that time, and brought me to Sassuolo, for both men and women loved me well; and afterwards they brought me to Reggio and then to Parma. And when we were come to Parma this Devotion was already there, for it flew as "an eagle flying to the prey," and lasted many days in our city, nor was there any so austere and old but that he scourged himself gladly. Moreover, if any would not scourge himself, he was held worse than the Devil, and all pointed their finger at him as a notorious man and a limb of Satan; and what is more, within a short time he would fall into some mishap, either of death or of grievous sickness.

—G. G. Coulton, *From St. Francis to Dante* (London: Duckworth, 1908), 190–91

New lay confraternities were likewise products of popular revivals. They increased significantly during the later Middle Ages, but the impulse to perpetuate a shared religious experience by institutionalizing it was nothing new. Groups of pilgrims returning from a shrine, such as Santiago de Compostela in Spain, would regularly establish local confraternities in honor of St. James. A similar remembrance of things past, as well as a desire on the part of former participants to continue to derive spiritual benefits from an extraordinary religious movement that had once so roused them, explains the remarkable proliferation of *disciplinati* confraternities in the wake of the flagellant movement of 1260, as well as Bianchi confraternities following 1399.

Less commonly than through confraternal institution-building, revivals perpetuated themselves by becoming fixed in collective memory. Here the chroniclers of medieval revivalism—borrowing from one another, adding to and embellishing what little information they disposed of—played an essential part in keeping ephemeral events alive. Even when they diffused half-truths, legends, and myths, as with the Children's Crusade of 1212, they kept obscure, short-lived episodes from disappearing from public consciousness; indeed, they endowed them with centuries of posthumous life. Kurt Vonnegut's best-selling *Slaughterhouse-Five; or, The Children's Crusade: A Duty-Dance with Death* was published in 1969.

OUTCOMES

Institutionalization and cultural memorialization were just two possible outcomes for revivalist movements whose endings were remarkably diverse and unpredictable, varying from successful fund-raising or church-building campaigns to anti-Judaic or anticlerical massacres. Nor can it be forgotten that medieval collective religious enthusiasm, especially when it was not inaugurated by ecclesiastical authority, could be divisive, attracting converts while distracting or repelling others. Furthermore, it is undeniable that certain heretical movements, the early-thirteenth-century, pantheistic Amalricians among others, were revivalist in their missionary zeal and prophetic fervor. It is also true that medieval crusading revivals like the first-crusade peasant armies of Peter the Hermit (1096) or the hordes loyal to Jacob, the Master of Hungary—a prominent leader of the Shepherds' Crusade of 1251—slaughtered Jews and, in the latter case, priests as well. But official crusades, which, after all, fused piety and violence, also provoked officially unsanctioned attacks on nearby Jewish communities. Such violent episodes apart, the overwhelming majority of medieval revivals were peaceful and orthodox in intent and did not set out to subvert religious authority. As their name implies, medieval revivals, on the whole, were aimed at revitalizing rather than overthrowing the religious structures of Christian society.

The inherently populist nature of medieval revivalism has been affirmed more than once. The crusade decree of the Council of Clermont (1095) reinforces that point, underscoring the populist character of crusading. Highlighting its intended all-inclusiveness, the decree began with the word *quicumque*, whosoever, which signifies that the offer to crusaders of remission from penance was to be made available to anyone who assumed the burden of the cross, every believer regardless of social status. Crusade revivalism was thus populist from its inception, in spite of contemporary and subsequent efforts to limit participation in the crusading host to the military professionals, that is, the knights.

Christian populism not only figured at the birth of revivals, as with the mixed religious crowd, but also often featured as an aspirational outcome. At the same time, contrary to Norman Cohn's *Pursuit of the Millennium*, in medieval revivalism there exists very little evidence of millennial yearnings for an egalitarian Garden of Eden. On the other hand, the dream of moral crusaders within the monastic and civic worlds was that of a religious house or city purified and restored to virtue. This ideal was no respecter of status when it came to individual or collective moral accountability. Perhaps its best exemplification can be seen in the work of the fifteenth-century preacher-revivalists, the Observant friars, Franciscans like Bernardino of Siena, and Dominicans like Girolamo Savonarola. Here we encounter a new Christian populism, a populism at once civic, puritanically reformist, and theocratic. The key was the reform of civic statutes in keeping with a puritanical legislative program directed against perceived social evils, such as Perugia's bloodthirsty civic game called the battle of stones, which Bernardino's new civic statutes abolished. The obvious precedent for this was the work of the friars during the Lombard Great Hallelujah of 1233, when they became the moral legislators of communities in disarray. Like revivals themselves, however, such reforms were relatively short-lived. What they do indicate, however, is that an underlying impulse in medieval revivalism was the desire to construct a morally renewed Christian community.

FOR FURTHER READING

Bornstein, Daniel E. *The Bianchi of 1399: Popular Devotion in Late Medieval Italy.* Ithaca, N.Y.: Cornell University Press, 1993.

Cohn, Norman Rufus Colin. *The Pursuit of the Millennium: Revolutionary Millenarians and Mystical Anarchists of the Middle Ages.* Rev. ed. London: Pimlico, 1993.

Cowdrey, H. E. J. *Popes, Monks and Crusaders.* History Series 27. London: Hambledon, 1984.

Dickson, Gary. *Religious Enthusiasm in the Medieval West: Revivals, Crusades, Saints.* Ashgate, U.K.: Aldershot, 2000.

———. "Revivalism as a Medieval Religious Genre." *Journal of Ecclesiastical History* 51 (2000): 473–96.

———. *The Children's Crusade: Medieval History, Modern Mythistory.* New York: Palgrave Macmillan, 2008.

Mayer, Hans Eberhard. *The Crusades.* 2nd ed. Oxford: Oxford University Press, 1988.

Origo, Iris. *The World of San Bernardino.* New York: Harcourt, Brace & World, 1962.

Riley-Smith, Jonathan. *The First Crusade and the Idea of Crusading.* London: Athlone, 1986.

Thompson, Augustine. *Revival Preachers and Politics in Thirteenth-Century Italy: The Great Devotion of 1233.* Oxford: Clarendon, 1992.

Weinstein, Donald. *Savonarola and Florence: Prophecy and Patriotism in the Renaissance.* Princeton: Princeton University Press, 1970.

CONTROLLING SEX

Part 3

CLERICAL CELIBACY AND THE LAITY

ANDRÉ VAUCHEZ

CHAPTER SIX

S imony and Nicolaitism: these terms, heavy with negative connotations, mysterious as they are troubling, designate the chief moral failings that were thought to afflict the clergy of the tenth and eleventh centuries, until the Gregorian Reform (which takes its name from that of Pope Gregory VII, who held office from 1073 to 1085) put an end to them.

"Simony" is defined as the act of paying money to acquire ecclesiastical office, a practice that was commonplace throughout the earlier Middle Ages, but from the middle of the eleventh century was considered illicit, even criminal, and denounced as heresy by the reforming papacy. It takes its name from Simon the Magician, who, according to the Acts of the Apostles (Acts 8:9-35), sought to buy from St. Peter the power to heal the sick that had been granted to him by the Holy Spirit; Peter brutally rebuffed him, declaring that the gifts of God are not for sale.

The origin of "Nicolaitism" is less clear. The author of Revelation denounces in two verses (Rev. 2:6, 15) the works and teachings of the Nicolaitans, whom later Christian tradition came to identify with a certain Nicholas, a deacon in Antioch who gave himself to impure acts. Augustine of Hippo eventually specified what exactly these "impure acts" were: Nicholas had prostituted his own wife and advocated men's having all women in common. In the sixth century, Isidore of Seville further blackened Nicholas's image by saying that he had embroiled in these sexual disorders "not only the laity, but also those who assumed the priestly function" (*Etymologies* 8.5). Nothing

179

more was needed to make Nicholas the symbol of the moral perversion of the clergy.

One notes, however, the curious fact that the term "Nicolaite" does not appear before the tenth century, when this accusation began to flow from the pens of certain ecclesiastical authors, and that it hardly was employed again after the end of the twelfth century. Should we then conclude (as certain surveys of church history have rashly asserted) that clerical morality declined markedly during the feudal age because of the control that lay lords then exercised over the church, and that subsequently, thanks to the beneficent effects of the reform measures undertaken by the papacy, this evil was overcome, and the practice of sexual continence was steadily established among the clergy? We should immediately observe that such a presentation of events contains a fundamental contradiction. If the pattern of development between the eleventh century and the thirteenth was, in fact, as I have just described, how could it be that diatribes against

Fig. 6.1. St. Augustine presents the Augustinian hermits with the book of his rules for monastic life. Church St. Stephen, Jerusalem. Photo: © Erich Lessing / Art Resource, N.Y.

priestly "fornicators" (as Nicolaites were now called) were heard more loudly than ever from the end of the fourteenth century and that the misconduct of the clergy would still today be presented, in countless books, as one of the age-old abuses that made necessary the Protestant Reformation? All the evidence indicates that this moralizing point of view is outmoded and unacceptable and that the question urgently needs to be reframed.

THE POSSIBILITY OF CLERICAL MARRIAGE

To understand the medieval situation, we must quickly sketch the broad outlines of how ecclesiastical discipline developed up to the eleventh century, which marked a decisive turning point in this area. From the origins of the church up to the beginning of the fourth century, no canon law—whether general or particular, in the East or the West—obliged married bishops or priests (and we know of many such clergy) to renounce sexual relations with their spouses. The only rule that seems to have existed regarding such matters was the injunction forbidding widowed clergy to remarry, in keeping with Paul's comment that the person responsible for the Christian community—the *episcopos*, or overseer—must be "the husband of one wife" (1 Tim. 3:2). After the end of the persecutions and the emergence of the church as a public institution, canonical legislation grew more substantial: priests and deacons were forbidden to marry after their ordination, and in the West married priests were called upon (by Pope Siricius, in particular, in 385–386) to abstain from conjugal relations with their spouse and live with her "like brother and sister." At the end of the sixth century, Gregory the Great (who was pope from 590 to 604) even specified that a married priest should "love his wife like a sister, but distrust her like an enemy," and so avoid cohabitation by maintaining separate bedrooms.

The Eastern churches, for their part, adopted on this point a different standard, ratified by a council held in Constantinople in 691, which they have maintained to this day: only the bishop is obliged to remain celibate; priests can marry so long as they do so before being ordained and can carry on normal marital relations. In both cases, the goal was the same: to see to it that the secular clergy—that is, the priests, bishops, and and other clergy engaged in pastoral care, whereas monks were known as the religious or regular clergy—stood out for its worthy manner of life and irreproachable conduct. But the Eastern churches thought that this could be attained within the framework of marriage, whereas the West held that a priest, whether married or not, could find safety only in sexual continence.

This choice must be seen in relation to the evolution of priestly duties, for it was then that priests began to celebrate the sacrifice of the Mass every day; they had to keep themselves pure in order to consecrate and handle the holy species of bread and wine. The fathers of the Latin church, St. Jerome and St. Augustine, had emphasized the impurity that results from sexual relations—*omnis coitus immundus* (all sexual relations are unclean), Jerome had written in his *Against Jovinian* (1.20)—and Pope Siricius voiced the same conviction in invoking Paul's assertion that "those who are in the flesh cannot please God" (Rom. 8:8). Since God is pure spirit, those who wish to approach him and claim to contemplate him must renounce their own bodies and abstain from all sexual relations. In this connection it is significant that clergy in minor orders—who, unlike those in major orders (priests, deacons, and subdeacons), did not take part in the consecration and distribution of the sacraments—were not subject to any limitations on their conjugal life.

During the early Middle Ages, these prohibitions ran up against stiff resistance and even seemed to have been quickly forgotten. Gregory of Tours (ca. 539–594) mentions numerous married bishops in Merovingian Gaul, whereas the church councils of that time frequently deplore the misconduct of unmarried clergy and the dubious company they kept. The church continued to ordain married men right down to the eleventh century, and the late-eighth-century collection of canon law known as the *Dionysiana-Hadriana*, which Charlemagne adopted to regulate clerical life and comportment in his empire, specified clearly that a married priest who returned to his wife was to be excommunicated. As late as 1010, the German bishop Burchard of Worms, in his *Penitential*, condemned those believers who scorned married priests and used this pretext to refuse to give them the offerings owed to the church.

This last viewpoint gives us a hint of the changes taking place in customs and outlook. Ever since the Carolingian epoch, in effect, the church had defined a favored path to salvation for each category of Christians in accordance with their place in the church and in society. In this perspective, marriage and family life had been proffered to lay-people as means of salvation at the same time that celibacy was presented to the clergy as the instrument of their sanctification. In addition, bishops tended to encourage single young men who under-

Fig. 6.2. Abelard and Heloise, 1325–1350. Scene from the story of the French lovers Abelard and Heloise who married in secret. Abelard was Heloise's tutor, and when their relationship was discovered, Abelard was castrated and became a monk. Heloise became abbess of Le Paraclet. From the poems of Charles, Duke of Orleans. ID: Roy 16.II, fol.137. British Library, London. Photo: © Erich Lessing / Art Resource, N.Y.

took to remain continent to enter the priesthood, rather than ordaining married men.

Unfortunately, the surviving documents from this period are too few and too imprecise to allow us to trace this development in detail. Nevertheless, the statistics that the Italian historian Gabriella Rossetti has compiled from the parchments of the diocese of Lucca seem fairly convincing: between 774 and 885, sixty-six cases of legally married priests are mentioned in them, alongside fifteen concubinary priests; in the tenth century (890–1101), on the other hand, one finds in these records only seven legally married priests, as opposed to 106 with concubines.[1] The results of this study are confirmed by the admonitions addressed to his clergy by Atto of Vercelli (924–961), one of the rare reforming bishops of the tenth century, in which he called upon them above all to abstain from frequenting prostitutes. Thus the prospect of marriage seemed to be increasingly closed to Italian clergy, even if certain churches that were especially attached to their traditions, like that of Milan, still had substantial numbers of married priests in the middle of the eleventh century.

THE END OF CLERICAL MARRIAGE

In the first decades of the eleventh century, the problem of the sexual lives of the clergy, which until then had barely merited a passing mention, became a burning issue and the object of numerous measures on the part of the highest church authorities. In less than a century, these measures brought about a complete reversal of the standards of clerical conduct that had prevailed until this point. In 1022, a Lombard church council, meeting in Pavia, decided that the children born to incontinent clergy would become slaves of the church that their father served and could not inherit their father's goods; a similar measure was adopted at Bourges in 1031. Above all, from the moment that the reforming impulse took root in Rome, with the pontificate of Leo IX (1048–1054), such measures—coupled with sanctions for those who contravened them—multiplied.

In 1050, a Roman synod ordered priests to send away their wives and live henceforth in continence. In 1059, Nicholas II (who was pope from 1058 to 1061) forbade the faithful from attending Mass celebrated by priests who refused to leave their wives or concubines—a very significant decree, since (contradicting all previous canonical legislation on this point) it implied that the sacraments celebrated by those priests who did not live chastely were worthless. Gregory VII pressed the issue further in 1074, declaring that all clergy who did not immediately abandon their female companions would ipso facto be deposed from their priestly office; he urgently called on all bishops throughout Christendom to apply these new regulations in their dioceses without delay and in their full rigor. Very few dared to do so, and those rare prel-

Fig. 6.3. Monk and a woman in stocks, ca.1300–ca. 1325. From the Smithfield Decretals, an illuminated copy of the decrees of Pope Gregory IX. Roy.10.E.IV, fol. 187 (detail). British Library, London. Photo: © HIP / Art Resource, N.Y.

ates who made the attempt, such as the archbishop Jean of Rouen or the Bavarian bishop Altmann of Passau, were nearly stoned by their subordinates.

In parallel to these canonical decrees, the most ardent advocates of reform waged a campaign of polemics. In his *Liber Gomorrhianus* (Book of Gomorrah), Peter Damian (1007–1072) denounced in the harshest terms the loose conduct of the clergy and lashed out especially at their female companions, whom he condemned as "seducers of clergy, lures of the devil, scum of heaven, poison of souls," and so on. It is noteworthy that in this literature, the legitimate wives of priests are no longer distinguished from concubines; rather, all are lumped together as "prostitutes." From this moment on, in effect, the Roman Church rejected any form of clerical marriage and tacitly refused to acknowledge that a marriage entered into by a priest had any validity.

The culmination of this development was signaled by canons 6 and 7 of the Second Lateran Council (1139), which declared that any priest who cohabited with a woman (other than his mother, aunt, or sister, or a female servant who had reached the "canonical age" of sixty) would be deprived

General Ecclesiastical Legislation on Clerical Celibacy

First Lateran Council (1123), Canon 7

We absolutely forbid priests, deacons or subdeacons to live with concubines and wives, and to cohabit with other women, except those whom the council of Nicaea permitted to dwell with them solely on account of necessity, namely a mother, sister, paternal or maternal aunt, or other such person, about whom no suspicion could justly arise.

Second Lateran Council (1139), Canons 6 and 7

We also decree that those in the orders of subdeacon and above who have taken wives or concubines are to be deprived of their position and ecclesiastical benefice. For since they ought to be in fact and in name temples of God, vessels of the Lord and sanctuaries of the Holy Spirit, it is unbecoming that they give themselves up to marriage and impurity.

Adhering to the path trod by our predecessors, the Roman pontiffs Gregory VII, Urban, and Paschal, we prescribe that nobody is to hear the masses of those whom he knows to have wives or concubines. Indeed, that the law of continence and the purity pleasing to God might be propagated among ecclesiastical persons and those in holy orders, we decree that where bishops, deacons, subdeacons, canons regular, monks and professed lay brothers have presumed to take wives and so transgress this holy precept, they are to be separated from their partners. For we do not deem there to be a marriage which, it is agreed, has been contracted against ecclesiastical law. Furthermore, when they have separated from each other, let them do a penance commensurate with such outrageous behaviour.

—*Decrees of the Ecumenical Councils*, vol. 1, *Nicaea I to Lateran V*, ed. Norman P. Tanner (Washington, D.C.: Georgetown University Press, 1990), 191, 198

of his office and his ecclesiastical benefice, and above all that any marriage contracted by secular or regular clergy who held the rank of subdeacon or higher was not only illicit but invalid. The Roman Catholic Church has upheld this standard ever since, and to this day ordination remains (to use the terminology of the canon lawyers) a diriment impediment to marriage. Even if a cleric and his companion could find a priest who was willing to marry them, the resulting union would be null and void.

We should reflect on the reasons for this storm that broke so brusquely over the priesthood. Why did the problem of clerical incontinence—the famous "Nicolaite heresy"—acquire such importance that it ended by becoming, along with the struggle against simony, one of the principal concerns of the reform movement in the Western church? Could it be because clerical immorality had reached a truly unbearable level at that moment? That has long been the position held by traditional scholarship, which takes at face value the accusations hurled by the most extreme of the Gregorian reformers in their polemical works. But despite their assertions, we have no particular reason to think that the situation had changed significantly, for better or for worse, with respect to the preceding centuries.

On the contrary, it seems more exact to say that what had changed was the way people viewed behavior that until then had been commonly accepted: in certain sectors of the church—sectors that were not limited to the ecclesiastical hierarchy—the idea that persons dedicated to the ministry of the altar might engage in sexual activities had become an intolerable scandal. As often happens, the causes of this hardening of attitudes were complex. The first (and perhaps, at the outset, the most fundamental) was interest in preventing the hereditary transmission of clerical offices and the ecclesiastical benefices attached to them. In this period, it often happened "that the rectory was full of children who, when they were old enough, helped their father at the altar while waiting to serve there themselves."[2] This process, which was becoming commonplace at the beginning of the eleventh century, carried a mortal peril for the church, since the creation of priestly dynasties claiming for themselves ecclesiastical functions and goods might lead in the end to a complete dissolution of the church's patrimony, already threatened by the encroachment of lay lords.

It is thus significant that the first disciplinary measures taken to combat this slippage struck above all at priests' children and wives. The former were declared illegitimate, even when they were the product of a legal marriage, and barred from inheriting their father's goods, entering the priesthood (unless they obtained a dispensation), and contracting a legitimate marriage. Everything suggests that the aim in thus punishing the sons for the sins of their fathers was to discourage certain behavior on the part of the clergy. The latter were treated no better, since they could be reduced to bondage by the local lord or bishop. Thus the former companions of Roman priests were appropriated as servants at the pontifical palace of the Lateran; elsewhere, they were thrown out on the street and fell into prostitution. A certain number of them can be found in the popular religious movements of the early twelfth century, such as the one that gathered in about 1100 in western France around Robert d'Arbrissel—himself the son and grandson of priests who had broken with his familial setting and thrown himself into the struggle for reform.

It would, however, be incorrect to explain the church's change in attitude simply in terms of social and economic interests, however important their role may have been. We must also take into account the growing hostility of the papacy toward the patriarch of Constantinople, which reached the point of formal schism in 1054. One of the fiercest opponents of any form of clerical marriage was the monk Humbert de Moyenmoutier, from Lorraine in northeastern France; when he became a cardinal of the Roman Church, he did not hesitate to accuse the Greek Orthodox Church of having fallen into the Nicolaite heresy because it allowed the ordination of married men and did not require that they be continent. His personal role in the struggle for clerical celibacy, like that of his contemporary and colleague Peter Damian, brings out clearly the importance of monastic influence. The program of monastic reform, promoted and exemplified by Cluny and by the Italian hermit-monks, made virginity a central concern and called all those entering the cloistered life to imitate the angels.[3]

In an age in which the prestige of the secular clergy was at its nadir and that of the monks at its zenith, it was inevitable that the monastic ideal would come to affect expectations of priests. In fact, at the

Local Ecclesiastical Legislation on Clerical Celibacy: The Synod of Valladolid (1322)

Since some clerics squander their reputations and their salvation by living an exceptionally dissolute life in public concubinage, we, desiring to correct such a life and abolish their infamy, admonish each and every clergyman, whatever office, dignity, or title they might hold, that they not dare to keep any concubine publicly in their own home or anyone else's. With the approval of this holy council, we proclaim that any beneficed cleric who continues to keep a concubine or concubines in the aforesaid manner two months after the publication of these synodal constitutions and admonishments by his archbishop or bishop or their vicars, in his church or in synod—or who, having dismissed her or them, takes another or others—shall ipso facto be deprived of one-third of the revenues of all benefices that he may hold for that time. If he persists in this filthy life of sin for another two months after the aforesaid two months, he shall be deprived of another third of his revenues. If perhaps, scorning the fear of God, he persists in the sin mentioned for another two months following the aforementioned four, we deprive him of the remaining third—all under the pain of excommunication, warning him that he not place rash hands on any portion of the said revenues once deprived of them, as explained above, for that period of time. . . . In parish churches, we allocate half of the seized revenues to the maintenance of the church building and the other half to ransoming captives held by the infidels.

—Joannes Dominicus Mansi, *Sacrorum Conciliorum nova et amplissima collectio* (Graz: Akademische Druck u. Verlagsanstalt, 1961 [1767]), vol. 25, cols. 700–701

same time that he issued the repressive measures already mentioned, Gregory VII called on the clergy—starting with the canons and those associated with collegial and cathedral churches—to live in common according to the model provided by the group of texts known as the Rule of St. Augustine. By holding all their goods in common, they would avoid any private appropriation of ecclesiastical property; by observing the discipline of eating in a common refectory and sleeping in a common dormitory, they would prevent any cohabitation with women and enable themselves to live chastely. This program did not receive an enthusiastic welcome from those for whom it was intended. Certain individuals or groups of clergy who were more fervent than the rest rallied to it and founded communities and even orders of regular canons (such as that of Prémontre, founded by St. Norbert in 1121), but the vast majority of secular clergy remained deaf to this appeal.

In the final analysis, the most fundamental reason for the campaign waged by the church in favor of clerical celibacy surely lies in the redefinition of relations between clergy and laity that took concrete shape, at the beginning of the eleventh century, in the schema of the "three orders" of society, whose significance has been effectively demonstrated by Georges Duby and Jacques Le Goff.[4] Around the year 1000, in effect, texts of clerical authorship that classified the members of Christian society into three categories or "orders"—those who pray (the clergy), those who fight (the knights), and those who work (everybody else)—began to appear throughout Western Europe. Specialists in social history have been especially alert to the appearance, within the laity, of a distinction between lords and peasants. But it is no less interesting to note that the secular clergy (bishops, priests, deacons, and so on) found themselves grouped with the monks in a single category, defined by the practice of prayer and, in a hierarchical perspective, placed at the head of the body of society. This tripartite schema thus expressed an unmistakable assertion of the emancipation and primacy of the spiritual estate, which became established over the course of the eleventh century: the spiritual must be freed from the grasp of the temporal authorities, because the spirit is superior to the flesh.

But this preeminence of the spiritual estate was only justified, in the eyes of people of that time, if those who comprised it lived in purity, far from the carnal life—which was likened, in a perspective more Neoplatonic than Christian, to a moral blemish. The advocates of clerical celibacy emphasized the need to raise the status of clergy above that of the laity. Insofar as most of the laity lived within the bonds of marriage and procreated children, priests, who were called to be their leaders and guides, must abstain from doing the same and confirm their superiority by the evidence of their irreproachable purity, whether they were monks or parish clergy. It was only at this price that the church could regain its liberty and fulfill its mission, which consisted in leading the faithful to salvation.

This argument bore all the more weight in that it rested, in certain parts of Christendom (such as northern and central Italy), on broad popular foundations. In Milan and in Tuscany, religious movements uniting large numbers of laypeople with some reforming clergy emerged around 1050 to 1060. These groups—labeled Patarines by their enemies—boycotted religious services performed by married or concubinary priests and rejected their sacraments as ineffective and even pernicious for the salvation of the soul. It is certain that the desire to have worthy and morally uplifting priests was widely shared in this period, including among the ordinary faithful. But serious differences emerged within Latin Christendom over how best to achieve that ideal. For the Gregorian reformers (who eventually carried the day), only celibacy, lived like a heroic struggle, could lead the clergy back to chastity.

Within the clergy, however, differing opinions were voiced in a whole series of treatises—particularly numerous in Germany and in Normandy—that argued that one would have a better chance of obtaining the same result by allowing those priests who so wished to live honestly as married men, and that family life constituted a much more effective remedy for incontinence than did celibacy imposed in authoritarian fashion. But since this current of opinion was linked with circles favorable to the emperor or hostile to papal centralization, it was stifled fairly quickly and, after the victory achieved by the Roman Church in the investiture controversy, no longer managed to make its voice heard.

THE PROGRESS OF CELIBACY

From the first decades of the twelfth century, the debates and conflicts over Nicolaitism, which throughout the previous epoch had held so prominent a place in the life of the church, slipped into the background. Even the term itself soon disappeared. From this relative silence of the texts, some historians have concluded that clerical celibacy had slowly but steadily become part of the priestly way of life in the course of the twelfth century and in any case had ceased to be a problem. This is a rather optimistic view of things, as we shall see.

We should note first of all that the campaign against clerical marriage waged by Gregory VII and his successors had been restricted largely to Italy, France, and Germany. Elsewhere, papal decrees forbidding priests from marrying long remained unknown or at least ignored in practice. Thus in England at the end of the eleventh century and beginning of the twelfth, two archbishops of Canterbury, Lanfranc and Anselm—both of them former abbots of Bec, in Normandy—took various measures to put an end to the marriage of priests and punish those who broke the rules. For the most part, these decrees remained a dead letter, done in by the passive resistance of the English clergy. Things became more complicated with the intervention of King Henry I, who, in 1129—on the pretext of supporting the efforts of the ecclesiastical hierarchy, but really to fill his coffers—hit incontinent priests with a fine that bore the revealing name of *culagium*, or ass tax. But far from putting an end to the evil it claimed to combat, this annual tax was viewed by those who paid it as an authorization to keep their wives, so long as they paid the fee. Even at the end of the twelfth century (if we can trust the testimony of a British intellectual, Gerald of Wales), nearly all of the parish priests in England had the habit of living with a *focaria* (hearth-mate) who served them by day as a cook and by night as a concubine.[5]

Certain bishops, like that of Hereford (which bordered on Wales, where clerical marriage long remained very widespread), petitioned the Holy See for permission not to apply fully the sanctions against incontinent priests. Pope Alexander III (1159–1181) effectively granted it, insofar as it concerned (as the text of the papal bull says) "a savage region and a primitive people."[6] But we must recognize that there were many such "primitives" in the Christianity of this time, since the same text applied equally to Hungary, Castile, and a certain number of other places where the clergy showed such opposition to the Roman legislation that forcing them to obey it was unthinkable—unless one was willing to compromise the entire structure of pastoral care. In Scandinavia, it wasn't until the thirteenth century that pontifical legates introduced clerical celibacy into local practice. But the lamentations of St. Birgitta of Sweden (d. 1373) about the moral condition of the Swedish clergy show how far they still were, a century later, from having accepted and absorbed the canonical requirements.

Such clerical resistance was much stronger and longer lasting than is generally admitted, and it

---

Legislation against Laymen Who Favor Clerical Concubinage: The Synod of Valladolid (1322)

In the judgment of divine as well as human law, not only those who sin, but also those who induce others to sin should be subjected to a suitable penalty. Thus it happens that some laymen compel clergy who have received the major clerical orders to take women as their concubines and live with them in public cohabitation, contrary to what is fitting for clerical orders and commanded by canon law. Detesting such wickedness in all its forms, we decree that a sentence of excommunication shall automatically apply to any person, of whatsoever status or condition, and a sentence of interdict to any group or community whatsoever, who induces any ecclesiastical person to do such a thing by compelling him to take any woman as his concubine. Indeed, we wish and order that the preceding decree be announced in diocesan synods, and frequently in parish churches.

—Joannes Dominicus Mansi, *Sacrorum Conciliorum nova et amplissima collectio* (Graz: Akademische Druck u. Verlagsanstalt, 1961 [1767]), vol. 25, col. 703

often found support among the laity. Thus in Alsace in the middle of the thirteenth century, according to a Dominican chronicler, "the peasants say that a priest cannot live alone and that it is therefore preferable that he have his own wife, since otherwise he would chase after other men's wives and sleep with them."[7] This attitude, expressing a sort of crude common sense, can be documented in any number of other places until the end of the Middle Ages. On the other hand, public opinion harshly condemned those flighty and lecherous priests whose escapades provided fodder for daily gossip, as evidenced by any number of French fabliaux and Italian novellas. In these cases, the faithful did not hesitate to denounce their priests to the ecclesiastical authorities, as attested by this passage from a pastoral visit in the English diocese of Hereford, concerning the rector of Coddington: "The parishioners say that the rector is too careless and negligent of the divine office, and that his pigs devastated the cemetery. . . . Item, that he is absent from the parish too often: that is the reason why the parishioners go elsewhere to baptize their children. Item, that he openly keeps in his house a concubine, whose name they don't know. Item, he fills the bell-tower with hay and keeps his calves there."[8]

In fact, what seemed to have troubled the parishioners was not clerical concubinage itself (so long as it only involved single women or widows extraneous to the village community) but rather the priest's appropriation for personal use of goods pertaining to the church, such as the bread and wine that the community gave him as part of the tithe, or installing his companion in a house that belonged to the church. The confusion of the rector's personal possessions with those of the parish, which were furnished by the local community, and their consumption by a household that (including children) might have many mouths to feed: these could provoke outrage. But so long as he maintained good relations with his flock and performed properly his religious duties, especially the regular celebration of Mass, a priest who had a stable and discreet relationship with a female companion could easily pass unnoticed by the ecclesiastical authorities and avoid their sanctions.[9]

Thus when the bishop of Geneva, Jean de Bertrand, inspected his diocese in the years 1411–1414, he discovered that the curate of Chenex, who was nearly a hundred years old, had been living with a woman for the past fifty years, without giving anyone any grounds for gossip. Perhaps struck by such touching fidelity, he let the priest off with a reprimand.[10] Obviously, in this case it was far too late to make a show of enforcing the rules! The situation was a little different in cities, but not necessarily better. Because the authorities could exercise control more easily, the urban clergy rarely lived openly with a female companion. But the registers of municipal judges and officials show that plenty of priests—and monks and friars as well—frequented bathhouses, brothels, and other places of debauchery. In 1494, in the diocese of Sens, Archbishop Tristan de Salazar punished roughly thirty clerics for incontinence; only four of them were responsible for the care of souls in the countryside, clearly demonstrating that the urban clergy, which in principle was better trained, did not for that reason show any greater respect for the law.[11]

On the whole, one can say that the legislation concerning clerical celibacy seems to have been better known and respected by the secular clergy starting in the thirteenth century—at least on certain points. Throughout Christendom, the church managed to put an end to the hereditary transmission of parochial duties, which had long been its obsession. Of course, if he obtained from the pope a dispensation releasing him from the restrictions that weighed on him because of his illegitimacy, the son of a priest could still hope to make a career in holy orders, but that procedure was now more closely supervised by the hierarchy. What is more, in the wake of the Gregorian reform, the religious orders and cathedral chapters had taken control of countless parish churches, effectively shifting the responsibility for naming their clergy from the hands of laypeople (who were often little concerned with priestly celibacy) to those of monks and canons, who, in general, knew and applied the ecclesiastical legislation in this regard.

Finally, and most important, the marriage of priests disappeared almost entirely. From the twelfth century, the wedding ceremony itself, which was by now restricted to the laity, became more and more formal and solemn. The prestige of marriage, whose sacramental character was emphasized by the church, was thereby further enhanced and more clearly distinguished than before from simple cohabitation. On the other hand, clandestine unions grew rarer after the Fourth Lateran Council, in 1215, required that the spouses, before celebrating their marriage, publicly announce their intentions in the parish church. In these circumstances, a cleric could no longer have sexual relations

Eudes Rigaud, Archbishop of Rouen, Inspects His Clergy (1248)

January 19. We visited the priests of the deanery of Foucarmont, whom we convoked at St.-Léger. We found that the priest of Nesle was defamed of a certain woman who is said to be with child by him; that he is engaged in trade; that he treated his own father, who owns the advowson [patronage right] of his church, in a most disgraceful manner; that he fought a certain knight with drawn sword, making a great clamor, and was supported by a following of friends and relations. Item, the priest at Basinval is ill famed of a certain woman, and although he has been disciplined by the archdeacon he continues to have relations with her and even takes her to the market; he also frequents taverns. Item, the priest at Vieux-Rouen is ill famed of incontinence, and although he was disciplined by the archdeacon in the matter of one woman he has not ceased to carry on with others; he goes about girt with a sword and wears unseemly clothes. Item, the priest at Bouafles does not wear a gown, is ill famed of a certain woman, and sells his grain at a rather advanced price because of the poor harvest. Item, the priest at Hesmy, reported to be a leper, is ill famed of incontinence. Item, the priest at Ecotigny plays at dice and quoits, and was unwilling to publish the marriage banns of a certain person who had not restored his father's legacy; he frequents taverns, is ill famed of incontinence, and continues his evil ways though he has been disciplined. Item, the priest at Mesnil-David is disobedient and has his children at home and a concubine elsewhere; item, two women fell upon each other in his house; they fought with each other and because one was fond of roses the other cut down the rose bushes.

—*The Register of Eudes of Rouen*, trans. Sydney M. Brown, ed. Jeremiah F. O'Sullivan (New York: Columbia University Press, 1964), 24

with a woman except in the framework of concubinage or prostitution. Moreover, if their relationship came to light and provoked the intervention of the civil or ecclesiastical authorities, his companion risked being expelled from the rectory and perhaps even being shaved and placed in the pillory for public derision, which could not help discouraging such involvement.

The campaign against clerical incontinence also became more systematic after 1215. One of the most effective means employed to impose this new discipline was the practice of pastoral visits, conducted at regular intervals (in theory, every three years) by bishops or their representatives. The visitor, as soon as he arrived in a given parish, made inquiries among the parishioners concerning the moral condition of the curate or his vicar. If nothing out of the ordinary was mentioned, he dropped that line of questioning. On the other hand, if (as sometimes happened) he was greeted by a priest surrounded by his children or the parishioners informed him of the presence of a "priestess" in the rectory, he took action. Generally, in the first instance that meant imposing a fine. If he did not mend his ways, the offending priest could be deprived of his benefice at the end of a more or less lengthy process. Thus the archbishop of Rouen, Eudes Rigaud, who visited his vast diocese assiduously between 1248 and 1264, had notoriously incontinent clerics sign a letter of resignation; if, on a subsequent visit, their situation had not changed, he suspended them. In the course of his pastoral visits, this prelate took action against eighty-six clerics out of the 705 whom he inspected—a figure that should be taken as a minimum baseline for calculating the incidence of concubinage, since many cases of clerical incontinence could have escaped detection.

Nonetheless, most bishops preferred to close their eyes to this sort of infraction rather than enter into open conflict with priests whom they would have had a hard time replacing. Alternatively, they were satisfied with urging such priests to observe a certain discretion in their behavior, in keeping with a Latin adage that saw wide and long-lasting use: *Si non caste, tamen caute* (If you can't live chastely, at least live discreetly). The strict application of the penalties stipulated in canon law for concubinary priests was, in effect, a step pregnant with consequences: not only did it threaten to throw the parish ministry into turmoil by depriving the faithful of their priest, but it could also be an occasion for scandal that might damage the prestige of the entire clergy as a privileged order. As far as possible, then, bishops avoided excessive rigor in the measures they employed, preferring to impose monetary fines on incontinent clerics, shift them from one parish to another, or even send them off to school to pursue their studies. The leadership of the church was convinced, in effect, that there was a close tie between ignorance and immorality and that those priests who had received a more advanced education would be that much more respectful of the rule of celibacy. In 1298, Pope Boniface VIII enacted measures aimed at allowing clerics to obtain leave to pursue their studies for several years, while still retaining the revenues of their benefice. This policy certainly bore fruit for the lower echelons of the ecclesiastical hierarchy, but it seems to have hardly touched the parish priests, whose ranks in the fifteenth century still included few university graduates.

The abandonment of pastoral visits by bishops during the period of the Avignon papacy (1305–1377) and the crisis of clerical recruitment in the second half of the fourteenth century, after the Black Death, brought in their wake a general relaxation of ecclesiastical discipline.

Investigation of a Concubinary Priest in Cortona (1337)

Guiduccio the farrier, son of the late Piero of Cortona and neighbor of the said priest Vollia, a sworn witness examined as above, when questioned on the first article of this inquest stated the extent of his knowledge: that is, that this priest Vollia keeps with him as concubine in the house where he resides a certain woman named Biagia, and that he has had children with her. Asked how he knows this, he replied because he saw it, and he saw the priest Vollia carry on his shoulders a certain child that he treated as his son, who was born from that woman, and whom people regarded as his.

Item, asked what was said about this, he said that the aforesaid is common knowledge and report. Asked how he knew, he said that this is what is said throughout Cortona, especially in the neighborhood where the priest lives.

Bartolo the kettle-maker, son of the late Orlando of Cortona, a sworn witness examined as above, when questioned on the first article of this inquest stated the extent of his knowledge: that is, that the witness heard it said that the priest Vollia kept a woman named Biagia as concubine and that he had fathered children with her, and that he saw her residing in the said Vollia's home, and that she maintained there a dutch oven for cooking bread and that the witness himself baked bread with her.

Item, asked what was said about this, he replied that the aforesaid is common knowledge and report, especially in the said priest Vollia's neighborhood. Asked how he knew, he said that he had heard this from his relatives and from other people.

—Translated from Noemi Meoni, "Visite pastorali a Cortona nel Trecento," *Archivio storico italiano* 129 (1971): 253

The lamentations of Jean of Varennes, Nicholas of Clamanges, Pierre d'Ailly, and Jean Charlier de Gerson—who, around 1400, bemoaned the catastrophic moral condition of the French clergy—all bear witness to this. Even allowing for a certain exaggeration and the unsupported generalizations inherent in ecclesiastical rhetoric, the situation seems in fact to have degenerated markedly in this area, and the case of France is certainly not an isolated one. The measures undertaken by the councils of Constance and Basel, in 1415 and 1435, aimed at improving the manner of life and morality of the clergy, did not meet with great success. One can even find certain authors, such as the seneschal of Provence, Guillaume Saignet, who in 1417 wrote his *Lamentation about Human Nature* addressed to Pope Martin V, willing to invoke the notion of natural needs that cannot be made light of without hypocrisy and to assert that church reform should proceed by abolishing clerical celibacy—an obligation that was contrary to the law of God, who wanted his children to be fruitful and multiply.[12]

Jean Gerson answered Saignet in 1423 with his *Dialogue in Defense of Clerical Celibacy*, in which he mixes spiritual and material arguments in not very convincing fashion.[13] According to Gerson, only chastity allowed meditation and contemplation of divine matters; the clergy, who were vowed

Fig. 6.4. The Holy Communion (detail), Chronicle of the Council of Constance (1414–1418) by Ulrich von Richenthal (fifteenth century C.E.). Ms. 32, p. 276. Germany, c.1450–1470. Spencer Collection. Astor, Lenox and Tilden Foundations. Photo: © New York Public Library / Art Resource, N.Y.

to God, must practice it to a heroic degree, by abstaining from sexual relations, in order to devote themselves fully to their vocation. In effect, celibacy allowed them to flee the domestic and economic cares involved in maintaining a family, as well as marital worries, and guaranteed the ritual purity a priest needed in order to celebrate the sacraments worthily. Chancellor Gerson recognized that certain clergy did not live up to this rule, but he affirmed that that was no reason to reject it: many principles of Christian morality are violated on a daily basis by the faithful, yet that does not stop the church from continuing to uphold these standards.

In the end it was Gerson's point of view that won out: celibacy must go hand in hand with the priesthood, even while acknowledging that this ideal could only be attained by raising the cultural level of the clergy and tightening the standards for admission to holy orders. This eventually led—though only after the Protestant Reformation, which abolished all vows of clerical chastity or celibacy, and the Catholic response to it at the Council of Trent (1545–1563)—to the creation of seminaries, those schools of theological science and virtue through which all future Catholic priests were obliged to pass, starting at the end of the sixteenth century or the beginning of the seventeenth.

IDEALS AND REALITIES

If one attempts to draw up a balance of the state of affairs at the end of the Middle Ages, the status of clerical celibacy in Western Christianity presents some sharp contrasts. We must start by emphasizing that actual practice varied from one region to another and even sometimes within a single diocese. Thus the inspection of 235 parish priests carried out by Andrea Corsini, bishop of the Tuscan diocese of Fiesole from 1349 to 1373, revealed that at least 20 percent of the priests in his diocese lived with concubines. But a closer look at their geographical distribution quickly reveals that the percentage of concubinary priests was much higher in remote and mountainous regions than in the center of the diocese, which was more urbanized and better supervised.[14]

By the same token, in the northern half of France, one notes a marked difference between the diocese of Paris or that of Châlons in Champagne, where in the fifteenth century, the cases of clerical incontinence punished by ecclesiastical courts are few and far between (1 to 3 percent of the clergy) and constitute a marginal phenomenon, and dioceses in the southeast, such as Lyons, Geneva, or Grenoble, where between 15 and 20 percent of priests were penalized for their weaknesses of the flesh. Concubinage was even more common in Normandy, as indicated by the fact that sexual infractions constituted fully 70 percent of the crimes for which clergy were punished by church courts in Rouen.[15]

What is more, it is sometimes difficult to assess the real incidence of sexual misconduct among the clergy, since pastoral visitations— which, together with the curial registers, constitute our principal source of information—changed in character. In the fourteenth century, visitations (when they existed) were generally conducted carefully by the bishops themselves or their representatives, and witnesses were subjected to thorough and detailed questioning. In the fifteenth century, in contrast, they were often far more perfunctory, directed at purely administrative concerns, and sometimes even reduced to a simple questionnaire concerning the possessions of the church and the conditions of the buildings. Nonetheless, one can make two observations that may seem contradictory but in reality are not: on the one hand, a significant percentage (which varies from place to place) of clergy continued to flout the ecclesiastical legislation, and on the other, their numbers tended to shrink.

If clergy persisted in rejecting clerical celibacy for centuries after it was officially mandated, it was not because of mere disobedience. Rather, they rejected the model imposed by the Gregorian reform and clung to another model, one different from that defined by canon law. The medieval priest was certainly a cleric and hence a man of the church, but most of the time, especially in rural settings, he was isolated from other clergy and tended to respect the norms and needs of the milieu to which he belonged and in which he lived his daily life. The prevailing social model there was the familial one, and it was hard to live as a single person in an environment where everything—from patrimonial property to the notion of honor that played an essential role in social relations—revolved around married couples and lineages.

Moreover, even if some parishioners might have wished to chide their priest for his conduct, the faithful—who had thoroughly absorbed the distinction, clearly affirmed by the church ever since the twelfth century, between the efficacy of the sacraments and the personal sanctity of those who administered them—knew by experience that they could not demand moral perfection of their pastors without running the risk of finding themselves accused of heresy, which induced them to refrain from criticizing them in public. The leadership of the church itself often set a bad example: many bishops were young men from aristocratic circles whose conduct inclined to notable looseness, which certainly did not inspire their fellow clergy to greater zeal in this respect. Ecclesiastical courts themselves long demonstrated a certain flexibility in their treatment of offenders, and the penalties they assigned were often more proportional to the amount of scandal the conduct might have provoked than to the objective seriousness of the offense. Thus spiritual incest—that is, sexual relations between a priest and one of this parishioners or someone in his spiritual care— was punished more severely than concubinage with a woman who was not his parishioner or the rape of a vagabond.

In the course of the fifteenth century, in any case, and especially after the end of the Great Schism (1378–1417) and the Hundred Years' War (1337–1453), which had weakened ecclesiastical structures in many regions, the clergy seem to have developed greater respect for maintaining celibacy. The reasons for this change are manifold. For one, there developed in this period all sorts of little priestly communities—chapters, colleges, confraternities—that grouped together the priests or chaplains of an entire village or small town, reducing their isolation and making them less susceptible to the influence of the society that surrounded them. With the resumption of economic growth, the upper fringe of the lower clergy—and in particular those priests who held title to an ecclesiastical benefice—attained a certain level of ease and tended to become local notables. This improvement in their level of material comfort led to a certain gentrification in their recruitment and in their social comportment, such that notions of self-restraint and respectability ended by taking the upper hand over the unbridled passions and even violence that had prevailed hitherto.

Priesthood and Purity in the Morality Play *Everyman*

Five Wits:
There is no emperor, king, duke, ne baron,
That of God hath commission
As hath the least priest in the world being;
For of the blessed sacraments pure and benign
He beareth the keys, and thereof hath the cure
For man's redemption—it is ever sure—
Which God for our soul's medicine
Gave us out of his heart with great pine.
Here in this transitory life, for thee and me,
The blessed sacraments seven there be:
Baptism, confirmation, with priesthood good,
And the sacrament of God's precious flesh and
     blood,
Marriage, the holy extreme unction, and penance;
These seven be good to have in remembrance,
Gracious sacraments of high divinity.

Everyman:
Fain would I receive that holy body,
And meekly to my ghostly father I will go.

Five Wits:
Everyman, that is the best that ye can do.
God will you to salvation bring,
For priesthood exceedeth all other thing:
To us Holy Scripture they do teach,
And converteth man from sin heaven to reach;
God hath to them more power given
Than to any angel that is in heaven.
With five words he may consecrate,
God's body in flesh and blood to make,

In a parallel development, the attitudes of both bishops and the laity grew more moralistic. From the 1450s on, those priests who continued to lead a family life came to be suspected of heresy or viewed as apostates who had renounced the Catholic faith, and the repression of abuses became more rigorous. In particular, the fines levied by ecclesiastical courts grew so heavy that a cleric who did not hold a benefice could no longer afford to maintain a lasting relationship with a woman. What's more, by now bishops viewed recalcitrant clergy as ipso facto excommunicate and did not hesitate to encourage the faithful to inform on them—for instance, as at Amiens in 1454, by promising twenty days of indulgence for anyone who denounced clerical fornicators.[16]

One can observe a similar change in how the faithful viewed those priests who lived as if married. It had long been the custom, when a rural priest was notoriously involved with a local young woman, for the youths of the village to organize a *charivari*, gathering at night to make noise and call out insults around the couple's house—a sort of symbolic protest against the intrusion of a male who should, by rights, have been excluded from the competition for brides (one of the fundamental challenges facing poor young men in rural society). But in the fifteenth century, these demonstrations came to be accompanied more often with violence against

Everyman (continued)

And handleth his Maker between his hands.
The priest bindeth and unbindeth all bands,
Both in earth and in heaven.
Thou ministers all the sacraments seven;
Though we kissed thy feet, thou were worthy;
Thou art surgeon that cureth sin deadly:
No remedy we find under God
But all only priesthood.
Everyman, God gave priests that dignity,
And setteth them in his stead among us to be;
Thus be they above angels in degree.
Knowledge:
If priests be good, it is so, surely.
But when Jesus hanged on the cross with great
    smart,
There he gave out of his blessed heart
The same sacrament in great torment:
He sold them not to us, that Lord omnipotent.
Therefore Saint Peter the apostle doth say
That Jesu's curse hath all they
Which God their Saviour do buy or sell,
Or they for any money do take or tell.
Sinful priests giveth the sinners example bad;
Their children sitteth by other men's fires, I have
    heard;
And some haunteth women's company
With unclean life, as lusts of lechery:
These be with sin made blind.
Five Wits:
I trust to God no such may we find;
Therefore let us priesthood honour,
And follow their doctrine for our souls' succour.
We be their sheep, and they shepherds be
By whom we all be kept in surety.
—*Everyman and Medieval Miracle Plays*, ed. A. C.
    Crawley (London: J. M. Dent, 1993), 219–21

women who engaged in liaisons with clergy and with punitive expeditions against priests who transgressed against social norms: priests who were caught in the act had to pay a ransom to the band of villagers that captured them in order to escape being beaten.

Finally, religious factors pertaining to the moral and spiritual order no doubt played a role as well in this shift in outlook, especially in urban settings. The diffusion of new devotional currents (such as that of the *devotio moderna* in Flanders and the Netherlands) helped introduce into the domain of religious life higher standards of private morality, making the control of one's speech and behavior more imperative. The urgent need for social order, after the disorders of the fourteenth century and the early fifteenth, blended with the yearning for salvation, which itself was linked with the notion that each Christian must respect the moral rules governing his or her own condition of life. Thus the church, which had treated its members with such tolerance and even laxity, found itself constrained by public pressure to respond more vigorously to their transgressions, even if only to avoid having lay authorities strip it of its judicial prerogative to discipline the clergy.

All in all, the results of the medieval church's age-old campaign against clerical incontinence betray a certain ambiguity. On the one hand, its energetic actions, in the eleventh century, against the legal marriage of priests had a salutary effect, allowing it to block the process by which priestly dynasties threatened to privatize churches and treat church property as a familial patrimony. In so doing, the church without any doubt assured its own survival as an independent institution within a society that was being feudalized. On the other hand, the authoritarian imposition of celibacy on all clergy dedicated to the service of the altar from the twelfth century onward makes it not at all certain that the Church did a better job of promoting chastity than it had earlier, between the fourth and eleventh centuries, when it had obliged married priests "to live with their wives as if they didn't have them," in Pope Leo the Great's expression.

In the long run, by dint of repetition and sanctions, the idea that the priesthood was incompatible with active sexuality came to be accepted by both clergy and laity. By the end of the fifteenth century, helped by a new social and religious climate, the precepts of the church in this regard seem to have been observed by most priests, at least in the central regions of Christendom. But this increased respect for the official standards of conduct did not mean that the underlying issue was entirely resolved, as soon became clear when a good portion of the secular and regular clergy joined in the Protestant Reformation.

FOR FURTHER READING

Barstow, Anne L. *Married Priests and the Reforming Papacy: The Eleventh-Century Debates*. New York: Edwin Mellen, 1982.

Bornstein, Daniel. "Parish Priests in Late Medieval Cortona: The Urban and Rural Clergy." In *Preti nel medioevo*, 165–93. Verona: Cierre, 1997.

Brundage, James A. *Law, Sex, and Christian Society in Medieval Europe*. Chicago: University of Chicago Press, 1987.

Frassetto, Michael, ed. *Medieval Purity and Piety: Essays on Medieval Clerical Celibacy and Religious Reform*. New York: Garland, 1998.

Heath, Peter. *The English Parish Clergy on the Eve of the Reformation*. London: Routledge & Kegan Paul; Toronto: University of Toronto Press, 1969.

Swanson, R. N. "Angels Incarnate: Clergy and Masculinity from Gregorian Reform to Reformation." In *Masculinity in Medieval Europe*, ed. Dawn Hadley, Women and Men in History Series, 160–77. New York: Addison Wesley Longman, 1999.

———. *Church and Society in Late Medieval England*. Oxford: Blackwell, 1989.

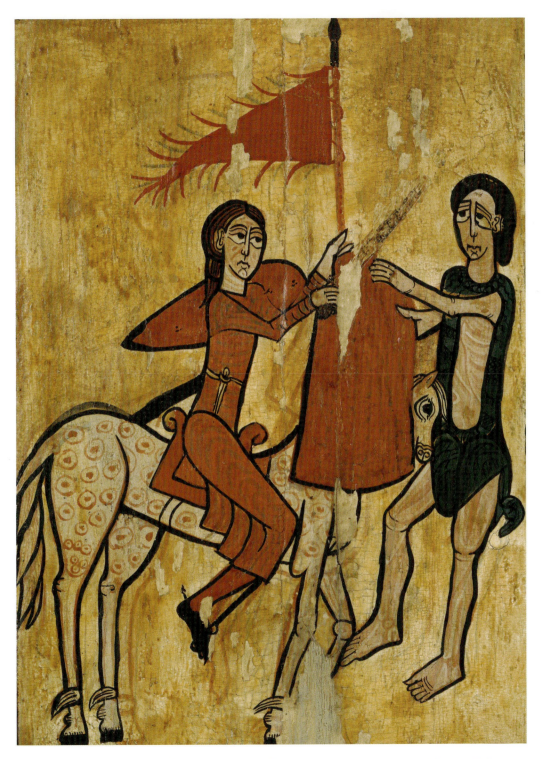

A. St. Martin of Tours sharing his cloak; altar frontal from St. Martin de Puigbó, twelfth century (detail); Episcopal Museum, Vich, Spain. This common image of charity shows Martin cutting his cloak to give half of it to a beggar. That night, in fulfillment of the biblical promise that "as you did it to one of the least of these my brethren, so you did it to me" (Matt 25:40), Jesus appeared to Martin wearing the cloak he had given to the beggar. Photo: © Scala / Art Resource, N.Y.

B. (Left) The Blessed Andrea Gallerani receiving pilgrims; exterior of the diptych of the Blessed Andrea Gallerani, Guido da Siena (thirteenth century CE); Pinacoteca Nazionale, Siena, Italy. A network of routes linked the major shrines of Europe. The scallop shell badges worn by some of these barefoot pilgrims indicate that they have already made the pilgrimage to Santiago de Compostela in Galicia. Photo: © Alinari / Art Resource, N.Y.

C. The building of Tavara monastary; Commentary on the Apocalypse by Beatus of Liebana; Spain (Burgos), dated 1220 CE; MS. M.429, F.183; the Pierpont Morgan Library, New York. The construction of monasteries, cathedrals, and other churches involved all sorts of skilled labor, from stonemasons, bricklayers, carpenters, and glaziers to the clerics who drew up plans and kept the accounts. Photo: ©The Pierpont Morgan Library / Art Resource, N.Y.

D. The tree of vices, fourteenth century; Psalter of Robert de Lisle; Arundel.83, British Library, London. The vices are listed in Latin, spread through the tree in seven groups, corresponding to the deadly sins. Such images served as mnemonic devices, to help people recall their sins in preparation for confession. Photo: © HIP / Art Resource, N.Y.

E. Detail (1470); from volume IV of a biblical history of Guyart des Moulins; British Library, London. Increasing literacy in the later Middle Ages meant that more people, including women, were able to use devotional books to guide their prayers, in domestic settings as well as in church. Photo: © HIP / Art Resource, N.Y.

F. The fall of the damned (detail); Dieric Bouts the Elder (c.1415–1475); oil on wood, 1450; Musée des Beaux-Arts, Lille, France. In the late Middle Ages, vivid images of nightmarish demons and the torments of the damned reflected and fed fears of the Last Judgment and eternal damnation. Photo: © Réunion des Musées Nationaux / Art Resource, N.Y.

G. Angels Raphael and Gabriel; altar frontal of St. Michael (thirteenth century); Museu d'Art de Cataluna, Barcelona. Worshipers watched their priests say mass before brightly colored altarpieces and altar frontals such as this. Here the archangels Raphael and Gabriel lift up a naked soul as it faces divine judgment and wrap it protectively in a white cloth. Photo: © Art Resource, N.Y.

H. Listening to an Augustinian preach; detail of a fresco by the Master of Tolentino (fourteenth century); Cappellone of San Nicola, Tolentino, Italy. Audiences flocked to the sermons of famous preachers, which offered entertainment as well as religious instruction and inspiration, but not everyone listened with the same degree of attentiveness and engagement. Photo: © DeA Picture Library / Art Resource, N.Y.

I. Pilgrims before the tomb of St. Sebastian (1497–1498); Josse Lieferinxe (fl.1493–1508); Galleria Nazionale d'Arte Antica, Rome. Petitioners appealed to the saints for relief from their physical ailments and spiritual anguish. Photo: © Nimatallah / Art Resource, N.Y.

J. Host desecration according to the case of Paris; detail of altarpiece for the monastery of Sijena, Catalonia, Spain; Jaime Serra (c. 1400). This image condenses two stages of an incident of host desecration: a Jew stabs the consecrated eucharist, which bleeds profusely, and throws it into a boiling cauldron from which the Christ-child rises unharmed. Graphic stories and images such as this sharpened anti-Jewish sentiments in the fourteenth and fifteenth centuries. Museu d'Art de Cataluna, Barcelona, Spain.

K. Four praying nuns, from the Herlin Altarpiece; Friedrich Herlin (1459–1491); Stadtmuseum, Noerdlingen, Germany. In the fifteenth century, the use of rosaries became common among laypeople as well as cloistered nuns. Photo: ©Erich Lessing / Art Resource, N.Y.

L. (Above) Wailing women and mourners; detail of the tomb of Don Sancho Saiz Carrillo; Museu d'Art de Cataluna, Barcelona. Women often took the lead in mourning the dead by wailing and tearing their hair and clothes. In the late Middle Ages, sumptuary legislation attempted to restrain these expressions of grief, which were held to be unseemly and disruptive. Photo: © Erich Lessing / Art Resource, N.Y.

M. (Right) The burial of a plague victim at Sansepolcro; anonymous votive tablet, sixteenth century; Pinacoteca Comunale, Sansepolcro, Italy. Lay confraternities engaged in a variety of devotional and charitable activities: feeding the hungry, dowering poor girls, visiting prisoners, comforting the dying, and burying the dead. Photo: © Scala / Art Resource, N.Y.

HEARING WOMEN'S SINS

ROBERTO RUSCONI

CHAPTER SEVEN

THE OBLIGATION OF ANNUAL CONFESSION

At the end of 1215, the Fourth Lateran Council, convened at Rome by Pope Innocent III, approved constitution 21, known from its opening words as *Omnis utriusque sexus*, which made the annual confession of one's sins to a priest a general obligation for all Christians. It specified very clearly that this obligation applied to all the faithful, both men and women: "All the faithful of either sex, after they have reached the age of discernment, should individually confess all their sins in a faithful manner to their own priest at least once a year, and let them take care . . . to perform the penance imposed on them."

The same constitution, moreover, enjoined the priest to question thoroughly the penitent who presented himself or herself before him, following a practice that had developed over the course of the preceding decades, and in sharp contrast with what had been the prevailing method of confession in the earlier Middle Ages: "The priest shall be discerning and prudent, so that like a skilled doctor he may pour wine and oil over the wounds of the injured one. Let him carefully inquire about the circumstances of both the sinner and the sin, so that he may prudently discern what sort of advice he ought to give and what remedy to apply, using various means to heal the sick person." Naturally, the priest was obligated to keep secret what he heard in confession, under pain of deposition from his office.[1]

If the confessor thus had to question the penitent—first of all, to ascertain the nature and circumstances of the sin committed, and then

The Fundamental Canon Law on Confession: Fourth Lateran Council (1215)

All the faithful of either sex, after they have reached the age of discernment, should individually confess all their sins in a faithful manner to their own priest at least once a year, and let them take care to do what they can to perform the penance imposed on them. Let them reverently receive the sacrament of the Eucharist at least at Easter unless they think, for a good reason and on the advice of their own priest, that they should abstain from receiving it for a time. Otherwise they shall be barred from entering a church during their lifetime and they shall be denied a Christian burial at death. Let this salutary decree be frequently published in churches, so that nobody may find the pretext of an excuse in the blindness of ignorance. If any persons wish, for good reasons, to confess their sins to another priest let them first ask and obtain the permission of their own priest; for otherwise the other priest will not have the power to absolve or bind them. The priest shall be discerning and prudent, so that like a skilled doctor he may pour wine and oil over the wounds of the injured one. Let him carefully inquire about the circumstances of both the sinner and the sin, so that he may prudently discern what sort of advice he ought to give and what remedy to apply, using various means to heal the sick person. Let him take the utmost care, however, not to betray the sinner at all by word or sign or in any other way. If the priest needs wise advice, let him seek it cautiously without any mention of the person concerned. For if anyone presumes to reveal a sin disclosed to him in confession, we decree that he is not only to be deposed from his priestly office but also to be confined to a strict monastery to do perpetual penance.

—*Decrees of the Ecumenical Councils*, ed. Norman P. Tanner, S.J. (London: Sheed & Ward; Washington, D.C.: Georgetown University Press, 1990), 245

to impose in consequence an appropriate penance, suited to the goal of healing the sinner's soul—hearing women's confessions posed at least two sorts of problems for priests as they wrestled with how to apply in practice the directive to "carefully inquire." In order to devise an efficacious medicine for the soul adapted to the particular penitent, they needed to ascertain in detail the circumstances of the transgression committed, and this not only to judge whether it involved a more or less serious—mortal or venial—sin. Even when the sin did not happen to be sexual in nature, the inevitable intimacy of confession made this a perilous task for priests, who were obliged to remain celibate.

One problem concerned how exactly the priest was to listen to a woman's confession. He was supposed to confirm by the visible blush of shame that the penitent was truly contrite, yet discretion—especially when dealing with a female penitent—cautioned him against looking her in the face. In addition to this, synodal legislation and handbooks on penance repeatedly instructed that confession should be heard in some sort of public place and yet remain confidential. A fairly typical image of how priests heard women's confessions in late medieval Europe was used as the frontispiece of *General Confession* by the Observant Franciscan friar Michele Carcano of Milan, a booklet printed in Venice in 1506 and intended as a guide to the annual confession of sins typically made in preparation for Easter communion (which that same canon 21 of the Fourth Lateran Council also made obligatory for all Christians). In the interior of a small rural church, a priest seated beside the altar listens to the confession of the female penitent kneeling beside him, with her bowed head veiled and a rosary in her hands. Behind her, we see a seated woman keeping her company, while in the background appears a small group of men talking among themselves. The confessor's right hand steadies a book that rests on his knee, suggesting that this handbook is the source of his own capacity for discernment; his raised left arm lets the ample sleeve of his robe form a curtain between himself and the woman, while at the same time he averts his gaze from her.[2]

Fig. 7.1. Frontispiece from Michele Carcano da Milano's *Confessione generale* (Venezia: Melchiorre Sessa, 1506).

This image offers a visual synthesis of established practice, as described (for instance) in John Myrc's *Instructions for Parish Priests*, written at the beginning of the fifteenth century. In a section dedicated to hearing confession, which repeats the advice offered in the *Oculus sacerdotis* of William of Pagula from the previous century, Myrc warns the priest confronted with a female penitent:

But when a woman comes to thee,
Look that her face thou not see,
But teach her to kneel down thee by,
And turn thy face from her somewhat awry.

Once settled into this pose of aloof intimacy, with ears pricked but gaze averted, the priest should encourage the penitent to speak freely and fully, addressing her in words like these:

Take thee good advice
And what manner sin thou art guilty of,
Tell me boldly and make no scoff.
Tell me thy sin, I thee pray,
And spare nothing, by no way.
Do not hesitate for any shame;
Perhaps I may have done the same.[3]

In fact, even before the general council summoned by Pope Innocent III, the synodal constitutions redacted between 1200 and 1208 by the bishop of Paris prescribed that confession—particularly of women—should be heard in an open space within the church so that priest and penitent could be seen, and that out of respect for due modesty, the priest should not look the penitent in the face.[4] After the approval of the constitution *Omnis utriusque sexus*, similar directives multiplied in provincial councils and diocesan synods throughout the thirteenth century, clarifying the precise steps to be followed in hearing confession (especially from women) for a parish clergy who certainly had not previously received any special training for that task, as the mendicant friars had.[5] Thus between 1217 and 1219, Richard Poore, bishop of Salisbury in England, prescribed that women's confessions, in the period leading up to Easter, should be heard *extra velum et in propatulo*—that is to say, in front of a cloth that ensured their public visibility while closing off the presbytery "from sight but not from hearing," a phrase that was repeated word for word in other synodal legislation.[6] Analogous prescriptions can be found (for instance) in the synodal constitutions of Paris in 1234 and Nîmes in 1252.[7]

A few decades later, these reiterations of minimal guidelines began to be supplemented with more detailed instructions, such as those contained in a diocesan synod held in 1280 at Cologne, in Germany, which summarized in its own directives the particular shape given to the ritual of hearing confession when it involved the confessions of women:

Item, we admonish priests that under no circumstances should they sit to hear confession before sunrise or after sunset, except in cases of great urgency, and then in a well-lighted place and with others present.

Practical Guidance on Hearing Confessions (ca. 1224–1237)

A priest should make a brief interrogation of those whose flesh is weak in the following manner: "Either you knew that the woman whom you approached for sex was unmarried or you didn't. If you knew she was single, you are due a lesser penance; if you didn't know then you are obliged to do a greater penance because she might have been a married woman, a nun, or related to you through affinity, or she may have had relations with your father." Likewise, prostitutes are prone to lie with lepers which can endanger their unborn children or their own health. Also, they should be asked about the number of people they have sinned with and the number of times if they can remember. Also whether they had sexual relations with widows who have taken religious vows, with virgins, with married people, or with nuns. Then they should be asked whether it was with a professed nun because those who have relations with nuns must be sent to the bishop for absolution since a bishop customarily excommunicates such people. If perhaps they do not wish to go to the bishop, the priest should go to the bishop and get his authorization. Likewise, if they had sexual relations with someone related to them by blood or through a spiritual affinity they should be asked in what degree they are related: removed or near. They should be asked whether they had sexual relations with a pregnant woman or a menstruating woman (which is dangerous due to the child that is born since a corrupted fetus is conceived by corrupted semen). Likewise, whether they had relations with a woman near childbirth, for then there is a danger that the infant could be killed. Also ask them whether they had relations with another man or with animals. And this penance should be enjoined on those who had relations with animals above and beyond any other penances that are enjoined: they must never eat that animal's meat. To sum it up briefly: Whenever semen is spilled it is a mortal sin except if it happens when one is sleeping or with one's own wife (and then this must be done legitimately according to the needs of nature). According to the diversity of the circumstances a variety of penances should be enjoined.

—"A Tract on Hearing Confessions (c. 1224–37)," in *Medieval Popular Religion, 1000–1500*, ed. John Shinners, 2nd ed. (Peterborough, Ont.: Broadview, 2006), 21–22

Item, we admonish under penalty of excommunication that priests keep a humble expression while hearing confession, with their eyes lowered to the ground; nor should they look in the face of the person confessing, especially women.

Item, priests should admonish those entrusted to them and teach them, so that they may confess humbly and contrite of heart, with eyes fixed on the ground. And women should confess their sins fully, in a lowered voice, with their head and neck covered.

Item, under no circumstances should priests hear the confession of a woman who is alone in the church, but only in the sight of respectable company. Anyone who consciously disobeys this shall ipso facto incur a sentence of excommunication, and in addition three days on bread and water.[8]

JUDGING IN ORDER TO HEAL

The further problem posed by the actual practice of hearing women's confessions was the specific array of questions that needed to be asked. This was shaped by the way that male clergy (who wrote the penitential literature in use in the late Middle Ages) categorized women's roles and the behavior associated with them, especially behavior they considered sinful.

On the eve of the introduction of this ecclesiastical legislation concerning the obligation of annual confession of sins, which applied equally to men and women, the first collections designed for the priests who faced the challenge of hearing confession—or, rather, of interrogating the faithful about the sins they had committed—began to appear in reforming circles in England and northern France. From that point on, the central action of this sacramental rite was a sort of inquest into the penitent's thoughts and actions, aimed at bringing to light the circumstances of his or her fault and hence the character of the sin involved.

This new manner of hearing confession transformed what had been the accepted approach for several centuries previously, an approach summarized at the beginning of the eleventh century, between 1008 and 1012, in the *Decretum* of Burchard of Worms. Book 19 of the *Decretum* (a section also known as *The Corrector, or rather Physician*) limited itself to dealing with marital issues, dedicating a chapter titled "On the Female Penitent" entirely to the problem of a widow who wished to remarry, the regulation of marital sex, and prescriptions concerning women's monthly "impurity."[9] Even as late as the first half of the twelfth century, the collection of ecclesiastical legislation contained in the *Decretum* of the Camaldolese monk Gratian—the so-called *Concordance of Discordant Canons*—gave scant attention to women.

Between 1199 and 1213, Robert of Flamborough, a regular canon at the abbey of St. Victor in Paris, where he was the penitentiary, composed two versions of his *Book of Penitence*, cast as a dialogue between priest and penitent and designed to teach clergy how to hear confession. Robert devoted the first section to how the priest should go about receiving the penitent, with no mention of gender (though he clearly had a man in mind), and specifying that the penitent should make confession "in orderly fashion, step by step," taking as a guide the seven deadly sins and their various expressions. He then noted that whereas in dealing with clergy the confessor confronts simony and ecclesiastical affairs, in dealing with laypeople he must concern himself with matrimony. For this reason, Robert dedicated an entire book to the topic, which he addressed primarily in terms of marital status, centering his discussion around the legal impediments to marriage.[10]

In these same years, Thomas of Chobham, the vice deacon of the chapter of Salisbury and (like Robert) a member of the Parisian circles around Peter the Chanter, wrote his *Summa for Confessors*. Peter the Chanter's circle shared a strong interest in the connections between theology and law, so it is no surprise to find that Thomas composed a guide to the art of preaching, a collection of Latin sermons, and a treatise on the virtues, as well as his summa for confessors. In his survey of the different juridical statuses that the priest must bear in mind, women appear explicitly only in the role of prostitute. Thomas offers, however, one reflection concerning the penance to be imposed on a woman:

> Priests must therefore keep many things in mind in imposing penance on married persons. . . . However, wives must always be enjoined in penance to be preachers to their husbands, for there is no priest who can so soften a man's heart as his wife can. For

this reason the sins of a man are often imputed to his wife, if on account of her negligence the husband did not mend his ways. Accordingly, she should speak enticingly to her husband in the bedroom and in the midst of their embraces.

It is no accident that shortly thereafter he reminds the reader that a husband must treat his wife well and cherish her more than anything else.[11]

The *Book of Penitence* by the Cistercian monk Alain de Lille (ca. 1128–1202) shows great concern with assigning to the faithful penances proportionate to their sins, a project requiring that the priest take into account the penitent's gender. Alain's outlook, however, is marked by the fierce misogyny typical of monastic settings, and his handbook repeats the shopworn stereotype of feminine weakness: "The sex should also be taken into consideration—that is, whether it be a man or a woman—since according to whether it is the stronger or weaker sex, the guilt is greater or lesser." He even goes so far as to treat the beauty of the woman involved as a mitigating circumstance when evaluating the gravity of a man's sins of the flesh: "It should also be taken into consideration whether the woman with whom he sinned was beautiful or not, since a person who has relations with a beautiful woman sins less than with an ugly one, because that which is beautiful is more compelling: where the compulsion is greater, the sin is less."[12]

Although the Lateran decree of 1215 and the penitential literature it inspired continued (especially throughout the thirteenth century) to employ a medical metaphor to describe the relations of confessor to penitent, that gradually gave way—both in theological and legal thinking and in priestly practice—to a juridical metaphor. The confessor changed from a doctor to a judge, and his inquests grew ever more probing. In effect, over the course of the later Middle Ages, we can observe in different arenas the parallel development of fine-combed investigations into beliefs and behavior, with the annual confession of sins sharing certain features with antiheretical inquisitions. Nor should we forget the special horror felt for female exponents of heterodox beliefs and adherents of heretical movements, condemned in the literature as "ignorant women burdened with sin."[13]

An important consequence of this shift in the focus of sacramental confession was that just as contrition (that is, heartfelt regret for one's sins) had supplanted the attrition (regret inspired by fear of punishment) expected by the handbooks of penance, now satisfaction—making recompense for the harm caused by one's sins—faded in significance compared to the very act of confessing them orally. In point of fact, the confessor's attempt to require a woman to perform certain actions in order to repair the damage done by her sins posed all sorts of problems, since it could have the undesirable consequence of revealing the sins she had confessed. While this concern did not extend to publicly notorious moral infractions, since they were already known to all, it was an especially delicate issue in the case of a sexual sin known only to the other party, who himself bore responsibility for disclosing his own transgressions to a priest. The penitential literature and synodal legislation thus contain cautions against imposing on a married woman (or man, for that matter) a penance that might reveal the wife's misdeeds to her husband.

A great aid to priests struggling with these complexities came from members of the mendicant orders, especially Dominican friars, who developed a penitential literature designed to facilitate the detailed application of the Lateran injunctions. One early and authoritative guide to the practice of hearing confession was the pioneering *Summa on Penitence* by the Catalan friar Raymond of Penyafort, which he first drafted in 1224–1227 and then revised in 1236, after the publication in 1234 of the collection of Pope Gregory IX's *Decretals*, which Raymond himself had edited. (It is no accident that Raymond also prepared a *Summa on Marriage*, redacted on the basis of the same considerations that a few years earlier had inspired Robert of Flamborough.[14]) For the most part, later authors followed and repeated the guidelines Raymond laid out in the section "On the Manner of Making Inquiries":

> He should thus begin by asking the penitent whether he knows the *Our Father*, the *Creed*, and the *Hail Mary*, and if he does not, he should teach him or at least admonish him to learn them. He should also teach him the form to be followed in confession. Then he should tell him that he should seat himself humbly at the foot of the priest whenever he confesses. Item, if it is a woman, he should instruct her to always seat herself transversely. Item, the priest should not look at a woman's face in confession, because

as it says in Habakkuk [1:9], "Her face burns like a wind from the east," and in Hosea [2:2]: "That she put away her harlotry from her face, and her adultery from between her breasts."[15]

The seven deadly sins provided one interpretive framework that shaped how the confessor organized his questions, and in them we can observe how certain kinds of sinful behavior were identified as being closely connected with women, even if the penitential literature of the thirteenth and fourteenth centuries in fact lacked rubrics dedicated specifically to women's sins. This was due in large measure to the tendency to classify women exclusively according to their marital status—unmarried virgin, wife, widow—and hence essentially in relation to their exercise of their capacity to procreate: infanticide, for instance, was a sin (and also a crime) typical of women. Men's status, in contrast, depended primarily on their social position or profession. If we look outside the genre of penitential literature, it is possible to find works, such as the early-fourteenth-century treatise *Behavior and Customs of Women* by Francesco da Barbarino (1264–1348), that at least give some modest consideration to the activities women engaged in beyond their primary social identity as "married women."[16]

Fig. 7.2. The benefits of abstinence: a glutton drinks to excess, while the sober man, with hands in his sleeves, nourishes virtue and controls the flesh. From *Le Livre de bonnes moeurs* by Jacques Legrand. France, ca. 1490. Illuminated manuscript page. Parchment, 22.4 x 17.0 cm. Ms. 297, f. 35v. Photo by René-Gabriel Ojéda. Photo: © Réunion des Musées Nationaux / Art Resource, N.Y.

Over time, the relative importance assigned to the various sins tended to shift in response to major social changes. Thus the commercial revolution of the twelfth century brought new social prominence to merchants, who claimed a place of authority alongside the traditional warrior nobility. As a consequence, in the course of the thirteenth century, avarice (the besotting sin of merchants) gradually supplanted pride (the characteristic vice of knights) as the principal preoccupation of preachers and confessors confronting the sins of men. In dealing with women, however, pride continued to have (so to speak) pride of place—perhaps not so much in purely quantitative terms of which questions were most often put to them by confessors, but in qualitative terms of their relative prominence. It is also significant that starting in the fourteenth century, the framework used in assessing the inherent sinfulness of certain behaviors, as well as in evaluating the "circumstances" surrounding the transgression, was no longer exclusively or even primarily that of the seven deadly sins. With the passage of time, the seven deadly sins gradually came to be supplemented, and eventually supplanted, by the Ten Commandments. This was not without its consequences, given the particularly feminine character ascribed to some of those mortal sins, and the corresponding virtues, in penitential literature.

Even if these texts—and, in all likelihood, the practitioners who turned to them for guidance—generally failed to take into consideration the specific features of women's social situation, at the center of the prescriptions of this penitential literature lay the female body. Everything came back to the body, whether it was the enduring consequences of Eve's sin, which made woman by definition "the temptress" (even, paradoxically, within the marital union), or the peculiar character ascribed to women's vices: not only lust (which would be associated with breaches of the seventh and tenth of the Ten Commandments) but envy, gossip, spite, and all the other "sins of the tongue," and everything that, within the broader rubric of pride, fell under the heading of vanity.

Typical of this outlook are the *Little Sermons on Sin* that the archpriest of Talavera,

---

The Dangers of Involvement with Women
How the priest and even the layman are destroyed by love.

Here is another argument that should persuade you to shun dishonest love, and it is that I have never seen an ecclesiastic (nor have you, for that matter, nor will you ever hope to see one) who has succumbed to dishonest love and won benefices or honors in God's Church. On the contrary, those who have succumbed and yielded to unbridled love have been ruined and will continue to be ruined, to their great shame, thinking to love a woman who does not and never could love them. For there is no woman, of whatever station she may be, who loves an ecclesiastic for any purpose other than to get something from him, such is the insensate greed of women to acquire and possess, and to go about in their mad finery vaingloriously. This is the reason they pretend to love them, but love them not. For example, there is not a woman in the world who does not hate ecclesiastics worse than poison, insulting them, scolding them, and gossiping about them, and this holds true for women who have got something from them, as well as for those who have not. And from this rule I do not except the laity, even though they are the sons of priests, for their mistresses never cease from vexing them, demanding presents and begging loans.

—Alfonso Martinez de Toledo, *Little Sermons on Sin: The Archpriest of Talavera*, trans. Lesley Bird Simpson (Berkeley: University of California Press, 1959), 37

Alfonso Martinez de Toledo, completed in 1438. After discussing men's sins, classified first according to the Ten Commandments and then according to the seven deadly sins, the archpriest turns to "the vices, blemishes, and evil ways of perverse women," all of which can be summed up as sins of lust, of vanity, and of disordered speech. Women, he says, are gossips and backbiters, envious, devious, and two-faced, lying, boastful, and disobedient, chatterers and scolds, greedy and lustful. These last two vices are, in his mind, closely connected: in her desire to fill her chest with fancy clothing, fine jewelry, and makeup, a woman will sleep with anyone who offers her some new adornment.[17] In their endless denunciations of what they held to be excessive luxury in women's clothing, it was as if the authors of penitential literature were trying to repress and suppress the one area of expression available to women, who were confined by church and society to a legally, culturally, and religiously subordinated position.

In point of fact, the sacrament of penance was administered by men and regulated by the relevant writings of clerical authors, for whom the frame of reference was in any case "man" understood as male. In hearing women's confessions, therefore, a fundamentally misogynous attitude prevailed, in light of which a soul—which in theological doctrine was asexual—assumed its body's sex where sin was concerned. In this connection it is revealing that in the penitential literature, the sexual identity of a female penitent always comes into consideration when addressing the circumstances of her sin, even when her actions themselves had nothing directly to do with sex. The universal emphasis on the centrality of women's bodies, both in the realm of sexual conduct and in that of childbearing, left them inescapably sexualized. Vernacular preaching to the faithful and hearing confession of their sins combined to reinforce this attitude, and it certainly did nothing to question the legal and social subordination of women in late medieval and early modern Europe. Nor was this reduction of women to their sexual and reproductive functions in any way limited to the penitential literature. That literature merely reflected and sanctioned the social concerns of the period, which were ruled by the desire to preserve the familial patrimony and transmit it to legitimate heirs.

A PENITENTIAL LITERATURE FOR WOMEN?

The collections of *exempla*, or edifying stories, made for use by preachers (and which often claimed to be derived from confessors' reports of actual cases) contain an ample array of commentary on women's sins—commentary that, in its didactic purpose, clearly reflects the contents of the penitential literature. Numerous exempla make reference to an attitude that they present as typical of women: that is, women's reluctance to confess certain sins, especially those involved in sexual activity, because of the shame that such behavior entailed for them. This reluctance features in exempla included in some Latin sermons collected in Paris in the course of the thirteenth century[18] and in a *Liber exemplorum* of Irish origin, one of whose tales is about "a certain woman, devout in prayer and in charity and outstanding in all good deeds, who had committed one sin in the flower of her youth that, out of shame, she always kept hidden."[19] In a story attributed to the Cistercian monk Caesarius of Heisterbach, a woman who has not confessed a very serious sin hangs herself upon her return home.[20] In fact, in collections of exempla, the stories dealing with incomplete confessions almost always have to do with women.

The penitential literature of the late Middle Ages oozes misogyny on every side. Even in such a context, however, the peculiar anti-litany that Antonino Pierozzi recorded in the first decades of the fifteenth century stands out for its virulence. Antonino claimed to have found in an unpublished commentary on the biblical book of Ecclesiastes written by his fellow Dominican, Giovanni Dominici, a veritable ABC of female sinfulness:

> And so that that bitterness which is women's malice might be clearly exposed, he fashioned an alphabet which he taught to his students, by which women's character and wickedness could be grasped. . . . This, then, is woman: Avid animal. Bestial abyss. Concupiscence of the flesh. Dolorous duel. Ever-burning fever. False faith. Garrulous gullet. Hateful harpy. Invidiousness inflamed. Kaos of calumny. Luring pestilence. Mendacious monster. Nurse of shipwrecks. Odious operator. Primal sinner. Quasher of quiet. Ruler of realms. Savage in pride. Truculent

tyrant. Vanity of vanities. Xerxes' insanity. Ymage of idols. Zealous in jealousy.[21]

Despite what would seem to be women's pervasive and irreducible wickedness, revivalist preachers and religious authors tirelessly denounced sin (which they expected to find everywhere) and urged their audiences to greater virtue (which they nonetheless continued to believe was an achievable goal). The road to spiritual improvement, of course, ran through the proper use of sacramental confession. With the introduction of printing with movable type—the "art of artificial writing"—a new genre of penitential literature emerged in Renaissance Italy: little handbooks intended to help sinners prepare for sacramental confession, published in the vernacular and aimed especially at an audience of female readers. Some of these were mere pamphlets, like the six-page *Confession: Brief and Useful Instructions on How to Prepare Oneself and Confess*, prepared for the use of a group of women in Faenza by their spiritual director, the Servite friar Paolo da Faenza, and published in Bologna around 1500.[22] There were others that, even if they bore titles such as *Examination in the Vernacular* (like that by an anonymous Observant Franciscan friar, printed at Milan in 1493), in reality belonged to the far more general category of devotional books.[23]

Despite their titles, we can also leave aside texts like the *Useful and Necessary General Confession for Religious Women and for Married Women, Widows, and Girls*, which appeared in Venice in the first half of the sixteenth century. This work was prepared by a Benedictine monk and intended for use by nuns, and while it confirms the long-established dominance of the cloister as the ideal model for women's religious life, the inclusion of ordinary women in its announced audience seems to have been merely the publisher's attempt to increase sales.[24] That notwithstanding, many a *General Confession*—that is, a booklet containing a list of all possible sins—also included a questionnaire specifically directed at behavior deemed typical of women's social circumstances.

In 1510, the Observant Franciscan friar Francesco da Mozzanica published in Milan his *Very Brief Introduction for Women Who Want to Confess Well*, which he addressed to the marquise Beatrice d'Avalos Trivulzio and the countess Paola Gonzaga Trivulzio—two devout women of high social status, like many of those for whom such booklets were intended. The innovative feature of this work consisted in its introduction, at the beginning of the usual formula for confession that could be used by any sort of penitent, of a preliminary section addressed specifically to women of various marital and social conditions. It takes into consideration a number of social groupings: young girls and virgins; maids, domestics, and other servants; peasant women, townswomen, and others of similar condition; married women, brides, and widows.[25] The author starts with the Ten Commandments and, in his discussion of the first commandment, lingers over the issue of "superstition," evidently something to which women were thought to be especially inclined.

When he comes to the subject of sexual sins, he prudently leaves some examples in Latin, to avoid causing embarrassment for (or giving ideas to) his less sophisticated readers. As he applies the analytical framework of the seven deadly sins, it is vanity above all that claims his attention: he dedicates page after page to the topic, enumerates fully seven ways in which vain women sin mortally, makes a heartfelt plea urging vain

A Priest Troubled by What He Hears in Confession

When I was a young man and, although unworthy, had advanced to the order of priesthood (although I was not yet a member of the Order of Preachers), I was compelled—without just cause and beyond my strength—to replace a bishop in the hearing of confession. I began this duty with great fear in my heart and after my ears had been troubled externally by what I was hearing, internally I became agitated with stirrings of temptation. Seized with the greatest fear and horror because of this, I went to the righteous Lutgard as though to my most special mother and, touched with sorrow, revealed my burden to her. After she had showed compassion to me, she gave herself over to prayer and then returned and said with great security, "Go back to your own place, my son, and expend due labor for the care of souls. Christ will be present to you as protector and teacher and He will powerfully snatch you from the attacks of the enemy in the hearing of Confession and will add a greater grace to make up for the defect of knowledge which you fear." Wondrous thing! Although I report this about myself with embarrassment, yet I will not be silent about what happened for the sake of praise of Christ and His handmaid. From that day until the present and for as long as I have been engaged in this office which was imposed upon me—sixteen years have passed since then—I have experienced in myself this truest prophecy of the righteous Lutgard. And even when it has not been the time for hearing confessions and I am not being attentive, I am often unbearably disturbed and the more unclean the things are that I hear, by so much the less do I care about them and am less moved in hearing them.

—Thomas de Cantimpré, *The Life of Lutgard of Aywières*, trans. Margot H. King, rev. ed. (Toronto: Peregrina, 1991), 79–80

women to mend their ways, and concludes by listing still further examples of vanity that remain to be treated. His discussion invokes a dozen exempla by various authorities, culled from preachers such as his Franciscan brethren Bernardino da Feltre and Battista da Siena, from friars noted for their work as confessors, and from the widely respected Dominican archbishop of Florence, Antonino Pierozzi.

Far from being peculiar to him, Francesco da Mozzanica's obsession with female vanity is entirely in keeping with the temper of his times. Throughout the fifteenth century, wandering Franciscan preachers had repeatedly lit "bonfires of the vanities" in the piazzas of Italian cities (and across the Alps in Germany as well), in which they publicly burned such instruments of the devil as playing cards and gambling tables but especially the innumerable ornaments with which women adorned themselves and ensnared men.[26] (See also chapter 5 in this volume for further discussion of these bonfires in the context of revivalism.)

WHAT WAS CONFESSED AND HOW?

In the popular genre of the Italian novella, hearing confession offers an opportunity for seduction, a weaving of amorous intrigues by both priests and women (who take turns deceiving one another), in a parodic narrative context that swiftly degenerated into stereotypical tales.[27] Several of these stories offer confirmation that the methods recommended for hearing women's confessions were actually employed in practice. For instance, the fifth story of day seven in the *Decameron* by Giovanni Boccaccio (1313–1375)—an author who was thoroughly familiar with the penitential literature of his time—describes a scene that faithfully reflects the image in the frontispiece of Michele Carcano of Milan's *General Confession*, which we examined at the beginning of this chapter. In Boccaccio's comic tale, a jealous man disguised himself as a priest so that he could hear his wife's confession: "When Christmas morning came, the lady got up close to dawn, prepared herself, and went to the church. . . . The jealous husband . . . arriving there before her . . . quickly put on one of the priest's robes with a hood that came down to his cheeks, like those we often see priests wearing, and after pulling it forward a bit, he went to sit down in one of the pews."[28]

In the middle of the following century, in the famous story of the breeches of San Griffone by Masuccio Salernitano (Tommaso Guardati, ca. 1420–1475), we find a woman's confession described in these terms: "And when they had withdrawn themselves somewhat aside, and the friar had taken up his position in the place where they were accustomed to hear confessions, and the lady had gone down on her knees before him, she began to confess herself according to the accustomed rule."[29] Drawing aside in this manner preserved the privacy of confession, which canon law required. But it also, as in this tale, provided an opportunity for seduction.

Well aware of this risk—to their souls and to their reputations—even those religious orders that were most dedicated to hearing confession (such as, in Italy, the Observant Franciscans) wrestled ever more explicitly with the problem of how to go about hearing the confession of women.[30] The regulations issued by the provincial chapter of Genoa echoed the constitutions of the Franciscan order approved back in 1354, under the minister general Guillaume Farinier, when they prescribed: "Item, the constitution of Farinier about hearing confessions shall be followed. That is, that no friar shall remain standing or seated next to a woman, for hearing confession or for any other reason whatsoever, unless he and his companion friar can see each other; and let them beware of long conversations with women; and whoever is guilty of doing this shall be denounced by his companions."[31] The friars thus had to come to grips with the problem of identifying and equipping a suitable place for hearing women's confessions. In 1467, the provincial chapter of the Observant Franciscan province of Sant'Antonio del Veneto issued this decree on the subject: "Item, that in each place where confessions of women are heard, there be placed iron bars with cloth attached, which cannot be removed."[32] A few years later, in 1471, their brethren in Bohemia similarly ordered: "Places for confession should have grates made of iron, and thick"—a measure that was repeated in 1480.[33]

It is entirely likely that in the gradual identification of an appropriate structure for hearing laywomen's confessions, the Observant friars let themselves be guided by the arrangements made for hearing the confessions of nuns entrusted to their spiritual guidance. That, at least, is what is suggested by the design that Francesco di Giorgio developed for the convent of San Bernardino in Urbino. In his plans for the convent church, the architect, in his own hand, labeled two adjoining rooms that also connected with the convent cloister: "place for the confessional" and "place for the women, where they confess."[34]

This was evidently not the best solution, even if it was designed specifically to maintain discretion in hearing women's confessions. Shortly after the conclusion of the Council of Trent (1545–1563), in the course of his 1565 pastoral visit to the diocese of Brescia, Bishop Domenico Bollani (1514–1579) received complaints about those rooms from the men of Chiari: "that the cells in which the friars of San Bernardino are accustomed to hear confessions should be looked at, because in them they do various inappropriate things, and on account of certain murmuring they would not willingly see their wives be confessed in those cells."[35] The concerns of ordinary laymen in this small northern Italian town were shared in Rome, at the highest levels of the ecclesiastical hierarchy. On August 27, 1575, Cardinal Bernardino Maffei wrote to Cardinal (and future saint) Carlo Borromeo: "Our lord [Pope Gregory XIII] has ordered the generals of the mendicant orders to eliminate this abuse of hearing confession in cells inside a convent, which have grates in the wall of the church through which they hear the penitents, considering it for many sound reasons appropriate that the priest and the penitent be visible to people."[36]

A solution to the problems priests faced in hearing women's confessions—including the physical arrangements—had already been articulated in Verona, in the *Constitutions* published in 1542 by the reforming bishop Gian Matteo Giberti. Giberti's *Constitutions* explicitly invoked the biblical passage about women's faces used three centuries earlier by Raymond of Penyafort. Then, after having repeated the traditional warnings about the need to hear women's confessions in a part of the church where both parties could be seen, as well as the basic guidelines concerning the conduct of a good confessor, they concluded by prescribing: "Whenever he has to hear a woman in confession, we want there to be a panel between the priest hearing confession and the woman, with a little window in which there is a grate or a thin sheet of perforated metal; we call this panel a confessional."[37]

The process reached its conclusion, in the wake of the Jubilee proclaimed by Pope Gregory XIII for the year 1575, with the invention of a new article of liturgical furniture: the confessional. Its inventor was that emblematic figure of the Counter-Reformation, the cardinal-archbishop of Milan, Carlo Borromeo (1538–1585), who laid out its features in the *Instructions Concerning Ecclesiastical Buildings and Furnishings* that he published in 1577.[38] Borromeo's guidelines were then incorporated in the *Roman Ritual* redacted by Cardinal Giulio Antonio Santoro and published there in 1584.[39] With the publication in 1614 of the definitive version of this text, the confessional became an essential item of furniture in all Catholic churches, and so it remained to the time of the Second Vatican Council (1962–1965).[40]

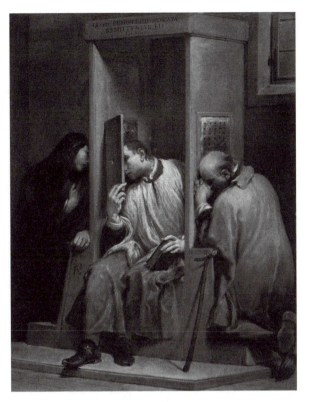

Fig. 7.3. Giuseppe Maria Crespi (1665–1747), St. John of Nepomuk confessing. Galleria Sabauda, Turin. Photo: © Scala / Art Resource, N.Y.

Giberti, Borromeo, and other ecclesiastical reformers championed the use of confession as a spiritual exercise and encouraged recourse to it well beyond mere fulfillment of the obligatory annual confession to one's parish priest. Paradoxically, however, the social control exercised over women in late medieval and early modern Europe hampered the full realization of the reformers' program, as certain social expectations of women impeded their practice of sacramental confession. The *Instructions for Priests* written on behalf of the bishop of Verona, Gian Matteo Giberti, by one of his closest collaborators, Tullio Crispolti of Rieti, comment in this regard:

> Another great defect found especially in women is that they do not confess more than once; and even if they have forgotten some sins, they don't go back again so as not to appear to be sinners, because they say that people notice when they do so. . . . And they also strive to be quick about it, even leaving out sins that they are

well aware of, so as not to give others reason to remark that they have spent a long time in confession.[41]

Another thing that troubled women about confession can be documented more clearly after the middle of the sixteenth century, thanks to the not-at-all disinterested solicitude of the Roman Inquisition. In its attempt to subject the administration of sacramental penance to its control, the Inquisition extended its own criminal jurisdiction to include "solicitation of obscene acts"—that is, priests' attempts to seduce penitents in the privacy of the confessional. Pope Paul IV's bull *Cum sicut nuper*, of February 18, 1559, confirmed the Inquisition's power to take action against this violation of trust and abuse of authority.[42] Yet even while it intervened to defend women's virtue, the Holy Office's fears for the purity and propriety of confessional practice led to an increased emphasis, in both penitential doctrine and practice, on sins of a sexual nature, especially on the part of women.

From the initial enunciation of the requirement that all persons of both sexes individually make annual confession of their sins to their parish priest, the church had at its disposal a marvelously flexible and far-reaching tool for instructing and disciplining the faithful. In theory, a rigorous examination of one's conscience, under the guidance of a sensitive and astute confessor, would make the penitent duly aware of his or her moral faults; performance of the penance imposed by the priest would both assuage the sinner's sense of guilt and encourage better behavior in the future. The introduction of the confessional, vernacular handbooks to guide penitents in making confession, better training for the priesthood in hearing it, and more rigorous control over sacramental doctrine and practice all helped the Counter-Reformation church to wield this tool more effectively. Inevitably, however, the goal—a perfectly disciplined society under the moral and spiritual guidance of the church—remained an elusive

Fig. 7.4.
Alberto Arnoldi
(fl. 1351–1364),
the sacrament of
Confession. Panel from
the Campanile of Giotto.
Relief. Museo dell'Opera
del Duomo, Florence,
Italy. Photo: © Scala /
Art Resource, N.Y.

ideal. In its effort to establish a clerical hegemony through the systematic application of the sacrament of penance, it may well be that the church achieved greater success in fostering a sense of guilt (especially in women) than in providing a means to deal effectively with that guilt. Such, at least, is the conclusion clearly suggested by the rueful remark of Elisabetta, daughter of the late Sebastiano, who, when summoned to appear before the vicar of the Inquisition in Modena on April 17, 1649, testified, "I know how to commit sins, but not how to confess them."[43]

FOR FURTHER READING

Elliott, Dyan. *Proving Woman: Female Spirituality and Inquisitorial Culture in the Later Middle Ages.* Princeton: Princeton University Press, 2004.

Hughes, Diane Owen. "Sumptuary Law and Social Relation in Renaissance Italy." In *Disputes and Settlements: Law and Human Relations in the West*, ed. John Bossy, 69–99. Cambridge: Cambridge University Press, 1983.

Karras, Ruth Mazo. "Gendered Sin and Misogyny in John of Bromyard's *Summa Predicantium.*" *Traditio* 47 (1992): 233–57.

Murray, Jacqueline. "The Absent Penitent: The Cure of Women's Souls and Confessors' Manuals in Thirteenth-Century England." In *Women, the Book, and the Godly*, ed. Lesley Smith and Jane H. M. Taylor, 13–25. Cambridge, U.K.: D. S. Brewer, 1995.

———. "Gendered Souls in Sexed Bodies: The Male Construction of Female Sexuality in Some Medieval Confessor's Manuals." In *"Handling Sin": Confession in the Middle Ages*, ed. Peter Biller and Alastair J. Minnis, 79–93. York, U.K.: York Medieval, 1998.

Payer, Pierre J. *Sex and the Penitentials: The Development of a Sexual Code, 550–1150.* Toronto: University of Toronto Press, 1984.

Rusconi, Roberto. *L'ordine dei peccati: La confessione tra Medioevo ed età moderna.* Bologna: Il Mulino, 2002.

Tentler, Thomas N. *Sin and Confession on the Eve of the Reformation.* Princeton: Princeton University Press, 1977.

DEFINING
BOUNDARIES

Part 4

HERESY AND DISSENT

GRADO G. MERLO

CHAPTER EIGHT

In the early Middle Ages, heresy was a matter for educated elites. Of course, the illiterate peasants who comprised the vast majority of Europe's population could not explain correctly the doctrine of the Trinity or the dual nature of Jesus. No one expected them to do so or even to be able to do so. Expositions of Christian doctrine intended for a broad public were appropriately elementary and concentrated at least as much on controlling behavior as on shaping belief.

At the start of the fifth century, Bishop Maximus of Turin insisted on the need to regulate Christian conduct, calling on the lords of great estates to see to it that peasants on their properties abstained from ritual activities that smacked of paganism. Around 574, when Bishop Martin of Braga prepared an aid for preachers engaged in proselytizing the peasantry, his model sermon provided a simple summary of basic Christian belief, outlined the course of sacred history, and proclaimed the fundamental articles of faith without explaining their scriptural underpinnings or entering deeply into any of their theological complexities. The result of such efforts to convert the countryside was a rural Christianity—in an overwhelmingly rural world—defined by universal reception of baptism, regular attendance at Mass, and deference to clerical authority in matters of doctrine. In return, the clergy generously imputed orthodoxy to the laity. That is, they presumed that ordinary believers implicitly accepted whatever the church defined as orthodoxy and would gladly have declared their orthodox convictions to anyone who asked, if only they had been capable of doing so correctly and coherently.

All this changed in the eleventh century. The Gregorian reform movement refashioned the Catholic Church into a centralized hierarchical organization whose head, the pope, claimed spiritual authority over all of Western Christendom. At the same time, however, the thriving economy, expansion of trade and commerce, and revival of urban life produced a laity that was wealthier, more literate, and more conscious of its own social and cultural identity—which included an interest in experimenting with new forms of religiosity. The inevitable result was tension between, on the one hand, the multiplication of religious experiences in a thousand directions and, on the other, the growing ecclesiastical intolerance of any form of autonomy. A resolution was not always possible, nor was it achieved. Some groups were reincorporated, while others were excluded, often violently; both inclusion and exclusion were pregnant with consequences.

With the exception of the dualist Cathars, both repression and incorporation were accomplished within a theoretical framework that conceived of heresy primarily in juridical and disciplinary terms, rather than theological ones. Heresy—beliefs contrary to orthodox teaching, publicly proclaimed and stubbornly maintained—ceased to be a purely intellectual concern, as the debate over what it meant to be truly Christian involved large numbers of people and broad segments of society. For the first time in half a millennium, heresy could properly be termed "popular"—though we must bear in mind that heresy is a label assigned by religious opponents who present themselves as defenders of orthodoxy. The dualist heretics known in orthodox sources as "Cathars" did not use that term for themselves: they simply spoke of themselves as the "good Christians."

THE "GOOD CHRISTIANS":
DUALIST TENDENCIES AND CATHAR CHURCHES

The dualism imported into Western Europe can be classified into moderate and radical stances. The moderate version is linked with the religious ideas of the Bulgarian priest Bogomil. He elaborated a peculiar notion of the origins of humankind, which he traced to Satan's revolt against God: defeated and cast down into the material world together with his rebellious angels, Satan gave shape to lifeless human creatures. Through God's infinite goodness, these inert forms were given life by means of the rebel angels, who thus became imprisoned in matter. God opened a prospect for liberation by sending one of his angels, Christ, who showed the way to escape the chains of matter through a life of rigorous penance and total detachment from the world. "Christ's brethren" should in turn be perfect or pure, leading an apostolic life of prayer, fasting, and itinerant preaching; they should renounce sexual relations, consumption of food derived from the flesh, and all worldly activity.

This moderate dualist myth of creation eventually took on more radical features. Exactly how and when it became radicalized remains unclear, though it may have happened in the eleventh century through the influence of ancient Manichaean ideas. Satan became the wicked creator of this material world, the antithesis of the good God of heaven. The spirit of darkness deceived the eternal God of light, taking on the appearance of the most splendid of angels but secretly using this opportunity to expose the other angels

---

Ecclesiastical Legislation against Heresy: The Canon *Excommunicamus* of the Fourth Lateran Council (1215)

We excommunicate and anathematize every heresy raising itself up against this holy, orthodox and catholic faith that we have expounded above. We condemn all heretics, whatever names they may go under. They have different faces indeed but their tails are all tied together inasmuch as they are all alike in their pride. Let those condemned be handed over to the secular authorities present, or to their bailiffs, for due punishment. Clerics are first to be degraded from their orders. The goods of the condemned are to be confiscated, if they are lay persons, and if clerics they are to be applied to the churches from which they received their stipends. Those who are found only suspect of heresy are to be struck with the sword of anathema, unless they prove their innocence by an appropriate purgation, having regard to the reasons for suspicion and the character of the person. Let such persons be avoided by all until they have made adequate satisfaction. If they persist in the excommunication for a year, they are to be condemned as heretics. Let secular authorities, whatever offices they may be discharging, be advised and urged and if necessary be compelled by ecclesiastical censure, if they wish to be reputed and held to be faithful, to take publicly an oath for the defense of the faith to the effect that they will seek, in so far as they can, to expel from the lands subject to their jurisdiction all heretics designated by the church in good faith. Thus whenever anyone is promoted to spiritual or temporal authority, he shall be obliged to confirm this article with an oath. If however a temporal lord, required and instructed by the church, neglects to cleanse his territory of this heretical filth, he shall be bound with the bond of excommunication by the metropolitan and other bishops of the province.

—*Decrees of the Ecumenical Councils*, ed. Norman P. Tanner, S.J. (Washington, D.C.: Georgetown University Press, 1990), 233–34

to the seductive pleasures of his realm (the earth), in particular the dazzling beauty of women and the fascination of power. Led astray by him, the angels were imprisoned in matter, which would have been their eternal hell if an angel, Christ, had not agreed to fully share the human condition, right down to his sacrifice on the cross, in order to reveal the way of salvation to humankind—or, rather, to the angels entrapped in this material hell.

These two principal myths were adapted and modified to respond to the changing needs of the Cathar churches, which never achieved a fully developed dogmatic system; the opportunity for their doctrine to evolve independently or in dialogue with the tradition of Catholic thought was cut short. Almost immediately persecuted and forced to go underground, the "good Christians," as they called themselves, had to grapple with issues of survival and martyrdom rather than theological and philosophical speculation. Still, there is no denying that the variegated Cathar beliefs all shared a dualistic orientation, whether that dualism was moderate (with a single creator) or radical (with two creators).

Many scholars over the centuries have debated the question, were the Cathars Christian? Perhaps the most satisfying answer is the simplest: the Cathars defined themselves as "good Christians," and we should accept their self-identification. But these good Christians found themselves at the intersection among different, sometimes contradictory traditions of thought, which they tried to meld to meet the double need for a more authentic form of Christian religiosity and a logical answer to fundamental questions about human and divine nature.

Eastern dualism offered a global response to the religious needs of people in the West, in the form of a complement to and explanation of the Gospel texts. Catharism did not arise from some daily obsession with the problem of evil, nor did it produce a pessimistic outlook. If anything, it led to a detachment from the earthly world and its materialist values in favor of a luminous celestial world with completely different values. The Cathars proclaimed a message of *liberation*: liberation of the divine element in every individual from its material prison. Imitating Christ, by opting for penitence and even martyrdom, was the way to remove the chains of this world from the souls of the pure. The Cathar leaders—the "Perfects"—were motivated in their rigorous asceticism by their need to keep the spirit from contamination by material pleasures and to bear witness to the way of salvation that Christ had initiated among and for humankind. Catharism thus meant a true knowledge of the cosmic struggle between God and Satan and the need to choose one side or the other.

Cathars were not concerned with the destiny of the physical world. What mattered was maintaining the acquired insight, by means of which souls could be freed. They bore witness to this insight, challenging monks and clergy with their personal commitment—a commitment to the apostolic life and evangelical poverty, which they carried to its logical extreme. Catharism thus constituted an intellectual and institutional rival to the dominant church, structured in imitation of that church. The Roman Catholic Church saw it as a threat that had to be eliminated at any cost.

The Cathar peril emerged, with varying intensity, in some of the most economically active, socially mobile, and culturally vibrant regions of Europe: southern and northern France, eastern Spain, northern and central Italy, Burgundy, Flanders, and the Rhineland. Societies experiencing rapid development and convulsive transformations invited and allowed countless innovations in every arena of human activity. Dualism figures as another expression of the general creative ferment that enlivened Western Europe from the eleventh century to the thirteenth. Established systems and rigid hierarchies were shaken: a butcher, like Marco of Lombardy, could become a Cathar bishop; nobles who had converted to Cathar Perfects became weavers; women participated intensely in religious life;

Fig. 8.1. Expulsion of the Albigensians from Carcasonne in 1209, in the course of the crusade against the Albigensians, or Cathars (ca. 1300–1400). From Les Chroniques de France, British Library, London. Photo: © HIP/ Art Resource, N.Y.

learned ideas elaborated in cultivated circles were appropriated by the uneducated, even peasants. Catharism took root in these dynamic contexts because it offered a religious alternative for individuals and groups who were already spontaneously searching for autonomous identities.

The impact of the Cathar Perfects' witnessing thus derived from their engagement with a widespread religious and cultural ferment, as well as their detachment from deep-rooted material interests and from established political and social connections. The Cathars were poor in every sense, individually and collectively. Cathar churches did not own buildings with vast estates and rights of lordship, and this lack was no minor consideration in a time and place when political and social elites, both old and new, were locked in a struggle with ecclesiastical and monastic potentates and attempting to sap the structural foundations of ecclesiastical power.

The spread of dualist heresies and number of dualist heretics were determined by specific local concerns. In Languedoc the good Christians—known also as Albigensians, from the city of Albi—attracted such broad social support that the Cathar churches threatened to become the dominant presence on the religious scene. This underlying concern pushed Innocent III to proclaim a crusade against the Cathars of southern France in 1208. The murder of a papal legate by armed followers of the count of Toulouse offered the occasion, but Innocent's crusade against the Albigensians fit into a preconceived plan of action and a sharpening program of repression. The idea of a massive military expedition to root out the heresy where it flourished most virulently was nothing new (and would find its fullest expression in the canon *Excommunicamus* of the Fourth Lateran Council in 1215). The decision was taken after the failure of other measures: the mission of Cistercian monks preaching as papal legates, the removal and replacement of many local prelates, and public debates over doctrine. Some of the Cistercians themselves apparently called for a radical and definitive solution to the Albigensian problem. Innocent decided on the crusade, in which most of the participants were knights from northern France.

Military operations in the south began in June and July of 1209 and dragged on, with occasional pauses, for two decades. Violence and slaughter are only to be expected in war, however "holy" it may be, and the contemporary sources describe it in all its gory drama. The papal legates Arnald Amalric and Master Milo reported to Innocent III the conquest of Béziers, an event deemed so important that their letter was inserted into the official register of papal correspondence: "The city of Béziers was taken; and since our troops cared nothing for clerical status nor sex nor age, nearly 20,000 people died by the sword. With great slaughter of people, the city was sacked and burned: in this manner, wondrous divine chastisement struck it."

The crusade became a war of conquest by the barons of northern France, led by Simon of Monfort, and an opportunity for the king of France to extend royal power over an area that previously had been developing an independent political and institutional identity. The heresy had put down roots in the cultural soil of a region on the verge of developing a national identity, and the associations that formed around Cathar Perfects in the wake of the crusade did so as expressions of a shared cultural identity. The Cathars were thus not the only ones to suffer; the

---

Cathar Beliefs Described by a Catholic Opponent

It should first be understood that the heretics postulated two creators, to wit, one of the invisible world, whom they called the benign God, and one of the visible world, or the malign god. They ascribed the New Testament to the benign God, the Old Testament to the malign one; the latter book they wholly rejected, except for a few passages which have found their way into the New Testament and which on this account they esteemed worthy of acceptance. . . . The heretics even affirmed in their secret assemblies that the Christ who was born in terrestrial and visible Bethlehem and crucified in Jerusalem was evil, and that Mary Magdalen was his concubine and the very woman taken in adultery of whom we read in the Gospels; for the good Christ, they said, never ate nor drank nor took on real flesh, and was never of this world, except in a spiritual sense in the body of Paul. . . . They held as naught the sacraments of the Church to the point of teaching publicly that the water of baptism differs not at all from water of a river; that the consecrated bread of the most holy body of Christ is no different from ordinary bread; . . . that confirmation, extreme unction, and confession are trifling and silly matters; and that holy matrimony is nothing else than harlotry, nor can anyone fathering sons and daughters in that state achieve salvation. They denied the resurrection of the body; they concocted certain unheard-of fables, averring that our souls are those of angelic spirits who were thrown out of heaven because of the apostasy of pride and who left their glorified bodies in the ether. These souls, after successive indwellings in any seven terrestrial bodies whatsoever, return again to those bodies which they had left, as though they had completed their penance.

—"A Description of Cathars and Waldenses by Peter of Vaux-de-Cernay," in *Heresies of the High Middle Ages: Selected Sources*, ed. Walter L. Wakefield and Austin P. Evans (New York: Columbia University Press, 1969), 237–39

development of Occitan civilization itself was brutally truncated. The Cathar churches of southern France were decapitated; the surviving Perfects took refuge in exile or in a clandestine existence. Political and cultural circumstances never again encouraged a revival of Catharism to match the way it had flourished in Languedoc in the last quarter of the twelfth century.

The antiheretical repression continued long after the crusade had come to an end, becoming a quotidian presence with the establishment of the inquisition, entrusted to Dominican friars. In fact, the new Dominican order, or Order of Preachers, was born in the midst of the struggle against the Cathars on the initiative of Dominic of Caleruega, a canon of the cathedral chapter of the Castilian diocese of Osma. In 1206, in southwestern France, he decided to dedicate himself to apostolic poverty and evangelical preaching with the specific aim of assisting the papal legates in their mission against the Cathars. Having obtained approval first from the bishop of Toulouse and then from the pope, Dominic's group of preachers grew fairly quickly and organized itself into a true mendicant religious order.

His inspiration of combating the heretics with their own weapons—an exemplary life of poverty and complete dedication to evangelical preaching—was combined from the start with the performance of pastoral functions that went well beyond a simple, albeit fierce, confrontation with heresy. Dramatic battles gave way to a steady and subtle exercise of social control managed by specialists and not left solely to local bishops. With the authority granted him by the papal legate, Dominic could impose penance on converted heretics and take coercive action against them. For long decades, southern France witnessed a far-ranging effort of Catholic "reacculturation," as diocesan clergy and the Dominican order collaborated in pastoral activity aimed at preserving the region from heterodox beliefs. What survived of French Catharism was more a romantic myth than history.

By the second quarter of the thirteenth century, the center of Cathar belief was no longer the Balkan peninsula or southern France; rather, its area of greatest concentration and diffusion was the Po Valley of northern Italy. Only in northern and central Italy had some peculiar local sociopolitical conditions allowed Catharism to survive as a significant presence. This was not due to any imagined alliance between Catharism and the papacy's Ghibelline political opponents (that is, those aristocrats who supported the emperor), nor to some implausible protection extended to dualist preachers by the urban ruling classes. More simply, the Cathars posed no threat to the urban authorities' uncompromising assertion of jurisdictional autonomy: these good Christians did not accumulate landed wealth, nor did they claim to exercise lordship over their estates, nor did they intervene in any way in public life. There was thus no reason to worry about their presence.

Such attitudes prevailed until the ecclesiastical hierarchy recognized the urgent need to remind civic authorities of their duty to uphold orthodoxy. This awareness took shape and grew slowly, amid the myriad difficulties created by a fragmented and unstable political situation. The idea that the problem of heresy required a political solution emerged early on, during the conflict between Frederick I and the papacy. In 1184, Pope Lucius III's decretal *Ad abolendam* ordained that all "counts, barons, rectors, [and] consuls of cities and other places" who did not join in the struggle against heresy when called upon to do so would be excommunicated and their territories placed under interdict—and declared that these provisions joined the apostolic authority of the church with the sanction of imperial power.

Soon thereafter, the papacy set about articulating and sharpening the legal steps to be taken against heretics, steadily refining the juridical measures for isolating and criminalizing heterodox believers themselves, their offspring, their other kin, and all those who supported them in any way. The ultimate goal was to get the constituted authorities to recognize the existence of a heretical threat and accept the need for an antiheretical strategy. In southern France, the struggle was transformed into a crusade. In northern and central Italy, where no such undertaking would have been possible, the ecclesiastical hierarchy adopted a less confrontational but no less effective approach.

Historians agree that the decisive role in this was played by Innocent III. On the one hand, he reintegrated into the Catholic Church those groups that were willing to place themselves at the service of the church and accept its authority; on the other, he increased the repressive violence directed against obstinate and unredeemable heretics. Innocent also understood clearly that the struggle against heresy would be decided by the ability of the institutional church to reaffirm its own Christian legitimacy by extending a welcome to authentically evangelical initiatives, as well as by organizing the faithful more effectively. During his pontificate, Dominic of Caleruega formed the Order of Preachers, and Francis of Assisi conceived of the Order of Friars Minor, groups destined to leave an enduring mark on the religious and ecclesiastical history of the late Middle Ages. In them, the apostolic life and evangelical poverty—the guiding ideals of the religious movement of the twelfth century—were interpreted afresh and instituted with conspicuous support from the papacy, restoring Christian legitimacy to ecclesiastical authorities and institutions that had not managed on their own to develop pastoral initiatives beyond an orderly and ordinary performance of rites and sacraments.

In tandem with the mendicant orders, the ecclesiastical hierarchy took on a pastoral role that infused the church with renewed credibility: presenting itself with a fresh face, free from old entanglements; establishing privileged relationships with social elites while acquiring prestige with the lower classes; identifying values and behaviors suited to mediating conflicts and strengthening the social fabric. With the Franciscans and Dominicans, groups of hermits and of penitents, confraternities and charitable associations, the Roman Catholic Church spoke to people's everyday concerns; and it did so through individuals and groups with a holy aspect that felt at home in the church and defended it. The decline of the Cathar churches was correspondingly swift, apart from a few scattered survivals, and by the dawn of the fourteenth century, the Cathar question had been effectively resolved. The inquisitors could easily mop up any remaining pockets of resistance.

VALDÈS OF LYONS: RENEWAL OF THE APOSTOLIC MISSION

In the mid-1170s, Valdès of Lyons (often referred to erroneously as Peter Waldo) pioneered a route that many would follow, with varying success and differing outcomes. His conversion was one of those religious crises experienced by more or less wealthy merchants who, at a certain point in their lives, stripped themselves of possessions and gave their belongings to the poor and to churches, rendering themselves poor for Christ. Thus Valdès was not peculiar in his wish to rid himself of worldly goods. The originality of his action lay rather in its inspiration and purpose, and in the immediate response his religious decision evoked.

Rather than founding a charitable institution or entering into a special relationship with a monastery, Valdès set out to proclaim God's Word, since he believed that those who bore the institutional responsibility for that task were rendered evangelically ineffective by their wicked behavior. This priestly silence was all the more serious in that, at the same time, Cathar dualists were energetically spreading their heterodox teachings. Valdès's calling to become an instrument of orthodoxy met with incomprehension and opposition from the clergy. Priests failed to see the signs of divine will, and Valdès and his companions were declared heretics for usurping a task that did not fall to them. They were therefore forced to fight on two fronts: against the dualist "good Christians" and against the Roman Catholic priesthood. "We do not excuse the improper acts of priests or of others," wrote Valdès's disciple Durand of Huesca in response to Cathar criticism, "but rather in disapproval do we resist them," emphasizing the orthodoxy of their effort to remind priests of their duties and recall them to a worthy ministry.[1]

Valdès demonstrated a concern for orthodoxy from the moment when, moved by desire

The Conversion of Valdès of Lyons

There was in that city [of Lyons] a rich man named Waldes [Valdès], who was not well educated, but on hearing the Gospels was anxious to learn more precisely what was in them. He made a contract with these priests, the one to translate them into the vernacular and the other to write down at his dictation. This they did, not only for many books of the Bible but also for many passages from the Fathers, grouped by topics, which are called Sentences. When this citizen had pored over these texts and learned them by heart, he resolved to devote himself to evangelical perfection, just as the apostles had pursued it. Selling all his possessions, in contempt of the world he broadcast his money to the poor and presumptuously arrogated to himself the office of the apostles. Preaching in the streets and the broad ways the Gospels and those things that he had learned by heart, he drew to himself many men and women that they might do the same, and he strengthened them in the Gospel. He also sent out persons even of the basest occupations to preach in the nearby villages. Men and women alike, stupid and uneducated, they wandered through the villages, entered homes, preached in the squares and even in the churches, and induced others to likewise.

—"Stephen of Bourbon on the Early Waldenses," in *Heresies of the High Middle Ages: Selected Sources*, ed. Walter L. Wakefield and Austin P. Evans (New York: Columbia University Press, 1969), 209

for an unmediated encounter with the Gospels, he had two priests translate some biblical texts and patristic authorities for him and write them in the vernacular. After pondering them, "he resolved to devote himself to evangelical perfection, just as the apostles had pursued it." His concern for orthodoxy led Valdès and his companions to seek the approval of the ecclesiastical leadership, going to Rome at the time of the Third Lateran Council in 1179 and, perhaps, meeting with Pope Alexander III himself.

The pope seems to have expressed sympathy and even admiration for their proposal for a life of evangelical poverty, though he was not inclined to accept their request to be preachers of the Word. Valdès and his companions declared their complete orthodoxy and expressed their wish to renounce the world and be poor for Christ, but the hierarchical church could not devise a framework that would allow the exercise of the preacher's role by a person who did not belong to the priesthood. The matter was complicated by the fact that women too participated in this mission. Laymen and women who took it upon themselves to preach, and in the process gradually became aware that they represented a new departure, presented nearly insurmountable problems for clerical culture and tradition.

How could the institutional church accept such an innovation without setting in motion processes of self-transformation with unforeseeable outcomes? The aristocratic canon Walter Map, representing King Henry II of England at the Lateran council in 1179, grasped this perfectly. These Waldensians, he said, "have no fixed habitations. They go about two by two, barefoot, clad in woolen garments, owning nothing, holding all things in common like the apostles. They are making their first moves now in the humblest manner because they cannot launch an attack. If we admit them, we shall be driven out."[2] The clerical order did not choose to change; indeed, it dug in to defend its special status.

In 1184, Pope Lucius III sanctioned this institutional hardening with *Ad abolendam*, lumping together in the general category of heterodoxy a wide assortment of religious groups: "In the first place, therefore, we lay under a perpetual anathema the Cathars, Patarines, and those who falsely call themselves Humiliati, or Poor Men of Lyons, Passagines, Josepines, and Arnaldists." For some of these groups and churches, excommunication might be seen as justified. But why excommunicate individuals who lived simply and evangelically in harmony with the Catholic theological tradition? The reason lies in the fact that Valdès's followers, like the Humiliati, persisted in their unauthorized preaching, an act that in itself sufficed to indicate a heretical bent, as the decretal specified.

In short, in only a decade, any possibility of accommodating Valdès's religious inspiration within the existing institutional framework had evaporated. Valdès fought steadily and resolutely to hold his followers to the orthodox line he had chosen from the outset, while perhaps clinging to the hope of overcoming ecclesiastical opposition. Despite the papal condemnation, the Waldensian movement continued to expand in southern France, northern Italy, and certain parts of Germany. We do not know exactly how *Ad abolendam* was applied. We do know, however, that Valdès's followers persisted in their program of orthodox preaching before, during, and after the crusade against the Albigensians. In southern France, the Cathar heartland, they established themselves in many localities; they founded centers of worship and study, engaged in charitable activities, produced books, celebrated their own rites including the Lord's Supper, and pressed their antidualist polemic in churches and in town squares.

Northern Italy witnessed quite different developments. There the Waldensian groups were significantly more organized, did not oppose the Cathars, and sometimes even lived together with other dissidents. These early indications show that the Waldensian movement rapidly developed multiple variants that Valdès struggled to keep together and, above all, hold true to his convictions. To no avail: around 1205, while Valdès was still alive, a substantial portion of the Waldensians in Lombardy broke off angrily from the rest, giving rise to an autonomous group known as the Poor Men of Lombardy and inaugurating a crisis in the Waldensian movement.

Valdès died between 1205 and 1207, having known the bitterness of the schism with his Lombard followers and failed to resolve the problems of his relations with the Roman Catholic Church. Personally faithful to orthodoxy as to the church of Christ, he had witnessed the steady distancing of his followers from his theoretical and practical stance. Some of them had begun to reject the ecclesiastical

An Educated Cleric's View of the Waldensians

At the Roman council held under Pope Alexander III, I saw simple and illiterate people called Waldenses, after their leader, Waldes [Valdès], who was a citizen of Lyons on the Rhone. They presented to the lord pope a book written in French which contained the text and a gloss of the Psalms and many of the books of both Testaments. They most urgently requested him to authorize them to preach because they saw themselves as experienced persons, although they were nothing more than dabblers. It is the way of birds who see not the fine snares or the nets to suppose that everywhere there is free passage. Do not men who engage in sophistical discourse all their lives, who can trap and only with difficulty be trapped, who are probers of the most profound depths, do not they, for fear of giving offense, speak with reverence all the thoughts which they reveal about God, whose state is so exalted that no praises or powers of prayer can mount thereto except as mercy may draw them? In every letter of the sacred page, so many precepts fly on wings of virtue, such riches of wisdom are accumulated, that anyone to whom God has granted the means may draw from its fullness. Shall pearls, then, be cast before swine? Shall the Word be given to the ignorant, whom we know to be incapable of receiving it, much less of giving in their turn what they have received? Away with this, erase it! Let the precious ointment on the head run down upon the beard, and thence to the skirt of the garment. Let waters be drawn from the fountain, not from puddles in the street.

—"Walter Map's Account of the Waldenses," in *Heresies of the High Middle Ages: Selected Sources*, ed. Walter L. Wakefield and Austin P. Evans (New York: Columbia University Press, 1969), 203–4

hierarchy, which they deemed sinful and wicked, and had taken the place of the priesthood in administering sacraments such as baptism, Eucharist, and penance. Others had organized themselves into communities that did not adhere to the institutional and ideological characteristics Valdès desired, choosing to adopt instead a certain internal hierarchy and dedicating themselves to manual labor. Evidently, Valdès's legacy was open to differing interpretations, raising the possibility of finding different solutions to the opposition it faced.

The leading spokesman of the original Waldensianism, Durand of Huesca, took part in a theological debate held at Pamiers in 1207 in the presence of important ecclesiastical officials, including Bishop Diego of Osma, the friend and collaborator of St. Dominic of Caleruega. In its aftermath, he perceived the possibility of finally winning recognition for the essential nucleus of his religious beliefs. In fact, in 1208, Innocent III confirmed Durand and his companions in their apostolic mission, creating a new religious order known as the Poor Catholics, which actively sought to realize the dream of reintegrating the Waldensians within the ecclesiastical body. This met with some success, as groups of Waldensians in Milan and elsewhere in the Po Valley affiliated themselves with the

Poor Catholics. In parallel fashion, in 1210 a group led by Bernard Prim obtained papal authorization constituting it as a religious order named the Reconciled Poor.

Did this mean that the orthodox orientation stemming from Valdès had been definitively reaffirmed? In a certain sense, yes: the papal bulls on behalf of the Poor Catholics and the Reconciled Poor incorporated the profession of faith and proposal for a way of life that Valdès had accepted in 1180 at the synod of Lyons. However, the original apostolic impulse of Valdès and his companions was significantly modified and even obliterated. The right and duty to preach—which Valdès claimed for whoever made himself an apostle of Christ, whether or not he held clerical status—was gone, replaced by a reaffirmation that only those with papal authorization and permission from the local bishop had the right to announce the gospel. This was granted to Durand of Huesca and his associates, emphasizing their qualifications as educated clerics. Bernard Prim's group apparently struck a harder bargain with the papacy, allowing it to preserve some markedly Waldensian symbols and ideas: submission to the teachings of the only authentic teacher, Jesus Christ, and his vicar, the pope; continued use of the Waldensian sandals to indicate their status as preachers; preservation of the original mission of preaching and of recruiting new preachers.

Despite their papal approval, however, the Poor Catholics and the Reconciled Poor confronted problems and faced opposition at a local level, as well as competition from the new (and rapidly growing) mendicant orders, the Franciscans and Dominicans. The Reconciled Poor had only a brief existence. Since they did not attract any new members, they eventually joined one or another of the existing religious orders before the middle of the thirteenth century. The Poor Catholics lasted until 1256, when they were absorbed into the great mendicant family of the Augustinian Hermits.

Thus far we have followed the more conservative wing of the Waldensian movement. But what about the Waldensian mainstream, the groups that the sources refer to as Poor Men of Lyons or the Ultramontane Poor, but which in 1218 were called simply "companions of Valdès"? Their very existence indicates that Durand of Huesca's plan had failed, since only some of the Waldensians chose to reenter into

Fig. 8.2. Etching of the burning of 224 Waldensians at Toulon in 1243, by Jan Luiken (1649–1712), from the *Martyrs' Mirror* (1685), a Mennonite work in which that religious minority, persecuted by Protestants and Catholics alike during the Reformation, invoked the memory of earlier groups presented as martyred for defending the true teachings of Christ. From website: http://www.bethelks.edu/mla/holdings/scans/martyrsmirror/.

communion with Rome. After the split in 1205 and the defections of 1208–1210, to which must be added the further complication of Valdès's death, the Waldensian movement faced the challenge of resolving its internal disagreements and divisions, which may have been due in part to the sharpening of ecclesiastical repression. Thus, in 1218, the remnants of those who deemed themselves "Valdès's company" (*societas Valdesiana*) assembled at Bergamo in hope of restoring unity. The brethren from north of the Alps presented themselves as the authentic interpreters of the founder's intentions, a role that was not challenged by the Italian brethren.

A decade after his death, the figure of Valdès was again at the center of attention, but as the bearer of notably different meanings. For the northern brethren, Valdès still represented the ideal model, virtually the essential touchstone of Waldensian identity. For them,

the redemptive value of Valdès's conversion was beyond discussion: "We say that Valdès is in paradise," the northerner Pierre de Relana declared at Bergamo, adding that they could not come to an agreement with anyone who did not share that conviction. The Italian response was very different in tenor: they held that Valdès would be saved only if before his death he had done penance to God for all his sins and offenses.

The figure of Valdès here underwent its first significant reevaluation, the beginning of a process that would end by erasing the very founder of the Waldensian movement. Valdès as a historical person would be forgotten, or at least relegated to the background, even while his original ideal—the drive to become apostles of Christ—retained its force. Thus was born the myth that the Waldensians were descendants of the first apostles: a myth that was understood in various ways but always invoked to justify and legitimize people who insisted that they were preaching the true Christian faith, even though they now had to do so clandestinely. In the historical memory of inquisitors and Roman Catholic polemicists, in contrast, Valdès remained very much alive, as the founder of this most stubborn heresy. From that memory, he passed into Protestant historiography as one of the "witnesses to the truth" repressed in the dark ages of papal tyranny, even if in the little reformed world of the Italian and French alpine valleys his role as founder of the Waldensians would often be cast aside in preference for the persistent (and far more appealing and empowering) myth of the Waldensians' apostolic origins.

THE HUMILIATI: A BRIEF HERETICAL FLING

At roughly the same time that Valdès experienced his religious crisis in Lyons and decided to become a poor missionary for Christ, a similar evangelical ferment was bubbling in the Po Valley. Around 1200, the anonymous author of the *Chronicon universale* of Laon described it in these terms:

At that time there were certain citizens of Lombard towns who lived at home with their families, chose a distinctive form of

religious life, refrained from lies, oaths and law suits, were satisfied with plain clothing, and argued for the Catholic faith. They
approached the pope and besought him to confirm their way of
life. This the pope granted them, provided that they did all things
humbly and decently, but he expressly forbade them to hold private meetings or to presume to preach in public. But spurning
the apostolic command, they became disobedient, for which they
suffered excommunication. They called themselves Humiliati
because they did not use colored cloth for clothing, but restricted
themselves to plain dress.[3]

The parallels with the Poor Men of Lyons seem exact: the same desire
to have their religious commitment recognized by the Catholic leadership; the same papal sympathy for ideals of evangelical poverty; the
same rejection of the request to preach; even the same condemnation in 1184, when the decretal *Ad abolendam* lumped the Humiliati
together with the Poor Men of Lyons, excommunicating both groups
as heretics. This shared experience of condemnation encouraged a
certain solidarity between the two groups, and with other heretics as
well. In 1203, Humiliati, Poor Men of Lyons, and Cathars could be
found sharing a house in the Veronese countryside. But this was probably an extreme case.

The initial character and later developments of the Humiliati
were not heretical, nor did they take a confrontational attitude toward
ecclesiastical institutions. They were certainly autonomous, but with
full respect for the Catholic tradition and ecclesiastical hierarchy.
They were declared heretics hastily, in all probability because they
had persisted in preaching without authorization, and Innocent III
recognized that this condemnation was not at all justified. Not long
after he became pope, in late 1198 or early 1199, the Humiliati took
the first step toward reconciliation, sending two representatives to the
papal court to seek reconciliation with the Catholic Church. Innocent,
who was generally quite sympathetic to any aspect of these varied
religious movements that seemed authentically Christian, responded
by welcoming them back into the fold.

We shall pursue this reconciliation in a moment. For now, let
us return briefly to that passage in the Anonymous of Laon, which

described the Humiliati as citizens who, while continuing to live with their families, abided by strict ethical principles, gathering for collective worship and evangelical witnessing. Scholars have accepted this image, even if the origins of the Humiliati (in the absence of an individual founder) remain obscure and their later developments seem rather less unified than we have been accustomed to think. Beyond any doubt, the Humiliati originated as one of those spontaneous manifestations of lay religiosity that sprang up over the course of the twelfth century in various forms, whether linked with churches and monasteries or engaged individually or collectively in charitable works and hospital administration. We know that in the Po Valley, as early as the 1130s, some laymen left their homes in the middle of the night to attend worship services and collective prayers celebrated in monasteries.

It is entirely possible that the Humiliati shared in various of the religious initiatives that enlivened the Po Valley, dedicating themselves from the start to assorted undertakings and following equally diverse manners of life. Some remained in their own homes, but others formed small or large communities, supporting themselves by artisanal or agricultural work. Although their earliest activities may well have been located primarily in cities, as the Anonymous of Laon indicates, the Humiliati also had a documented rural presence.

Despite the condemnation of 1184, the Humiliati continued to spread. They even received papal privileges: in 1186 Urban III renewed the papal protection extended to the *fratres regulari vita professi* of San Pietro of Viboldone, though he carefully phrased the bull to avoid mentioning the term "Humiliati"—a necessary ploy, since that name carried the taint of heresy. Even Innocent III, while handling the definitive reconciliation and formal organization of the Humiliati, avoided using that term in official documents until 1211. Nonetheless, the number of Humiliati and of their establishments in Lombardy continued to grow. At the end of the twelfth century, they were found in the dioceses of Milan, Como, Pavia, Brescia, Bergamo, Piacenza, Lodi, and Cremona, and extended their reach toward Piedmont and the Veneto. Despite the papal approval of their way of life, the Humiliati themselves continued to be called heretics by some. Evidently, the old ambiguities were not resolved, at least at the local level.

Settled distrust and rancor persisted, probably among that segment of the clergy that had never grown accustomed to these new forms of religious life.

In a famous text dating to 1216, the northern prelate Jacques de Vitry praised the Humiliati for their antiheretical activities in cities like Milan, which swarmed with heretics and heresies. Already receptive to the lay religiosity of the Beguines in his native Flanders, he looked more favorably on the Humiliati, voicing his admiration for a religious order that was relatively young, active, filled with missionary zeal, and rapidly growing. He wrote: "The name of Humiliati is given to those who, leaving everything for Christ, gather in various places, live from the work of their hands, frequently preach God's Word and listen to it eagerly, perfect and firm in faith and active in works. Now this order has so multiplied in the diocese of Milan that they have constituted 150 conventual congregations, with men on one side and women on the other, not counting those who remain in their own homes."

While we certainly cannot take these numbers literally, the Humiliati were without a doubt extraordinarily diffused throughout the diocese of Milan, forming a thick network of presumably small settlements. It has been suggested that their rapid spread reflected recruitment from the lowest levels of society, among people pressed to form religious associations to defend themselves from oppression and exploitation by the early entrepreneurial "capitalists" of the wool industry (and, one might add, by the owners of agricultural estates). The hypothesis is fascinating but lacks solid documentation. On the other hand, those who object that Humiliati communities included rich citizens, nobles, and clerics do so on the basis of equally faint traces found in scattered sources.

In fact, the question of the social origins of the Humiliati and their possible ideological motivations remains open, even if it seems highly unlikely that the truly poor—that is, people born to and living in poverty—would generate a movement based on voluntary poverty for Christ. Of course, it is entirely plausible that once the Humiliati were established in some form, their ranks might have been swelled by individuals from the lower orders of society. Perhaps one of the reasons the Humiliati proved so attractive was precisely their willingness to recruit members from social groups traditionally excluded from ecclesiastical careers or the monastic profession.

Innocent III deserves credit not only for having drawn the Humiliati out of the heretical shadows but also for crafting a calibrated structure that suited the various forms of religious life present among them. Beginning in 1201, a series of bulls defined the new religious order, organizing it in a threefold structure: clergy, unmarried laymen and women living in communities, and married laypeople living in their own homes. Innocent also devised a solution for the problems of lay preaching and meetings for worship: "It shall be your custom to come together to hear the word of God every Sunday in a suitable place, where one or more brothers of proven faith and expert in religion who 'are mighty in words and deeds' [Luke 24:19], with the authorization of the bishop of the diocese, shall offer words of exhortation to those who have assembled to hear the word of God, admonishing them and encouraging them to good conduct and works of piety, in such a way that they do not speak of the articles of faith and the sacraments of the church."[4] Innocent's provisions thus removed barriers to lay preaching so long as it was limited to moral exhortation and avoided doctrinal issues. But they also sought to soften opposition to the Humiliati, since in the same bull he specifically warned bishops against obstructing the free exercise of this ethical preaching.

In short, the pope foresaw continued resistance at the local level, which in fact occurred. Despite their resolute stand against the heretics in Milan, the Humiliati—"holy men and religious women"—were themselves still considered heretics by some people fully fifteen years after obtaining papal approval. Perhaps these critics recalled that just a few years earlier, not all of the Humiliati had opted for orthodoxy.

GERARD SEGARELLI:
THE NEW APOSTLES BECOME HERETICS

In Parma in 1294, four individuals—two men and two women—were burned to death as heretics of the Order of the Apostles. In the same year, however, their leader was instead condemned to life in prison:

had Gerard Segarelli received a special deal (so to speak)? The bishop of Parma at the time was Obizzo Sanvitali, who during his long episcopate had gotten to know Gerard and his followers well. After having imprisoned him briefly, Obizzo invited Gerard to be his table companion, moved by sympathy for these new apostles as well as amusement at their leader's idiosyncratic behavior. In 1269, he even encouraged the faithful to support the Sisters of the Apostles, granting an indulgence of forty days to anyone who made a donation to them. It is not surprising that the elderly prelate would not send to the stake a man he had known for so long and perhaps even admired.

After Obizzo moved on to the archbishopric of Ravenna, Gerard was finally condemned to the stake. His execution in 1300 marked the culmination of a sweeping campaign, waged by inquisitors in the Po Valley, to put an end to a religious movement that had escaped ecclesiastical control. Forty years had passed since this young man of modest birth, an immigrant to Parma from the nearby countryside, had decided to become an apostle of Christ. In the course of those forty years, Gerard had seen the rise and fall of his religious movement—and its transformation from perfect orthodoxy into heresy as a result of ecclesiastical action.

The turning point was the decision taken by the church fathers at the Council of Lyons in 1274. The canon *Religionum diversitatem nimiam* aimed to put an end to the confusing proliferation of new orders, while at the same time confirming the crucial role of the Dominicans and Franciscans. Invoking the canon of the same name issued by the Fourth Lateran Council in 1215, the Second Council of Lyons prohibited the formation of any new order and insisted that all those that had sprung up since 1215 halt their growth, cease founding new houses, put an end to recruitment, and allow their members to transfer to one of the religious orders approved by the papacy. When Gerard and his followers refused to abide by these injunctions, their action was taken as a sign of heretical tendencies. Shortly thereafter, the process of making them into heretics began.

In March 1286, Honorius IV issued the bull *Olim felicis recordationis*. Invoking the memory of Gregory X, whose pontificate had included the Second Council of Lyons, he called on ecclesiastical authorities to seek out members of the so-called Order of the Apostles and compel them to abandon their habits or enter a recognized order; if they refused, they should be imprisoned or struck with other penalties. Four years later, Nicholas IV renewed his predecessor's provisions, establishing that judicial authority in these cases rested with the inquisitors; in 1296, Boniface VIII repeated pretty much the same declaration.

These papal pronouncements, aimed at putting into effect the conciliar canon, transformed its disciplinary concerns into doctrinal ones. Once again, those who had simply disobeyed ecclesiastical norms were cast as heterodox. The standard accusations were dusted off and launched against the Apostles: they were feigning sanctity, meeting in secret, preaching against the Roman Church, undermining the faith of simple folks. On the tactical level, the inquisitors, moving from this ideological base, would do the rest. "Because the error and the heresy of the Apostles grew ever greater with the passage of time, by authority of the holy see the inquisitors into heretical depravity began to seek out and proceed against them in Italy." So wrote the Dominican Bernard Gui, recalling the mobilization of Roman Catholic forces that followed the bulls of Honorius IV and Nicholas IV. Such was the course of events. But what inspired such rancor against people who wanted to follow an apostolic life in evangelical poverty?

For light on this question, we turn to the Franciscan Salimbene de Adam, who devoted an entire section of his famous chronicle to Gerard Segarelli and his followers.[5] This is undoubtedly the best source on the origins and development of the Apostles. We must, however, bear in mind one key consideration in reading Salimbene's treatment of the Apostles: it is not a simple report of events as they occurred, but an interpretation crafted after the fact, in keeping with the decision of the Second Council of Lyons concerning new religious orders. When the Apostles did not comply with this decision, they not only entered into disciplinary conflict with the ecclesiastical authorities but became illegitimate institutional competitors of the canonically approved Franciscans. At stake was the question of who were the "true mendicants." The Franciscan chronicler saw Gerard's interpretation of evangelical poverty and penitence as fundamentally incompatible with the cultural, religious, and existential choice he himself had made. Thus Salimbene sought not to investigate but to denounce and combat. For

A Franciscan Critic Describes the Origins of the Apostles

This group got its start in Parma. For when I was living in the convent at Parma, a priest and preacher, there came a young citizen of Parma to the convent beseeching the Friars Minor to receive him into the Order. And he was a man of base family, an illiterate layman, ignorant and foolish, by the name of Gerard Segarelli. But because they would not accept him, he used to spend the whole day in the church of the Brothers, where he thought out what he later performed in his foolish way. For there was a painting on the lamp-cover in that church, on which were depicted the Apostles with sandals on their feet and mantles around their shoulders, as they have traditionally been painted from ancient times down to the present day. There, this man sat in contemplation and, having thought out his plan, he let his hair and beard grow long, and put on the sandals and cord of the Friars Minor, because, as I said above, whoever wishes to start a new order always steals something from our Order. Moreover, he had a garment made for himself of rough gray cloth and a white cloak of course woolen fabric, which he wore thrown over his shoulders, thinking in this way to imitate the dress of the Apostles. And having sold his little house, he took the money which he received for it and stood on the stone which had been used by the podestà of Parma from ancient times as a rostrum for proclamations. Then holding his sack of money in his hand . . . he called out to the rascals who were there gambling in the square, and threw his money among them, crying out in a loud voice: "whoever wants it may have it!"

In the days when these things took place, the Friars Minor of Parma had a certain servant named Robert, a disobedient and shameless young man. . . . Gerard Segarelli persuaded this man to leave the Brothers and become his companion. . . . Then these two went day after day sauntering throughout the city in their apostolic garb to the amazement of the citizens of Parma. And, behold, suddenly their numbers multiplied to thirty, and they gathered together into a single house, eating and sleeping together.

—*The Chronicle of Salimbene de Adam*, trans. Joseph L. Baird with Giuseppe Baglivi and John Robert Kane (Binghamton, N.Y.: Medieval and Renaissance Texts and Studies, 1986), 250, 252–53

these reasons, he presents Gerard and his followers as transgressors of both religious and civil order.

The urbane and aristocratic friar Salimbene disparages the Apostles with terms such as lewd, foolish, ignoble, swineherds, cowherds, country bumpkins, hicks, idiots, beasts, ignoramuses, swindlers, thieves, and fornicators. How could people of that ilk claim to preach the gospel and put themselves on the same level as Franciscans and Dominicans? Fortunately, at the Council of Lyons, Gregory X had unified and reorganized a church order threatened by fragmentation and disintegration. Everyone was once again in their proper place, in harmony with the divine will: Franciscans and Dominicans on high, Gerard Segarelli and his Apostles at the bottom. They belonged on the bottom because they were false apostles, even hicks, and therefore ought to be relegated to wielding hoes and looking after pigs and cows—tasks that they, being lazy scoundrels, wished to avoid, even though they were worthy of nothing better than "cleaning latrines and doing other vile chores."

Disruption of the ecclesiastical and sociopolitical hierarchies and violation of the divine and human order were, for the Franciscan Salimbene, simply unacceptable. As far as he was concerned, "this order was rightly destroyed because these men served no function for the Church: they were useless for preaching or singing the Church offices; they could not celebrate Mass, nor hear confession, nor teach in the schools, nor give counsel, nor even seek out benefactors. Rather, they spent every day running through the cities seeking out women. What good they were, therefore, for the Church or the Christian people, I find it impossible to understand."

Invert these negative assertions, and we have a positive description of Salimbene's true mendicants, the Franciscans and Dominicans. The reversal holds true for the personal history of Gerard Segarelli as well. Every action that might attest the radically evangelical character of his conversion is seen instead as foolishness, a distortion of the biblical message. Gerard literally distorted that message: when he urgently echoed the scriptural call to conversion, he mispronounced the Latin *Penitentiam agite* as *Penitençagite*. What mattered for Friar Salimbene was the correct pronunciation rather than the intrinsic value, however phonetically distorted, of the evangelical call to do penance.

This Franciscan chronicler, rejecting a certain Franciscan populism, heaped scorn on Gerard's religious experience by invoking language and images derived from carnival celebrations. An actor, juggler, mime: such was this character who had deluded himself into thinking that he should take on an evangelical mission, imitating the apostles and assuming their dress and appearance as these were depicted on a lamp cover in the Franciscan church of Parma, where as a youth he had often stopped to pray. The Franciscans had not granted his wish to enter their order, in all likelihood because of his low social status. What's more, even if he had been accepted, his ignorance and crudeness would have made him barely suitable for waiting on table, washing the dishes, or begging alms from door to door. These are harsh words and ideas, coming from the pen of a follower of St. Francis. They attest to the ongoing transformation of the Franciscan order, at that time led by the most illustrious and learned scholars and eager to extract the maximum advantage from its relations with social elites.

It is thus quite logical that Gerard's earliest audiences, according to Friar Salimbene, would be a bunch of scoundrels to whom he distributed the money he got from the sale of a small parcel of land. It was equally logical that his first disciple would be a former servant of the Franciscans, "an unruly and disobedient youth." Things did not improve when his followers increased in number. Meeting in a house, his disciples acclaimed Gerard in puerile words and gestures, chanting, "Father, father, father," over and over again, like schoolchildren whose teachers make them repeat new words. On that occasion, Gerard had his companions take off all their clothes and stand against the walls, while their clothes were gathered up and bundled together in the center of the room; a woman then entered and handed out the clothing at random. Salimbene did not deny that this gesture of complete denuding, both real and symbolic, dramatically conveyed their decision to "follow naked the naked Christ." However, he emphasized the impropriety of the ceremony, conducted in the presence of a woman. In short, Salimbene used every polemical weapon available, even if he could not manage to completely conceal some positive aspects of his adversaries' religious experience.

Salimbene reported that the Apostles, being uncertain what institutional form to take, sought the advice of Master Alberto of Parma, one of the seven notaries of the Roman curia, who asked the abbot of Fontevivo in Parma to respond in his stead. The abbot laid "down the rule that they should have no convents whatsoever, but they should travel through the world with their long hair and beards, bareheaded, with their cloaks over their shoulders, simply seeking hospitality at whatever convent happened to be at hand." Evidently, the Apostles were not those "lewd, foolish, and ignoble swineherds" that Salimbene dismissed, if a papal protonotary and a Cistercian abbot had taken an interest in them, and if they had not been blocked in their endeavor but rather encouraged to go forward in the peculiar form in which they had conceived it.

Even the hostile friar-chronicler noted two positive aspects to the movement: for one thing, the Apostles had made their own the image of the apostles of Christ transmitted by the iconographical tradition;

for another, they had appeared in 1260, the year of the flagellant movement, when (according to Joachim of Fiore's vision of history) the third age of the world—the age of the Holy Spirit—was supposed to begin. Moreover, if the citizens of Parma lavished more alms on them than on the Franciscans and Dominicans, the Apostles clearly enjoyed a certain measure of success. That very success posed problems of organization and leadership. In keeping with the evangelical conviction that everyone was responsible for his or her own actions, Gerard Segarelli steadfastly refused to transform his position of personal prestige into one of institutional authority, and as a consequence the new religious movement was troubled by internal tensions and conflicts.

Around the time of the Second Council of Lyons, the Apostles were thus facing difficult times. Obizzo Sanvitali, bishop of Parma, bent under the weight of conciliar and papal provisions and finally expelled from his diocese those Apostles he "had long supported because of Friar Gerard Segarelli." Elsewhere, for a time, they continued to receive recognition and support. In Bologna the city government allocated financial contributions to the Order of Apostles right down to the 1290s. But here too the situation changed abruptly following the intervention of the Lombard inquisitors, who were eager to see that ecclesiastical norms were respected.

A Dominican Inquisitor Lists the Errors of the Heretical "Apostles"

Also, they say that only those who are called Apostles of the aforementioned sect or congregation are the Church of God. They have that state of perfection in which the first apostles of Christ lived. And they declare themselves not bound to obey any man, the supreme pontiff or any other, inasmuch as their rule, which they claim came directly from Christ, is one of freedom and of a most perfect life. . . .

Also, [they say] that no pope of the Roman Church can absolve anyone, unless he be as holy as was the blessed apostle Peter, living in complete poverty, without property of his own, and in humility, not engaging in wars or molesting anyone, but permitting everyone to live as he likes; also, that all the prelates of the Roman Church, the greater as well as the less important, from the time of St. Sylvester (for since that time they have fallen away from the mode of life of the first saints) are liars and seducers, with the exception of Brother Peter of Murrone, who took the name of Pope Celestine; also that all monastic orders and all the hierarchy of priests, deacons, subdeacons, and prelates are an offense to the Catholic faith; also, that laymen should not be and are not bound to give tithes to any priest or prelate of the Roman Church who does not observe a state of perfection and poverty like that of the first apostles; likewise, they say that no tithes should be given to any but to those who are called the Apostles, who are the poor of Christ.

—"Bernard Gui's Description of Heresies," in *Heresies of the High Middle Ages: Selected Sources*, ed. Walter L. Wakefield and Austin P. Evans (New York: Columbia University Press, 1969), 405–6

Heretics started to be burned at the stake. Gerard was imprisoned by his old friend Bishop Obizzo and finally went to the stake as the new century dawned. By then, his "religious order" was developing in new directions under the stimulus of Dolcino, a new leader destined for lasting fame.

DOLCINO OF NOVARA: THE DREAM OF SPIRITUAL REBIRTH

Dolcino—more commonly known as Fra Dolcino—was probably born in Novara or its territory; he may have been the son of a priest. We do not know his exact birth date or indeed anything else about him before 1300, the year in which he drafted the first of the three letters he addressed "to all Christ's faithful and especially to his followers." In the three or four years following, Dolcino led a semi-clandestine religious life, preaching in private meetings to partisans of Gerard Segarelli and making converts in an unknown number of localities in northern and central Italy.

The final phase of his existence began in 1304. Dolcino and some of his followers moved to the Sesia Valley, in northern Piedmont. There, strengthened by the arrival of more followers, under pressure from the troops sent against them and, perhaps, with a heightened apocalyptic expectation of the imminent end of time, his religious movement gradually became an armed resistance. The Dolcinians' troubles increased when Clement V announced a crusade against them. In March 1307, after a winter spent in the mountains, pressed by an ever tighter siege, the surviving Dolcinians were defeated. Some were killed on the spot, others captured and handed over to the inquisitors. Condemned by an ecclesiastical tribunal, Dolcino and two of his leading followers were handed over to the secular authorities for the inevitable death sentence.

Such are the bare bones of the course of events. And yet no medieval heretic has enjoyed such enduring fame as Dolcino. The reasons are many, ranging from the essentially sociopolitical to the more properly religious and owing more than a little to Dante's poetic masterpiece. In *Inferno* 28.55–60, Dolcino appears as a heretic and sower of discord, with the accent on the military rather than the religious aspect. The famous Florentine chronicler Giovanni Villani, who died in the great plague of 1348, shared this orientation, and his description fed countless interpretations of Dolcino's movement as a peasant revolt.

The ecclesiastical tradition concerning Dolcino derives above all from the brief tract about the Order of the Apostles written in 1316 by the Dominican inquisitor Bernard Gui and from the *History of Friar Dolcino the Heresiarch*, an anonymous little work attributed to a contemporary witness of the final stages of Dolcino's adventure. The anonymous *History* originated in Vercelli and reflects the interests and concerns of that local setting; ironically, its self-satisfied yet moving description of Dolcino's martyrdom unintentionally encouraged admiration for a man who fought to the bitter end and accepted death in the name of an ideal. Gui's tract is the work of a learned and dedicated man of the church. He placed the Dolcino episode in a broader framework, using information derived from his experience as an inquisitor to draw out its legal, ecclesiastical, and theological implications, all with the aim of creating a useful tool for identifying and prosecuting the Apostles.

Dolcino of Novara came to the fore after Gerard Segarelli went to the stake in Parma in 1300. In that same year, Dolcino gave a decisive spin to the religious ideas of the Apostles. Their condemnation as heretics had probably provoked personal crises and led them to rethink their beliefs. Dolcino offered a solution, influenced, perhaps, by the spread of Joachimite and pseudo-Joachimite ideas and the sharp polemics that erupted in ecclesiastical circles over the worldliness of the church. Under his influence, the Apostles grew more conscious of their identity and more coherent in their program, affecting not only their organization and ideals but also their theoretical underpinnings.

These changes emerge clearly in Dolcino's two letters of 1300 and 1303, as reported by Bernard Gui. Even though the *History* tried to present the heresiarch as a despotic leader, Dolcino did not seem to have held any leadership role. He figured rather as a prophet, a man illuminated by God to announce the swift approach of the last days. The original charismatic spontaneity of the movement did not seem to have disappeared, even if it was joined to a more complex conception of the history of salvation. The call to conversion that Gerard had issued in garbled Latin took on new urgency. The decision could no longer be deferred: one could either cling to the worldly reality that would soon pass away, with its negative connotations of irredeemable corruption, or convert to the spiritual reality that resists corruption and was about to triumph everywhere.

Dolcino knew that the fourth of the ages of the saints, in which the Holy Spirit would descend anew upon the apostles as it had in the primitive church, had begun with Gerard Segarelli and that this age would endure until the end of the world. The Apostles, as a "spiritual congregation" that lived in poverty on the model of Christ's first disciples and governed itself by bonds of fellowship (rather than external, formal, and juridical bonds), would be joined by "all the spiritual men who are in all the other orders." For all those who belonged to or supported the corrupt church, and thus were not spiritual persons, the time of chastisement and extermination was at hand.

Like other medieval apocalyptic thinkers, Dolcino drew from the Apocalypse of John and other Old and New Testament passages of eschatological character the information and symbols that allowed him to identify the signs and protagonists of the end-time of history. The events were foretold in precise stages with specific actors. Dolcino prophesied that Frederick III of Aragon, king of Sicily, would crush Boniface VIII, his cardinals, and the regular and secular clergy between 1303 and 1305. Then an age of peace would dawn, and God would place a holy pope at the head of the Apostles and, in general, of all spiritual persons. That things in fact turned out differently did not reduce the significance of Dolcino's dream of spiritual rebirth, though it seems to have encouraged a millenarian radicalization of the Apostles' eschatological expectations. Their withdrawal into the mountains drew on biblical inspiration to assume the aura of a sign of the last times, suggesting possible links between the final phase of armed struggle and Dolcino's concepts of church reform.

In his letter of 1300, Dolcino explained the Apostles' clandestine character by their need to escape persecution by the corrupt church. Once that church was destroyed—in the near future—the Apostles would resume preaching freely and publicly. In the meantime, their voluntary isolation in mountainous solitude would be the necessary period of waiting while the prophecies were being fulfilled: that is, while Frederick III was eliminating the ecclesiastical hierarchy and its supporters. The fact that this did not come about presented the Dolcinians with theoretical quandaries and practical difficulties. Because the text of the third letter, which Dolcino supposedly wrote after his adversaries had begun their military operations, has not survived, we cannot speak with any certainty on the subject. We can, however, dismiss the notion that Dolcino intended an armed revolt from the moment he withdrew into the Alpine valleys. It was to others, and not to himself and his brethren, that he ascribed responsibility for military and political action.

What is more, the guiding principles of the movement of the Apostles—imitation of the lifestyle of Christ's first disciples and apostolic poverty—could hardly inspire a resort to violence. We might recall in this connection that the Apostles believed that papal authority depended on the pope being "as holy as St. Peter," living in absolute poverty, and "not waging war nor persecuting anyone, but allowing everyone to live in liberty." It is unthinkable that the obligation to refrain from any form of coercive action could apply to the pope and not be an equally valid imperative for the Apostles.

The Dolcinians' desperate circumstances, surrounded as they were on every side, may well have forced them to take up arms rather than surrender. Alternatively, Dolcino and his followers, refusing to accept the defeat of their dream of spiritual renewal, could then have made themselves instruments of the divine plan to destroy the corrupt church, moving up the awaited emergence from clandestinity and—in response to the changed circumstances—turning their passive role into an active one, militant and military. Finally, many historians have suggested that local economic, social, and political conditions themselves transformed the peaceful Apostles into ferocious rebels. The pressures of self-defense, millenarian dreams, and peasant revolt: these are three possible explanations to be considered.

We can start with a glance at the social provenance and cultural formation of the Apostles. Dolcino had a better training in scripture and a better knowledge of history and current events than did Gerard. Dolcino shared the literate culture of the clergy, whereas Gerard communicated through symbolic gestures. The Apostolic movement thus passed from the leadership of an individual guided by his intuitions (which could be brilliant) to that of someone with the cultural capacity to develop elaborate intellectual models. Around 1300, the Apostolic movement had spread widely in northern and central Italy, in both urban and rural settings, but with some significant differences: in the cities it appealed to isolated individuals from artisan and commercial circles, whereas in the countryside it involved entire family groups of day laborers and small and middling landowners. Dolcino and his prophecies even attracted the interest of some intellectuals, including, in Bologna, a doctor of physics, a master of the notarial arts, a medical doctor, and a schoolteacher. Some of the Apostles knew Latin, engaged in debates in that language of learning, and wrote commentaries on Dolcino's manifestos. In Florence, eminent members of the aristocracy of arms and wealth supported Dolcino, even sending him money when they knew he was besieged by the inquisitors. In short, the Dolcinians belonged to social classes that were far from the lowest. What is more, individuals from all over northern and central Italy flocked to join him in the mountains of Piedmont, and it is hard to imagine that these individuals had any particular socioeconomic reason to rebel against the lords of the Alpine valleys above Vercelli and Novara.

With good reason, however, some scholars have wondered whether the Dolcinians could have resisted their attackers for almost two years without the support of the local population. The locals, in this view, would have become aware of their own state of exploitation and come to constitute the peasant wing (so to speak) of the Dolcinian movement, transposing Dolcino's religious ideology into a program for social and political struggle, albeit of a utopian character. The documents do show a limited local involvement, but at the same time they register negative reactions by the inhabitants of the Valsesia and nearby areas who had to defend themselves against raids by Dolcinians in desperate search for essential provisions. If it is difficult to see the Dolcinian episode as a form of peasant resistance, it is equally problematic to take Dolcino's ideas as an ideology of class conflict. His denunciation of the corrupt church and call to conversion did not contain any appeal against the holders of power, nor against the rich as a social class. When Dolcino lumped prelates and clerics together with "many of the people and the powerful and tyrants" as God's enemies and servants of Satan, he did not voice a class consciousness so much as chastise and denounce laypeople who supported the corrupt church and for that reason were destined to be swept away by the divine plan.

Of course, a radical religious stance might have implications for its social and political setting, and such a stance might evoke a stronger response among people already dissatisfied with the existing order. The Apostles' teachings asserted above all the right of each person to live his or her personal relationship with God according to the logic of the Gospels, which is not the logic of this world; in this sense they had the potential to upset established social relations and threaten the structures that governed those relations. Gerard Segarelli's original decision to live according to the letter of the Gospels survived in Dolcino but was complicated by apocalyptic and millenarian expectations. The movement of the Apostles thus shared a variety of elements and ideals with other proponents of evangelical poverty, such as the mendicant orders, and especially with Franciscans of rigorist orientation and Joachimite tendency. These similarities even worried the radical elements in the Franciscan order who were themselves the targets of ecclesiastical repression. For example, Angelo Clareno, one of the leading figures among the Franciscan Spirituals, went out of his way to insist vigorously that he and his followers had no contacts or relations whatsoever with Dolcino's Apostles.

The Dolcinians were left isolated. Perhaps the transformation of their apocalyptic expectations into a millenarian military campaign can best be understood not as a desperate attempt to save their lives—after all, when condemned as heretics, they could have abjured their beliefs and avoided going to the stake, yet they chose to die in the flames—but as the only way to fulfill their role in the history of salvation. Even if the prophecies concerning Frederick III had not come true, the Dolcinians could well have continued to believe firmly in the visions of their charismatic leader. What mattered was that with Gerard Segarelli, the long wait for Christ's second coming had entered the fourth stage, the era in which the church would be restored to its pristine condition at the time of the very first apostles. Whether or not the king of Sicily played the role foretold for him, this drama was approaching its inevitable climax. The biblical and apocalyptic texts on which the Dolcinians (or at least their leaders) drew contained plenty of passages that could justify or even, in those extraordinary circumstances, stimulate a resort to arms.

HERESY'S CONTRIBUTIONS TO MEDIEVAL CHRISTIANITY

The dramatic conclusion of this dream of spiritual rebirth brings to a close the story of late medieval heresy and heretics, a story of people wounded by violence and by hope. Heretics and heresy had forced the Roman Catholic Church to change; having changed, it succeeded in eliminating both heretics and heresy, in the process closing off every opportunity for experimentation or even for a certain evangelical dream. Here and there in Europe, a few Waldensians, Fraticelli, Beghards, and Beguines remained, to be joined eventually by the Lollards and Hussites. But the Hussites were an expression of national identity, in a situation with prospects that were not even imaginable in earlier centuries. The others, of necessity, survived only by hiding at the margins of society.

The beginning of the fourteenth century marked the end of two centuries of innovation in Christian life, the last froth of the great wave of reform that, starting in the second half of the eleventh century, had traversed and transformed the entire body of the church. We should not think of this movement as unified and coherent: its progress was neither uninterrupted nor linear, and the hierarchical church, headed by the papacy, had to take into account multiple contexts as it responded to its various components and diverse expressions. That response was often confrontational, encouraged, no doubt, by fear of heretics and hesitation to make radical changes in an eccle-

Fig. 8.3. Burning of a group of vagabonds accused of heresy, Paris, 1372. Ms. 677, f. 103v, Bibliotheque Municipale, Besancon, France. Photo: © Erich Lessing / Art Resource, N.Y.

siastical organism believed to be fully and perfectly developed. At the same time, however, the papacy cooperated with groups it saw as sincerely attempting to realize a life of evangelical poverty.

Genuinely Christian aspirations and violently repressive reactions mingled in a church sustained by an elaborate system of canon law, rigorous theological reflection, a powerful bureaucratic structure, and a fine strategic and tactical sense. Spontaneous and autonomous religious impulses could be expressed so long as the fragmentation of power encouraged experimentation in every field of human activity. In the last two centuries of the Middle Ages, however, political and social trends—toward the formation of political entities on a vast territorial scale, with correspondingly grand ambitions, and the steady crystallization of the social order—called for religious structures that were equally robust and certainly not for fluid aggregations of unpredictable apostles of Christ.

With church and society tightly sealed, the only spaces open to heresy were the inner world of conscience and the social fringes of marginalization. Thus ended a long historical period that had witnessed the expression, often in convulsive and confused forms, of an exceptionally vibrant culture that included the articulation of a religiosity developed self-consciously for all Christians. Its key point of reference was the text of scripture, a text that many people strove to know directly. Among those many scriptural enthusiasts were heretics who drew from the Bible spiritual nourishment and reasons for their own intellectual and moral autonomy. And that autonomy, which led them to approach the established intellectual and institutional order with a certain belligerence, provoked a chain of reactions, some of which became explosive, particularly when they encountered cultural forces oriented in a dramatically different direction. Orthodoxy emerged triumphant, but in the process a valuable religious force was lost.

FOR FURTHER READING

Andrews, Frances. *The Early Humiliati*. Cambridge: Cambridge University Press, 1999.
Audisio, Gabriel. *The Waldensian Dissent: Persecution and Survival, c. 1170–c. 1570*. Cambridge: Cambridge University Press, 1999.

Barber, Malcolm. *The Cathars: Dualist Heresies in Languedoc in the High Middle Ages.* Harlow, U.K.: Pearson Education, 2000.

Given, James B. *Inquisition and Medieval Society: Power, Discipline, and Resistance in Languedoc.* Ithaca, N.Y.: Cornell University Press, 1997.

Heresies of the High Middle Ages: Selected Sources. Translated by Walter L. Wakefield and Arthur P. Evans. New York: Columbia University Press, 1969.

Lambert, Malcolm D. *Medieval Heresy: Popular Movements from the Gregorian Reform to the Reformation.* Oxford: Blackwell, 1992.

Lansing, Carol. *Power and Purity: Cathar Heresy in Medieval Italy.* Oxford: Oxford University Press, 1998.

Merlo, Grado Giovanni. *Eretici ed eresie medievali.* Bologna: Il Mulino, 1989.

Moore, R. I. *The Origins of European Dissent.* Oxford: Blackwell, 1985.

Pegg, Mark Gregory. *The Corruption of Angels: The Great Inquisition of 1245–1246.* Princeton: Princeton University Press, 2001.

———. *A Most Holy War: The Albigensian Crusade and the Battle for Christendom.* Oxford: Oxford University Press, 2008.

Strayer, Joseph R. *The Albigensian Crusades.* Ann Arbor: University of Michigan Press, 1992.

JEWS, MUSLIMS, AND CHRISTIANS

TEOFILO F. RUIZ

CHAPTER NINE

The long and complex relationship among Jews, Christians, and Muslims in medieval Europe cannot be fully told in this short essay. Throughout the medieval West, whenever two or more religious groups coexisted in a distinct temporal and geographic space, how the dominant religious group interacted with religious minorities varied according to local circumstances. How numerous the religious minorities were influenced the nature of the relationship among these different groups, as did changing social, economic, political, and cultural contexts. Above all, the manner in which religious groups related to each other was never simple or monochrome. The nature of the relationship changed from place to place and from century to century. This was also the case with the boundaries and contours of such relations. Sometimes they were rigid and sites of strife and violence; other times the boundaries between the different religious groups were porous and allowed for exchanges and positive contacts.

In the past, the tendency has been either to describe these relationships as marked by unrelenting persecution, subordination, and rising intolerance or to depict them (in a view few would subscribe to nowadays) in somewhat idealized terms of cooperation and mutual understanding. Anecdotal accounts of friendships, intellectual partnerships, and economic bonds illuminate this latter vision of Jewish, Christian, and Muslim encounters. The literary scholar cum historian Américo Castro coined the term *convivencia* in the mid-twentieth century to describe the social and cultural fact that followers of the three religions lived in close proximity in Iberia. As deployed in the historical

How Jews Should Live among Christians— from the Laws of Alfonso X, the Wise

Jews should pass their lives among Christians quietly and without disorder, practicing their own religious rites, and not speaking ill of the faith of Our Lord Jesus Christ, which Christians acknowledge. Moreover, a Jew should be very careful to avoid preaching to, or converting any Christian, to the end that he may become a Jew, by exalting his own belief and disparaging ours. Whoever violates this law shall be put to death and lose all his property. And because we have heard it said that in some places Jews celebrated, and still celebrate Good Friday, which commemorates the Passion of Our Lord Jesus Christ, by way of contempt; stealing children and fastening them to crosses, and making images of wax and crucifying them, when they cannot obtain children; we order that, hereafter, if in any part of our dominions anything like this is done, and can be proved, all persons who were present when the act was committed shall be seized, arrested and brought before the king; and after the king ascertains that they are guilty, he shall cause them to be put to death in a disgraceful manner, no matter how many there may be.

We also forbid any Jew to dare to leave his house or his quarter on Good Friday, but they must all remain shut up until Saturday morning; and if they violate this regulation, we decree that they shall not be entitled to reparation for any injury or dishonor inflicted upon them by Christians.

—*Las Siete Partidas*, vol. 5, *Underworlds: The Dead, the Criminal, and the Marginalized,* trans. Samuel Parsons Scott, ed. Robert I. Burns, S.J. (Philadelphia: University of Pennsylvania Press, 2001), 1433–34

literature, the term has come to be laden with complex overtones and to focus on an idealized vision of these relations. In Castro's paradigmatic formulation, in Spain Jews, Muslims, and Christians lived together in relative peace, in some specific localities—Seville, Toledo, Barcelona, and other cities—engaging in significant and fruitful intellectual cooperation.

The reality, of course, lies somewhere in between. Periods of persecution and violence were interspersed with periods of relative calm. Ghettos, an early modern creation, did not yet exist, and Jews, Christians, and Muslims often shared social, physical, economic, and celebratory spaces. But, of course, not too many regions in Europe had substantial numbers of religious minorities throughout the Middle Ages. In Western Europe, Christians met and coexisted with other religious groups principally in Iberia, Sicily, and, to a lesser extent, Hungary. Jews could be found throughout most of the Christian West, but by the late thirteenth century, they had been expelled from England and some parts of southern Italy, and by the early fourteenth century, from parts of France. It is paradoxical that although Jews were not to be found at all in many parts of Western Europe after the 1320s, and Muslims rarely, except in the places indicated above, religious minorities played a heightened role in the literary and theological imaginings of Western European Christians. That is, often the fewer Jews living in an area, the greater their symbolic role or the more pejorative the literary representations that could be found of them. Think, for example, of Chaucer, who lived in a country where Jews had not been seen for at least three generations but assigned them a negative role in one of his *Canterbury Tales*.

MINORITIES IN THE CHRISTIAN WEST

It may be useful to provide a brief summary of the relations between Christians and religious minorities throughout the West before focusing on the unique circumstances found in medieval Spain. Jewish presence in some areas of Western Europe dated as far back as Roman times, and Jewish lives and activities were deeply intertwined with the rhythms of Christian observance. Throughout this period, Jews occupied a particular location in the Christian theological explanation of the world, and this had important implications for the daily life of Christians. At least in theory, Jews could not be forced to convert. Christianity itself was founded upon Jewish roots. Jesus and his disciples were Jews; Christian sacred history was inextricably linked to that of the Jews. But Jews in their stubbornness, as Christian polemicists tended to argue, had refused, and continued to refuse, to accept and worship Jesus as the Christ, the Messiah.

Early Christianity liked to posit itself as the true Israel and to claim the rich heritage of the Old Testament—as explicated in numberless homiletic texts—as its own. But the church also taught that the Jews had rejected and killed the Christ. This contradictory position—Jews as valuable ancestors, Jews as enemies of Christ—allowed for the survival of Judaism under Christian rule: the Jews were to be the indispensable witnesses to the second coming of Jesus. But it also prompted anti-Jewish sentiments and, from time to time, bouts of violence. Antagonisms were articulated in anti-Jewish legislation that sought to segregate Jews from Christians. They also led to legal measures—legitimized by pejorative representations of Jews as the killers of Jesus and blood libels about Jews as murderers of Christian children—that regulated, to the advantage of those who ruled, Jewish social and economic activities.

Fig. 9.1. Cupola of the Mezquita Mosque and Cathedral in Cordoba, Spain, erected in 961 by Umayyad caliph al-Hakam II. After the fall of Cordoba in 1236, King Ferdinand III consecrated the mosque as the city's cathedral. Photo: © Erich Lessing / Art Resource, N.Y.

Because Jews were fairly mobile, because they had entry to established Jewish communities in the East, and because Jewish relations with Muslim rulers were, on the whole, fairly good, they occupied a unique niche in the economy of the West as conduits for trade with Eastern markets (until the Italians monopolized most of these activities). As financiers they provided capital for Christian enterprises and royal governments, and they formed associations with Christian moneylenders—for whom they usually provided the public face to protect them from injunctions against lending at interest. We should not be misled, however, by the usual stereotyping of Jewish economic activities as being restricted to money lending, tax collecting, and other limited pursuits, which, although necessary for economic life, were often despised by the dominant Christian population. Variety in Jewish economic activities and lives was not restricted to places such as Iberia, Hungary, and Sicily, where Jews filled many different occupations. Even in places where their presence was not as prominent, their social and economic roles were far more complex than most general accounts have been willing to admit.

But most of all, the Jews of medieval Western Europe belonged to the kings, lords, and bishops. Their dependence on rulers was, in some respects, beneficial. It meant that most Jews enjoyed a great

deal of autonomy from their Christian neighbors and counted on the protection of those on top who benefited from taxes on Jews or from their services. But this autonomy from local rule and dependence on the Crown and lords proved to be quite prejudicial in the long run. It defined the Jews as a religious group, which in the Middle Ages had nefarious associations with ethnicity and race. It meant that Jews were inextricably tied to those in power, whether local, regional, or—eventually—national, and their fate was linked to that of the rulers and their whims. As "servants" of constituted political power, they often became alternate targets for popular opposition to the existing order. Attacking the Jews could be a way of assailing and resisting the power of kings and bishops, as was the case in southern France during the revolt of the Pastoreaux in the 1320s or throughout most of central Europe (wherever any Jews were left) during the great plague of 1347–1351.

Thus throughout most of the early and central Middle Ages, roughly from the end of the Roman Empire to the eleventh century, the treatment of Jews oscillated between neglect and persecution. It is clear, however, that the deep changes in Europe's system of values, as well as the social, economic, and political transformations that took

Fig. 9.2. Above left. Allegorical figure of the Church. Thirteenth century, Strasbourg Cathedral, France. Photo: © Foto Marburg / Art Resource, N.Y.

Fig. 9.3. Above right. Allegorical figure of the Synagogue. Thirteenth century, Strasbourg Cathedral, France. Photo: © Foto Marburg / Art Resource, N.Y.

Interrogation of a Muslim Prostitute, Mariem (1491)

She was asked with whom did she come [to Valencia]. She answered that [she came] with a procurer by the name of Cutaydal [a Muslim], whose place of origin, she said, is unknown to her.

She was asked if she is with that one [Cutaydal] freely or by compulsion. She answered that she is no longer with him, since he mistreated her; however, previously she was and came with him out of her own free will, for he had promised to make her his wife.

She was asked if he [Cutaydal] put her to work [as a prostitute] with her free consent or by compulsion. She answered that in the beginning she, the said defendant, traveled with the said Cutaydal voluntarily, for he had promised to make her his wife.

She was asked if she, the said defendant, is in the brothel voluntarily or if the said Cutaydal was forcing her to be there. And she answered that before she, the said defendant, became a prostitute, the said Cutaydal threatened her, telling her that the agents of the Lord Cardinal [of Valencia; a major landholder in the kingdom with a reputation for mistreating Muslims] would enslave her. And therefore it was decided [by Mariem and Cutaydal] that she should be sold to the noble Don Altobello [de Centelles] and that thus she would be secure [that is, safe from the Cardinal's men as Don Altobello's slave, a more benign master]. And so she was led to believe that she had been sold to Don Altobello, and thus they have put her in the brothel. And thus she has to endure being there and is there voluntarily.

She was asked if she would like to return to the custody of her husband or of her mother and return to freedom, instead of being where she is. She answered that she does not wish to return to her husband, but that she desires to return to her mother rather than being where she is.

—*Medieval Iberia: Readings from Christian, Muslim, and Jewish Sources*, ed. Olivia Remie Constable (Philadelphia: University of Pennsylvania Press, 1997), 341

place in the late twelfth and early thirteenth century, had a dramatic negative impact on Jews. As larger and more encompassing political communities began to be forged throughout the West, processes of identity formation left little room for outsiders. This affected Jews, lepers, and other marginalized groups in painful ways.

In many respects, the edicts of the Fourth Lateran Council (1215) articulated the new social and cultural anxieties sweeping the West—and the impact of the council's dispositions on Jews was felt deeply. Canon 68 required Jews to wear a distinct sign on their clothing, typically a yellow circle. By inscribing difference on the body of Jews or lepers (who were also forced to wear distinctive clothing and to separate themselves from their healthy neighbors), Christian society in the West defined Jews and other marginal people as polluted and sought to segregate them from the larger community. Fear of sexual intimacy and bodily contact between Jews and Christians drove these new attitudes. Although the council's edicts were not applied fully in many parts of Europe, as for example in Castile, they played a significant role in shaping attitudes toward Jews and led to increasingly pejorative representations of marginalized people and religious minorities.

Christians in the medieval West had long cast Muslims and Jews in a negative light. Polemical and vitriolic descriptions of both religious minorities were quite common. In the case of the Muslims, however, few Christians (except for those in the Holy Land, Iberia, Sicily, and Hungary) had ever set eyes upon one. Nonetheless, Muslims were often viewed as worthy foes and even (by the Byzantine Empire, for example) as intellectual and political equals. This was not the case with Jews, who had no state and rarely commanded arms. Violence against them was always possible. Random localized or individual violence was part of the ambivalent negotiations between Jews and Christians. Sometimes, as was the case in the wake of the first crusade, Jews in Germany lost their lives and property to the wrath of easily aroused mobs, despite the attempts of bishops and princes to protect them as valuable fiscal resources for those in power.

When combined with rising social tensions, economic changes, and the growing power of kings, these novel anti-Jewish discourses led to nefarious consequences. As elaborated in literary and polemical works, in public disputations between Christians and Jews, and in popular culture, these anti-Jewish sentiments were powerfully articulated in the early thirteenth century by the preaching of the recently founded Franciscan and Dominican orders and by the far-reaching policies of feudal kings. Royal fiscal needs and the popularity of targeting Jews led to a series of expulsions that removed Jews from entire regions of Western Europe. Some areas, such as the papal states, Germany, Hungary, and elsewhere, retained a Jewish

Fig. 9.4. Scenes from the Old Testament, ca.1350. The Hebrews crossing the Red Sea with the Egyptians in pursuit, above; Miriam the prophetess beating the timbrel and watching a group of dancing girls, below. From the Sister Haggadah, a Hebrew service book read on Passover Eve. Northern Spain. Shelfmark ID: Or 2884. Folio 16 v. British Library, London. Photo: © HIP / Art Resource, N.Y.

presence, but nowhere did medieval Christians come into contact with Jews and Muslims as frequently as they did in Iberia. It is to that special setting that we turn now.

MUSLIMS, JEWS, AND CHRISTIANS IN MEDIEVAL SPAIN

Unlike most of western medieval Europe, believers of the three religions of the Book had substantial representation in Iberia. As noted earlier, the nature of the relationship of these three groups varied according to specific time periods, social and economic contexts, and, most important, who was on top. One can identify several broad periods of interaction: (1) from the beginning of the Middle Ages, roughly coinciding with the settling of the Visigoths in the peninsula, to the Arab invasion of 711; (2) from the Muslim conquest of Spain to the collapse of the Caliphate in 1035; (3) from the beginnings of Christian hegemony to the battle of Las Navas de Tolosa; (4) from 1212 to 1391, a year of untold violence against Jews; and finally, (5) to the very end of the Middle Ages, a period marked by the expulsion of the Jews in 1492 and the forced conversion of Muslims in the first years of the sixteenth century.

The interaction of the three religious groups took place along overlapping and intersecting vectors: sporadic or frequent (depend-

Fig. 9.5. Seventh-century Visigothic church of San Juan Bautista, Baños de Cerrato, Spain. Photo: © Vanni / Art Resource, N.Y.

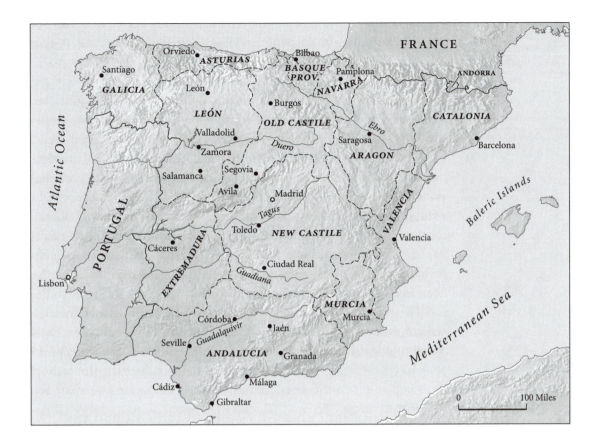

Fig. 9.6. Regions of medieval Spain.

ing on where and when) antagonism and violence, peaceful coexistence, persecution, and conversion. During some periods, as was the case in the early eighth century and in the late fourteenth, there was a great deal of fluidity between religions, and numerous conversions took place, some of them voluntarily. Religious conversion was perhaps the most significant category of relation in the long and conflictive histories of Christianity, Islam, and Judaism in the Iberian peninsula.

Visigothic Spain, 400–711

Jews could be found in Roman Spain from the first century of the Common Era (CE). Roman law and practice granted them a protected status, but the first years of Christianity as the official religion of the empire in the late fourth century coincided with the rapid decline of imperial authority in Hispania and elsewhere throughout the western empire. This did not bode well for the Jews. A series of Germanic tribes—Vandals, Suevi, and Visigoths—came into Spain during the late fourth and early fifth centuries, and by the 440s, the Visigoths had established their undisputed rule over most of the peninsula. We do not know a great deal about how Jews were treated in the early years of Visigothic rule. Iberia's new German masters were Arian Christians and as such were considered heretical by the Ibero-Roman "Catholic" population. The Visigoths therefore had to contend with diverse religious groups: orthodox Christians; "pagans" of various sorts, including those still faithful to the old imperial religion, followers of the cults banished by the emperor, and people in the northern parts of the peninsula who had never been conquered by Rome or by the Visigoths, such as Basques and Cantabrians; and Jews.

The Visigoths were not easy masters, and their own heterodoxy did not prevent them from antagonism against the Jews. Early Visigothic legislation—some of it predating Recared's conversion to Roman Christianity in 589—shows how harshly the Visigoths treated the Jews. Already in 505, Visigothic law restricted Jewish life. Jews were not allowed to marry Christians, to hold Christian slaves, to serve in municipal or royal offices, or, far more onerous, to open new synagogues. Once the Visigoths embraced orthodox Christianity, conditions for the Jews changed for the worse. Early in the seventh century, under King Sisebut, these earlier restrictions were reissued and conversion to Christianity was encouraged. Conversely, any Christian converting to Judaism was to be punished with death. The parallels between Visigothic legislation and that of the Christian kingdoms of the late Middle Ages are eerie indeed, for they point to a historical continuity in anti-Jewish measures. Although the Visigothic legislation was not very effective, it set a pattern for future Christian regulatory policies toward Jews and, later on, Muslims.

> **Penalty for Conversion to Judaism—from the Laws of Alfonso X, the Wise**
>
> Where a Christian is so unfortunate as to become a Jew, we order that he shall be put to death just as if he had become a heretic; and we decree that his property shall be disposed of in the same way that we stated should be done with that of heretics.
>
> —*Las Siete Partidas*, vol. 5, *Underworlds: The Dead, the Criminal, and the Marginalized*, trans. Samuel Parsons Scott, ed. Robert I. Burns, S.J. (Philadelphia: University of Pennsylvania Press, 2001), 1435

Muslims on Top

In 711, the growing antagonism between Christians and Jews came to an end, as did the Visigothic Empire. In swift and unexpected victories, a motley group of Berbers, Arabs, and other Muslims crossed the Straits of Gibraltar and smashed the Visigothic Empire into pieces. The victory of Islam in Iberia dramatically altered the lives of Jews and Christians in the region and reversed the traditional hegemonic relationship between Christians and other religious groups. Conditions for the Jews improved greatly. Though Islamic rulers in Spain were not always tolerant, the early centuries of Muslim rule proved particularly beneficial for Jews. Under the protection of Islam, Jews, as people of the Book, rose to positions of influence and power. Christians, especially in southern Iberia, flocked to the new religion, adopting not only Islam as their faith but also Arabic as their language and Muslim dress, dietary customs, and lifestyle. A small number of Christians fled to the northern mountains and over the next centuries waged war on Muslim lands. Other Christians remained under their new masters and, although retaining their faith, assimilated into the higher civilization of Islam, benefiting from its culture and expansive economy. A few resisted and sought martyrdom.

In general terms, one could say that when Muslims were on top in the Middle Ages, they often behaved with far more tolerance toward Christians and Jews than Christians did toward Muslims and Jews when they had the upper hand. This was the case in Egypt in the late seventh century and in Iberia in the eighth, ninth, and tenth centuries. During the early decades of Islamic rule

---

Penalties for Sexual Relations between Muslim Men and Christian Women— from the Laws of Alfonso X, the Wise

If a Moor has sexual intercourse with a Christian virgin, we order that he shall be stoned, and that she, for the first offense, shall lose half of her property, and that her father, mother, or grandfather, shall have it, and if she has no such relatives, that it shall belong to the king. For the second offense, she shall lose all her property, and the heirs aforesaid, if she has any, shall obtain it, and if she has none, the king shall be entitled to it, and she shall be put to death. We decree and order that the same rule shall apply to a widow who commits this crime. If a Moor has sexual intercourse with a Christian married woman, he shall be stoned to death, and she shall be placed in the power of her husband who may burn her to death, or release her, or do what he pleases with her. If a Moor has intercourse with a common woman who abandons herself to everyone, for the first offense, they shall be scourged together through the town, and for the second, they shall be put to death.

—*Las Siete Partidas*, vol. 5, *Underworlds: The Dead, the Criminal, and the Marginalized*, trans. Samuel Parsons Scott, ed. Robert I. Burns, S.J. (Philadelphia: University of Pennsylvania Press, 2001), 1441–42

in Spain, relations were still sufficiently fluid, and the Muslim invaders were few in number and heterogeneous enough that conversion provided significant social, economic, political, and cultural benefits. Promotion within Muslim society could also be swift for recent converts and even for those who retained their religion but cooperated with the ruling Muslim groups. Christians and Jews, though often still at odds, were placed in a new situation in which cooperation and willingness to get along were necessary, and often rewarded, under Islam. How did this work in Muslim Iberia?

Jews under Islam

Jewish communities in Lucena, Toledo, Barcelona, Tarragona, and other communities grew in number under Muslim protection. Jewish merchants, in association with Muslims or sometimes even with

Fig. 9.7. Game of chess between a Crusader and a Saracen, thirteenth century. From a Spanish manuscript of a treatise on chess by Alfonso X the Wise (1221–1284), king of Castile and Leon from 1252. The game of chess reached Spain with the Moors in the tenth century. Ann Ronan Picture Library, London. Photo: © HIP / Art Resource, N.Y.

Fig. 9.8. This Toledo synagogue, designed and built in Mudejar style by Muslim workers in the thirteenth century, became the church of Santa Maria la Blanca in the fifteenth century. Photo: © Vanni / Art Resource, N.Y.

Christians, enjoyed the advantages of Islamic control over the Mediterranean and access to profitable eastern markets. Documents from Cairo show the far-flung commercial ties joining Spanish Jews to their brethren and other trading communities in the eastern Mediterranean. Jews were also found in prominent administrative positions in eighth-century Islamic Spain and even more so after the formation of the Caliphate of Cordoba in the ninth century. Jewish communities enjoyed jurisdictional autonomy and the right to practice their faith (subject to a special tax). European Jews migrated to Spain, finding there a haven from the harsh conditions faced by Jews in Christian northern Europe. Yitzhak Baer even reports that a Christian cleric named Bodo traveled to Zaragoza, converted to Judaism, and married a Jewish woman in 839.[1]

The first Jew for whom we have sufficient information to fully trace his life and activities under Islamic rule is Abu Yusuf Hasdai ibn Shaprut (ca. 917–970). A physician at the court of Caliph Abd-ar-Rahman III (912–961), he not only treated the caliph and other Muslim notables (as well as Christian kings who came to Cordoba in search

Fig. 9.9. Conquest of Mallorca. Museu d'Art de Cataluna, Barcelona, Spain. Photo: © Werner Forman / Art Resource, N.Y.

of cures for their ailments—or, in one case, to lose weight) but also served as a special legate to Christian courts. Hasdai ibn Shaprut also collected taxes and may have supervised the activities of foreign merchants. Other scholars and teachers, such as Dunas ibn Labrat (ca. 920–980) and Judah ibn Daid Hayyuy (ca. 940–1010), contributed to the splendor of Jewish culture in this period. It was a culture deeply intertwined with Muslim or Arabic culture, and often articulated in the Arabic language.

Christians and Muslims until 1035

If Jewish life under Islam was generally peaceful and prosperous, Christians did not always fare equally well. From the mid-eighth century into the tenth, a series of small Christian realms began to emerge in the northern areas of the peninsula: the kingdoms of Asturias, Leon, Galicia, Navarre, Aragon, and Castile. These fledgling Christian kingdoms defined themselves in opposition to the Muslim Caliphate. Although they were as yet no match militarily, economically, or culturally for the sophisticated Cordoban Caliphate, they provided an alternative and a glimmer of hope for Christians in the south.

Many Christians had converted to Islam shortly after 711. There is no reason to believe that their conversions had not been sincere: in fact, although there were few conversions from Islam to Christianity, the contrary was not uncommon. Other Christians embraced many aspects of Islamic civilization without abandoning their faith. These became known as Mozarabs, developing their own language (Mozarabic), their own Christian liturgy, and a distinctive cultural identity. They prospered and even held positions of power in the caliph's court and, above all, in the city of Toledo, a place that became strongly identified with Mozarabic culture and politics. When unrest flared up, as it did in the tenth century, some Mozarabs fled to the Christian north, where they played a significant role in shaping Asturias and Leon's political culture in the tenth and eleventh centuries.

A few other Christians challenged Islamic rule directly by provocative denunciations of the religion and of Muhammad's teachings. The most notable of these forms of resistance was that of the so-called martyrs of Cordoba, a group of Christians who sought martyrdom in Cordoba in the early 800s. Although Christian authorities often condemned their actions, the martyrs, through the hagiographical

Fig. 9.10. Turks and Moors. Photo: © Giraudon / Art Resource, N.Y.

Penalty for Intercourse with a Christian Woman—from the Laws of Alfonso X, the Wise

Jews who live with Christian women are guilty of great insolence and boldness, for which reason we decree that all Jews who, hereafter, may be convicted of having done such a thing shall be put to death. For if Christians who commit adultery with married women deserve death on that account, much more do Jews who have sexual intercourse with Christian women, who are spiritually the wives of Our Lord Jesus Christ because of the faith and the baptism which they receive in His name; nor do we consider it proper that a Christian woman who commits an offense of this kind shall escape without punishment. Wherefore we order that, whether she be a virgin, a married woman, a widow, or a common prostitute who gives herself to all men, she shall suffer the same penalty which we mentioned in the last law in the Title concerning the Moors, to which a Christian woman is liable who has had carnal intercourse with a Moor.

—*Las Siete Partidas*, vol. 5: *Underworlds: The Dead, the Criminal, and the Marginalized*, trans. Samuel Parsons Scott, ed. Robert I. Burns, S.J. (Philadelphia: University of Pennsylvania Press, 2001), 1436

writings of two Cordoban Christians, Eulogius and Paulus Alvarus, who witnessed the events, became emblematic of Christian resistance to Islam. Their actions, the ideological support they garnered from some Christians, and the language of Christian chronicles written from the mid-eighth century onward—in both Muslim Spain and the Christian north—created a discourse of opposition to Muslim occupation. The 711 invasion and defeat of the Visigoths came to be seen as a catastrophe, the invaders as cruel and barbaric (even cannibals), Muhammad as a false prophet, and the teachings of the Qu'ran as a pack of lies. Admiration for, and assimilation into, Islam were tempered by these antagonistic attitudes.

As the power of the Caliphate began to wane as a result of internal dissension, growing pressure from the Christian north, and a harsher and more fundamentalist religious stance in the Muslim south, some Christians and Jews began to migrate to the Christian realms in the north, hoping either to find better opportunities to practice their religion or to benefit from the growing prosperity there. By 1035, the Caliphate fragmented into a series of small kingdoms known as the kingdoms of *taifas*, and the context in which Muslims, Jews, and Christians interacted changed.

From 1035 to 1212

The period between the collapse of the Caliphate and the early thirteenth century was marked by important changes. Some of the taifa kingdoms—those of Seville, Zaragoza, Granada, Valencia, and Murcia—prospered in spite of the growing Christian threat. Some Jews, such as the great Solomon ibn Gabirol (ca. 1020–1058), could still produce seminal works such as his *Fons vitae*, written in Arabic at Zaragoza. Maimonides (1135–1204) taught, wrote, and tended to his duties as a physician in the court of the Muslim ruler in Cordoba before migrating to Egypt in search of a less volatile society. In many respects the period between 1035 and 1085 represented a liminal period in the relationship among the three religions.

The slow process by which Christians made territorial gains at the expense of the Muslims—the so-called Reconquest—was never a simple affair. Christian gains often led to Muslim reactions, including invasions from North Africa: the Almoravids in the eleventh century, the Almohads in the twelfth. Spanish Muslims were caught in a bind. On the one hand, they did not cherish these North African invaders. The Almoravids and Almohads brought with them harsher measures, stricter interpretations of religious rules, and an end, or at least a threat, to the independence of the taifa kingdoms. On the other hand, without these invaders, the Muslim kingdoms would have become easy pickings for the Christians. One of the results of these political changes within Islamic Spain was a growing intolerance of Jews and Christians and a growing demand for a more faithful observance of Islam. That meant no wine, less flexibility, more antagonism.

Christianity in Spain underwent a similar transformation, which had dire consequences for the future. The rapid growth of the pilgrimage to Compostela in the eleventh and twelfth centuries brought numerous northern Europeans into Iberia. Cluniac monasteries rose along the pilgrimage road, and Cluniac monks began to play a significant role in the culture and politics of Iberian kingdoms. The Reconquest, which until then had been a complex process of shifting alliances and conflict over territory and tribute, became now a crusade, acquiring an ideological bent that led to growing hostility between different religious groups. Even if reality was often otherwise and Christians could pragmatically ally themselves with Muslims against Christian enemies and vice versa, a crusading discourse pervaded the writings and actions of rulers and, most of all, ecclesiastics. This gave a hard new edge to Christian attitudes toward Muslims and Jews.

This change was most obvious in Alfonso VI of Castile's conquest of Toledo in 1085. As a young exile, Alfonso had lived in the city, and his relations with the Muslim rulers of the kingdom of Toledo had been

Provisions for Converting Muslims—from the Laws of Alfonso X, the Wise

Christians should endeavor to convert the Moors by causing them to believe in our religion, and bring them into it by kind words and suitable discourses, and not by violence or compulsion; for if it should be the will of Our Lord to bring them into it and to make them believe by force, He can use compulsion against them if he so desires, since He has full power to do so; but he is not pleased with the service which men perform through fear, but with that which they do voluntarily and without coercion, and as He does not wish to restrain them or employ violence, we forbid anyone to do so for this purpose; and if the wish to become Christian should arise among them, we forbid anyone to refuse assent to it, or oppose it in any way whatsoever. Whoever violates this law shall receive the penalty we mentioned in the previous Title, which treats of how Jews who interfere with, or kill those belonging to their religion who afterwards become Christians, shall be punished.

—*Las Siete Partidas*, vol. 5, *Underworlds: The Dead, the Criminal, and the Marginalized*, trans. Samuel Parsons Scott, ed. Robert I. Burns, S.J. (Philadelphia: University of Pennsylvania Press, 2001), 1438–39

amicable and even close. His mistress, Zaida, was a Muslim woman. When he conquered the city in 1085, he granted rights to the conquered Muslims and to the many Jews who lived in the city and its territory—the largest Jewish population in Iberia. He proclaimed himself the "emperor of the three religions" and envisioned a city where the three groups could live in harmony and understanding. But the northern knights (mostly from France) who had joined the siege of the city wanted to kill all the "infidels," actions that the king had to prevent by great effort. Within days of his coming to power in Toledo, his hand was forced by his Cluniac ecclesiastical advisors. The main mosque of the city became a Christian cathedral. Faced with the king's anger against this breach, the Muslims, to avoid further conflict, acquiesced in the action. Tolerance was replaced by hostility.

As for the Jews, they fared poorly under the Almoravids and even worse under the Almohads. Although Jews continued to engage in trade and other activities in the great cities of al-Andalus, many fled to the urban centers coming into being along the road to Compostela in Castile, to Catalonia and Aragon (mostly to Barcelona, Zaragoza, and Girona), and to the new cities settled along the advancing frontier of the Reconquest (Avila, Segovia, Cuenca, and others). Jews in Christian Spain engaged in a variety of economic pursuits: from farming to mercantile activities and crafts, medicine, soldiering, money lending, and financial or fiscal occupations. As possessions of the Crown, they paid substantial taxes to the kings while enjoying autonomy from municipal jurisdiction and taxes. Jewish communities (*aljamas*) were self-governing, responsible only to royal authority. In many respects, their organization paralleled that of the Muslims living now under Christian rule, known as Mudejars: they too lived in their own self-governing communities (*morerías*), enjoying autonomy from local governments but paying a tax to the Crown. The Muslims' economic profile, however, became different. In Aragon, many of these Mudejars became a semi-servile peasant population, tied to great lords and constituting the basis of their wealth. In Castile, they could be found in agricultural labor and as small traders and craftsmen.

By the twelfth century and afterward, pejorative representations of Jews and, to a lesser extent, Muslims were on the increase, and these two groups suffered from stereotyping. The classical example is that of the *Poem of the Cid* (ca. 1206). It depicts two Jews of Burgos, Raquel and Vidas, as greedy moneylenders who, in the end, are cunningly and (in the eyes of the author) rightly deceived by the Cid. The same text, like its mid-twelfth-century predecessor the *Historia Roderici*, reflected the ambivalence of Christians toward Muslims: respected warriors, neighbors, and even friends, but also infidels and enemies. This ambivalence was particularly marked in the period when, following the demise of the Caliphate, the Christians began to make gains against the fragmented taifa kingdoms and to extort substantial tribute. Nonetheless, Christians understood the complex nature of their relations to the Muslims. In reality as in the *Poem of the Cid*, Muslims could be enemies, but they could also be friends and allies. Equals in the battlefield, they were to be treated with respect. The tide of war had not yet turned decisively in favor of the Christians, and thus certain proprieties had to be maintained. Enemy cities that surrendered were treated leniently. Rights of property and of religious practice were protected in the treaties that regulated conquest and surrender. Christians knew that harsh measures would stiffen resistance and would be returned in kind. Although ecclesiastical propaganda and literary representations often vilified Muslims and their religion, the reality on the ground was different, at least until 1212.

From 1212 to 1391

The early thirteenth century witnessed the confluence of two signal events. One was the great victory by an international Christian army over the Almohads at Las Navas de Tolosa in 1212. This victory changed the peninsular political landscape forever. After the Christian victory, the relationship between Christians and Muslims (but also between Christians and Jews) underwent a dramatic transformation. The battle for control of the peninsula was essentially over. Although Granada was not conquered for another 280 years, the Christians were now securely on top. The second development, affecting all of medieval Christendom, has already been summarized in the introduction to this essay: in 1215 the edicts of the Fourth Lateran Council also reached the Spanish kingdoms. Together with the recent victory at Las Navas de Tolosa, these edicts provided the impetus for harsher treatment and growing resentment of religious minorities.

But once again, we should not be misled into seeing any particular period as being one of either great tolerance or unrelenting persecution. Despite the establishment of Christian hegemony in the peninsula and growing church militancy and intolerance, the thirteenth and fourteenth centuries witnessed both tolerance and intolerance. At the court of Alfonso X (1252–1284) of Castile and, to a lesser extent, those of other Iberian kings in this period, Muslim, Jewish, and Christian scholars worked together in ambitious cultural programs. In fact, the court of Alfonso X, known as Alfonso the Wise, has long stood as a model of *convivencia*.

The Castilian king had an abiding interest in Arabic science and magic and promoted the work and scholarly cooperation of religious minorities. Jews also played an important role in the fiscal affairs of the kingdom. Great Muslim lords accompanied the peripatetic royal court, witnessed royal charters, and often proved to be reliable and faithful allies in Castile's internal strife. When Alfonso X fought a losing civil war against his own son, the Infante Sancho, in the late 1270s and early 1280s, he sought refuge among Andalusi princes and military support from them. Jewish and Muslim music; the artistic and architectural forms known as the Mudejar style; agricultural practices such as irrigation and vertical watermills; craftsmanship in silk, iron, and leather work; Arabic words; types of food; and forms of eating, dress, and other aspects of cultural and material life were deeply woven into Spanish society.

Forced Baptism and Attacks on *Conversos*

Heretical Mosaic depravity reigned for a long time, hidden away in corners, not daring to show itself; and it was allowed to exist through the negligence of the prelates—namely, the archbishops and bishops of Spain—who never acknowledged or denounced it to the kings or the popes as they were obliged to do.

This Mosaic heresy had its start in the year of Our Lord 1390, at the beginning of the reign of King Henry III of Castile, when the plundering of the Jewish quarter occurred as a result of the preaching of Friar Vincent Ferrer, a holy, Catholic, and learned man, of the Order of St. Dominic. At that time, Ferrer wanted to convert all the Jews of Spain through preaching and proofs from the Holy Law and Scripture, and to put an end to that obstinate, stinking synagogue. He and other preachers preached a great deal to the Jews in synagogues, churches, and fields; the Jewish rabbis, completely convinced by the Scripture of the Law and its prophecies, did not know how to reply. But they were deceived and misled by that gloss called the Talmud . . . made after the birth of Our Lord, in the year 400. . . . There were very great lies and intricate arguments in that Talmud. . . . The Jews deny the truth and are ignorant of it; thus it is said, "There is no argument against those who deny the truth."

As a result, Friar Vincent Ferrer could convert only a few Jews, and the people spitefully put the Jews in Castile to the sword and killed many, and this occurred all over Castile in a single day, Tuesday. Then the Jews themselves came to the churches to be baptized, and so they were; and very many in Castile were made into Christians. After their baptism, some went to Portugal and to other kingdoms to be Jews; others, after some time had passed, returned to being Jews in places where they were not known. Many unbaptized Jews and synagogues still remained in Castile, and the lords and kings always protected them because of their great utility.

The baptized Jews who stayed were called *conversos*; this is the origin of the name "*converso*," which means those converted to the Holy Catholic Faith. The *conversos* observed the Faith very badly . . . for the most part they were secret Jews. In fact, they were neither Jews nor Christians, since they were baptized, but were heretics, and [yet] without the Law [of Moses].

—Chronicle of Andrés Bernáldez, in Lu Ann Homza,
The Spanish Inquisition, 1478–1614: An Anthology of Sources
(Indianapolis: Hackett, 2006), 1–3

The Structures of Everyday Life

Muslims, Jews, and Christians met every day in the streets of Spanish cities and small towns: there were, after all, very few places without representatives of one or both of the religious minorities. They made purchases in each other's stores, lived close to each other (there were no ghettos in Spain), joined in mercantile and business enterprises, and benefited from the craftsmanship of others.

In early-fourteenth-century Avila, almost all the artisan trades and small shops were run by either Muslims or Jews. In a town with just over four thousand inhabitants, Jews and Muslims ran over forty different shops, including those of a locksmith, a cloth seller, weavers, painters, fruit dealers, and other essential goods and services. The Jew Mossé de Dueñas and his wife, Çid Buena, sold half of their house to the dean of the city's cathedral chapter. Two other Jews, Halaf and Alazar, sold property in Avila to the dean as well. Yuzef, a Muslim, sold his stores to a Christian. And these are only a few examples from many such activities in Avila and elsewhere.[2]

In most large Spanish medieval towns, it would have been impossible for Christians not to shop in Muslim or Jewish shops or vice versa. In addition, censuses of property and property transactions throughout the peninsula allow us an entry into how Christians, Muslims, and Jews interacted as buyers, sellers, and neighbors. In 1305, a Muslim couple, Audalia and Doña Çienso, sold their houses in Burgos to Don Pedro de Mena, a Christian and municipal official. The houses, which commanded a very high price for the period, were located on the street of Tintes (dyes) and were bounded by houses inhabited by Muslim dyers. The Muslim couple had rented one of the houses to two Jews, Vellido and Yhuda. Christians and Muslims signed as witnesses to the transaction.[3] These economic exchanges, while not necessarily engendering tolerance, provided points of contact with other people, cultures, and religions. In litigation among members of the three religions—and lawsuits were frequent—each swore on his or her own sacred book: Christians on the Bible or the Gospels, Muslims on the Qu'ran, Jews on the Torah. There was no ignorance as to what the other believed or their rituals and language of devotion.

In the Crown of Aragon, as David Nirenberg has brilliantly shown, sexual relations between adherents of the three religions were not rare, though they were often tinged with violence.[4] Though intermarriage was legally forbidden, Jews, Muslims, and Christians seduced one another, raped one another, and visited brothels where they may have had intercourse with prostitutes of another religion. The porous boundaries of sexuality brought these different groups together. So did conversion, the act that brought different religions most directly face-to-face with the beliefs of others.

So much, I fear, for the good news. The flip side of these exchanges was dark indeed. From the early thirteenth century onward until the end of the Middle Ages, the legislation of the *Cortes*, enacted at almost every meeting of these parliamentary assemblies, promoted harsh measures against the Jews and, to a lesser extent, against the Muslims. These edicts sought to segregate religious minorities from Christians, demanding types of clothing and hairstyles that would make

Fig. 9.11 The Jewish quarter of Seville. Jewish architecture developed in the Mudejar fashion, which characterized domestic building as well as resulting in several handsome synagogues. Seville, Spain. Photo: © Werner Forman / Art Resource, N.Y.

Jews and Muslims easily identifiable as such. Jews and Muslims could not serve as nannies to Christian children, and their economic activities were severely restricted. Jews suffered the most from this, as debts to them were canceled or reduced. Urban representatives to the Cortes continuously requested an end to Jewish and Muslim exemption from municipal jurisdiction and taxation. In the *Siete Partidas*, the great Roman-based legal code from the second half of the thirteenth century, the sections dealing with Jews and Muslims were particularly restrictive. In *Partida* VII, title 24, while providing the usual bans on sexual intercourse with Christians or holding Christians as slaves, evokes some of the worse aspects of anti-Jewish rhetoric, even though tempered by the requirement of proof:

Socializing and Violence
on Corpus Christi Day (1491)

On 3 June 1491, before the court of the bailiff general of the kingdom of Valencia, Mariem, widow of the murdered Abdalla Centido, and Abdalla's two sisters, Axa and Nuça, all Muslims of the village of Alacuas, with the assistance of the royal prosecutors, make the following accusations against the defendant Açen Muça, Muslim of the village of Serra.

. . . Some time ago the defendant had conceived, for no reason, great hatred, rancor, and ill will against the said Abdalla Centido, thinking about how he might kill or gravely wound him. . . . On the day of Corpus Christi —on which day is made a great celebration and ceremony of the precious blood of our [the scribe's] Lord God Jesus Christ [and] on which day many Muslims and Christians from diverse parts of the kingdom come to see the great celebration—the said Abdalla Centido, along with his wife and others from the village of Alacuas, came to the present city [of Valencia] to see the said celebration simply and without any fear of the said defendant. . . . The said defendant, knowing that the said Abdalla Centido was in the present city to see the celebration without fear of him and therefore without carrying arms, seized a large dagger and went searching for the said victim [Abdalla] in the *boçería* [pursemaking center] and other places where the Corpus Christi procession passed in order to kill him. . . .The defendant, seeing the said Abdalla Centido standing near the butcher shop of the *morería* [Muslim quarter] and watching the said procession, drew his dagger from under his cape and approached Abdalla Centido. . . . And so the said defendant . . . stabbed Abdalla Centido in the chest . . . from which the said Abdalla Centido quickly died and passed from the present life into the next. . . .

Because of the very foul deed committed by the said defendant on the person of the said Abdalla Centido, a great disturbance was caused in the present city, especially in the *boçería*, *morería*, and other places near where the said foul deed was done, inasmuch as all the [Christian] people moved to take arms against the Muslims.Were it not for the assistance of the officials of the present city, a very great inconvenience would have occurred in the present city.

—*Medieval Iberia: Readings from Christian, Muslim, and Jewish Sources*, ed. Olivia Remie Constable (Philadelphia: University of Pennsylvania Press, 1997), 338–39

And because we have heard it said that in some places Jews celebrated, and still celebrate Good Friday . . . stealing children and fastening them to crosses, and making images of wax and crucifying them, when they cannot obtain children, we order that hereafter . . . [if] anything like this is done and can be proved, all persons who were present when the act was committed shall be seized, arrested and brought before the king; and after the king ascertains that they are guilty, he shall cause them to be put to death in a disgraceful manner.[5]

Title 25 deals with Moors in only slightly kinder fashion. Although prohibitions on sexual intercourse remained, the thrust of the law was to foster gradual conversion of Muslims to Christianity and to prevent Christian conversion to Islam. The constant reissuing of these legal measures tells us that they were not easily enforced, but nonetheless something had changed for the worse.

Between the 1230s and the 1260s, the Christian kingdoms of Castile, Aragon, and Portugal conquered most of southern Iberia. By the late 1260s, only Granada remained as a Muslim outpost in the peninsula. How the Christians dealt with the conquered Muslims tells us a great deal about changing policies in dealing with religious minorities. In Castile, Muslims were expelled from Cordoba and Seville after the Christian conquests in 1236 and 1248, respectively, and, after 1264 and a Mudejar rebellion, from the countryside as well. The top layers of Muslim society had long opted for removal to either Granada or North Africa, choosing to live in exile rather than under Christian rule. Those at the bottom who had remained behind after the conquests were expelled from Andalusia. After 1264, though there were Muslims in Castilian cities and countryside in the north, few or none were found in the south. In the east the pattern of conquest was very different. Mudejars remained on the land in Aragon and Valencia, but they did so as marginalized and semi-enserfed rural labor.

As for the Jews, even those close to the king could easily find themselves in mortal danger. Alfonso X had his top Jewish fiscal agent killed, sacrificing this scapegoat to appease popular complaints about oppressive taxation. So did his son and heir, Sancho IV (1284–1296), and his grandson, Alfonso XI (1312–1350).

On the whole, as Castile and the Crown of Aragon sank into civil wars, demographic dislocations, social upheavals, and severe economic downturns, attitudes toward Jews and Muslims hardened. There were, of course, some important nuances. The antagonism against Jews was quite different from that against Muslims. Moreover, not all social groups shared equally in the hatred of religious minorities. One could say that the high nobility, clerical dignitaries, and the Crown were generally far less hostile than the lower classes. The bourgeoisie and urban middle class were in constant competition with Jews for control of financial resources, and they spearheaded the petitions against the Jews at the meetings of the Cortes. Hostility against Islam was particularly strong in frontier areas, but it frequently alternated with trade and other peaceful contacts. Sporadic outbreaks of violence against the Jews took place in Navarre in 1277, 1321, and 1328; in Girona (Catalonia) in 1285; in Castile in 1295, 1335, and 1360; and in Valencia in 1348, in the wake of the Black Death. Muslims lived throughout Christian Castile (except for the south) and Aragon, albeit in communities that were increasingly segregated and diminished in size. They served as farm labor, unskilled and skilled labor in the building trades, and craftsmen, their activities and lives becoming but a shadow of the greatness that Islam had once achieved before 1035. Only in Granada did the flame burn brightly still, though the future was ominous indeed.

1391 and Beyond

1391 was a true watershed in the relations between Christians and Jews. Social and political tensions, resulting from the political instability of the realm, had long been building, but no one could have predicted the wave of violence that swept many towns throughout the peninsula. Some cities, such as Avila, did not witness any violence, and their Jewish and Mudejar communities were not disturbed. But in the great cities of the south (Seville, Cordoba, Andujar, Baeza, and Jaén), in some of the most important urban centers of the Castilian heartland (Cuenca, Burgos, Toledo, and Palencia), in Galicia, and in the

The First Auto de Fe in Toledo (February 12, 1486)

All the reconciled went in procession, to the number of 750 persons, including both men and women. They went in procession from the church of St. Peter Martyr in the following way. The men were together in a group, bareheaded and unshod, and since it was extremely cold they were told to wear soles under their feet which were otherwise bare; in their hands were unlit candles. The women were together in a group, their heads uncovered and their faces bare, unshod like the men and with candles. Among all these were many prominent men in high office. With the bitter cold and the dishonour and disgrace they suffered from the great number of spectators (since a great many people from outlying districts had come to see them), they went along howling loudly and weeping and tearing out their hair, no doubt more for the dishonour they were suffering than for any offence they had committed against God. Thus they went in tribulation through the streets along which the Corpus Christi procession goes, until they came to the cathedral. At the door of the church were two chaplains who made the sign of the cross on each one's forehead, saying, "Receive the sign of the cross, which you denied and lost through being deceived." Then they went into the church until they arrived at a scaffolding erected by the new gate, and on it were the father inquisitors. Nearby was another scaffolding on which stood an altar at which they said mass and delivered a sermon. After this a notary stood up and began to call each one by name, saying, "Is X here?" The penitent raised his candle and said, "Yes." There in public they read all the things in which he had judaized. The same was done for the women. When this was over they were publicly allotted penance and ordered to go in procession for six Fridays, disciplining their bodies with scourges of hempcord, barebacked, unshod and bareheaded; and they were to fast for those six Fridays. It was also ordered that all the days of their lives they were to hold no public office such as *alcalde*, *alguacil*, *regidor* or *jurado*, or be public scriveners or messengers, and that those who held these offices were to lose them. And that they were not to become moneychangers, shopkeepers, or grocers or hold any official post whatever. And they were not to wear silk or scarlet or coloured cloths or gold or silver or pearls or coral or any jewels. Nor could they stand as witnesses. And they were ordered that if they relapsed, that is if they fell into the same error again, and resorted to any of the aforementioned things, they would be condemned to the fire. And when all this was over they went away at two o'clock in the afternoon.

—Henry Kamen, *The Spanish Inquisition: A Historical Revision* (New Haven: Yale University Press, 1997), 207–8

Crown of Aragon's most important cities (Valencia, Barcelona, Lérida, Palma de Mallorca, Teruel, Girona, and others), violence against the Jews erupted with unprecedented ferocity.

Owing in part to the vitriolic preaching of mendicant friars and other clerics, Jewish communities were attacked, synagogues burned, and the Jews given the choice of converting or being killed. Thousands of Jews—according to some estimates, as many as 60 percent of the roughly 200,000 Jews living in the peninsula—converted in 1391. And they continued to convert for the next two decades. Many Jewish communities were completely erased, most notably that of Burgos, the second-largest Jewish community in Spain. There the great rabbi of the city, the learned Selomah ha Levi, converted in 1390 (a year before the violence), went to Paris to study theology, returned to Burgos, and became the bishop of the city. Obviously, factors in addition to violence were at work in the Jews' massive conversions to Christianity. The opportunity for social and economic mobility, the growing attachment to secular lives, and the desire to avoid further violence all served as incentives for conversion.

Those Jewish communities that survived the pogroms of 1391 did so greatly diminished and impoverished. Withdrawing or forcibly expelled from large cities, the Jews sought refuge from the violence and the uncertainties of the time in small towns, placing themselves under the protection of lords strong and independent enough to withstand the anarchy of the period. By the fifteenth century, the Muslims too played a lesser role in the affairs of the Spanish kingdoms, though in rural Aragon and Valencia they remained an important economic and demographic presence as skilled and thrifty farmers and as a significant source of revenue for their lords. Castile's intermittent wars against Granada created a volatile frontier in the south. Raids against each other's territories, kidnapping and enslaving of the enemy, and occasional conversions helped to maintain a growing level of hostility.

Conversions represented an important aspect of the interaction of the three groups. Religious conversion is a complex and difficult topic that is not central to this narrative, but it was an important historical and religious phenomenon with an undeniable presence in the relations among Jews, Muslims, and Christians. The conversions we know best are those from either Judaism or Islam to Christianity.

Ferdinand and Isabella Expel the Jews from Spain (March 31, 1492)

You know well, or ought to know, that whereas we have been informed that in these our kingdoms there were some wicked Christians who Judaized and apostatized from our holy Catholic faith, the great cause of which was interaction between the Jews and these Christians, in the cortes which we held in the city of Toledo in the past year of 1480, we ordered the separation of the said Jews in all the cities, towns, and villages of our kingdoms and lordships and [commanded] that they be given Jewish quarters and separated places where they should live, hoping that by their separation the situation would remedy itself. . . . And since we are informed that neither that step nor the passing of sentence [of condemnation] against the said Jews who have been most guilty of the said crimes and delicts against our holy Catholic faith have been sufficient as a complete remedy to obviate and correct so great an opprobrium and offense to the faith and the Christian religion, because every day it is found and appears that the said Jews increase in continuing their evil and wicked purpose wherever they live and congregate, and so that there will not be any place where they further offend our holy faith, and corrupt those whom God has until now most desired to preserve, as well as those who had fallen but amended and returned to Holy Mother Church, the which according to the weakness of our humanity and by diabolical astuteness and suggestion that continually wages war against us may easily occur unless the principal cause of it be removed, which is to banish the said Jews from our kingdoms. . . .

Therefore, we, with the counsel and advice of prelates, great noblemen of our kingdoms, and other persons of learning and wisdom of our council, having taken deliberation about this matter, resolve to order the said Jews and Jewesses of our kingdoms to depart and never to return or come back to them or to any of them. And concerning this we command this our charter to be given, by which we order all Jews and Jewesses of whatever age they may be, who live, reside, and exist in our said kingdoms and lordships, as much those who are natives as those who are not, who by whatever manner of whatever cause have come to live and reside therein, that by the end of the month of July next of the present year, they depart from all of these our said realms and lordships, along with their sons and daughters, manservants and maidservants, Jewish familiars, those who are great as well as the lesser folk, of whatever age they may be, and they shall not dare to return to those places, nor to reside in them, nor to live in any part of them, neither temporarily on the way to somewhere else nor in any other manner, under pain that if they do not perform and comply with this command and should be found in our said kingdom and lordships and should in any manner live in them, they incur the penalty of death and the confiscation of all their possessions by our Chamber of Finance, incurring these penalties by the act itself, without further trial, sentence, or declaration.

—*Medieval Iberia: Readings from Christian, Muslim, and Jewish Sources*, ed. Olivia Remie Constable (Philadelphia: University of Pennsylvania Press, 1997), 353–55

Recently converted Jews sometimes engaged in bitter polemics against their former coreligionists. Joshua Halorqui, later known as Jerónimo de Santa Fe, even led the Christian side at the Disputation of Tortosa in the early fifteenth century. Some Muslims converted to Judaism and even to Christianity and vice versa, but Muslim conversion out of Islam was rare. On the whole, our data on conversion from Christianity to one of the minority religions is scant. The penalties for such actions were heavy indeed, and such actions required secrecy. But they did happen—above all on the Jaén frontier with Granada, where some Christians converted to Islam and fled to Muslim territory, to the shock and outrage of Christians they left behind—creating liminal spaces and zones of contact on the confessional borders.

Moreover, Jews and Muslims played special, and necessary, roles in Christian religious and secular spectacles. As David Nirenberg has shown, Jews, and sometimes Muslims, became important players in Holy Week celebrations. The Jews became the targets of ritualized violence and humiliation, but these ceremonial performances were, while dangerously exclusive, also a way to integrate religious minorities into the broader compass of Christian society. Jews and Muslims were compelled to attend the great Corpus Christi processions, serving as permanent reminders of Christian hegemony. And in a wonderful evocation of the manner in which the three religions could still coexist in ludic performances, a Castilian royal chronicle tells us of the ceremonial entrance of Princess Blanca into Briviesca in the 1440s, when she came to marry the heir to the Castilian throne. Upon entering the small town, she was received by the guilds with their *tableaux vivants*, displays, and music and by the Jews dancing with the Torah and the Mudejars with the Qu'ran, as was the custom, the chronicler tells us, when foreign princes came into the realm.[6]

THE END OF RELIGIOUS PLURALISM IN SPAIN

By the second half of the fifteenth century, a great deal of the animosity felt against Jews shifted to the *conversos*—Jews who had converted to Christianity, whether freely or under threat of violence. Conversos came in many different categories, from exceedingly well-to-do and aristocratic new converts to artisans and poor ones. Most of the upper echelons of converso society escaped both popular ire and the eventual attention of the Inquisition. The brunt of these attacks was borne by conversos living in the same old neighborhoods, preserving some rituals and customs of their ancestral religion (keeping the Sabbath, washing on Fridays, lighting candles, refusing to eat pork), and marrying endogamously.

Riots against conversos broke out in the mid-1440s, most noticeably in Toledo. In the 1460s, they swept Jaén and other locations with large converso populations, while still other localities witnessed no violence. To a large extent, the economic structure of individual towns determined the level of violence against religious minorities or against those who were thought to practice their former religion in secret (in the case of the conversos, who were Christian). Towns where the local Christian elites—the so-called Old Christians—derived their income from land rents or from transhumance sheep-raising, and where Jews, Muslims, and, later on, conversos dominated local trade, escaped most of the sectarian violence that dominated the late Middle Ages.

By 1474, the Catholic Monarchs were firmly in control of Castile and began a thorough reform of Castilian society. Their most notable achievement was the restoration of order and the centralization of power in Castile. (The Crown of Aragon was left to its own devices and allowed to continue in its complicated institutional fragmentation.) Isabella and Ferdinand were personally openly sympathetic to Jews and Muslims. Their court was populated by Jewish financial advisors and Muslim vassals. Conversos played a unique role in the court and in the cultural revival of the period. Ferdinand himself was said to descend from an aristocratic converso family. Foreign travelers journeying through Spain in the late fifteenth century often reported on the number of religious minorities at court, accusing the queen herself of being a Jewess. Nonetheless, the same accumulation of power that allowed the Catholic Monarchs to put an end to the random violence against Jews and conversos, and to formalize the campaigns against Granada, also allowed for new restrictive measures and for realm-wide policies to regulate the lives of religious minorities.

The assault on Jews, conversos, and Muslims took several forms. First, the Jews became increasingly marginalized and their economic roles diminished. By one estimate, only around 80,000 Jews were left in the peninsula by 1492. Even if that figure is a bit on the low side, this is a remarkable decline in population from the high point before the 1391 pogroms. Fiscal activities such as tax collection and tax farming came to be ever more in the hands of conversos or even Old Christians. In fact, one could argue that despite the continued presence of Jews at the royal court as treasurers and financiers, Jewish economic advantages had been transferred, to a large extent, to conversos. Moreover, those Jews who remained in the peninsula became far more observant than they had been in the past. Shaken by the events of 1391, many of those who did not convert returned to a stricter observance of Jewish law and rituals. Finally, Jews were perceived, often incorrectly, as a permanent temptation to conversos. The latter were believed to continuously fall back into Judaic practices and to observe their former religion in secret. Even if in reality by the 1470s many Jewish religious scholars had declared conversos to be non-Jews, Christians still feared conversos would welcome, and be welcomed by, the religion of their ancestors.

One answer to the alleged backsliding of the conversos was the establishment of the Inquisition. Although the Spanish Inquisition, which took shape in the late 1470s and was officially established only in 1484, came into being for a complex set of reasons, it is certainly true that in its first three decades of operation, it targeted conversos almost exclusively. To be more precise, it targeted certain groups of conversos, mostly from the middle and lower classes. Inquisitorial activities, the Catholic Monarchs' conquest of Granada in 1492, and a renewed sense of religious fervor among the Christian population led to the fateful Edict of Expulsion. On March 31, 1492, in spite of the pleas of their Jewish advisors and their offer of substantial bribes to rescind the edict, Isabella and Ferdinand ordered that Jews choose between conversion to Christianity or exile from their beloved Sefarad (the Jewish term for Spain).

The reasons behind the Edict of Expulsion, how many Jews left, how many chose to convert, and how many returned to Spain and converted after a brief exile are all topics of endless controversy among historians. The fact remains that after 1492, Jews, who had lived in the peninsula for almost a millennium and a half, who had coexisted with

Muslims and Christians, who had built beautiful synagogues and contributed to Spain's economy and culture, were no longer allowed to remain on Spanish soil as Jews and had to choose a bitter exile if they wished to practice their religion.

Muslims did not fare much better. By the early 1480s, the Catholic Monarchs had committed to annual campaigns against Granada. The purpose was no longer to exact greater tribute or to conquer a few towns but rather to bring an end to the last remnant of Muslim political autonomy in the peninsula. The war was fought over a decade, at great cost in human life and money. Surrounded by rough mountains, the Muslims in Granada mounted a stiff resistance to the Christian advance, and conversions to Islam continued along the fractured frontier. The Christian armies, mostly from Castile, took one small town at a time, one mountain pass, until Granada was encircled. On the evening of January 1, 1492, the last Muslim ruler of Granada surrendered the city to Ferdinand and Isabella. The terms of surrender—a treaty bitterly opposed by the inhabitants of the city—guaranteed the defeated Muslims their property and right to worship Islam freely. It also granted them the right to remain in the city and the countryside.

But as had been increasingly the case, the treaty was cast aside and punitive measures against the practice of Islam put into place, even though the bishop of the city, Hernando de Talavera, preferred a policy of peaceful relations and lenient treatment of the Muslims. In 1499, the Muslims rose up in arms against the occupiers in both city and countryside. The Catholic Monarchs defeated the rebels in the mountains of the Alpujarras, in the Granada hinterland, and then, in a series of edicts in 1501 and 1502, ordered the forced conversion of all Spanish Muslims. From that date, at least legally, Spain became a monolithic Christian kingdom. The practice of another religion, which had been allowed for centuries, was no longer possible.

THE AFTERLIFE OF JEWS AND MUSLIMS IN IBERIA

The edicts of 1492 and 1501–1502 did not necessarily bring an end to Jewish and Muslim life in Spain. Conversos continued to be assailed by the Inquisition for their alleged practice of Judaism. Although not every converso was a "Judaizer" (the term used by the Inquisition), there were certainly some who did continue to practice Judaism in secret. Many conversos fled Spain and the Inquisition and relocated to Italy, Amsterdam, and other places. In some cases they reverted to Judaism; in others they remained Christians. Their world was a complex and difficult one, standing as it did between two religions. As John Edwards has shown, many of them had become skeptics and what we may call today proto-atheists.[7] But conversos also integrated very well into Spanish society, especially after 1525, when the Inquisition's attention turned toward Protestants. Their untold history is one of assimilation. Some of the most signal literary figures and saints, most notably St. Teresa of Avila, were the descendants of conversos. One could not imagine the Golden Age of Spanish literature, nor the politics of the age, without their contribution.

For the Muslims the story was quite different. With only a few exceptions, the Muslims refused to assimilate. They retained their language, their customs, their diet, and their dress, and they practiced Christianity not at all. In areas of Aragon, as in the hinterland of Granada, there were entire towns inhabited by Moriscos (the name given to the Muslims who had converted to Christianity) where Islam was practiced openly. Their numbers growing by leaps and bounds, thought of by Christians as a fifth column always ready to ally with the Ottoman Turks, the Moriscos became the favored object of Christian anxieties. In the 1560s, Philip II ordered their integration into Christian society by a series of punitive and restrictive measures, including taking Morisco children into Christian homes. In 1568, the Moriscos in the Alpujarras rose up in arms once again. The war, marked by unprecedented cruelty and savagery, lasted for two years. At the end, the Moriscos were defeated and dispersed throughout Castile, their lands given to Christian settlers.

The war of the Alpujarras was only one major event in a century of persecution and violence against Moriscos in Valencia, Aragon, and elsewhere. Between 1609 and 1619, 300,000 Moriscos were expelled from Spain. Their final exile brought to an end any hope of religious pluralism in Spain, leaving a Catholicism steeped in an ideology of crusading vigor and confessional purity. Nonetheless, Jewish and Muslim culture and civilization endure in every aspect of Spanish life to this very day, and in one of those ironies of history, with the influx of immigrants from North Africa, synagogues and most of all mosques once again dot the Spanish landscape.

FOR FURTHER READING

Baer, Yitzhak. *A History of the Jews in Christian Spain.* Translated by Louis Schoffman. 2 vols. Philadelphia: Jewish Publication Society of America, 1961–1966.

Beinart, Haim. *Conversos on Trial: The Inquisition in Ciudad Real.* Translated by Yael Guiladi. Hispania Judaica 3. Jerusalem: Magnes, 1981.

Fletcher, Richard. *Moorish Spain.* New York: Holt, 1992.

Freund, S., and T. F. Ruiz. "Jews, *Conversos,* and the Inquisition in Spain, 1391–1492: The Ambiguities of History." In *Jewish-Christian Encounters over the Centuries: Symbiosis, Prejudice, Holocaust, Dialogue,* ed. Marvin Perry and Frederick M. Schweitzer. American University Studies 9. New York: P. Lang, 1994.

Gampel, Benjamin R. *The Last Jews on Iberian Soil: Navarrese Jewry, 1479–1498.* Berkeley: University of California Press, 1989.

Kamen, Henry. "The Mediterranean and the Expulsion of Spanish Jews in 1492." *Past and Present* 119 (1988): 30–55.

Meyerson, Mark D. *The Muslims of Valencia in the Age of Fernando and Isabel: Between Coexistence and Crusade.* Berkeley: University of California Press, 1991.

Nirenberg, David. *Communities of Violence: Persecution of Minorities in the Middle Ages.* Princeton: Princeton University Press, 1996.

Smith, Colin, ed. *Christians and Moors in Spain.* 2 vols. Hispanic Classics. Warminster, U.K.: Aris & Phillips, 1989.

ACCESSING
THE DIVINE

Part 5

Medieval Christianity

DOMESTIC RELIGION

DIANA WEBB

CHAPTER TEN

It might be said that Christianity began in the home. This was not just out of necessity, because the early Christians were sporadically persecuted and obliged to conceal their activities. In antiquity it was normal for the religious observances that most intimately concerned the individual worshiper to take place in his or her domestic surroundings. The Roman emperor himself had his household gods in his bedchamber. The great temples of the ancient Mediterranean and Near East were for the most part dedicated to the public or state cult and had little to do with the needs of individual worshipers, although some major sanctuaries ministered to a broader pilgrimage clientele. Christianity had its origins within Judaism, and both early synagogues and early churches were adapted from dwelling houses, as at Dura-Europos in Syria in the third century.

Nonetheless, whereas the home has always played a central role in Jewish religious practice, Christianity later followed a somewhat different path. During the fourth century, it ceased to be persecuted and moved quite rapidly from a position of official acceptance, and indeed favor, to one of monopoly. Christians, whose predecessors had been liable to persecution, became empowered to persecute not merely outright unbelievers but those within their own ranks who subscribed to false dogma. A Christian's faith had to stand up to public scrutiny.

The church was the visible embodiment of this public identity, and churches became multipurpose buildings, uniting functions that had often been kept separate in pagan practice. Not only was the consecrated host, a material memento of Christ's bodily sacrifice, kept in an honored place within the church building, the Christian equivalent of the holy of holies, but churches were built around and above the remains of the saints, the dead heroes and heroines of the faith. This fact, and the practice of burying ordinary Christians in the neighborhood of these sacred relics (although not usually within the building), contravened the ancient Roman practice of strictly separating the world of the dead from that of the living. The offensive against pagan shrines also meant that the demand for healing and problem solving was as far as possible brought under the umbrella of the church, to be satisfied by the saints, present in their bodily remains.

The church was the location for the offering of solemn prayer and the enactment of a central mystery on an altar consecrated by the presence of relics. Only qualified personnel were able to perform this ritual. Much private religious practice must have been swept away with the altars of the household gods as paganism withered, for no mere head of household could offer the sacrifice of the Mass within his own four walls. No less important than all these developments, the social and geographical expansion of Christianity to take in more and more illiterate believers had the inevitable consequence that prayer of any but the most elementary repetitive kind became less likely to be central to the lives of the mass of Christians, while the actual reading of the scriptures was a near monopoly of monks and clergy.

In the course of the early medieval centuries, Christianity thus became a religion that, so far as the mass of worshipers was concerned, was practiced in public, on licensed premises. In 1215, the Fourth Lateran Council set the seal on this development, imposing on adult Christians the minimum requirements of annual confession to the parish priest and reception of communion. At this date, with heresy flourishing in certain parts of Europe, private religion more than ever looked like clandestine and possibly erroneous religion. The faithful could derive additional nourishment from sermons, especially after the appearance of the orders of friars early in the thirteenth century, but this too was a public recreation. The basic requirements laid down in 1215 were amplified by custom and sometimes by additional regulations. In 1287, for example, the bishop of Exeter laid it down that all those age fourteen or older must make an offering at their parish church four times a year. Some of the devotional literature produced in the later Middle Ages, such as the English *Lay Folks Mass Book*, was intended to guide the believer through the central public ritual of the church, and preachers reinforced the message that this was at the heart of Christian practice.

For the mass of its practitioners, Christianity became a visual and oral culture. At no time, perhaps, was there a conscious intention that there should be levels of devotion accessible only to a social and intellectual elite, but the observable facts tended to breed an acceptance that this was the case. In the mid-fourteenth century, the Dominican friar Jacopo Passavanti could declare that there was no need for either the laity or the lower clergy (that is, the ordinary parish priests who ministered to the mass of the faithful) to know more than the bare minimum of religious formulae.[1] For those who shared his way of thinking, this was not just the outcome of history but positively desirable, a safeguard against heresy and idle questioning of the faith by the unqualified. That the brute multitude were superstitious and ignorant of their religion was a commonplace grouse, sometimes directed as much against the priests and pastors who failed to teach the flock as against the flock itself, but it often also reflected a complacent professional pessimism about the unregenerate masses. Such attitudes both stemmed from and reinforced engrained perceptions of social status.

For all this, it is possible that our picture of medieval domestic religion is fatally skewed. Perhaps there was a wealth of homemade, nonliterate, yet specifically Christian devotion (as distinct from magical or other folk practices of doubtful character) that flourished in the lower reaches of the social scale but about which we know little or nothing. The recitation of memorized prayers, the Paternoster or Ave Maria, would not have left much trace in the historical record; there may be a world of devotion here that we are unable to see clearly. There was nothing in theory to prevent ordinary Christians from surrounding themselves with religious imagery in their own homes, and many of them did indeed do so in the later medieval centuries, but such ownership was bound to be limited by material poverty. Even the more opulent medieval home would have looked to us extraordinarily bare of furniture and objects of all kinds. Before the advent of the cheap woodcut, the religious image was likely to remain, as books remained, the perquisite of the few and, of course, of the church. If

churches were the favored target of Viking raiders in the ninth century, it was for the very sensible reason that in a world short of material wealth, they contained a relatively high concentration of precious
objects. Before about 1000, furthermore, imagery was less abundant
even in churches than it would later become. The quantity of goods,
notably including devotional objects, undoubtedly increased greatly
in the later medieval centuries, but purchasing power still rationed
the possession of them.

There was, of course, always a lay elite who possessed that purchasing power and who had contact with literate culture through their
priests and chaplains, even if they themselves were not personally
literate. These advantages enabled them to import into their homes
something of the practices and paraphernalia of public worship.
There were chapels in the very greatest residences, and gradually they
penetrated the dwellings of individuals lower down the social scale.
Around 1100, a chapel was incorporated into the wonderful timber
house built over the castle of Ardres, described by the chronicler
Lambert a century later.[2] The evidence for the possession of portable
altars and private chapels multiplies, as we shall see, in and after the
thirteenth century.

Our principal focus here is on people who lived in the world and
had homes to go to when they were not engaged in their public or professional activities. We are not concerned with monks and nuns, who
inhabited specialized accommodation with distinctive architectural
features, but it is important to remember that there was an unknow-
able number of individuals, male and female, who lived a great variety
of forms of the religious life in ordinary dwelling houses or in cells
adjacent to churches. Some of the late Roman pioneers of the religious
life had remained in their own homes, in effect converting them into
monasteries of a rather loosely regulated kind. Something resembling
this expedient reappeared in the urban setting in the late Middle Ages,
with the Beguines of northern Europe, who often lived together either
in ordinary houses or in purpose-built accommodation, and the
Humiliati of northern Italy and the third orders sponsored by the friars, whose members tended to remain in their own homes. Anchorites
and anchoresses were also exceedingly numerous in medieval towns.

Few devout layfolk would have been unaware of one or more

such individuals, especially in the urban environment. They provided accessible models for those who wanted to import a little more religion into their day-to-day lives. The ordinary priest, as distinct from the monk, lived in an ordinary house and shared the social environment of his parishioners, much as the bishop usually shared the lifestyle of the lay aristocracy, living like them in large houses open to the world and ministered to by chaplains and other servants. Abbots inhabited separate lodgings in which they entertained guests lay and ecclesiastical, which the *Rule of Saint Benedict* stated to be one of their duties. Priests, bishops, and monks alike had parents and other kin in lay society with whom they remained in contact; monks had patrons and benefactors; anxious laypeople consulted pious nuns about the state of their souls. There never was a hermetic seal between the worlds of the clergy and the laity, and the seal on the monastic world was not as watertight as some would have liked it to be. With the coming of the friars, society was, so to speak, invaded by a new group of religious professionals who combined a quasi-monastic regimen with a specific mission to the laity. The thirteenth century was a crucial period in the development of lay spirituality.

There were a hundred and one ways, then, in which the knowledge of devotional practices and devotional literature could seep into the lay household.

Excerpt from Jean Gerson's Eleven Rules for His Sisters

There follows here some advice that I have provided for my five sisters who are living with their father and in accord with his will. . . .

Go to confession each week at least once and receive the body of our Lord each month.

Again, if one of you says a harsh or unpleasant word to the other, then she is to be obliged to ask for forgiveness, or else you will not eat or drink with her until she has done so.

Again, each day read aloud a part of a good book among you in order to strengthen you more and more in your holy endeavor. Consider especially carefully the books that deal with God's commandments, such as the *Summa of Vices and Virtues*, and other such treatises. . . .

Again, when you are at work, you can at times say prayers together, especially after eating, in order to remove any evil melancholy and temptation.

Again, do not sleep in the nude without having any article of clothing. What you wear should be sufficiently roomy so that it does not irritate you, or at least you should wear your slip. . . .

Again, you are to say your hours and other prayers at certain regulated times, as at matins, terce, vespers, bedtime, and at midnight, if you can get up for a while. You are to go to mass as often as this can be done, and especially on the feast days that are ordered, for these are days of obligation. The rest of the time you are to work diligently, not so much in order to gain riches as to rid yourselves of idleness, laziness and indolence, which are the mothers and causes of all evils.

—*The Mountain of Contemplation*, in Jean Gerson, *Early Works*, trans. and ed. Brian Patrick McGuire (Mahwah, N.J.: Paulist, 1998), 125–27

On the eve of the Reformation, significant differences of wealth, status, and education still limited the extent of this influence. If relatively few could read or afford to possess a prayer book or a manual of devotion, fewer still would be able to build a private chapel in their home or employ a chaplain, not to mention a staff of chaplains. The devout domestic routine of the widowed Cicely, duchess of York, the mother of two kings (Edward IV and Richard III), is well known; not only could she afford all these things, but her household arrangements were more likely to be recorded than those of a lesser lady.

It is easy, therefore, to see that for most if not all of the Middle Ages, the evidence for private religious practice comes from a restricted stratum of the population. Before 1500, the home life of the upper classes is not chronicled in the detail that memoirs, diaries, letters, and other sources make possible in later ages, but that of the lower classes is hardly chronicled at all. On the evidence we have, however, the stratum of those who lived an active religious private life enlarged and deepened in the course of the later Middle Ages, and this must be regarded as a significant indicator of the changes that overtook Western society in the last centuries before the Reformation.

We can try to follow several threads through the medieval period in our search for this domestic religiosity, among them private prayer, the use of religious books, and the presence of images, altars, and even private chapels in the home. If by 1500 there is significantly greater evidence for all these things, there are also some striking continuities, modes of behavior that were perhaps so simple and so obvious that they were bound to be widely adopted by those who had the capacity to do so.

PRAYER AND READING

At its most basic, for example, prayer required neither special equipment nor special accommodation. In the mid-ninth century, the lady Dhuoda, the wife of the nobleman Bernard of Septimania, wrote a manual of advice for her son William, anxious that he should lead the life appropriate to an educated lay noble. William was to practice the virtues, such as hospitality and charity, that befitted his rank and was to be unquestioningly loyal to his father, but his mother also described the religious practices he should adopt.

Prayer, Dhuoda emphasized, was always possible: "Offer your prayer not only in church but wherever circumstances take you." William was to call upon God as he lay quietly in his bed, but Dhuoda did not rely on him to extemporize: she probably took it for granted that prayer was best offered in words that had been reflected on and polished, such as the Lord's Prayer. The little routine that she suggested culminated in making the sign of the cross "on your forehead and over your bed," accompanied by a declaration of adoration of the cross and the invocation of God's blessing. A similar routine was to be followed "when with God's help you get up in the morning or at whatever hour the good Lord permits you do so." Furthermore William was to observe the daily canonical hours, fulfilling the requirement of Psalm 119:164, "Seven times a day I have given praise to thee." More nourishment was to be obtained from reading: "You already have books— and you will have them—in which to read, ponder, contemplate, study and understand."[3]

Presumably William was personally literate and capable of performing this reading for himself, although much medieval "reading" meant listening to someone else reading aloud. Dhuoda refers to the learned men whom William has about him who can teach him, just as she herself doubtless had clerks at her elbow; her "writing" was probably dictation to a scribe. Books were few, and good and intensive use had to be made of them. Serious reading therefore meant, as it meant for monks, the repeated perusal of a very few texts, more closely resembling prayer and meditation than we may now find it easy to imagine.

The Ménagier of Paris

I have said that morning is called matins, and this I have said because the matins ring at that hour to waken the monks to sing matins and praise to God, and not because I mean that you, dear sister, nor married women, should rise at this hour. But I intend by this to have said that at the hour when you hear the matins ring then you should pray and praise Our Lord with some intercession, prayer or orison before going to sleep again; and for this purpose you will find hereafter fit prayers and orisons. So for waking at this hour of matins or for rising at dawn I have here written two prayers to say to Our Lord and two others for Our Lady. And first there follows one for midnight, in which you thank Our Saviour for his mercy in bringing you to this hour... These orisons may you say at matins, or at your awakening at morn, or at one and the other, whilst you rise and dress, and afterwards; they are good for all these occasions, and let it be with fasting and before all other tasks.

—*The Goodman of Paris (Le Ménagier de Paris)*, trans. Eileen Power (London: Folio Society, 1992), 35–37

Some five and a half centuries after Dhuoda counseled William, a rather different advice manual was produced in France. The book written by the so-called Ménagier de Paris around 1393 was ostensibly intended as guidance both moral and practical for a very young woman married to a man well on in years (himself). The Ménagier gave a great deal of practical advice on cooking, gardening, and cleaning, but he begins with his young wife's religious conduct, "with prayer and rising [from bed]." He did not expect her to rise like a nun for matins, but when she heard the matin bell, she should praise God by saying a prayer before she went back to sleep again. Like Dhuoda, he provided some appropriate prayers, three of them in Latin with a French translation and one in French alone. (These prayers, it has been noted, are to be found in several contemporary Books of Hours.) They were to be said either on awaking or while arising and getting dressed; at all events, they were to precede any other occupation. The other end of the day was of equal concern. The Ménagier recommended that his wife should after nightfall eat or drink little or nothing and "drive all earthly and worldly concerns from your mind. Retire into a private place by yourself and away from people, to walk there and think of nothing except the mass of the following morning which you will hear at an early hour, and also of the account which you will give to your confessor of all your sins."[4]

The environment in which the Ménagier's wife practiced her religion was different from that which we can imagine for Dhuoda's William. Whether in town or country, she lived in a world organized into parishes, which, nearly two hundred years after the Fourth Lateran Council, provided the official framework for her devotions. Devout practices at home were salutary but supplementary to this duty. The Ménagier's wife had at her side in the household a Beguine called Agnes whose role was as much to manage the household as to give spiritual advice, but there is no mention of a private chapel or a chaplain. She would go to church, respectably garbed in accordance with her husband's instructions: the Ménagier devotes a section of his book to the Mass, confession, the seven deadly sins, and the virtues. At the end of this section, he expresses his confidence that she will be assisted by "the natural intelligence with which God has endowed you," her pious disposition, the preaching she heard in the parish and elsewhere, "and, besides, the Bible, the *Golden Legend*, the *Apocalypse*, the *Life of the Fathers* and certain other good books in French which I possess and which you are free to take whenever you like."[5]

Another French *paterfamilias* of the same period, Geoffroy de la Tour-Landry, endorsed the Ménagier's advice. The knight's book for his daughters was more than once translated into contemporary English and published in 1484 by Caxton. Like the Ménagier, the knight begins with religious duty and gives similar advice:

> And because the first work and labor that man or woman ought to do is to adore and worship our Lord and say his service—that is, to understand that as soon as he awakes he ought to acknowledge him for his lord and maker and himself to be his creature. . . . Then we ought to pray for them that are dead before we go to sleep, and the dead pray for them that pray for them; and also forget not the blessed and sweet Virgin Mary who night and day prays for us, and also to commend yourself to the holy saints of heaven, and when this is done, then may you well go to sleep, for this ought to be done as often as you awake. . . .
>
> In the morning, when you rise out of your bed, then enter into the service of the high lord and begin your matins. This ought to be your first work and your first labor, and when you say them, say them with good heart, and think on no other thing if you may, for you may not go two ways at once.[6]

The knight believed firmly that "hours and prayers devoutly said" were "pleasant" to God and that it was a good thing to wake often in the night to say them. At all events, his daughters were not to break their fast until they had done so. They were to hear all the masses that they could, and he strongly advised that they should fast three or four days in the week until they were married. By fasting he meant, as a minimum, abstinence from flesh: "If you fast it not to bread and water, at least take nothing that suffers death." This, as he clearly appreciated, was to surpass the church's minimum requirements, but it was simply a matter of exercising willpower and establishing good habits: "I say to you for truth that it shall be a light thing to you if you accustom yourselves therein, for it is but custom to hear mass and the service of God, to say your hours and to do all other holy works as have done these holy women, as is contained in the legends and in the lives of the saints of heaven."[7] It is a pity that the book the knight wrote for his sons does not survive; his counsels to them would have nicely complemented the examples of advice to women that we do have, as well as Dhuoda's to William centuries earlier.

The knight referred to the examples that his daughters might find "in the legend of holy confessors, of virgins and of other holy women" who had taken steps to ensure that they slept little. This implies that, like the Ménagier's wife, they had access to some devout reading matter. Another contemporary, Christine de Pizan, advised that a young girl who was waiting to be married "should especially venerate Our Lady, St. Catherine and all virgins, and if she can read eagerly read their biographies." In broad terms Christine endorsed the knight's recommendation of fasting "on certain days" and enjoined moderation in eating and drinking as a general rule. These counsels were directed at young women of a certain standing. The artisan's wife was to put her children to school so that they might learn to serve God; women of this class could follow the advice that had already been given to the upper bourgeoisie with due regard for the wealth and standing of their husbands, which, as Christine noted, varied from trade to trade.[8]

Her observations on servants and peasant women are of interest for her assumption that little in the way of religious observance could be expected or indeed demanded of them, at church or elsewhere. Both labored under severe disadvantages, although in partial compensation they were screened from many of the vices that threatened their betters. Often serving-women had been put to work at a very young age, which "prevented them from knowing as thoroughly as other people things that concern the salvation of their souls." Fasting might be quite out of the question for individuals who worked hard on a poor diet. Yet there was variation between servants, as there was between tradeswomen, and some had no excuse: "There are chambermaids with more leisure in all respects than many housewives who fast for the love of God." Christine's picture of the servant who "will be able to say her Our Fathers and her devotions" even while doing her duties recalls the description, written about a century earlier, of the Tuscan servant-saint Zita of Lucca (d. 1278), who was so intent on her prayers that her housework suffered. Both the serving-woman and the peasant might be restricted in their attendance at church. Of the latter Christine acknowledges that "you who must help the world with your labor, which is for the sustenance, life, and nourishment of every human being, cannot vacate your post or try to serve Him by making fasts, saying prayers, or going to church like other women in large towns." They should go as often as they could, pay their tithes, and "say their Our Fathers."[9]

Christine makes no explicit reference to one disadvantage the servant and the peasant labored under: their illiteracy, which she doubtless took for granted. Even the relatively affluent young girl could only study the *Lives* of the saints "*if* she could read." Catherine of Siena (d. 1380), a dyer's daughter, determinedly led a religious life in her father's home; she wanted to learn to read so that she could enlarge the range of her devotions, but she needed miraculous assistance in order to do so. The Our Fathers and Ave Marias that were within the compass of the lower social classes would have been learned by ear. The contrast with the top of the social scale is marked: Christine evidently believed that the daughter of a princess would be taught to read, and "after she knows her religious offices and the Mass, she can be given books of devotion and contemplation or ones dealing with good behavior."[10]

About the Life of Catherine of Siena

Since reference has been made to reciting the Psalms, I must tell you, reader, that this holy virgin knew how to read without being taught by human beings. I say "read"; she could never speak Latin, but she could read the words and say them properly. She told me that when she decided to learn to read so that she could say the Divine praises and the Canonical Hours, a friend of hers wrote the alphabet out and tried to teach it to her, but after spending many fruitless weeks over it she decided not to waste any more time over it and to turn to heavenly grace instead. One morning she knelt down and prayed to the Lord. "Lord," she said, "if you want me to learn to read so that I can say the Psalms and sing your praises in the Canonical Hours, deign to teach me what I am not clever enough to learn by myself. If not, thy will be done; I shall be quite content to remain in my ignorance and shall be able to spend more time in meditating on you in other ways." Then a marvel happened—clear proof of God's power—for during this prayer she was so divinely instructed that when she got up she knew how to read any kind of writing quite easily and fluently like the best reader in the world. . . . I believe that the Lord meant this to be a sign of the miracle that had taken place. From then on Catherine began to hunt for books of the Divine Office and to read the Psalms and anthems and the other things fixed for the Canonical Hours.

—Blessed Raymond of Capua, *The Life of St. Catherine of Siena*, trans. George Lamb (London: Harvill, 1960), 96–97

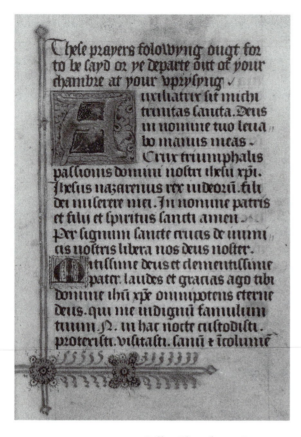

Fig. 10.1. Illuminated leaf from an Hours for Sarum Use, late fifteenth-century English, Pierpont Morgan Library Ms M. 24, fol. 14r (reproduced in Roger S. Wieck, *Painted Prayers: The Book of Hours in Medieval and Renaissance Art* [New York: Braziller, 1997], p. 12). The opening of the text declares: "These prayers folowyng ougt for to be said or ye departe out of your chambre at your uprysyng. . . ."

The Ménagier's little list gives some idea of what a man of rank in late fourteenth-century France might have on his shelves. The pragmatic literacy of the merchant and notary could also be turned to religious purposes. The Merchant of Prato, Francesco di Marco Datini, who died in 1410, had a fair number of books. The Merchant needed some prodding, notably by his friend the pious notary Ser Lapo Mazzei, who gave him a number of his books, to practice his religion and thus make the best use of the literacy he may well have valued principally for business purposes. Among the books found in a chest in the bedroom of his house in Florence on his death were a worn-out child's psalter (which may have been used for teaching reading), a *Life of the Saints*, the Gospels, the Epistle of St. James, and writings of the thirteenth-century Franciscan Jacopone da Todi and the Vallombrosan monk Giovanni delle Celle. Elsewhere Francesco had a *Life of Christ* and translations of the letters of St. Gregory and St. Jerome and of the Epistles of St. Paul. Ser Lapo once asked for the return of the loan of a copy of the *Little Flowers of St. Francis* so that he could read it to his children on winter evenings; he also urged Francesco's wife, Margherita, to provide her Book of the Hours of the Virgin with a respectable cover.[11] Margherita's literacy had been very hard-won. If images were more universally legible by young and old, the book was increasingly important, whether it was a psalter, a more or less personalized Book of Hours, a collection of saints' lives in the vernacular, or some other manual of devotion.

CHAMBERS AND IMAGES

Christine, the knight, and the Ménagier combine to give a picture of a world of devout domestic possibilities in France around the year

1400. These possibilities differed greatly according to social rank, wealth, and the different degrees of education, which to a large extent (certainly for women) depended on rank. The space and privacy that were available to individuals varied similarly. To read and to discover new prayers and other edifying material that could nourish religious fervor, one required both the access to books that was conferred by affluence and the right conditions in which to study them. Seclusion was helpful, if not essential, to prayer. Servants lacked both time and private space.

We are told that Zita of Lucca had a bed, although she rarely slept in it, but she may not have had a room to herself; when she wanted to pray, she sought out a rather ill-defined "place" in the house, from which others could see a light shining.[12] If one was fortunate enough to possess one's own bedchamber, it was a fit location for private devotions. It is impossible to state when pious layfolk first began to use their bedrooms in this way. We do not know precisely where the Emperor Otto III (d. 1001) or his successor Henry II contemplated the sumptuous prayer books that were made for them, or where the high-ranking ladies for whom Anselm late in the eleventh century composed prayers and meditations read them, probably with the assistance of their chaplains. Anselm's readers included the countess Matilda of Tuscany and Adela, the daughter of William the Conqueror, neither of whom is likely to have lacked the necessary amenities.

The bedroom was obviously the location for prayers said on retiring or on rising as the Ménagier and the knight recommended. At such moments, even if only for a very brief time, the bedchamber approximated the cell of the anchorite or those full-time religious enthusiasts who lived their lives in a domestic setting. The early thirteenth-century English author of *Ancrene Wisse*, a guide for anchoresses, imagined that the anchoress spent most of her time in a chamber that contained her bed together with her altar and images. The anchoress on first awaking was to begin the *Veni Creator Spiritus* (Come, creator spirit) "with eyes and hands lifted toward heaven, bowing forward on your knees on the bed."[13] Such women, who had taken formal vows of lifelong enclosure, were instructed in a quasi-monastic regimen in which gesture and posture had both symbolic and disciplinary significance. Pious lay individuals doubtless adopted their own routines, under direction from their spiritual advisors. In modern times, individuals praying at bedtime not infrequently do so on their knees. Zita's knees were calloused from kneeling in prayer, both at home and in church.

The religious possibilities that the friars helped to open up, especially to women, were not to everyone's liking. As a very young widow, the Florentine Umiliana dei Cerchi (d. 1247) refused remarriage and in the teeth of her father's hostility retired to a room in his tower-house, where she lived under Franciscan guidance, although she continued to go out to church and sometimes to perform errands of mercy and visit like-minded friends. She had in her chamber (which her Franciscan biographer likes to call her "cell") an image of the Virgin and Child that played an important part in her devotions; she used to keep a lamp burning by it at night. Her imitation of the saints, although she was not a nun and technically still lived "in the world," was underlined by the trouble she had from the devil, who frequently invaded her sanctum.[14]

Some other Italian saints of the period, by contrast, received support from their families, and their *Lives* include attractive, if idealized, pictures of domestic religious practice. Benvenuta Boiani, a native of Cividale del Friuli (d. 1292), ultimately became a Dominican nun, but she had earlier lived a devout life in her father's home. Her sister, with whom she shared a bedroom, seems to have been scarcely less devout; we get a glimpse of the two of them in the courtyard of the house, exclaiming at the beauty of the stars and the works of God. Benvenuta used both her bedchamber and the garden for her devotions. One evening she had retired to her room to pray when her father too left the fireside in order to complete the recitation of the Hours of the Virgin, which he performed every day. He paused outside the door of his daughter's room and to his surprise heard voices within, which proved of course to be those of heavenly visitors.[15]

A male Dominican saint, the great preacher Ambrogio Sansedoni (d. 1289), came of an aristocratic Sienese family. His early religiosity was revealed when his mother recited her Hours in his presence, and he would cry inconsolably until she gave him her prayer book. His father also played an important part: he commissioned illustrated books for the use of the saintly prodigy.[16]

The bedroom could be an important spiritual resource. When the young Catherine of Siena aroused the ire of her parents by her refusal to consider marriage, she was significantly deprived of her own bed-chamber and even forbidden to be in a room by herself with the door closed. Her parents were obviously alert to the religious possibilities of privacy. Catherine of course got her way, and when her bedroom was restored to her, she in effect converted it into a "cell" within the household that she continued to inhabit.[17] Catherine, we have seen, became literate; it is not clear whether or not Umiliana could read. The spirituality that she nourished under Franciscan direction in her chamber-cell was essentially one of prayer, meditation, and mortification. Fasting or the wearing of a hair shirt or tightly knotted girdle next to the skin were in principle available to lay devotees: Zita of Lucca wore such a girdle.

Men or women whose days were spent in worldly occupations normally had to moderate their indulgence in such practices, but for them, too, the bedchamber afforded religious opportunities. An unusually intense and personal example of this use of private space for religious purposes was recorded by the Florentine merchant Giovanni di Paolo Morelli. In 1407, bitterly reproaching himself for having allowed his young son to die a year earlier without the comforts of religion, he performed a penitential routine of his own devising in his bedroom, before a painted image of the crucifixion with the Virgin and St. John; in his nightshirt, barefoot, and with a halter round his neck like a public penitent, he addressed himself to each of the holy personages in turn, apologizing for his unpolished speech. Comfort eventually came from his personal favorite among the saints, Catherine of Alexandria, who came to him in a dream and brought him together with the soul of his dead son.[18]

As is well known, medieval living spaces tended to be unspecialized and multifunctional. Flemish fifteenth-century paintings of the Annunciation sometimes show the Virgin as a prosperous young bourgeoise anachronistically reading her prayer book not in a bedroom but in a well-appointed living room of the kind that served numerous purposes: conversation, recreation, the reception of guests, private family meals. In one such painting by a follower of Robert Campin, a woodcut image of St. Christopher is affixed to the wall above the spacious fireplace behind the Virgin. This is a visual pun, for the Virgin is about to become a "Christ bearer" as Christopher was, but it also hints at a relatively inexpensive way of importing religious imagery into the home. Another example is a panel by Petrus Christus, which shows a young man at his prayers in a room of indeterminate character with windows looking out over a landscape. He holds his prayer book, and behind him on the wall is a manuscript image of the head of Christ, of the type known as the "Veronica," with the text of the hymn *Salva Sancta Facies* ("Hail, Holy Face"), which was to be recited before or in honor of the image. Generous indulgences were available not only for seeing the Veronica itself exhibited at Rome but for devout recitation of the *Salva Sancta Facies*. That may explain its presence in the young man's room.

There were various possibilities of enjoying religious experiences vicariously and indeed even of earning indulgences in the comfort of one's own home. An interesting example occurs in the preamble to an anonymous fourteenth-century Tuscan account of the Holy Land: "These are the journeys which pilgrims who go Overseas must do to

Fig. 10.2. *The Annunciation* by Robert Campin (ca.1373–1444). Musee d'Art Ancien, Musees Royaux des Beaux-Arts, Brussels, Belgium. Photo: © Scala / Art Resource, N.Y.

save their souls and which every person can do standing in his house, thinking in every place that is written below, and in every holy place saying a Paternoster and an Ave Maria." Pilgrim narratives and so-called guidebooks may well have been thus intended not only to be of practical use to intending travelers but also to nourish imaginative "armchair travel" and even to bring secondhand spiritual benefit to the conscientious reader. The technique of visualization of holy personages and places, long familiar to the monk, was exported beyond the cloister by means of the dissemination and translation of treatises such as *Meditations on the Life of Christ*, originally written by a Tuscan Franciscan friar for the use of a nun but destined for a much wider popularity: it was translated into English by a Carthusian monk, Nicholas of Mount Grace, early in the fifteenth century.

Fig. 10.3. Petrus Christus, *Portrait of a Young Man* © National Gallery Collection. By kind permission of the Trustees of the National Gallery, London/CORBIS.

In the fifteenth century, woodcuts and later engravings clearly multiplied the possibilities of bringing into the domestic setting images accompanied by the promise of further spiritual benefits, including indulgences. It is difficult to know how deeply such images penetrated lay devotion at an earlier date. In the thirteenth century, it was certainly possible, if not common, to possess a painted Virgin and Child for one's own use, as Umiliana's image indicates. A growing wealth of artistic paraphernalia, from full-fledged carved or painted altarpieces to ivory figurines of the Virgin, gradually became available to those with a sufficient depth of purse. Around 1400, the Florentine Dominican Giovanni Dominici strongly favored the presence of religious pictures in the home. He thought it an excellent idea to surround young children with suitable representations of the Virgin and Child, of the infant Jesus, of the Massacre of the Innocents (rather alarmingly), and of the virgin saints (for girls). He also advised women to adorn their bedchambers with altars and religious images and even to encourage their little boys to play at being priests and acolytes around toy altars, imitating at home what they had seen done at church.[19]

ALTARS AND CHAPELS

It might not be enough, however, to bring religious images into the home or to possess the wherewithal for devout reading. Given the late medieval focus on the saving virtues of the sacrament, it was likely that lay householders would desire, if they could, to have it brought closer to them. They could not do as the Roman paterfamilias had done and sacrifice for themselves on their own altars, and not everyone could employ a staff of chaplains, but from at least the later thirteenth century, there is evidence for the increasing penetration of altars and even private chapels into upper-class households. The portable altar, often a small and plain object but always containing relics, was known from early times, used principally by monks and clergy on their travels. Toward 1300, the pope was granting increasingly numerous licenses to laypeople to possess such altars. At first the petitioners were men and women of the higher nobility, and their frequent journeying was clearly a relevant consideration.

Early in his pontificate, Clement V (1305–1314) made a flurry of grants to great men and women that sometimes suggest that their peripatetic households were little oases of ecclesiastical privilege. Eleanor de Montfort, countess of Vincennes, "when on a journey or afflicted by illness, may have mass celebrated in her chamber." Arthur Duke of Brittany, among others, was empowered to have Mass celebrated before daybreak when on a journey or impelled by some other necessity, and Robert Count of Flanders was permitted, for a period of five years, to have Mass celebrated "on his portable altar or in the oratory or chapel of himself or another," if he arrived in a place that happened to be under interdict. Persons of this rank had their own confessors, and the pope sometimes permitted them to hear the confessions of other members of the household; the Franciscan confessor of Henry, Earl of Lincoln, could do so when the household was "in transit."

In the course of the fourteenth century, the papal registers reveal the extension of some of these privileges to members of what in English terms might be called the gentry. On November 13, 1343, for example, Clement VI granted permission to two knights and a "donsel" (or squire) of the diocese of Exeter to use portable altars in a total of eleven named manor houses in that diocese and the neighboring diocese of Wells. Presumably these gentlemen carried their altars with them as they moved between their estates. Whether every one of these residences contained a purpose-built chapel or oratory, we do not know, but we do know that bishops were granting licenses for private chapels to persons of similar social standing already in the previous century. The sixteenth canon of a council held by the papal legate Cardinal Ottobuono Fieschi in London in April 1268 safeguarded the right of the "mother" church to the offerings made to other chapels in the parish and made it clear that this ruling applied also "whenever a private person wishes to acquire his own chapel and this is conceded for just cause." In 1287, the statutes of the bishop of Exeter specified that the sacraments were not to be administered or marriages celebrated in chapels that did not possess parochial rights, and (again) that all offerings were to go to the rector of the parish church: the same applied to "oratories constructed in some people's homes." The duty of repairing such oratories, furthermore, rested on the founders.[20]

Fig. 10.4. Mary of Burgundy and Maximillian of Austria with Virgin and Child. Cod. 1857, fol. 14v., Oesterreichische Nationalbibliothek, Vienna. Photo: Foto Marburg / Art Resource, N.Y.

Oliver Sutton, bishop of Lincoln between 1280 and 1299, granted a number of licenses for private chapels. He was often told that the petitioner's residence was a long way from the parish church and that the roads were difficult, especially in winter, or that the petitioner or members of his or her family were suffering from old age or some kind of infirmity; the bishop sometimes also acknowledged "your devotion to hearing the divine office." Sutton upheld the rights of the parish church, stipulating that the beneficiaries of his grants must attend the parish church on major feast days and certainly in the summer months. Some of these householders, although not grandees, had priests in residence with them. In 1290, Sutton told Adam

of Arden that every new chaplain on his arrival should take an oath to
the rector of the parish church to render the offerings to him, which
seems to imply such an arrangement. Other householders may simply
have invited a local or visiting priest to celebrate. Sutton insisted that
such celebrations could be for the benefit only of the grantee and his
immediate household—outsiders could not be invited to share the
experience—and that the sacrament could not actually be administered to them. (If the grantee was himself a priest, slightly different
conditions applied.) Chapels were to be inconspicuous from the outside and not distinguished by a bell tower, but they were also to be
decently appointed and had to be inspected.

Sutton clearly had occasional trouble with householders who
overstepped the mark. An extreme case was that of the oratory in
the manor house of the earl of Cornwall at Hambelden in Bucking-
hamshire, where miracles were alleged to have occurred and vigorous
action had to be taken to prevent Mass from being celebrated for the
pilgrims who were attracted by these happenings. Sometimes householders simply failed to obtain the episcopal license and had to be
reprimanded. A very detailed license for John Lord of Orby in 1298
may hint at earlier infringements, although the bishop acknowledged
John's "special devotion to the divine cult." Sutton insisted that household members, both sick and well, were to confess to the vicar of the
parish church, receive the sacraments from him, and be buried in
the parochial cemetery "as has hitherto happened"; their obligation,
and John's, to attend church on major feast days was to be strictly
observed.[21]

The rules applied by Bishop Sutton and his contemporaries
forbade not only the administration of the Eucharist but also the
performance of baptisms and nuptial blessings in nonparochial chapels. What householders gained, apart from the uplifting experience
of having a professional to recite the office for them, was something
that was increasingly valued in late medieval devotion: the ability
to behold the performance of the Mass, even if only the celebrating
priest was entitled to receive the sacrament. Soon, however, more
generous privileges were extended to the owners of private chapels.
As usual, the very great were the first to receive them. In 1352, Pope
Clement VI permitted Henry Duke of Lancaster and his wife to have

their chaplains administer the sacraments to themselves, their children, and their household and also to have nuptial blessings celebrated in their chapel.

In the course of time, similar privileges were granted to persons farther down the social scale, such as "John Baret, nobleman, esquire and lord in part of the town of Fornham All Saints" in the diocese of Norwich, who received one of a batch of such grants from Pope Eugenius IV in 1444. Fornham All Saints is in Suffolk, a little to the north of Bury St. Edmunds, of which the Barets were prominent merchants and citizens. John Baret mentions a chapel in his town house in his will, made in 1463. The house was to go to his nephew William, but he stipulated that his niece Jenette Whitwell was to have accommodation in it for her lifetime; she was given a choice of chambers, and if she chose the one above the kitchen with its adjacent drawing room, she was to "have her liberty at all lawful times to go into the chapel to say her devotions." Other late medieval English testators mention their chapels; it was common to leave the furnishings of one's chapel to one's son or other principal heir. Not all who possessed an altar had an architecturally distinct chapel: one York testator had been in the habit of setting up his altar in a parlor (*bassa camera*) of his house.[22]

John Baret is buried in the church of St. Mary in Bury, where his tomb and effigy are still to be seen. He made elaborate dispositions for his interment and left other bequests to the church, mentioning "the

---

Excerpt from the Will of John Baret of Bury St. Edmunds (1463)

Item I give and bequeath to Dame Margaret Spurdaunce of Norwich my crucifix, which is in my white chamber; and the celure [canopy] of cloth aloft, with the valance of scripture about the image, be not removed nor had away; and I will there be made at my cost such another crucifix, to be set up in the white chamber where the other crucifix was. Item I give and bequeath to the said Dame Margaret a double ring departed of gold, with a ruby and a turquoise, with a scripture written within, for a remembrance of old love virtuously set at all times to the pleasure of God. Item I give and bequeath to the said Dame Margaret a pair of beads with paternosters of gold, and on each side of the paternosters a bead of coral, and the Ave Marias of color after marble with a knob, otherwise called a tuft, of black silk, and therein a little nugget of gold, with small pearls and stones, beseeching the said Dame Margaret to pray for me, and that she will vouchsafe if her daughter live longer, then she to have the said beads after her decease.

—*Wills and Inventories from the Registers of the Commissary of Bury St. Edmunds and the Archdeacon of Sudbury*, ed. Samuel Tymms, Camden First Series 49 (1850), 36

pillar there I was wont to sit." The domestic religious practices of such a man were in no sense a substitute for his public involvement with his church, but it is clear that by the fifteenth century, layfolk who could not plead distance from the parish church had chapels in their urban residences. Cosimo de' Medici, a friend of Pope Eugenius IV and like Baret a businessman, if a grander and politically more powerful one, was among the first members of the Florentine patriciate to have a chapel in his urban palazzo. Whether in England or in Florence, private chapels seem to some extent to have shared the typical multifunctionality of other medieval apartments, being used, for example, for storing books and documents or for holding private meetings with estate officials. Cosimo used his not only for engaging in his private meditations but for receiving honored guests. At the same time, like other Florentine notables, he continued to attach great importance to the patronage he lavished on favored churches, for this was an arena in which the display of piety could reach a different and wider audience.[23]

Even if he was no Cosimo, John Baret's will is a lengthy and intriguing document that affords numerous glimpses of the possessions and the values of a pious fifteenth-century layman of some wealth and standing. It is apparent that rooms in his house other than the chapel were fitted out with religious objects; this was true also of the Medici palazzo. Dame Margaret Spurdaunce of Norwich was to have "my crucifix which is in my white chamber" but not the valance with scriptural quotations that surrounded it; the crucifix was to be replaced by another, as if Baret took it for granted that there must be one in this chamber. Dame Margaret also received a rosary (by no means the only one Baret possessed) that he hoped she would pass on to her daughter. Baret made several bequests of jewelry and other objects with religious inscriptions (his own motto was "Grace me govern"); he left to Master Robert Lawshull "my book called *Disce Mori*" (a guide to holy dying) and to Dame Joan Stones "my book of English and Latin with diverse matters of good exhortations." He must surely have possessed more books than he mentions in his will, although in the pre-print age even the most literate possessed fewer than we might expect. Baret's reading, whether for purposes of religion or of business, may have been facilitated by the silver-gilt spectacles that he bequeathed to a monk of Bury and also by the possession of a room called a "study" (one of the early instances of this word recorded by the *Oxford English Dictionary*).[24]

PUBLIC AND PRIVATE

For those who perhaps did not aspire to the possession of a private chapel, other possibilities remained open. The pious interplay between the ecclesiastical and the domestic space is vividly and touchingly illustrated in a letter written by Agnes Paston in 1453. Her neighbor Sir John Heveningham, she reported, had come home from church in good spirits and had told his wife that he would go say a little devotion in his garden before dinner. The poor man evidently had a stroke, for he felt a "fainting in his legs" and was dead "'ere noon."[25]

This little vignette may tell us quite a lot about private religion

Fig. 10.5. Chapel at Old Soar. Photo: Diana Webb.

at the end of the Middle Ages. First and foremost, it was not antithetical to public observance, but complementary. Sir John was in an elevated frame of mind, having just been to church. He wished to carry this devout state home with him and to nurture it there by private meditation. Perhaps he did not have a private chapel to go to, but perhaps anyway the sun was shining, and he was inspired to take his prayer book, or possibly just a mind well stocked with memorized prayers and meditations, into a peaceful outdoor space. Monks, after all, walked and read in the cloister; over a century earlier, both monks and laypeople liked to walk and meditate in the replanted cemetery at the great abbey of St. Albans. Indoors (failing a chapel),

Instructions for Devout Laypeople

When you dine, and also after dinner, say grace standing.

Let the book be brought to the table as readily as the bread.

And lest the tongue speak vain or hurtful things, let there be reading, now by one, now by another, and by your children as soon as they can read, and think of the wicked Dives [the rich man], tormented in hell in his tongue more than in any other members.

Let the family be silent at table, and always, as far as is possible.

Expound something in the vernacular which may edify your wife and others.

When there is no reading, have your meditations; and let there be these three at least this year, that is to say "Hail Mary," "Thou who hast made me, have mercy upon us and upon me," "In the name of the Father and of the Son and of the Holy Ghost may we be delivered Amen."

You can make a cross on the table out of five bread-crumbs; but do not let anyone see this, except your wife; and the more silent and virtuous she is, the more heartily you should love her in Christ.

After grace, said standing, go to that secret place, and send for William Bonet or Sir William Trimenel or others as you please, and confer with them there until vespers.

—W. A. Pantin, "Instructions for a Devout and Literate Layman," in *Medieval Learning and Literature: Essays Presented to Richard William Hunt,* ed. J. J. G. Alexander and M. T. Gibson (Oxford: Clarendon, 1976), 398–400

the bedchamber, or even an oriel window, might provide the desired peace and quiet.

Sir John Heveningham did not live long enough to take his dinner. If he had done so, and if he had followed some anonymous counsels that were offered to a contemporary "devout and literate layman," perhaps a London citizen, he would have stood for grace and would have kept silence at the table except for reading by his children, perhaps now and then breaking his own silence to expound something edifying in the vernacular. To conduct a private dinner in this manner was to import monastic decorum into the domestic space. This "devout layman" was given one curious piece of advice: he might make a cross on the table out of five crumbs of bread, but only his wife should see, and she should earn his love by making no comment.

This wife was a pious but passive onlooker. Many women led relatively secluded lives, centered on the household, which afforded them opportunities to make good use of what leisure and literacy they possessed. They also had a special responsibility for the upbringing of their daughters and of their sons at least when young; thereby they achieved an influence that, as Dhuoda clearly hoped, might prove enduring. The "devout layman," John Baret, Sir John Heveningham, and the father of Benvenuta Boiani all serve to remind us, however, that domestic religion was not an exclusively female preserve. As householders, husbands, and fathers, men too had opportunities, and indeed responsibilities, to direct and influence their family and their subordinates, and if they were devout, they took them to the benefit of their own souls. Erasmus later envisaged the perfect pilgrimage as being that of the paterfamilias going from room to room of his house seeing to the welfare of all its inhabitants. The prosperous widow, like Cicely, Duchess of York, might take on something of that role inasmuch as she had the direction of a household.

The domestic religiosity that has been evoked in this chapter was consciously orthodox in character and obedient to public norms; it was encouraged by churchmen of equally unquestionable orthodoxy. John Baret had an extensive devout acquaintance, lay and ecclesiastical; his only legitimate son became a monk of Bury, and he remembered monks, clergy, and laymen and laywomen in his will. He well illustrates the interplay between the world of the professed religious and that of the pious layperson, which, despite the theoretical separation of the cloister from the world, always characterized medieval society. The development of lay piety and an educated laity was in part an outcome of this interrelationship. That development certainly enlarged the possibility of the exercise of private judgment, which might be critical of the church and the clergy, but to think it inevitable that the outcome should be the Protestant Reformation is another matter. Later forms of Catholic domestic piety can equally well trace their ancestry to the beliefs and practices of men and women who, especially after the twelfth century, lived in a more urbanized setting, a more complex economy, and a society more deeply penetrated by literacy.

FOR FURTHER READING

Armstrong, C. A. J. "The Piety of Cicely, Duchess of York." In *England, France, and Burgundy in the Fifteenth Century*. History Series 16. London: Hambledon, 1983.

Dhuoda. *Handbook for Her Warrior Son*. Translated and edited by M. Thiébaux. Cambridge: Cambridge University Press, 1998.

Nuechterlein, Jeanne. "The Domesticity of Sacred Space in the Fifteenth-Century Netherlands." In *Defining the Holy: Sacred Space in Medieval and Early Modern Europe*, ed. Andrew Spicer and Sarah Hamilton, 49–79. Aldershot, U.K.: Ashgate, 2005.

Pantin, W. A. "Instructions for a Devout and Literate Layman." In *Medieval Learning and Literature: Essays Presented to Richard William Hunt*, ed. J. J. G. Alexander and M. T. Gibson, 398–422. Oxford: Clarendon, 1976.

Van Os, Henk. *The Art of Devotion in the Late Middle Ages in Europe, 1300–1500*. Princeton: Princeton University Press, 1994.

Webb, Diana. "Domestic Space and Devotion in the Middle Ages." In *Defining the Holy: Sacred Space in Medieval and Early Modern Europe*, ed. Andrew Spicer and Sarah Hamilton, 27–47. Aldershot, U.K.: Ashgate, 2005.

————. "Woman and Home: The Domestic Setting of Late Medieval Spirituality." In *Women and the Church: Papers Read at the 1989 Summer Meeting and the 1990 Winter Meeting of the Ecclesiastical History Society*, ed. W. J. Sheils and Diana Wood, 159–73. Studies in Church History 27. Oxford: Basil Blackwell for the Ecclesiastical History Society, 1990.

PARISH LIFE

CHAPTER ELEVEN

Religious life for medieval Christians was predominantly a communal experience. They practiced their faith in the context of a parish, the basic unit of public worship. Where one lived determined what parish one belonged to, and within its boundaries, a medieval Christian learned his or her creed, received moral instruction and correction, received the sacraments, and paid taxes, called tithes, to support the church. Communal life was both supportive and coercive, and much of the laity's parish involvement comprised balancing these two forces.

The formation of parish boundaries went hand in hand with the spread of Christianity. Some of the first parish churches were set up by rural lords after they and their families had converted to Christianity. Early monasteries also provided cure of souls to locals after converting them. These early parishes were often quite large, with one parish church serving many far-flung villages. Distance as much as ignorance hindered church attendance. To facilitate participation in church worship, a network of local chapels sprang up. These chapels remained legally subordinate to the primary or mother church of the parish and offered a limited array of religious services to local residents. People could hear Mass at the local chapel, and in many cases, after overcoming resistance from the parish church, which feared the loss of burial fees, they also won the right to be buried there, near where they lived. Baptism, however, remained the exclusive prerogative of the parish church.

**Papal Response to a Request
to Turn a Chapel into a Parish
(February 1427)**
Pope Martin V, to the Abbot of Holme
Coltrayne in the diocese of Carlisle:

Mandate—in response to the
recent petition of the parishioners
of Fishlake in the diocese of York,
dwelling on the bounds of the
said parish, complaining that they
dwell in places which are often
watery and miry and remote from
the said church, whose parish is
a wide one, and sometimes cannot go without danger to the said
church to receive the sacraments
and baptize their children, and that
they propose to found and erect a
chapel of Holy Trinity near the said
bounds within the parish, with a
font and parochial insignia, and to
endow it for a priest to celebrate
divine offices and administer sacraments and sacramentals—to
license them (if the said parishioners assign such an endowment) to
found and erect the said chapel
and cause it and its cemetery to be
consecrated by a catholic bishop
etc.; saving the rights of the said
church [of Fishlake].

—*Calendar of Papal Letters*, vol.
7, *1417–1431*, ed. J. A. Twemlow
(London: His Majesty's Stationary
Office, 1906), 521–22

In 1215, Pope Innocent III set out to reform parish life with the Fourth Lateran Council. This council reaffirmed the bishop's role in administering pastoral care to the laity and mandated that each Christian go to confession and receive communion at least once a year, usually at Easter. Fulfillment of these requirements meant that there had to be local churches easily accessible to the laity and they had to be staffed with properly ordained clergy. In the episcopal records of the thirteenth century, historians can sometimes make out the subdividing of large parishes into smaller ones, so that the laity could more easily attend church.[1] In effect, the dependent chapels where people had attended Mass were elevated to the status of independent parish churches. In these smaller parishes, village religious life centered on the village church, where infants were baptized, Mass celebrated, confession heard, Easter communion received, and the dead buried. In the process the parish fostered a stronger sense of religious community.

The communal nature of medieval Christian life grew in part out of the theological requirement for Christian charity. Indeed, medieval theology called specifically for the creation of what we think of as community. The second major commandment of Jesus, "You shall love your neighbor as yourself" (Mark 12:31), formed the basic moral doctrine of *caritas*—charity, in the broadest sense of the word. Charity required social integration and fraternity, and medieval preachers and the parish clergy directed their efforts to promoting the notion of Christianity as fraternity and community. One fourteenth-century English sermon declared that "the church is an ordained place where Christian people should come together in charity, to worship our God in peace, each one with the other."[2] Parishioners attended three mandatory services on Sundays and other holy days, which gave the laity ample opportunity for interaction in a parish context.

As the anonymous author of a fifteenth-century English didactic work wrote, "Singular prayer of one person is good in chamber and in oratory and better in church, but common prayer of a community in church is better than singular prayer, for Christ said in the gospel that if two or three be gathered together in his name that is charity, there is he in the midst of them."[3] Ecclesiastical authorities distrusted private worship, especially among peasants and artisans, fearing that the worshiper would fall into error and heresy without constant clerical supervision. Although aristocrats, gentry, and wealthy merchants often had private chapels in their houses, the bishop licensed them and made sure that a private chaplain supervised them. The licenses invariably stipulated that the licensees still had to attend their local parish church on holy days and major feasts and pay their tithes.

The communal nature of medieval parish life was further developed by the laity's legal obligations to maintain the parish church building and its contents. In many parts of Europe, ecclesiastical law divided responsibility for maintaining the church building between the laity and the clergy. The laity maintained and furnished the nave, while the clergy took care of the chancel. (See fig. 11.1.) Although ecclesiastical law may have assumed initially that landlords would provide much of these costs, by the fourteenth century these obligations had largely devolved to the peasants and townspeople who filled the congregations. To give the Eucharist a proper home and ensure that the laity lived in Christian charity, parish organizations, led by the laity, began to emerge in the late thirteenth and early fourteenth centuries. These

Fig. 11.1. Church at Yatton, Somerset, England (Conway Library B47/1988). The parishioners rebuilt the nave of this church in the fifteenth century, without much financial help from the local gentry. The large size of the nave relative to the chancel suggests how important the project was to the laity.

organizations varied tremendously across time and region. Although the precepts of Christian orthodoxy were the same throughout Western Europe, the implementation of this orthodoxy was locally specific, giving parish life in England a different flavor from that of parish life in Germany or Spain. The laity's behavior often fell short of the Christian ideal, but they still shared many common values that they expressed through different forms of parish participation.

SOURCES

Historians rely on a variety of sources to study medieval parish life. The creation and use of these sources by medieval parishioners and their overseers depended on the communal nature of parish life. Most medieval people were unable to read and write. To keep the records that ecclesiastical and legal authorities required, parishioners hired professional scribes or relied on those among them who were literate, including their priest. They not only recorded information but also read it back to the assembled community as necessary. The process of informing illiterate parishioners of the written contents of parish records constituted an important part of parish life, because it allowed the community to hear about members' contributions, the progress of parish projects, and the consequences of un-Christian behavior. Taken together, they show Christian charity at work in the parish.

The range of surviving sources reflects the administration that regulated and organized medieval parish life. Most of the surviving sources relate to issues of money or behavior, but from this information we can identify many of the characteristics of local religious life. Some of the best sources for studying parish communities are from England. However, the variety in parish life and organization in England alone is such that it can be taken as emblematic of the variety across Europe.

The most useful sources are the financial records the laity kept as they raised and spent money to maintain and furnish their parish churches (see fig. 11.2). In England these were called churchwardens' accounts, after the lay officers who kept them; they begin to survive in the fourteenth century and grow more common by the Reformation in the sixteenth century. There are nearly 250 sets from before the Reformation, of varying quality and details. English episcopal administrations required the laity to keep these records so that the community and the bishop's annual visitor could audit them. As the episcopal statutes for the diocese of Exeter, in southwestern England, explain, "The custodians should come before the rectors or vicars of the churches (or at least before parochial chaplains and five or six trustworthy parishioners, whom the rectors or vicars have selected for this) and they should render every year a faithful account of the stock of the churches. And it should be recorded in writing, which writing we order to be presented to the archdeacon of the place when he should visit."[4] Churchwardens' accounts reveal a great deal about how parishioners organized themselves and how they raised and spent money. Comparisons of churchwardens' accounts also show how parishes differed from one another. Parishioners recognized and celebrated these differences, making parish life a focus of the community's identity.

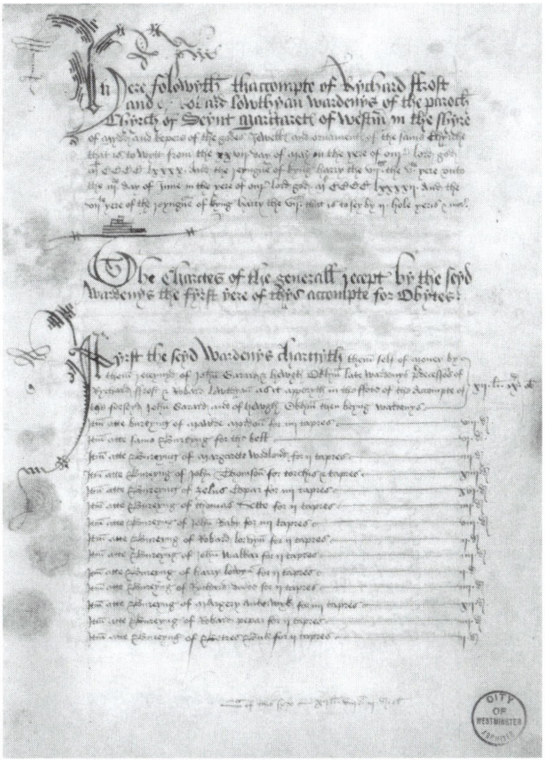

Fig. 11.2. Page from the churchwardens' accounts for St. Margaret's, Westminster, England (Westminster City Archive E1). These records are much more elaborate and complete than many sets of churchwardens' accounts. The fancy initial shows that this was the work of a professional scribe.

Visits by archdeacons and bishops generated another useful source for studying parish life, although survival of pre-Reformation visitation reports is sporadic. Ideally the bishop visited each parish once every three years to check on the condition of the church fabric, the behavior of the clergy and laity, and the performance of the liturgy. In reality, bishops often turned this duty over to their officials. In between episcopal visitations, archdeacons conducted visits of the parishes in their portion of the diocese, known as a deanery. For reasons of convenience (the official's, not the parishioners'), this might not always entail a physical inspection of the village and its church. Instead of traveling to each parish, the archdeacon received lay officials and maybe a parish clerk sent by each parish to a centrally located parish in the deanery. There the deacon asked each parish official a

Portion of a Churchwarden's Account for the Parish of Yeovil, 1516

This is the account of Thomas Nicket and Thomas Lane wardens and proctors of the goods and chattels of the parish of Yeovil Church, which was made the Sunday after the feast of the Purification of Our Lady . . . in the year 1516. . . .

— Received of a parcel of such money as was presented by Robin Hood from the devotion of the people - £5. . . .

— Received upon Easter Day of the good devotion of the people for to maintain the holy taper, which comes to - 9s. 7d. . . .

Seats:

— Received of John Gelat for a seat for his wife or himself which it shall please him in the middle range - 1s. 4d.

— Received of Joan Gloor for the change of a seat in the north side that Joan Lye sat in - 4d.

— Received of William Bently for the change of a seat in the south side - 4d.

— Received of John Bachelar, miller, for a seat in the middle range - 1s. 4d. . . .

Expenses: . . .

— For the covering and uncovering of the images of the church at Lent - 2d. . . .

— Paid for the making of the Easter taper and the font taper - 3d.

— Paid for watching of the [Easter] sepulcher: first to the priest, to the clerk, and to the wardens - 9d.

— Paid upon Corpus Christi for ringing [the bells] at time of procession - 2d. . . .

— Paid for John Bachelar for the scouring of the latten candlestick that stands before the high altar [and for] washing of the canopy - 16d.

—Somerset Record Office
D/P/yeo.j 4/1/6

series of questions designed to discover whether their church was a proper house for the Eucharist and whether their clergy performed the liturgy correctly.

In one set of surviving questions the visitors asked: "If the church's chancel, nave, or bell tower were well covered? If other parts of the chancel, nave, or bell tower were in ruin? If the churchyard might be well enclosed or if cattle grazed there?" The visitors also inquired after the moral character of the laity and clergy: "Did the parish chaplains and other clerks honorably celebrate in the church? Were they frequenters of taverns or were they scholars? Were the parishioners criminals, adulterers, or fornicators? Were the clergy or the parishioners heretics, usurers, or soothsayers, or other kinds of criminals?" The visitors also looked into the church's finances to determine whether the parishioners paid their tithes, if the priest were in residence, or if he were involved with usury.[5]

The records that resulted from visitations are lists of infractions that range from moral issues, such as bigamy or clerical incontinence, to financial impropriety, such as failure to keep the churchwardens' accounts, failure to pay tithes, or ruination of the church building. As with all such documents, the visitation records are far more informative about what was wrong with a parish than what was right. Parishioners tended to be far more vocal, and far more specific, about what irked them about their neighbors and their priest. A well-run parish might appear in the register with no more than a terse "All is well," whereas a more contentious one could generate pages of complaints, not all of them particularly serious (or necessarily well founded). This makes isolated lists of infractions derived from visitations notoriously difficult to evaluate and contextualize. Still, visitation reports show something of the concerns of parishioners with respect to their clergy and the behavior of the community. Maintaining a harmonious and cooperative parish clearly took great effort, and officials faced many challenges.

Visitors assessed fines and minor punishments for most problems. They referred the serious issues to one of the bishop's courts. Parishioners also tried cases in royal courts. Some parishes owned property, and all parishes in the course of maintaining the church building dealt with artisans and contracts of some kind. There was plenty that could go wrong that would bring parishioners into royal courts. For example, two parishioners from Basingstoke, Hampshire, stated in a petition to the English king's court of chancery that in 1506 they had contracted with a bell founder who "agreed . . . that the said bells should well truly and sufficiently accord, agree, and ring in good perfect tone with [the] other bells then being within the said parish church of Basingstoke." After consideration, however, they decided that "the greater bell of [the] two new bells did not accord nor agree in perfect tone with the other bells," and they wanted their money back.[6] Like episcopal court records, royal court records show something of the laity's concerns and expectations and often illuminate how parishioners worked together to reach decisions—and like the visitation records, court records tend to be skewed toward the negative. It was matters of contention, not general agreement, that ended up in court.

PARISH LEADERSHIP

One of the most important decisions facing a parish was who would lead the people. Keeping accounts, overseeing building maintenance, and attending visitations all required organization, and parishes gradually developed permanent administrations in the wake of the Fourth Lateran Council. The officer who came to oversee parish administrations was the churchwarden, a member of the laity. England was by no means unique in having this office; similar officers existed in Germany, Iberia, France, and the Low Countries. The earliest known reference to an English churchwarden is from 1261, when Alice Halye left the churchwardens of her parish of All Saints, Bristol, a house for the maintenance of a light in that church.[7] Although churchwardens were a ubiquitous office, the range of responsibilities and powers they exercised varied considerably from parish to parish. Local customs and surrounding institutions, such as manorial or civic government, also played a role in shaping this office and the resulting parish administration.

Most parishes seem to have had two churchwardens, although there are examples of parishes with only one and others with three or more. Because there were nearly nine thousand parishes in England in the late Middle Ages, many people served as churchwarden over the course of their lives. Typically churchwardens were householders of middle rank who had respectable reputations, neither the richest nor the poorest members of the parish. In rural parishes the gentry rarely served, and in towns most wardens came from the merchant or artisan class. In the cathedral city of Wells, in Somerset, nearly 20 percent of the men who were churchwardens were weavers, and another 18 percent were merchants. Of the men who served as churchwarden, 11 percent went on to serve as the city's mayor—a common pattern, as many men used the position of churchwarden as a stepping-stone to higher public office.[8] Women also occasionally served as churchwarden, but usually only when their husbands died while in office. In St. Petrock's, Exeter, a wealthy urban parish, six widows took over for their husbands between 1425 and 1515.[9] In 1426, two widows, Alice Cooke and Alice Pyppedon, even served together. This presence of women in a public office, unusual for the Middle Ages, reflects the broad level of community involvement that parish life fostered.

Churchwardens' accounts frequently say that the parish "chose or elected" their wardens, and this gave rise to the belief among some nineteenth-century scholars that the roots of English democracy lay in the medieval parish.[10] Recent research, however, has shown that parish communities appointed their churchwardens in a variety of different ways, most of them hardly democratic. Even within one diocese, parishes observed many different practices. A common method employed by town parishes was to have a junior and a senior warden. This system required the parish to elect one new warden each year for a two-year term. Staggering the terms of office allowed the senior warden to train the junior one and helped ensure a smooth transition from one warden to the next. In the London parish of St. Mary at Hill, the junior warden had control of the petty cash, while the senior one looked after the property and parish endowments.[11] Some town parishes, such as St. Cuthbert's in the cathedral town of Wells, had their wardens appointed by the city council. In contrast, the rural parish of Nettlecombe, in the same county, followed a rotation system among fifteen householders. In this system widows took over for their husbands if they died, so we also find more women serving as churchwardens. For example, with the death of James Mychell, his widow, Eleanor, assumed his place in the rotation for what would have been his term of office in 1523. She again served as warden in 1537 and died while in office. Other parishes appear more oligarchic, with the office remaining in the hands of one man or one family for many years. In the parish of St. John the Baptist, Peterborough, Northamptonshire, John Saberton served for twenty-five terms, from 1478 to 1506. Still other parishes relied on appointed parish councils to select their churchwardens. Holy Trinity, Cambridge, had a complex system where the curate chose two men, who in turn chose four others, and these six men then chose the churchwarden. The variety of appointment and tenure practices helped prevent chaos and dissent, and it gave churchwardens a variable amount of power within their communities. Some, such as the oligarchic ones, appear to be relatively powerful, both making and carrying out parish policy. Those serving for only one term or appointed by a council were less so: they only implemented, not made, parish policy.

Good intentions notwithstanding, community decision making and the role of the churchwarden could lead to many disagreements. In one particularly vivid instance, we can see quite clearly that different factions disagreed over the role and power of their churchwarden.

In the Devon town of Tavistock, John Amadas went to court over the parish's failure to pay him for a new silver cross he had purchased on their behalf. Court testimony reveals that no one's recollections agreed on how the parish had made the decision to purchase the cross in the first place. One faction maintained that it was "certain persons to the number of six or eight and not by the whole inhabitants and rulers of the said parish," while another group claimed that the priest had asked the whole community from the pulpit. Adding to the confusion was the fact that the decision to purchase a new cross was made while John Williams was churchwarden, and Amadas delivered it to his successor, John Guscote. The two wardens also disagreed over how to fulfill their job. Williams was accustomed to dealing with a small number of parish elite, Guscote less so. This case, when read in light of the different appointment procedures for churchwardens, suggests that the duties and influence of the churchwarden depended as much on local politics and personality as on law and tradition. The same can be said for parish decision making as well.

FUND-RAISING

One of the churchwardens' primary jobs was fund-raising. Parishes needed money to maintain the church building and furnish the liturgy. If the parish developed a new interest in a particular saint and wanted a new chapel, this too required money. Ordinary expenses included wax and oil for candles and lamps burning on the high altar and side altars; cleaning of the church, the vestments, and the liturgical items; general maintenance of the bells and masonry; and decorating for the holy days and saint days throughout the year. Special expenses might include new additions or renovations to the building, installation of new windows and pews, or replacement of liturgical items and vestments. Never far from any parish project was the idea that it was for God. Fixing the church made the building a worthy home for the body of Christ, and candles, altar cloths, and vestments added to the liturgy's splendor and furthered the veneration of the saints and the worship of God.

A parish's size, devotional interests, and resources combined with legal requirements to establish a parish's financial needs. Parishes employed a variety of fund-raising strategies, which determined the churchwardens' duties and shaped the relationships that members had to their parish as an institution. Different methods of fund-raising brought parishioners together in different ways and made contributing to the parish an expression of local interest and religious faith rather than simply a response to the demands of church doctrine. Some fund-raising activities tried to foster the same Christian charity that the Mass promoted by encouraging neighborliness, shared experiences, and spiritual well-being, adding to a sense of community membership and local identity.

Scholars often distinguish between parish income from the living, such as a church ale or fair, and income from the dead, such as rental property left as a bequest by a deceased member. Another way of looking at these differences is the role that regional economies and local resources played in fund-raising. In rural areas, parishioners donated grain and other produce, which the wardens sold. The rural Somerset parish of Trull supplemented its income by selling apples and grass growing in the churchyard.[12] The moorland parish of Morebath in Devon rented out a parish-owned flock of sheep, and coastal parishes such as Walberswick, Suffolk, often relied on income from fishing. The ease of property ownership that town law allowed made rental properties a common source of income for urban parishes. In the early fifteenth century, the parish of St. Michael's without the North Gate, Bath, acquired enough rental property so that by the middle of the century, nearly all of its income came from this one source. Taken together, churchwardens' accounts show that there were essentially five methods of fund-raising: gifts, rents, sales, collections, and entertainment, each involving its own set of administrative concerns and social interactions. Ales and entertainment were found more often in rural parishes. Common to all parishes were collections, gifts, testamentary bequests, and sales and rentals of items members needed.

Both in England and on the Continent, the most common method of parish fund-raising was making parish-wide collections. St. Margaret's in Westminster, just outside of London, held an annual collection to raise money for the wax for the large Easter taper. This parish also held other collections that helped cover the costs of decorating and maintaining the church on Christmas, Good Friday,

Pentecost, St. Margaret's Day (July 20), and Halloween.[13] Parishes also used collections as a way of paying for new building projects or purchasing new liturgical items such as a cross or a set of vestments. Sometimes specific groups in the parish organized the collection. For example, in the Bristol parish of St. Ewen's, the women raised the money for a new silver censer in 1466.[14] The maidens and young men of All Saints, Derby, solicited funds from members for a new bell tower.[15] As the women and youth collections suggest, entertainments and fund-raising often merged. Medieval people would have found some humor in respectable women going door-to-door soliciting funds for the church. In another context this behavior would have been scandalous.

Fig. 11.3. August, from a series of labors of the months, ca. 1450. English stained glass roundel, 21.5 cm. Presented by the National Art Collections Fund. Inv.: C.126-1923. Photo: © Victoria & Albert Museum, London / Art Resource, N.Y.

Medieval entertainment often involved ritual inversion, which also served up political or social commentary. A common parish festival that both raised money and critiqued the community was Hocktide, which fell on the second Monday and Tuesday after Easter.[16] Hocktide revels entailed the women capturing the men on Monday and the men paying a forfeit for their release. On Tuesday the men and women reversed roles. These rituals of inversion allowed men and women in the parish to comment on gender roles and the ways in which they determined participation in parish life.

Robin Hood revels are another example of social commentary and ritual inversion.[17] Many parishes in England used Robin Hood revels and plays to raise money. The earliest example of someone dressing up as Robin Hood can be found in the churchwardens' account of Croscombe, Somerset, where the festivities grew increasingly elaborate and earned more money. By the end of the accounts, Robin Hood appeared with Little John and his whole company.[18] There is a certain irony in linking Robin Hood with parish collections, since he was an outlaw known for using his criminal activities to help those in need. Giving the role of Robin Hood to the warden or some other prominent local figure created the social inversion. Role-playing transformed the warden from an upstanding member of the parish into a bandit. The revel became a form of commentary on the parish's continual financial demands and the wardens' insistence that members provide financial support. The laity generally supported their parish, but in some years it may have been with more resignation than outright enthusiasm.

Another common means of fund-raising was for parishes to rent out items such as brewing vats, ovens, or weights and measures. In the western part of England, called the West Country, church houses became common. They not only provided gathering space for parish functions but also could be rented out for either storage or brewing. Once parishes began to realize their church house's potential, they expanded them to make them even more useful. The Somerset parish of Yatton built its first church house in 1446, and in 1470, the parishioners added a second story, a kitchen, and a chimney. Although never a major source of income, they served a useful function for the community by supplying items that were too expensive for individuals to afford on their own.

For rural parishes throughout Europe, the most ubiquitous form of fund-raising was the church ale. Generally held in the spring when the weather was milder, ales often included other attractions such as a play, music and dancing, or athletic competitions, which helped draw visitors from outside the parish and raised profits. Whatever activities the parish provided, they offered participants a chance to gossip, tell stories, and visit with each other. Churchwardens and other parishioners frequently attended a neighboring parish's ales. Such visits provided opportunities for local comparisons and community solidarity, while also showing community conviviality and a spirit of neighborliness among parishes. The parish of Yatton, Somerset, in England regularly contributed to the ales held at the nearby parishes of Ken, Kingston, Wrington, and Congresbury, which all supported Yatton in return.[19]

Although bishops and authorities often condemned ales as drunken, violent affairs that led to bloodshed, sacrilege, or worse, successful ales united the community in the common purpose of supporting their

parish. They were financially successful and underscored the close connection between sociability and religious experience. Ales recreated the
bonds of charity and community that ideally the laity had also forged
at Mass. Those that fell after Easter drew upon the Lenten and Easter
themes of charity and reconciliation.

Financial support for the parish was not only a legal obligation
and a means of creating community solidarity; it was a religious work
that could shorten a soul's time in Purgatory. Many individuals left
money and goods in their wills for masses and other good works to
help ease their souls out of Purgatory. The church encouraged the
laity to understand giving as a good work through practices such as
bede rolls. A bede roll was a list of parish benefactors. A contribution
to the parish earned the benefactor's name a place on the roll. The
priest or clerk read the entire list from the pulpit four times a year and
maybe an abbreviated list every Sunday; the congregation would pray
for those named. Over the course of the fifteenth century, bede rolls
become increasingly popular. This money often found its way into the
parish coffers, which helped perpetuate the parish's spiritual and communal life and created a permanent bond between the living and the
dead. Large gifts could consist of houses for the parish to rent; lesser
gifts could be small amounts of money, jewelry, or a sheep for the parish flock. Gifts that the wardens rented out created endowments from
which the parish could draw.

Testators also gave material items to their parish. Wardens either
sold them and used the proceeds or incorporated gifts into the liturgical decoration. Much depended on the testator's wishes. What goods a
parishioner left reflected his or her wealth, gender, and relationship to
the parish. Many historians have observed that men and women left
different kinds of bequests, which reflects the gendered nature of parish life.[20] Men were more likely to give books and liturgical furnishings than women. Men had access to greater wealth and could better
afford costly chalices, pyxes, and candlesticks, and men were also more
likely to own books. Both men and women gave household goods,
but women gave them more often. The items women gave most often
were sheets, table linens, pots and pans, and dishes, while men, for
their part, tended to give tools and furniture. Women were also twice
as likely to leave clothing and jewelry as men.

Men and women seem to have expected their parishes to use their gifts differently. Women often left explicit instructions for how the parish could adapt their bequest or place it close to the body of Christ. Avice de Crosseby of St. Cuthbert's parish in Lincoln was very inventive. She left a wooden board to the parish clerk "suitable for making wax tapers," "one carpet . . . to cover the bodies of the dead," and "one very little leaden vessel to mend the eaves or gutter of the church."[21] Women's work often required them to piece together limited resources. Hard-learned frugality manifested itself in their instructions becoming expressions of their piety. The most common suggestion that women made for their bequests was that they adorn the statues of saints. They gave rings, kerchiefs, girdles, and dresses, which went around the base or on the statue itself. Agnes Awmbler of Barroby in Lincoln, for example, gave a kerchief to "the image of Our Lady within the choir," while in 1403, Sybil Pochon left St. Katherine "her best silk robe." She seems to have expected the wardens to clothe Katherine in it on special occasions.[22] Women also turned their sheets into altar cloths; gowns and dresses into copes and vestments; and kerchiefs into corporas, cloth envelopes that protected the host. (See fig. 11.4.) These donated household goods and clothing enriched the liturgy. At the same time, placing personal possessions close to the body of Christ elevated or sacralized the mundane items of a woman's everyday life. Historians have suggested that differences between men's and women's parish bequests grew out of the greater care and attention women paid to their parish's furnishings in their lifetime. Although women typically had less money than men, they were active in supporting the cult of the saints, cleaning and decorating the church, and attending Mass. The clergy often commented that more women than men attended Mass, and visitation reports cited men more often than women for absenteeism.

Fig. 11.4. The Erpingham chasuble with crucifixion, 1400–1430. Brocaded silk lampas. Woven in Italy, embroidered in England. Photo: © Victoria & Albert Museum, London / Art Resource, N.Y.

Parish fund-raising strategies both created and reflected different relationships that a parishioner had to his or her parish. These relationships not only incorporated local resources but also revealed class and gender concerns. The flexibility of parish fund-raising further underscores the corporate nature of medieval parish life.

BUILDINGS

The money parishes raised maintained the church and its liturgy, providing a good home for the host and a worthy place to venerate the saints. While the clergy warned parishioners against the sin of pride, it is clear that the parish church was often a source of pride and even competition for the local community. The English didactic text *Dives and Pauper*, a dialogue between a rich man and a poor man, addresses this very concern. Dives, the rich man, states, "I think that it would be better to give money to poor folks: to the blind and the lame whose souls God bought so dearly, rather than spend it in solemnity and pride on building a church or rich vestments or curious windows and great bells." Pauper responds that one should not spend money on a church for prideful reasons, but rather with the intent of glorifying God. He goes on to explain that both the Old and the New Testaments justified the expense of building a beautiful place of worship.[23] Even the widow's mite, given in support of the church, was a valuable and pious contribution, more important in the eyes of God than the rich man's gift. Pauper argues that a beautiful church should be a source of comfort and succor to all, and the support of the church was for all Christians, not just the rich.

With community life and worship in mind, parishioners rebuilt and adorned their parish churches. They expanded the naves, added chapels, updated the stained-glass windows and rood screens, and installed pew benches, new bells, new clocks, and sometimes an organ. Some of these initiatives were communal projects, others the work of wealthy individuals, who combined personal piety with family or self-aggrandizement. These projects blended and displayed communal and individual pride, religious interests, and the community's social priorities. The resulting buildings reflected both sacred and profane motivations and both communal and individual concerns.

Parish communities included men and women of all ages from a variety of social classes, and they incorporated these differences into their religious behavior. Status—lay or clerical, male or female, rich or poor—determined one's place in religious processions, church seating arrangements, and burial location. As the laity both expanded and furnished their churches, they inscribed into the building and displayed in the liturgy their competing ideas of Christian fellowship and social distinction. When we consider how the church's space reproduced the parish's social and gender hierarchies, we see that parish communities were far from egalitarian and not always harmonious. This realization, however, should not distract us from thinking of the parish as a community or parish involvement as a collective concern.

The clergy occupied the chancel, the laity the nave. Separating them was a rood screen, an elaborately carved fence with painted panels of saints on the bottom and "windows" on the top, through which the laity viewed the elevation of the host. Typically a large crucifix flanked by St. Mary and St. John stood on top of the screen, surrounded by candles. The painted images on the bottom panels that faced the congregation and the crucifix on the top made the rood screen "overwhelmingly the most important single focus of imagery in the people's part of the Church."[24] Often the iconography was quite complex, with smaller altars and or candles burning before some of the images painted on the screen. In some parishes, such as Ludham, Norwich, the saints on the left are paired with those on the right, so that virgin martyrs match virgin martyrs, and king saints match king saints. Local saints or saints who reflected a donor's interests were also common choices. At Ranworth, Norfolk, one section of the screen contains images of St. Margaret, the patron saint of childbirth, and the Holy Kindred: the three daughters of St. Anne—Mary Salome, Mary Cleophas, and the Virgin Mary—with their children. The image of the Holy Kindred affirmed and sanctified motherhood, fertility, and family. In front of these panels had stood an altar dedicated to St. Mary, which was the focus of women's offerings and prayers for fertility and safe childbirth.[25] (See fig. 11.5.)

Constructing a rood screen took money, planning, and time. The parish of Yatton, Somerset, started building their new rood screen in 1446, while they were expanding the nave. They did not complete it until 1460. Before starting, parishioners and the stone

Fig. 11.5. Rood screen in St. Helen's, Ranworth, Norfolk, England. The rood screen separated the chancel from the nave. The right-hand side, above the side altar, contains panel paintings of the Holy Kindred and St. Margaret, the patron saint of childbirth. Women prayed at this altar for safe delivery during childbirth. Photo: Katherine L. French.

carver traveled to neighboring parishes to compare their rood screens.[26] The final product had an elaborately painted loft adorned with sixty-nine images, which were probably mass-produced in a workshop and painted and installed on site. The loft housed a chapel and some organs. The screen, in both construction and existence, united the parish while hearing Mass, and its images and decorations expressed lay rather than clerical piety.

While the rood screen helped to divide the church interior into lay and clerical areas, the arrangement of the nave itself configured social interactions in terms of gender and social status. These concerns become especially visible when parishes started installing permanent seats.

Until the fifteenth century, most laity attending the liturgy stood or brought their own stools. The introduction of fixed seats is often associated with the rise of preaching and with the realization that the laity would not attend to long sermons if they had to stand. The resulting seating arrangements usually separated men and women, a practice that goes back as far as the third century.[27] The early church seems to have placed women in the back of the church, at the west end, to keep the threat of female pollution as far as possible from the priest in the chancel. By the late Middle Ages, however, the more usual arrangement placed women on the north side of the nave. The traditional explanation for this organization lies in the association of the north and women with things dark, damp, and demonic. An alternate interpretation is that women sat on the same side as Mary relative to her position to Christ on the cross as depicted on top of most rood screens. The association of Mary with the north side also carried over to other spatial arrangements within the nave. The Marian chapel was often on the north side of the church, usually behind or next to the chancel.

Parishes often re-created other social hierarchies with their seating arrangements. Rural communities such as Ashton-under-Lyne, Lancashire, based seating in the parish church on land holding; those with the most land sat in the best seats.[28] Many urban parishes sold seats as a way of raising money, and this tended to make seating arrangements in these churches a reflection not only of wealth but also of social aspirations. Parishes recognized that some seats were better than others, because of their good view of the high altar or proximity to a cult site, and better seats cost more. For example, in St. Lawrence, Reading, the most expensive seats were close to the chancel.[29] Good seats also might be near a favorite image. In 1519, Yeovil parishioners John Short and John Tressher both purchased seats on the south side of the nave "under St. Christopher."[30] The medieval bench ends in Braunton, Devon, have initials, heraldic devices, or occupational symbols that identified their occupants. Those seats with the best view of the high altar and chancel have the heraldic devices, meaning that those of highest status had the best seats.

Buying a seat demonstrated the connection between piety and social status. The purchase of a good seat not only demonstrated the occupant's piety or devotion but also advertised his or her wealth. Because of the dual meaning behind seating arrangements, those in civic office or those aspiring to civic office often purchased seats as a way of both displaying their piety and promoting their visibility. Piety was a qualification for civic office. When the parishes of Bridgwater, Somerset, and Westminster outside of London built new pews, they raised the prices; in response, civic officers and wealthy men began purchasing them, instead of the middling and infirm members who had occupied the older, less expensive seats.

Separating men and women during Mass may have prevented men and women from talking or flirting during the liturgy, but it also facilitated women's interaction with each other and marked out social divisions among women. In St. Margaret's, Westminster, many women changed seats or purchased their first seat when their husbands died, suggesting that there was a widows' section. In the London parish of St. Mary Woolchurch, unmarried women apparently sat together in their own section.[31] The records do not explain whether it was the women themselves or parish officials who felt the need to identify

---

**How to Behave in Church, from
Instructions for Parish Priests (Late
Fourteenth, Early Fifteenth Century)**

Yet you must teach them more:

That when they are inside the church door

Then bid them listen to these words:

Give up idle speech and jokes they have
heard,

And put away all vanity,

And say then the *Our Father* and then the *Hail
Mary*

No one shall stand in the church at all

Nor lean on a pillar, nor against the wall

But pray on their knees, they can't do more

Than kneeling down upon the floor.

And pray to God with heart so meek

For it is his grace and mercy they do seek.

Suffer them no noise to make

But be in their prayers for God's sake.

And when the gospel shall be read

Teach them then all to stand up instead.

And bless them well as everyone

When the *Glory to you* is begun.

And when the gospel is all done

Teach them to kneel down again as one;

And when they hear the bell ring

For that holy consecrating

Teach them to kneel down both young and old

And both their hands to up hold,

And say then in this manner

Fair and softly without chatter

"Jesu Lord, welcome be

In the form of bread as I now see;

Jesu! For your holy name,

Shield me today from sin and shame. . . ."

   —John Myrc, *Instructions for Parish Priests,*
ed. E. Peacock, Early English Text Society 31a
(London: Trübner, 1868), 9

---

women's marital status through seating. The policy for the parish of St. Lawrence, Reading, was to sit the wives of the mayor and city councilmen together up front, while in Westminster there is evidence that some women chose to sit next to friends.[32] In either case, seating arrangements served to group women together at Mass according to social categories of communal importance.

Seating arrangements made women's own concerns and priorities part of attendance at Mass, but these categories also may have served as a means of social control for women. The clergy worried about women's behavior in church. The Middle English poem "What the Goodwife Taught Her Daughter," which was probably written by a cleric, speaks directly to this anxiety:

When you sit in church, attend to your
   beads and prayers;
Do not talk to friends or to neighbors;
Do not laugh or scorn the old or the
   young
But be of fair bearing and of good
   tongue.[33]

The poet fears that women will use church attendance as an opportunity for gossiping and sparring, and that age and status—perhaps because seating arrangements emphasized them—were sources of tension and competition. Even if women followed the goodwife's advice, women's culture was not limited to conversation.

It also consisted of material displays. Attendance at Mass allowed women to show off rosaries, clothing, and jewelry, the very items that appear most frequently in women's wills.

By assigning seats that reflected marital status, the parish could also encourage the behavior expected of persons of that status. Newly married women could easily identify and emulate the demeanor, deportment, and dress of more experienced matrons or women from more socially prominent families. At the same time, seating arrangements could make it harder for women to "misbehave" and easier for authorities to identify absenteeism. Conformity was easier to enforce in an organized nave.

Pews and benches sported their own genre of carvings. Religious images on benches, such as the instruments of the Passion or the seven works of mercy, instructed both viewers who walked by and the occupants who sat in the seats. In some churches, bench carvings identified the women's section. In St. Mary Wiggenhall, Norfolk, figures on the bench ends in the southern half of the nave contain only male saints and those on the north female saints.[34] Similar schemes survive at Freckenham and Ufford, both in Suffolk. Depictions of the virgin martyrs in the late Middle Ages drew upon contemporary notions of women's proper behavior. Artists and carvers portrayed the virgin martyrs as courteous, demure, and refined in the face of persecution. These were the attributes of well-behaved women and especially appropriate models for young women. Seats with carvings of the virgin martyrs promoted both age- and gender-appropriate behavior for those sitting in the seats. Wall paintings also adorned parish churches, and these paintings often addressed those who sat nearest to them. A common image was "the warning to gossips": two women talk to each other while a lurking devil writes down their every word. This painting often appears in the back of churches,

Fig. 11.6 Langdale Rosary. Enamelled gold. English, late fifteenth century C.E. Inv.: M.30-1934. Photo: © Victoria & Albert Museum, London / Art Resource, N.Y.

Fig. 11.7. Madonna and Child. 1450–70. Hand-colored woodcut. Photo: © The Trustees of The British Museum / Art Resource, N.Y.

where the parishioners might think they could ignore the priest in the chancel.

Maintaining the parish church was a financial burden for the laity, but it was also a place for them to act out their own concerns. The arrangement of internal space in the parish church demonstrates the intertwining of piety and social status. Subgroups based on status, gender, and even occupation emerged as forums for the expression of piety. Piety was as much a prerequisite for civic office as wealth, and the parish provided a forum to display these attributes.

LOCAL CONCERNS IN A COMMUNAL SETTING

Through a balance of local priorities and religious conformity, parishioners created a communal religious life around their parishes. Because of the legal mandate to maintain their parish churches, the laity were obliged to draw upon the resources and skills they had at hand. As a result, parish life and worship reflected local social concerns, such as gender, status, and occupation.

It is easy to romanticize the community of the medieval parish. Many of the remaining buildings are beautiful, and the ceremonies and celebrations held inside them and in the churchyard were often picturesque. Yet it would be a mistake to overlook the coercive aspects of parish life that sought to regulate behavior based on social and marital status. Although parish life accepted the contributions of both rich and poor, those with money found it easier to promote their concerns and interests. Nevertheless, the communal nature of medieval parish life was a manifestation of Christian charity and integral to the practice of Christianity.

FOR FURTHER READING

Blair, John, and Richard Sharp, eds. *Pastoral Care before the Parish*. Leicester, U.K.: Leicester University Press, 1992.

Bossy, John. *Christianity in the West: 1400–1700*. Oxford: Oxford University Press, 1985.

Duffy, Eamon. *The Stripping of the Altars: Traditional Religion in England, 1400–1580*. New Haven: Yale University Press, 1992.

———. *The Voices of Morebath: Reformation and Rebellion in an English Village*. New Haven: Yale University Press, 2001.

French, Katherine L., Gary G. Gibbs, and Beat A. Kümin, eds. *The Parish in English Life: 1400–1600*. Manchester, U.K.: Manchester University Press, 1997.

———. *The People of the Parish: Community Life in a Late Medieval English Diocese*. Philadelphia: University of Pennsylvania Press, 2001.

———. *The Good Women of the Parish: Gender and Religion after the Black Death*. Philadelphia: University of Pennsylvania Press, 2008.

Gibson, Gail McMurray. *Theater of Devotion: East Anglian Drama and Society in the Late Middle Ages*. Chicago: University of Chicago Press, 1989.

Rubin, Miri. *Corpus Christi: The Eucharist in Late Medieval Culture*. Cambridge: Cambridge University Press, 1991.

Vauchez, André. *The Laity in the Middle Ages: Religious Beliefs and Devotional Practice*. Edited by Daniel E. Bornstein. South Bend, Ind.: University of Notre Dame Press, 1993.

Winstead, Karen A. *The Virgin Martyrs: Legends of Sainthood in Late Medieval England*. Ithaca, N.Y.: Cornell University Press, 1997.

THE BURDENS
OF PURGATORY

R. N. SWANSON

CHAPTER TWELVE

In 1274, presided over by Pope Gregory X, the Second Council of Lyons attempted to resolve the dispute that had separated the Greek and Catholic branches of Christianity since the mid-eleventh century. A formal scheme for reunion was approved at the council, but in the end the plan aborted. The profession of faith subscribed by the Greeks included a provision that at last gave doctrinal status to a concept that had been evolving and consolidating for some time and that subsequently became a mainstay of late medieval Catholicism: the doctrine of Purgatory.

Although the Greek profession of faith was not technically canonical, it was nevertheless a clear statement of what was to be accepted as Catholic doctrine. When dealing with the issue of those who fell back into sin after baptism, it affirmed that they "are not to be rebaptized, but that through true penitence they obtain pardon for their sins." Furthermore,

> if the truly penitent die in charity before having rendered satisfaction by worthy fruits of penance for the things they have committed or omitted, their souls . . . are purged after their death, by purgatorial or purificatory pains, and . . . for the alleviation of these pains they gain benefit from the suffrages of the living faithful, that is, by the sacrifice of the mass, prayers, and alms, and other works of piety which are customarily offered by the faithful for others of the faithful as instituted by the Church. The souls of those who, after receiving holy baptism, have contracted

absolutely no stain of sin, and also those who, after contracting the stain of sin, have been purified either while remaining in their bodies or after having cast them off, are ... immediately received into heaven.[1]

The emergence and identification of Purgatory had been a long process, whose early stages go back to Augustine. Later, ghost stories that related the efficacy of the Mass and charitable works in relieving the souls of the dead gave increasing strength to the notion that death was not the determining point for salvation, and that souls laden with sin might undergo some form of purgation in the afterlife. Between 1100 and 1250, as Catholic theology and doctrine were defined ever more precisely by the new academic method of scholasticism, Purgatory finally gained an identity as a location between Hell and Heaven. Although not actually identified as a precise place in 1274, twenty years earlier (and again during discussions on the doctrinal relationships between Greeks and Latins), Pope Innocent IV had employed the term "Purgatory" to designate the place of purgation, and he urged its future use. As a distinct place, it had clearly assumed a concrete and describable character when Dante included a guided tour in his *Divine Comedy* in the early 1300s. In the doctrinal precisions of the time, Purgatory was to be differentiated from Limbo, which, although not a place for torment, was technically a segment of Hell: the Limbo of the Patriarchs had been emptied by Christ during the harrowing of Hell in the days between his crucifixion and resurrection, but the Limbo of the Infants continued to receive the souls of unbaptized infants, burdened with original sin but undeserving of punishment.

Adumbrated in the context of the attempted reunion of the Greek and Roman churches in 1274, and formally restated in similar circumstances at the Council of Florence in 1439 (a restatement that was also at long last a formal legislative pronouncement), the doctrine of Purgatory was the foundation for some of the main aspects of Catholic devotional practice in late medieval Europe. As a late doctrinal accretion, and in practical terms a significant support for papal claims to spiritual authority, Purgatory was bitterly attacked by the sixteenth-century reformers in their rebellion against spiritual practices and religious structures that were largely thirteenth-century creations. Purgatory remained—and remains—part of Roman Catholic doctrine and practices, but it was expunged from the Protestant tradition.

While Purgatory was neither Heaven nor Hell, neither was it exactly a middle state. The point about Purgatory was that it was part of a cleansing process: it removed the lingering stain of sin and restored the soul to purity, precisely to qualify for admission to Heaven. That admission was guaranteed: Purgatory was a holding tank; once admitted, the question was not whether one was going to Heaven but when. Immediate access to Heaven was limited to those so pure that they needed no further qualifications, but the great majority of ordinary sinners required the preliminary stage of Purgatory before achieving salvation. That made death ever more significant, since the soul's state at death determined the ultimate destination, Heaven or Hell. Those doomed to the latter would be immediately consigned to an eternity of punishment with no hope of reprieve. Purgatory was also a place of punishment, but with every hope—indeed, the assurance—of its eventual termination and of admission to the company of the blessed.

Purgatory's definition marked a significant revolution in doctrine, whose implications were gradually worked out in the following centuries. It marked, if anything, a liberalization of attitudes among theologians to the laity's role within the church. It also generated notable changes in devotional practice.

Until around 1100, the general assumption was that most humans were, quite simply, without hope of salvation—they were just too sinful to be saved. Heaven was for a minority, a very small minority, of those nominally Christian. Contemporary ideas insisted that the pure could be saved, imposing extremely demanding penalties for sin that were effectively unsustainable. If penance was incomplete at death, the burden of unexpiated sin would weigh the deceased down to Hell. Only saints (however they were to be identified) were actually guaranteed Heaven. Besides saints, the only group generally thought of as likely—but not bound—to secure salvation were the monks, at that date usually committed from childhood to a round of liturgy, prayer, and mortification, in theory as *milites Christi* (knights of Christ) combating the world's burden of sin for the benefit of their fellow humans.

The depressing prospect of damnation for almost the whole human race did not lack challenges, notably the ghost stories that demonstrated that people could be saved after death. The mechanics of that process, effected through action by those left behind on earth, opened up a prospect of deliberate provision for salvation, what might be called a "strategy for eternity," if doctrine allowed. Purgatory did just that. Once accepted, it allowed everyone to work toward salvation as a long-term objective, even after death, as part of a concerted effort by the Church Militant, the church on earth. (Very few people in the late medieval period seem to have expected that they would go to Hell: that prospect was too awful to contemplate.) Purgatory allowed the rise of a tripartite definition of the Christian community: the Church Militant on earth; the Church Triumphant in heaven; and the Church Dormant, those awaiting their eventual triumph, the souls in Purgatory.

Fig. 12.1. Distribution of alms to the poor and lame (giving drink to the thirsty), ca. 1430–1440. Stained glass, 16.8 cm. Inv.: C.56-1953. Photo: Victoria & Albert Museum, London / Art Resource, N.Y.

Particularly important here was the relationship between the living and the souls undergoing purgation. Possibly the most evocative depiction of how Purgatory was felt to operate appears in a fifteenth-century English Carthusian manuscript, showing a kind of "salvation by civil engineering." Purgatory appears precisely as a holding tank, where souls are cleansed. They are winched up to Christ, to Heaven, in batches, by a pulley mechanism. Two different forces set the pulley in motion (and, although this is not actually indicated, identify the particular souls that are to be saved): the Mass, celebrated by the clergy (but available to be commissioned by the laity), and alms deeds, works of charity, which would generally be performed by the laity. These processes essentially summarize the "suffrages of the living faithful" mentioned in 1274, and they identify the two main ways in which Purgatory affected late medieval Catholicism. Both became aspects of the explosion of postmortem provision for souls that is characteristic of the period. Many of the living arranged for masses and charitable deeds to be performed after their deaths, strategically aiming to limit their time in Purgatory. The ramifications and implications of each of them require more extensive attention.

A third late medieval response to Purgatory's demands is missing from the Carthusian picture, as it is also absent from the 1274 statement, yet also requires discussion. Provision for masses and charitable works could be made by the living before death; they could also plan to bypass Purgatory, or at least limit their time there, by acquiring indulgences, which burgeoned as a result. Among Protestants, indulgences are almost instinctively considered one of the major abuses and signs of corruption in the pre-Reformation church; even Roman Catholics are not always happy with them. Yet they were important and can be considered a further aspect of the doctrinal liberalization that the consolidation of Purgatory itself reflected. They have to be taken seriously.

DEATH

Even with the acceptance of Purgatory, there were only two ultimate destinations for the human soul. Whatever happened at the Last Judgment, the immediate judgment at death—whether one went to Hell or to Purgatory—was decisive and crucial. Unsurprisingly, therefore, death was a critical point for late medieval Catholics. How one died was vital, to ensure that one embarked on the road to salvation rather than perdition. The late Middle Ages saw not only an explosion of concern with death in art but also an emphasis on death as a process, to ensure that as many as possible died a "good death." The notion of a "good death" was not itself new: it appears in many earlier descriptions of monastic deaths. Now, though, the extension of the offer of salvation beyond the cloister required the format of the good death to be made equally accessible.

From around 1350, what can be generalized as the *ars moriendi*, the art, craft, or skill of dying, was set forth in numerous books addressed mainly to the laity, detailing the prerequisites and procedures of the good Catholic death, one that ensured that the right decisions were

Prayer of Commendation at Death, from *The Book of the Craft of Dying*

Go, Christian soul, out of this world, in the name of the almighty father who made you from nothing; in the name of Jesus Christ his son who suffered his passion for you; and in the name of the holy ghost that was established within you. May holy angels and archangels, thrones and dominations, principalities, powers, and virtues, cherubim and seraphim, greet you; patriarchs and prophets, apostles and evangelists, martyrs and confessors, monks and hermits, virgins and widows, children and innocents, help you; the prayers of all the priests and deacons and all the ranks of holy church assist you; so that your place shall be in peace, and your dwelling everlastingly in that heavenly Jerusalem, by the mediation of our lord Jesus Christ who is the highest mediator between God and man. Amen.

—*Catholic England: Faith, Religion, and Observance before the Reformation*, ed. R. N. Swanson (Manchester: Manchester University Press, 1993), 146–47

taken at critical moments and the soul was guided through to Purgatory. The most widely distributed of these texts probably originated at the Council of Constance (1414–1418)—although its popular ascription to the major French reformer Jean Gerson cannot be maintained.

Such texts, several of which were among Europe's early printed books, gave both instruction and exhortation. The determination of a soul's fate was a delicate matter and a shared responsibility. A good death was at least a familial, possibly a communal, experience, a process of sustaining the dying and making the living aware of their duties to their neighbors. Death was the great test of faith; that faith had to be sustained to ensure that in the final moments the soul did not condemn itself through the pride of over-assurance or through a despair and self-abasement that rejected God's mercy. To lose hope, no matter how deserving one might otherwise be of salvation, was the irrevocable denial of God and the surest way to Hell. Around the deathbed, as shown in illustrations to printed texts or recounted from personal experience (as in the case of the English mystic Julian of Norwich), clergy, friends, and relatives nurtured and maintained faith, encouraging the dying as devils and angels waited to seize prey or grant rewards, and at the point of death (on the assumption that all had gone well) they began the cycle of prayers that, eventually, would secure liberation from Purgatory.

The mood in which people actually approached death, the mood in which they prepared for Purgatory, is difficult to determine. Certainly death weighed hard on the late Middle Ages, especially after 1347–1350 (the years of the Black Death), when the random ravages of plague were added to the previously predictable forms of death—from famine, accident, warfare, childbirth, the usual endemic

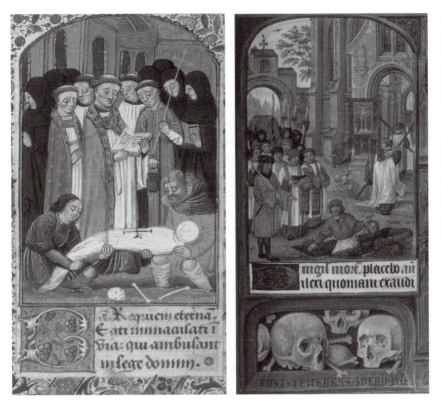

Fig 12.2. (Left) *Burial of the Dead.* Playfair Book of Hours. Ms. L.475-1918, fol. 125r. French (Rouen), late fifteenth century. Photo: © Victoria & Albert Museum, London / Art Resource, N.Y.

Fig. 12.3. (Right) Burial scene, fifteenth century. *Vigils of the Dead,* from a Book of Hours dedicated to the Virgin. Add. 35313. Folio 159, British Library, London. Photo: © HIP / Art Resource, N.Y.

seasonal illnesses, and the degeneration of old age. Awareness of the potential for the afterlife, always conditioned by a presumption of admission to Purgatory (and, therefore, of eventual access to Heaven), is often shown in wills, which survive fairly widely (but definitely not universally) from around 1350. The emphasis on death, and especially on the soul's postmortem commemoration to secure salvation, can be interpreted as a morbid obsession, both with death and with the self. It can also be considered an expression of hope and assurance, albeit tinged with a mechanistic approach to the basic problem that has led some to identify the period as one of "semi-Pelagianism" because of the emphasis on justification through works and an apparent assumption that individuals could control and bargain for their own salvation.

Wills have been much studied in recent years, from England to Avignon, from Catalonia to Tuscany, and elsewhere. Important as they are, they are not trouble-free sources. Their most obvious and

Fig 12.4. The Black Death. Death strangling a victim of the plague. From the codex called the Clementinum collection of tracts by Thomas of Stitny, 1376. University Library, Prague. Photo: © Werner Forman / Art Resource, N.Y.

significant drawback is that they usually exist in isolation, as the only surviving documents relating to particular individuals that offer insights into their spiritual concerns. As documents constructed for implementation after death, they are insecure guides to spiritual appreciations and actions during life, for which sources are much rarer. Wills are also often guides to aspirations more than achievements: they essentially transfer responsibility for saving the testator's soul to the executors, and a common late medieval trope was that executors could not be trusted. There is, therefore, no guarantee that any will's stipulations were ever implemented—whether that will was actually the last will, often written on the deathbed and proved a few weeks or months later (as is the general pattern in England), or exists as a draft in an Italian, French, or Spanish notarial register, with no certainty that it was in fact the final statement of bequests.

As the doctrine of Purgatory took hold, so its influence on religious practice increased. As the dead were incapable of self-help, the responsibility for procuring their speedy passage through Purgatory devolved to the living. Their actions, with the merit transferred to the credit of particular souls, would aid the process. The tasks undertaken for each of the dead, individually, may not have amounted to much, but cumulatively (especially when endowments were given "in perpetuity"), the scale and impact became considerable. By 1500, Catholicism had become in many ways "in large part a cult of the living in the service of the dead"[2]—but not completely.

PRAYER FOR SOULS

The institutionalized commemoration of the dead, especially the celebration of masses and other liturgical rites, is a defining characteristic of late medieval Catholicism. As the Carthusian illustration indicated, masses could free souls from Purgatory, and such commemorative and intercessory acts proliferated between 1300 and the Reformation. (They do appear earlier, but the evidence increases massively after 1300.)

The mass, the sacrificial reenactment of Christ's own self-sacrifice on the cross, was the most important and most vital component of medieval religion. By the doctrine of transubstantiation, developed from the Fourth Lateran Council in 1215, at the moment of conse-cration the bread and wine became, in substance if not in external appearance, the flesh and blood of Christ, making the divine present and concretely visible. Each celebration was a meritorious act, ben-eficial to the world in general; to commission a celebration therefore itself brought merit. If the Mass was said in intercession for a specific "intent," its merit was transferred to that end—and masses with the intention of aiding named souls in Purgatory added to the credit of those souls against the weight of their sins.

In the late medieval world, such masses were sought universally. The traditional postmortem commemorations were integrated into the process (the funeral itself, the "month's mind" or equivalent rite a few weeks later, and the marking of the anniversary a year after death), but more was demanded. The desire for masses was insatiable; how much it could be satisfied for any individual depended on resources, forward planning, the reliability of executors, and the availability of priests. The third of these was largely a matter of hit and miss, and it is usually untestable unless firm evidence survives that intentions had been fulfilled. The remaining factors can be considered in more depth.

The endowment of celebrations that leave their own evidence offers one route into appreciation of the first two factors: it required both resources and forward planning. However, few people had the resources to establish really long-term provision. For most, the masses celebrated after death—if there were resources to celebrate any—were arranged on a more ad hoc basis. In wills testators often ask that a priest be hired for brief periods, frequently less than a year, which would be as much as they could afford. Such hiring would be a mere cash transaction, requiring few formalities beyond agreement between

An Apparition Attests to the Efficacy of Intercessory Prayers

In the said year 1323, on the day of Epiphany, there appeared in Provence, in a place called Alès, the spirit of a man of that place who had recently died, and he came with a racket, speaking wildly, saying great and marvelous things about the after life and the pains of Purgatory. And the prior of the preaching friars [= Dominicans], a man of saintly life, came with many of his brothers and more than a hundred good men of that place to examine and exorcise him, secretly bringing with him the Lord's body, lest he should be a malign and false spirit. He recognized it immediately, and confessed that it was truly God, saying to the prior, "You have with you the Savior of the world." And while exorcising him through the power of Christ, he said more secret things, and how through the aid and merits of the said friar and his brothers he would swiftly have eternal rest.

[Note: This is an abbreviated version of a longer tale, which became widely dispersed across Europe during the later Middle Ages in the Latin text *De spiritu Guidonis*, and in assorted vernacular versions, including the Middle English *Gast of Gy*.]

—Giovanni Villani, *Cronica*, bk. 9, ch. 234

the executors and the celebrant. Masses for the dead in late medieval England were generally contracted at the rate of four pence each (roughly the equivalent of the standard daily wage), but sometimes, notably with block arrangements with members of religious orders, the cost went down to one penny. Masses could be purchased in set quantities, the trental (a series of thirty) appearing most often, and frequently requested from friars. In England a particular variant, the Trental of St. Gregory, requiring masses on a set series of feast days during the course of a year, was also relatively popular but more expensive (at least, if the celebrant was one of the ordinary, "secular" clergy, hired for a full year: the guaranteed living standards of members of the religious orders may have made purchase from them cheaper).

As such intercessory commemorations were procured to gain speedy release from Purgatory, those with sufficient wealth, or suffering from acute anxiety, might try to concentrate their masses immediately after death: wills of the wealthy call for anything up to 50,000 masses to be said as speedily as possible, presumably hoping that such a concentrated salvo would rapidly overwhelm the outstanding punishment due for sins.

While priests were often hired for less than a year, lengthier employment was not uncommon. Wills record bequests for priestly salaries for periods extending up to twenty years and longer. The organization and administration of such hiring imposed a considerable burden on the executors; there was every risk that arrangements would collapse. Far better to establish a more formal arrangement, especially if the services were meant to last "in perpetuity." Under such arrangements the commemoration would be set up either as a freestanding unit or under the auspices of an established body. Hence the many formal foundations creating annual commemorations ("obits," or anniversaries) or establishing a lasting daily Mass (a chantry).

The annual commemoration of the obit essentially reenacted the funeral, without the corpse. It demanded little investment but secured annual prayers, and it kept the memory of the deceased, if not alive, at least in mind intermittently. The merit of the Mass was often enhanced by using the endowment to secure additional prayers, effectively paying people to attend. Where detailed regulations for such obits survive, they often specify payments to identified attenders; attendance and prayers could also be enhanced by a general charitable dole.

Endowment could provide funding for annual obits, but ensuring that they occurred required more than financial resources. Someone had to make the arrangements to ensure that commemoration took place. Most obits were therefore placed under institutional oversight, for example, of local churchwardens or a cathedral, or were written into the obligations of a hospital or almshouse. Often the revenue-generating endowment was expected to produce a surplus beyond the stipulated expenditure, which was paid to the supervising body.

Like all endowments, those for obits might erode. Because they required few resources, many were funded through rent-charges, that is, payments levied on individual identified properties, especially in towns. Keeping track of such petty sums, of the liability to pay as well as the payments themselves, required effective oversight and administration. Changing property values and ownership meant that such income could easily be lost. Obits that were less haphazardly funded, from real property rather than rent-charges, were more secure, but even their continuity could not be guaranteed, especially if repairs were neglected.

Rather more securely funded, and more prominent in the records, were the chantries. In these the priest would celebrate daily for specified souls, ideally in perpetuity. Such a perpetual chantry could be a freestanding foundation, a full ecclesiastical benefice, giving its incumbent full freehold title to the revenues from the endowment. As with obits, however, a chantry could also be attached to another institution, its clergy less securely tenured. Many were tied to monasteries and hospitals (especially if the initial funding was a cash payment) or linked to cathedrals. Not all such priests had immediate personal access to the endowment; many were hired by the administrators and were removable at will. In the late Middle Ages, lay rulers sought to limit the amount of land passing into ecclesiastical hands—in England, for instance, through the Statute of Mortmain of 1279, originally applicable only to religious houses but later extended to cover chantries and other intercessory institutions. The response was a range of strategies to circumvent the restrictions, including establishing informal long-term chantries, whose endowment was held effectively by self-renewing bodies of trustees who administered the funds and engaged the priest to perform the ceremonies under appropriate contractual arrangements.

The scale, distribution, and visibility of perpetual chantries varied considerably. At the lowest level, they might amount to little more than endowing a priest to say Mass at whatever altar chanced to be allocated to him. Some ran to a formal chantry chapel within another institution—the many remaining, for instance, in English cathedrals and (more rarely) parish churches. Chantry chapels could be freestanding structures, often taking on other parochial or charitable functions, such as serving as chapels of ease. Almost all medieval university colleges were founded with chantry purposes, which in the statutes often had a higher status than the educational function: if funds eroded, the masses were to continue, but the other roles would wither. Indeed, a chantry could be the core of a wide range of benefactions. Many lay at the heart of hospitals and almshouses; others had schools annexed

Fig. 12.5. Anonymous fifteenth-century fresco. Redemption of the souls in purgatory, S. Francesco in Borgo, Todi, Italy. Photo: © Alinari / Art Resource, N.Y.

to them. They increased the provision of masses in busy churches and enhanced a parish's liturgical round (often, especially, the music). Moreover, always central to the process, they procured masses and prayers for their founders, assisting them through Purgatory.

While all chantries needed priests, many—perhaps, across Europe, most—remained under some kind of lay supervision; most were lay foundations. The rise of Purgatory and the demand for long-term masses for the dead thereby gave the laity a claim to greater involvement in ecclesiastical affairs, with considerable freedom. Chantries increasingly colonized ecclesiastical space; lay endowment allowed founders to impose their own liturgical demands and regulate clerical behavior; patronage gave laypeople influence over clerical careers. The chantry movement perhaps expresses more emphatically than any other aspect of late medieval Catholic practice the laity's increasing role within the church and how the church had to adapt itself to face and satisfy lay demands.

Such evolutions occurred across Europe, although with local differences. Space was most visibly dominated by the intrusion of tombs and the privatization of chapels within churches—not just the chantry chapels of England, but the family chapels of Italian churches, for instance. Private chapels built outside churches also acquired quasi-chantry purposes, with their liturgies including commemorative intercessory masses that hurried souls through Purgatory. Noble domestic chapels undertook such work; so did the chapels built for guilds and fraternities to benefit their members.

With the privatization of space went the privatization of liturgy. Chantry founders decreed the round of prayers and masses for their priests, reflecting their own preferences in their impositions. The intention to pray for souls meshed with contemporary spirituality in the cycles of prayer thus established, in the sequence of masses reflecting particular devotions (to the Virgin, the Cross, the Five Wounds, and so on), and in the selection of prayers and psalms. The regulations drawn up for chantries (and other institutions such as hospitals and schools that had chantry functions) often specify such activities in meticulous detail.

Finally, the spread of the chantry movement made clergy into employees who could be hired and fired. Chantry founders naturally

**A Spanish Indulgence
for the Dead**

In the name of God, Amen. May all Christ's faithful know how our most holy lord of happy memory Pope Innocent VIII [1484–1492] granted by special privilege and grace that the salvation of the souls of those who have departed this life in charity may be procured if, stirred by charity, their parents, friends, or others of Christ's faithful of any nation or province no matter where they might be shall give or send the twentieth part of a ducat for the soul of each of these dead in order to rebuild the great hospital of St. James Compostela and also for hiring two chaplains for the hospital, one for the men, the other for the women. Both those making a donation and the aforesaid dead are made to share in all the suffrages, intercessions, alms, fasts, prayers, disciplines, and other pious works and spiritual benefits currently pertaining to the said hospital and chapel according to the tenor of other letters from our most holy lord Pope Alexander VI [1492–1503]. And because you, [*blank left for name of donor*] have paid the aforementioned sum for the soul of [*blank left for name of deceased*], the Treasurer or his deputy grants you [this] testimonial letter. Sealed by the Treasurer's seal and signed by Alfunso de Lola, apostolic notary. A.D. *1488.*

—*Medieval Popular Religion, 1000–1500*, ed. John Shinners (Peterborough, Ont.: Broadview, 1997), 385–86

wanted effective prayers, assurance that the masses would be effective and the clergy up to scratch. When regulating their foundations, they often declared how their priests should behave. Some testators would simply stipulate that their priest be "good" or "honest," but more formal and detailed statements regularly appear in the provisions for full-fledged foundations. Here the lifestyle of the chantry priests was firmly controlled, their morality assured by strict disciplinary provisions against (for instance) dicing and tavern-haunting, and arrangements set out for formal deprivation and replacement if necessary.

The implications of such subordination for the clergy were considerable; their only consolations were the insatiable demand for their services and the willingness of the hirers to pay accordingly ("hirers" rather than "laity," because clerics were just as concerned with the future of their souls as any laypeople). In the generations after the Black Death, when clerical numbers declined considerably, chantry priests were in a sellers' market. To be such a priest had its benefits, and some clerics clearly preferred chantry employment to the demands and obligations of a parochial benefice. French villages accommodated communities of Mass priests, the *prêtres-filleuls*, local-born clerics praying for local souls. The major disadvantage of chantry posts was their common insecurity of tenure: if the chantry was not formally endowed and established as a proper ecclesiastical benefice, its occupant had few rights and often only a short-term contract.

Most chantries were established for individuals or small groups, but in medieval Europe the guilds and brotherhoods (or fraternities) that were possibly the most widespread social manifestations are often treated as "collective chantries." The full gamut of medieval guilds—from the small parish bodies in England dedicated to maintaining a light before an image, to the great Venetian *scuole* and confraternities of Florence—defies generalization. Many assumed the responsibility of providing post-mortem commemoration and intercession for their members, including masses, and so assisted their liberation from Purgatory. Such collectivities break away from the specificity and focus on individuals that is the hallmark of most chantries; they also offer a reminder that there was that broader collective that was, ultimately, the totality of the church. Masses for specific intentions emphasize the privatization, the segmenting and fragmentation, of religious experience, but no Mass could be so totally and exclusively focused. Whatever its specific intention, every Mass was of benefit to "all the faithful departed," to some degree relieving every soul in Purgatory.

CHARITY

The demands of charity, *caritas*, underpinned much of medieval Catholicism, which must be treated as a social system as much as a religion. Mutuality and reciprocity were central themes, emphasizing the interconnectedness of individuals who together created the unity that was the church in all its manifestations. That interconnectedness was firmly integrated into the attitude toward the souls of the dead, in the second method shown in the Carthusian illustration to help souls to pass from Purgatory to Heaven: alms-deeds.

The totality of charitable provisions cannot be covered in anything like adequate detail here; charity as a practice and a Christian doctrine simply encompasses too much. Charity was of course a basic precept for Christian living, an obligation imposed by Christ in his injunction to "love . . . your neighbor as yourself" (Luke 10:27), and ideally established among the living in the Corporal Acts of Mercy derived from Matthew's Gospel (25:34-40). The six listed there required the faithful to feed the hungry, give drink to the thirsty, house the homeless, clothe the naked, visit the sick, and visit the imprisoned. To these was added burying the dead, bringing the total to seven. All such activity secured merit and assisted the search for salvation: the standard exemplum illustrating the imperative of charity (or, rather, the dangers of being uncharitable) was the parable of the rich man and the leper—Dives and Lazarus—as recorded in the Gospel of Luke (16:19-31).

Charity also secured merit postmortem. Distributions, ordained in wills or left to the discretion of executors, sought prayers from the recipients and beneficiaries that would help the donor's soul through Purgatory to Paradise. Wills therefore contain innumerable bequests for such purposes. Their stipulations, occasionally impenetrable because they took for granted what executors were expected to do, vary with regional practice and over time. Donations went to secure prayers from religious houses (often friars in preference to monks), to fund education, to provide dowries, and for myriad other purposes. The reciprocity of student funding was highlighted by Edmund Dudley, Henry VII's minister, in 1509, when he urged such provision "for a better chantry shall you never found."[3] Much of this distribution was left to executors, administering the residue of the testator's goods "for the health of my soul." The scale and variety of such activity are indicated in the will of Thomas Fyneham, made in 1518. For a decade, 40 marks (£26, 6 shillings, 8 pence—when £10 was a decent annual income) was to be used annually "in works of mercy and deeds of charity by the discretion of my executors, that is to say for priests to sing for my soul, in repairing and making highways, in distribution to poor folk as need requires, to prisoners being in prison, and in ornaments and jewels to be given to churches, and for the maintenance of poor scholar students."[4]

Incalculable in their totality, and in their effects, such testamentary charitable distributions made a major contribution to medieval social provision. Obviously they were selfish, a process of gift exchange intended to benefit the deceased as much as the living. Some bequests were simply ostentatious, especially those for funerals, paying the poor to make a display. But their overall ramifications were important: the provision of wider social (and economic) benefits by maintaining roads and bridges, the constant monetary circulation that fueled the wider economy, the relief of destitution. The demands of Purgatory worked in mysterious ways.

INDULGENCES

The emphasis in the fifteenth-century illustration of the rescue of souls from Purgatory is very much on the living acting to relieve the dead: the release may be the result of forward planning by the deceased, but those plans only came into effect after death. Yet, as already noted, in addition to prescribing postmortem masses and charitable acts, there was a third way to try to ease the soul's fate: acquiring indulgences.

Indulgences have not had a good press, largely because Martin Luther's assault of 1517, traditionally taken as the start of the Reformation, has caused them to be seen as an overwhelming abuse in pre-Reformation Catholicism. In fact, however, it can justifiably be argued that indulgences were among the most widely spread, popular, and effective components of medieval religious life; their contribution and significance have been consistently underappreciated—by both Catholic and Protestant writers. Admittedly, they did cause problems and certainly could be abused, but their positive contribution cannot be disregarded.

The doctrine of indulgences developed slowly and was never quite fully worked out. Originally produced in response to a tariff system of penance, with set penalties for specific sins, the understanding of indulgences had to be reformulated as penitential practice changed and Purgatory developed. The penitential regime that emerged around 1200 emphasized priestly absolution, imposing token penances to be performed while living and postponing the full payment of satisfaction to God until the afterlife. In this context, indulgences were refashioned, although their absence from the Greek faith profession of 1274 suggests that even at that point the refashioning was incomplete, or that the hierarchs considered them limited privileges rather than something to be exploited by forward planning for the afterlife.

By 1300, indulgences were considered alleviations of the postmortem punishment to be suffered in Purgatory to complete the satisfaction for sin due to God. Technically, priestly absolution removed the *culpa* (guilt) of sin but did not abolish the physical punishment, or *pena*, that sin incurred. The terrestrial penance would be incomplete, so the full exaction would be completed in Purgatory, to an extent

The Utility of Pardon and Indulgences

(From a Carthusian devotional miscel-
lany; the original is in rhymed verse)

. . . Also I advise you to take good care
That you act to get yourself pardon
For all the sins you have done here
And with perfect penance not made
    yourself clear;
For so much pardon may a man
Purchase that he may then
In Purgatory acquit all the debt
Which may withdraw or inhibit him from
    bliss.
For so great is holy church's treasure
That it is enough to pay for it
And for all the penalties that are due
From all the people in Christendom.
Thus pardon aids in Purgatory.
But some clerk counsels thus,
That we should not use it and remain holy
Until we come to Purgatory,
And do penance here while we can,
So we may get away from Purgatory.
Here may you see that pardon is more fit to
    be valued
Than are all worldly riches.

—London, British Library,
Add. Ms. 37049, f. 24v.

that God alone could compute. However, the merit accumulated by Christ and the saints—particularly the merits of Christ's passion—could be drawn on to reduce individual postmortem liability through use of the power of the keys, the authority to bind and loose that Christ had granted to Peter and his successors in the church—the pope and bishops. After a lengthy period of evolution, this doctrine of the Treasury of Merits secured final definition from Pope Clement VI in 1343.

The capacity to draw on the Treasury was a matter of jurisdiction, essentially reserved for the pope, cardinals, and bishops. Popes could grant anything up to a plenary indulgence—the total elimination of the outstanding debt to God. Such power was invoked (rather unclearly at first) in the grant of plenary remission of sin to crusaders, regularly offered after 1095; the plenary indulgence offered to fund the rebuilding of St. Peter's at Rome in the 1500s sparked Luther's revolt. In contrast to the potential immensity of papal power, from 1215 the powers of bishops and cardinals were limited. Cardinals could grant only a hundred days (though some in the early sixteenth century broke that limit, including Wolsey), while bishops could give only forty.

Whatever the doctrinal, theoretical, and practical problems surrounding indulgences (and there were several), the central point is that their acquisition allowed individuals to plan for the afterlife by tapping into the Treasury of Merits and so by their own actions reduce the suffering due for sin after death. In general such pardons could only be acquired during life. Although pardon sellers suggested that they were transferable and could be gained by the living to benefit the dead, and despite odd grants that suggested that the dead could be beneficiaries, indulgences were only generally extended to the dead after 1476. Even then, how they would operate remained obscure; on the whole indulgences remained focused mainly on human action to stock up merit before death.

In this context, indulgences seem highly self-centered, exemplifying a doctrine of justification by works, perhaps suggesting that they tied God into a contract and that the living could actually control their souls' destiny by planning accordingly—an interpretation close to the heresy of Pelagianism. Things were actually more complex. The idea of control was probably widespread, but we have few signs of how individuals really understood the indulgences they busily accumulated. Technically, pardons required the recipient to be contrite and confessed; they could only kick in after absolution. More important, they could only kick in after death, making it absolutely essential—regardless of how many pardons had been accumulated—to die fittingly, ensuring initial admission to Purgatory.

The process contained many variables and uncertainties, and even the leading theologians disputed how and why pardons operated, their debates

---

Extract from a Printed Publicity Schedule of the Spiritual Privileges of Membership of the Confraternity of the Hospital of Santo Spirito, Rome (ca. 1520)

First, . . . [Pope Leo X] has granted authority to each of the . . . brothers whose names . . . are written in the book of the said confraternity . . . that they may choose as their confessor a secular or a regular priest, . . . [who may] give them at the point of death plenary remission of all their sins. . . .

¶ Item, our said holy father has granted that the bodies of all brothers . . . both spiritual and secular men and women (having their names written in the foresaid book) may be buried with Christen burial (without funeral pomp) during any interdict imposed by any authority, provided that they were not the cause of the interdict. . . .

¶ Item, to every Christian man and woman helping the said brothers from their possessions [Pope Innocent] . . . has released the seventh part of enjoined penance, and granted plenary remission at point of death to those who give or send any of their possessions to the said Hospital. . . .

¶ Item, . . . if any man gives according to his ability as aforesaid to the aforesaid hospital for the souls of his father and mother and of other dead men who died in sincerity of faith, and in the unity and obedience of our mother the holy church of Rome, contrite and confessed (or else willing to be confessed if they had had opportunity), [Pope Nicholas] has released all the pains of purgatory which they should suffer after their death for their sins.

—Edinburgh, National Library of Scotland, Crawford Indulgences, box 6, no. 3

running through the centuries. By the late fourteenth century, some writers, like John Wycliffe and John Huss, were advancing arguments against indulgences that foreshadowed Luther's assault. Theologians and lawyers moved cautiously, and their caution was often shared by confessors. A common refrain was that people should not rely on pardons to guarantee their salvation: it was far better, far more secure, to live a truly Christian life and acquire real merit than hope that going through the motions and piling up pardons was enough to get painlessly to Heaven.

Nevertheless, the amounts of pardon offered and available clearly did matter and were often set out in publicity leaflets and elsewhere. The resulting totals could be staggering, although the 39,245,120 years of indulgence associated with the relic collection of Albert of Brandenburg, elector and archbishop of Mainz at the start of the sixteenth century, does seem somewhat excessive. What people (other than critics) made of such figures is elusive; most probably did not bother with the arithmetic and simply acquired whatever indulgences they could. Given the sheer ubiquity of pardons, their integration into the routine of religious life, it was possible to build up massive amounts almost without thinking (although devotional pardons, as their name implies, required that the devotion be performed devoutly and therefore not unconsciously). The counting (and accounting) could be left to God.

In the terrestrial sphere, the mathematics of pardons is less important than the mechanics, the processes whereby people accumulated indulgence. This, however, is one of the many gray areas of medieval religion. That pardons were granted is clear from the sources—for example, the entries in English episcopal registers and among the papal archives—but how they operated in detail is rarely known. They had little administrative impact; their history accordingly remains elusive. Pardons offered in return for cash donations may leave traces in accounts, like the records of indulgence receipts in the archives of the Norwich Cathedral priory between 1400 and the 1530s.

When indulgence documents were printed (as they soon were when the technology became available), there is occasionally evidence of their print runs. Over 200,000 documents were printed for the Catalonian monastery of Montserrat in 1498–1500, but this was exceptional, and print runs would often be only a thousand or fewer. Usually the information is extremely limited, because once the church hierarchs had granted the pardon and authorized collection, it became someone else's responsibility and concern. The efficiency and archives of the administering bodies, and the information from private archives, dictate what can be known about indulgences in operation.

Many pardons were offered for money: they were firmly part of medieval charitable structures, functioning in effect as a marketing ploy (to put it crudely) for numerous causes while also having the characteristics of a gift exchange. Bishops authorized individuals requiring financial assistance following personal disasters to offer pardons in exchange for donations; such people might be those trying to rebuild their lives after a fire, individuals captured in war who needed to pay a ransom for their release, people reduced to poverty by business fraud, or lepers collecting alms to buy a place in a hospital. Local infrastructure—widely interpreted—might also need support. Indulgences were often granted (by bishops and popes) to solicit funds for the repair of roads and bridges, rebuild seawalls, or support other public works, as well as for explicitly ecclesiastical projects such as building or rebuilding churches, chapels, hospitals, and religious houses. Several English cathedrals conducted annual collections for their building maintenance funds that offered indulgences in return for gifts. There were drives to build shrines for newly canonized saints. The collection to rebuild St. Peter's at Rome was merely the most ambitious and most widely publicized of such projects.

Indulgences had partly developed from a concern for the defense and expansion of Christianity, first gaining prominence in the First Crusade of 1095–1099. They retained such associations in later centuries. Those who fought in crusades secured pardons; so did people who offered financial support. Debate about the validity of specific crusades embraced their accompanying pardons. The Italian crusades of the Avignon popes were criticized, Wycliffe's condemnation of the English campaign in Flanders in 1383 extended to the associated indulgences, and John Huss objected to the pardons distributed to fund Pope John XXIII's struggles against King Ladislas of Naples. Nevertheless, crusades and their indulgences still drew financial support, whether specific appeals like the one for funds to fight the Hussites (as proclaimed in England in 1428) or the repeated call to aid the Knights Hospitaller, who were holding out against the Turks in the eastern Mediterranean.

Crusade indulgences were offered for both active and passive involvement, for fighters and for funders. Those who prayed for the venture's success also secured some pardon: prayer was considered a potent weapon. Prayers, however, changed the emphasis to a different aspect of indulgences. Indulgences were usually dealt with as something bought and sold, a commodity whose marketing perhaps compounded the feeling that they were an abuse. The emphasis on cash ignores the second currency with which pardons were purchased, that of prayer. Many pardons—possibly the majority—were secured (or meant to be secured) by devotional activity: by saying prayers, by pilgrimages, by venerating saints and images. Such activity, unsurprisingly, leaves even fewer traces than the monetary transactions, yet for the history of Catholicism it may be more revealing and more important.

There is, of course, considerable overlap between the devotional and the cash aspects of indulgences: pilgrimages were devotional acts but often—maybe invariably—resulted in a donation. Indeed, while pilgrimages did not need pardons for their stimulation, they were frequently linked to each other. The fame and scale of an indulgence could affect the spiritual tourist trade: the holy places of Rome, Palestine, and Compostela attracted by their proffer of pardons; the pardon associated with St. Francis's church of the Porziuncola at Assisi became effectively a brand, which others sought to copy, legitimately or not. Late medieval popes often granted such branded pardons—named for the Porziuncola and other places—to churches across Europe, offered on set dates to visitors to stimulate pilgrimages and offerings.

Other pardons were simply rewards for devotional acts. Here again the range is considerable, the details often elusive. One major category, which leaves limited evidence, was pardons offered in return for prayers for particular souls. For instance, in 1316, Bishop John Dalderby of the English diocese of Lincoln offered a pardon of thirty days (at this point bishops still might not give their full forty) to all who prayed for the souls of John Belond of Northampton and Joanna his wife, both buried in the cemetery of St. Michael's Church, Northampton. The bishop also gave blanket ratification to other indulgences granted for prayers for their souls by other English bishops, thereby increasing the pardon available for the intercessions. The generic practice persisted throughout the period, but it is only intermittently recorded. Besides episcopal pardons (which, as in the Belond case, could be sought from several bishops), such indulgences were also sought at Rome, perhaps usually from curial cardinals after about 1450. The pardons acquired merit for the person saying the prayers and also worked to speed the prayed-for soul's liberation from Purgatory, functioning much like a chantry but exploiting a different kind of intercessory act.

Fig. 12.6. Pilgrim's badge: St. James the Major. Fifteenth-century molded tin, lead. 3.2 x 2.6 cm. CL5799. Musee national du Moyen Age, Thermes de Cluny, Paris. Photo: © Gérard Blot, Réunion des Musées Nationaux / Art Resource, N.Y.

Pardons also encouraged specific cults, rewarding prayers before named statues or when hearing bells. Such devotionalism expanded in the late Middle Ages, as pardons (and other spiritual privileges) were increasingly associated with particular prayers. Here the massive expansion in the amount of pardon supposedly available, particularly that offered for minor acts, serves to bring pardons into disrepute. Such criticism may be based on a misunderstanding, however. Insofar as pardons were a process of gift exchange, devotional pardons associated with prayers addressed to God and the saints function differently from pardons offered for donations or even for prayers for souls. All of those were charitable, with humans (living or dead) as the prime beneficiaries. Devotional pardons were granted explicitly for acts of worship but remained exchanges—with God and the saints. Divine generosity was incomparable with the merely transactional calculation of most other pardons: indulgences for prayers, even if mediated via the pope, were not merely exchanges but rewards, expressions of thanks, and acts of unconstrained generosity.

Like any good lord, God gave extravagantly to acknowledge even petty gestures, the extravagance acknowledging and highlighting the difference in status between the person praying and the divinity honored. This, paradoxically, made the devotion and the pardon commensurate, despite appearances. Nevertheless, many of the leading devotional pardons were in fact spurious, often foisted onto popes with no real historical justification. Yet that did not matter.

Many became traditional, circulating with the prayers or images (notably those linked to depictions of the Mass of St. Gregory, or of Christ as Man of Sorrows). Several were tied to recitation of the Rosary. All could be integrated into daily devotions, could become almost unthinkingly routine, yet would still enter the balance sheet for salvation.

The devotional pardons still need more investigation to determine their appeal and distribution. It seems likely, for instance, that England was little affected by many of them until the early sixteenth century, before which they were mainly a Continental phenomenon. While the prayers appear in earlier English prayer books, they are not automatically accompanied by the pardons. Only when Books of Hours were printed for the English market by Continental printers did the Continental indulgences take hold, their inclusion in the volumes and subsequent proliferation becoming a factor in the advertising and marketing of the books.

Fig. 12.7. Indulgence box for donations to win forgiveness of sins, 1522. Originally part of the altar of St. Sebastian, Sammlungen des Stiftes, Klosterneuburg Abbey, Austria. Photo: © Erich Lessing / Art Resource, N.Y.

A final category of indulgences was among the most important for individuals planning for Purgatory. From around 1250, if not earlier, many religious orders and several ecclesiastical institutions developed broad confraternities, exchanging spiritual benefits for annual donations. The benefits often included remissions of the purgatorial punishment for sins, accompanied by power to choose a confessor to grant plenary absolution at death, and the right to full ecclesiastical burial regardless of the manner of death (even during an interdict), so long as the beneficiary was not formally excommunicated by name. (The papacy also offered individual indulgences that gave the right to choose a confessor to grant plenary indulgence at death; these were granted throughout the period.) Such associations spread and proliferated after 1350: the confraternities tied to English cathedral building funds offered equivalent benefits; major hospitals did likewise; mendicant confraternities were similar (but had some practical differences).

From around 1400, the rather formulaic nature of such benefits is attested by mass-produced confessional letters distributed by the collectors and pardoners (and often printed after 1470), from institutions like the hospitals of St. Thomas and Santo Spirito in Rome or the London hospitals of St. Anthony and St. Thomas of Acon. The marketing arrangements for these letters were often complex; their proliferation and the competition between the issuing institutions were major factors in the indulgence market, producing a spiraling increase in the privileges offered that is perhaps best exemplified in the elaboration in England of the ever-increasing benefits of membership in the Guild of Our Lady at Boston.

The priorities of those who bought the pardons elude evaluation. The repeated purchases, the acquisition of several plenary indulgences from the same or different bodies, and the sense of accumulation and perhaps bargain hunting are hard to reconcile and assess. It may be wrong to attempt evaluation, beyond acknowledging that the pardons were acquired, were considered important, and were seen as part of a strategy to speed the soul on its way to Paradise by taking a shortcut through Purgatory.

THE END OF PURGATORY

The scale and ingenuity of the attempts to circumvent Purgatory attest to its importance in Europe's pre-Reformation religious life. The activities also had profound social implications and effects. Considerable funding and effort were plowed into provisions for souls; the economy of salvation played a significant part in the circulation of wealth yet also diverted and concentrated massive resources into ecclesiastical hands. This had important political results as resources were transferred to clerical possession and threatened to pass from lay control. The threat of a reduced tax base and lowered income from lordship pushed secular monarchs and civic rulers to act to prevent (or at least limit) the transfer of land into the church's "dead hand" (*mortmain*), which in turn generated confrontation with the ecclesiastical authorities. While even kings worried about their souls, extravagant testamentary provision could undermine royal resources and endanger political stability. King Philip IV of France made costly bequests for his own soul, but his successor Louis X ignored the obligations of filial piety—he could not afford to make the payments. England's Henry V earmarked the income from the duchy of Lancaster to fund his own chantry provisions, thereby seriously depleting the resources available to his infant son, Henry VI.

At some point, as such instances indicate, the demands of Purgatory became burdensome and might become intolerable and unsustainable. To meet all the requirements, especially the financial demands, could impose strains. Yet just how the equations were balanced out is a matter of interpretation. In some readings the demands associated with the doctrine of Purgatory reflected the development of a Western guilt culture, extending the burden of sin beyond life and making the assuaging of that guilt a dynamic force that skewed and tormented medieval social and spiritual life. Alternatively, Purgatory was a positive response to awareness of the nature of the burden of sin, a gift of hope that, while not relieving sinners of responsibility for their condition, did make Heaven more widely and securely accessible. Its contribution to social life, whether the charitable provision for relief of poverty and distress, the more mundane funding of infrastructure such as roads and bridges, or the ambitious underpinning of education, was incalculable.

Where cash was involved, people would calculate. For those anxious to get themselves through Purgatory, the strategic decisions reflected their own personal concerns: to have as many prayers said as possible, as permanently or speedily as resources allowed. The beneficiaries of any charity were viewed only as prayer providers, selected for quantity and quality. The social benefits resulting from charitable acts were directed not by social need but by the utility of the arrangements for the donor's or founder's soul. In consequence, provision was haphazard and episodic, not planned and comprehensive, its unevenness matched by its frequent lack of discrimination.

On the other hand, over time those paying for the long dead might resent the impositions and act to evade them. This would be particularly problematic if resources eroded but burdens remained static. Changing economic relations—like the reduced rents and increased priestly salaries of the fifteenth century—would undermine the provision for souls. Whether heirs were indeed growing more resentful of the demands of the dead by the sixteenth century is impossible to say, but the abolition of Purgatory in those countries that abandoned Catholicism at the Reformation certainly had its economic attractions. It is, nevertheless, surprising and notable that the attack on Purgatory was delayed until the sixteenth century: there is little sign of any consistent opposition or challenge to the doctrine among the heretical movements of earlier years.

For over three hundred years—from roughly 1200 to the Reformation—the doctrine of Purgatory was a formative influence on European religious and social life. The call for prayers for the souls of the dead resounded and reverberated through spiritual and social practice, its ramifications permeating social provision, unavoidably influencing every life—so much that it is hard to see how anyone could have avoided its effects. The fifteenth-century English Carthusian illustration gives a simplified picture of how Purgatory was understood, omitting indulgences as an approach that was potentially just as important as provision for souls through intercessory masses and alms-deeds (if not more so). The masses and the charity were appreciated on earth, but the symbiotic relationship between the living and dead that the picture expressed was central to the doctrine. Living and dead were bound together in mutual need, mutual dependence. The mutuality was perhaps best expressed in some Continental devotional practices, which made the souls in Purgatory themselves intercessors for the living, even before they had achieved the sainthood that awaited them in Heaven.

Purgatory fell in the sixteenth century when the reformers challenged its existence because it lacked scriptural foundation. By then it was also fully integrated, or entangled, with other aspects of Catholicism that similarly evoked the reformers' ire, especially papal authority, the efficacy and sacrificial nature of the Mass, and priestly authority over sin. Even more than this, in the thirteenth to early sixteenth centuries, Purgatory had also functioned as a core component of and stimulus for broader medieval Catholic practice, devotional and charitable, for medieval Christianity as a social and collaborative mutuality as well as an assortment of religious and devotional regimes and structures.

FOR FURTHER READING

Banker, James R. *Death in the Community: Memorialization and Confraternities in an Italian Commune in the Late Middle Ages*. Athens: University of Georgia Press, 1988.

Beaty, Nancy L. *The Craft of Dying: A Study in the Literary Tradition of the Ars Moriendi in England*. Yale Studies in English 175. New Haven: Yale University Press, 1970.

Binski, Paul. *Medieval Death: Ritual and Representation*. Ithaca, N.Y.: Cornell University Press, 1996.

Cohn, Samuel K., Jr. *The Cult of Remembrance and the Black Death: Six Renaissance Cities in Central Italy*. Baltimore: Johns Hopkins University Press, 1992.

Delumeau, Jean. *Sin and Fear: The Emergence of a Western Guilt Culture, 13th–18th Centuries*. Translated by Eric Nicholson. New York: St. Martin's, 1990.

Duffy, Eamon. *The Stripping of the Altars: Traditional Religion in England, c. 1400–c. 1580*. New Haven: Yale University Press, 1992.

Le Goff, Jacques. *The Birth of Purgatory*. Translated by Arthur Goldhammer. Chicago: University of Chicago Press, 1984.

Swanson, R. N. *Religion and Devotion in Europe c. 1215–c. 1515*. Cambridge Medieval Textbooks. Cambridge: Cambridge University Press, 1995.

———, ed. *Promissory Notes on the Treasury of Merits: Indulgences in Late Medieval Europe*. Brill's Companions to the Christian Tradition 5. Leiden: Brill, 2006.

Tanner, Norman P. *The Church in Late Medieval Norwich, 1370–1532*. Studies and Texts 66. Toronto: Pontifical Institute of Mediaeval Studies, 1984.

Wood-Legh, K. L. *Perpetual Chantries in Britain*. Cambridge: Cambridge University Press, 1965.

ABBREVIATIONS

BAR	British Archaeological Reports
d.	died
MGH	Monumenta Germaniae Historica
Ms.	Manuscript
SRG	Scriptores rerum Germanicarum
SRM	Scriptores rerum Merovingicarum

NOTES

Introduction. Living Christianity

1. Einhard's "Life of Charlemagne," in Einhard and Notker the Stammerer, *Two Lives of Charlemagne*, trans. Lewis Thorpe (Harmondsworth, U.K.: Penguin, 1969), 79.

2. Caroline Walker Bynum, *Jesus as Mother: Studies in the Spirituality of the High Middle Ages* (Berkeley: University of California Press, 1982), 8.

3. Peter Burke, "Editorial Preface," in Aron Gurevich, *Medieval Popular Culture: Problems of Belief and Perception*, trans. János M. Bak and Paul A. Hollingsworth (Cambridge: Cambridge University Press, 1988), ix.

4. *St. Francis of Assisi's Writings and Early Biographies: English Omnibus of the Sources for the Life of St. Francis*, ed. Marion A. Habig (Chicago: Franciscan Herald, 1983), 67.

5. *Two Memoirs of Renaissance Florence: The Diaries of Buonaccorso Pitti and Gregorio Dati*, ed. Gene Brucker, trans. Julia Martines (Prospect Heights, Ill.: Waveland, 1991), 132.

6. Daniel Bornstein, "Spiritual Kinship and Domestic Devotions," in *Gender and Society in Renaissance Italy*, ed. Judith C. Brown and Robert C. Davis (London: Longman, 1998), 191.

Chapter One. Converting the Barbarian West

1. Martin Goodman, *Mission and Conversion: Proselytizing in the Religious History of the Roman Empire* (Oxford: Clarendon, 1994).

2. *Theodosiani libri XVI cum sirmondianis et leges novellae ad Theodosianum pertinentes*, ed. Theodor Mommsen, Paul M. Meyer, and Paul Krüger (Berlin: Weidmannsche Buchhandlung, 1905), 16.10.10–11.

3. *Concilium Arelatense (314, Aug. 1)*, ed. and trans. Jean Gaudemet, *Conciles gaulois du IVe siècle*, Sources chrétiennes 241 (Paris: Cerf, 1977), 35–63, at 56–63.

4. Lewis Thorpe, *Gregory of Tours: The History of the Franks* (Harmondsworth, U.K.: Penguin, 1974), 309–10.

5. Arthur Darby Nock, *Conversion: The Old and the New in Religion from Alexander the Great to Augustine of Hippo* (Oxford: Clarendon, 1933), 7.

6. Ramsey MacMullen, *Christianizing the Roman Empire, A.D. 100–400* (New Haven: Yale University Press, 1984), 74.

7. Nock, *Conversion*, 7, 14.

8. Bede, *The Ecclesiastical History of the English People*, ed. Judith McClure and Roger Collins (Oxford: Clarendon, 1994), 57.

9. See R. A. Markus, "Gregory the Great and the Origins of Papal Missionary Strategy," *Studies in Church History* 6 (1970): 29–38; reprinted in R. A. Markus, *From Augustine to Gregory the Great: History and Christianity in Late Antiquity* (London: Variorum Reprints, 1983), ch. 11.

10. R. A. Markus, *The End of Ancient Christianity* (Cambridge: Cambridge University Press, 1990), 127; 125–35.

11. *Gesta Pontificum Autissiodorensium*, in *Les gestes des évêques d'Auxerre*, vol. 1, ed. Michel Sot et al. (Paris: Les belles lettres, 2002), c. 19, 70–77.

12. Jean-Charles Picard, "Espace urbain et sépultures épiscopales à Auxerre," *Revue d'histoire de l'Église de France* 168 (1976): 205–22; reprinted in *La christianisation des pays entre Loire et Rhin (IVe–VIIe siècle)*, ed. Pierre Riché (Paris: Cerf, 1993), 205–22, with an updated bibliography on 264–65.

13. *The Calendar of St. Willibrord*, ed. H. A. Wilson, Henry Bradshaw Society 55 (London: Boydell, 1918).

14. See, for example, Eve Picard, *Germanisches Sakralkönigtum? Quellenkritische Studien zur Germania des Tacitus und zur altnordischen Übelieferung* (Heidelberg: Winter Verlag, 1991).

15. Alexander Callander Murray, *From Roman to Merovingian Gaul: A Reader* (Peterborough, Ont.: Broadview, 2000), 594.

16. Alexander Callander Murray, "*Post vocantur Merohingii*: Fredegar, Merovech and 'Sacral Kingship,'" in *After Rome's Fall: Narrators and Sources of Early Medieval History: Essays Presented to Walter Goffart*, ed. Alexander Callander Murray (Toronto: Toronto University Press, 1998), 121–52; Ian N. Wood, "Fredegar's Fables," in *Historiographie im frühen Mittelalter*, ed. Anton Scharer and Georg Scheibelreiter, Veröffentlichungen des Instituts für Österreichische Geschichtsforschung 32 (Vienna: Oldenbourg Verlag, 1994), 359–66.

17. Janet L. Nelson, "The Lord's Anointed and the People's Choice: Carolingian Royal Ritual," in *Rituals of Royalty: Power and Ceremonials in Traditional Societies*, ed. David Cannadine and Simon Price (Cambridge: Cambridge University Press, 1987), 141; 137–80; reprinted in Janet L. Nelson, *The Frankish World, 750–900* (London: Hambledon, 1996), 101; 99–131.

18. J. M. Wallace-Hadrill, *Early Germanic Kingship in England and on the Continent*, Ford Lectures (Oxford: Oxford University Press, 1970), 47.

19. *Gunthramni regis edictum (585, Nov. 10)*, ed. Alfred Boretius, Monumenta Germaniae Historica, Capitularia Regum Francorum 1 (Hannover: Hahnsche Buchhandlung, 1883), no. 5, 10–12.

20. See Yitzhak Hen, "The Uses of the Bible and the Perception of Kingship in Merovingian Gaul," *Early Medieval Europe* 7 (1998): 277–90.

21. *Liber sacramentorum Romanae aecclesiae ordinis anni circuli (Sacramentarium Gelasianum)*, ed. Leo C. Mohlberg et al., Rerum Ecclesiasticarum Documenta 4 (Rome: Casa editrice Herder, 1960), 3.62, 217–18.

22. Cathwulf, *Epistola*, ed. Ernst Dümmler, Monumenta Germaniae Historica, Epistolae 4 (Berlin: Weidemann Verlag, 1895), 503–5.

23. Arnold Van Gennep, *The Rites of Passage*, trans. Monika B. Vizdom and Gabrielle L. Caffe (London: Routledge Paul, 1960).

24. Cornelius Tacitus, *De origine et situ Germanorum [Germania]*, in *Cornelii Taciti Opera minora*, ed. Michael Winterbottom and R. M. Ogilvie (Oxford: Clarendon, 1975), c. 13.1, 44.

25. Paulinus of Nola, *Carmina*, ed. Wilhelm von Hartel, Corpus Scriptorum Ecclesiasticorum Latinorum 30 (Vienna: Verlag der Österreichischen Akademie der Wissenschaft, 1894), 21.377–78, 170.

26. *Liber sacramentorum Gellonensis*, ed. A. Dumas and Jean Deshusses, Corpus Christianorum, series latina 159 (Turnhout: Brepols, 1981), c. 2499, 380.

27. See MacMullen, *Christianizing the Roman Empire*, 154 n. 25.

28. Ramsey MacMullen, "What Difference Did Christianity Make?" *Historia* 35 (1986): 322–43; reprinted in Ramsey MacMullen, *Changes in the Roman Empire: Essays in the Ordinary* (Princeton: Princeton University Press, 1990), 142–55.

29. For references, see Markus, *End of Ancient Christianity*, 103–6; Yitzhak Hen, *Culture and Religion in Merovingian Gaul, A.D. 481–751* (Leiden: Brill, 1995), 167–70.

30. *The Letters of Saint Boniface*, trans. Ephraim Emerton (New York: Columbia University Press, 2000), 59–60.

31. Markus, *End of Ancient Christianity*, 9.

32. R. A. Markus, "From Caesarius to Boniface: Christianity and Paganism in Gaul," in *Le septième siècle: Changements et continuités / The Seventh Century: Change and Continuity*, ed. Jacques Fontaine and J. N. Hillgarth (London: Warburg Institute, 1992), 154–72, esp. 171–72.

33. Markus, *End of Ancient Christianity*, 207.

Chapter Two. Death and Burial

1. Some devoted followers of the saints nonetheless saw such occasions as moments of great sorrow, such as recounted by Gregory of Tours in his description of Radegund of Poitiers's burial in 587, which could not be attended by the members of her monastic community since the cemetery was located outside the walls of the monastery in which they were cloistered. *Gregorius episcopus Turonensis, Liber in Gloria confessorum* 104, ed. Bruno Krusch, in MGH: SRM 1.2, new ed. (Hannover: Impensis bibliopolii Hahniani, 1969), 364–66.

2. T. Delarue and E. Thirion, "Amay (Liège): Le sarcophage de Chrodoara," in *L'archéologie en Wallonie: Découvertes récentes des circles d'archéologie,* no. 58 (Nivelles: Fédération des archéologues de Wallonie, 1980), 133–34. The gravestone may have been erected in the 730s, as much as a century after her death. Alain Dierkens, "A propos du sarcophage de Sancta Chrodoara découvert en 1977 à Amay," *Art et Fact: Revue des*

historiens de l'art, des archéologues, des musicologues et des orientalistes de l'Université de Liège 15 (1996): 30–32.

3. *Vita sanctae Geretrudis* B.7, ed. Bruno Krusch, in MGH: SRM 2, new ed. (Hannover: Impensis bibliopolii Hahniani, 1956), 461–62.

4. Ionas, *Vitae Columbani abbatis discipulorumque eius libri II* 2.12, ed. Bruno Krusch, in MGH: SRG 37 (Hannover: Impensis bibliopolii Hahniani, 1905), 261.

5. *Vita Sancti Cuthberti auctore anonymo* 13–14, in *Two Lives of Saint Cuthbert: A Life by an Anonymous Monk of Lindisfarne and Bede's Prose Life*, trans. and ed. Bertram Colgrave (New York: Greenwood, 1969 [1940]), 130–33.

6. Beda, *Vita Sancti Cuthberti* 37–41, in *Two Lives of Saint Cuthbert*, 270–89.

7. *Bede's Ecclesiastical History of the English People*, ed. Bertram Colgrave and R. A. B. Mynors, Oxford Medieval Texts (Oxford: Clarendon, 1969), 272–75.

8. Éric Rebillard, *Religion et sepulture: L'Église, les vivants et les morts dans l'Antiquité tardive*, Civilisations et sociétés 115 (Paris: Éditions de l'École des Hautes études en Sciences socials, 2003), 155–60.

9. Paul Willem Finsterwalder, *Die Canones Theodori Cantuariensis und ihre Überlieferungsformen* U2,5,1-7 (Weimar: Hermann Böhlaus Nachfolger, Hof-Buchdruckerei, 1929), 318–19.

10. Patrick Périn and Laurent Renou, "Les sarcophages mérovingiens de plâtre moulé trouvés à Paris: Technologie, ornementation, chronologie," *Bulletin de liaison: Association française d'archéologie mérovingien* 5 (1981): 49–52.

11. Howard Williams, "Cemeteries as Central Places—Place and Identity in Migration Period Eastern England," in *Central Places in the Migration and Merovingian Periods: Papers from the 52nd Sachsensymposium, Lund, August 2001*, ed. Birgitta Hårdh and Lars Larsson, Acta archaeological Lundensia Series in 8, 39 (Stockholm: Amqvist & Wiksell International, 2002), 341–62.

12. *Capitulatio de partibus Saxoniae*, ed. Alfred Boretius, in MGH: Leges 2, Capitularia 1.26 (Hannover: Impensis bibliopolii Hahniani, 1883), 68–70.

13. Cécile Treffort, *L'église carolingienne et la mort: Christianisme, rites funéraires et pratiques commemoratives*, Collection d'histoire et d'archéologie médiévales 3 (Lyons: Presses universitaires de Lyon, 1996), 139–41.

14. I have borrowed use of this concept from Frans Theuws, who has used it to describe the image of the dead created by burials. Frans Theuws, "Ethnicity, Grave Goods and the Rhetoric of Burial Rites in Late Antique Northern Gaul," in his forthcoming *Ethnic Identity and Power in the Greek, Roman and Late Roman World*. He in turn modified this idea from the rich analysis of late antique hagiography in Lynda Coon, *Sacred Fictions: Holy Women and Hagiography in Late Antiquity* (Philadelphia: University of Pennsylvania Press, 1997).

15. Martin Carver, "The Anglo-Saxon Cemetery at Sutton Hoo: An Interim Report," in *The Age of Sutton Hoo: The Seventh Century in North-Western Europe*, ed. M. O. H. Carver (Rochester, N.Y.: Boydell, 1992), 348–55.

16. Étienne Gilot, "Les sepultures de chevaux: Datations au 14C," in *Les fouilles du quartier Saint-Brice à Tournai* 2, ed. Raymond Brulet, Publications d'histoire de l'art et d'archéologie de l'Université catholique de Louvain 73 (Louvain: Département d'archéologie et d'histoire de l'art, 1990–1991), 47–49.

17. Bailey K. Young, "Paganisme, christianisation et rites funéraires mérovingiens," *Archéologie médiévale* 7 (1977): 16–24.

18. Mark A. Handley, *Death, Society and Culture: Inscriptions and Epitaphs in Gaul and Spain, AD 300–750*, BAR International Series 1135 (Oxford: British Archaeological Reports, 2003), 14–22.

19. Frans Theuws and Monica Alkemade, "A Kind of Mirror for Men: Sword Depositions in Late Antique Northern Gaul," in *Rituals of Power from Late Antiquity to the Early Middle Ages*, ed. Frans Theuws and Janet L. Nelson, Transformation of the Roman World 8 (Leiden: Brill, 2000), 444–70.

20. Sam Lucy, *The Early Anglo-Saxon Cemeteries of East Yorkshire: An Analysis and Reinterpretation*, BAR British Series 272 (Oxford: British Archaeological Reports, 1998), 42–43.

21. Cécile Treffort, "Vertus prophylactiques et sens eschatologique d'un depot funéraire du haut Moyen Age: Les plaques boucles rectangulaires burgondes à inscription," *Archéologie médiévale* 32 (2002): 31–53.

22. Hayo Vierck, "Folienkreuze als Votivgaben," in *Die Goldblattkreuze des frühen Mittelalters*, ed. Wolfgang Hübener, Veröffentlichungen des Alemannischen Instituts Freiburg 37 (Bühl: Verlag Konkordia, 1975), 134–42.

23. In a few instances, organic remains of cloth and flora have been found in particularly well-preserved elite graves in churches. Raymond Boyer et al., *Vie et mort à Marseille à la fin de l'antiquité: Inhumations habillées des Ve et VIe siècles et sarcophage reliquaire trouvés à l'abbaye de Saint Victor* 20 (Marseilles: Imprimerie Municipale, 1987).

24. Helmut Roth, "Archäologische Beobachtungen zum Grabfrevel im Merowingerreich," in *Zum Grabfrevel in vor- und frühgeschichtlicher Zeit*, ed. Herbert Jankuhn, Hermann Nehlsen, and Helmut Roth (Göttingen: Vandenhoeck & Ruprecht, 1978), 60–65.

Chapter Three. Relics, Ascetics, Living Saints

1. Athanasius, *Life of Saint Anthony*, in Karl F. Morrison, ed., *University of Chicago Readings in Western Civilization*, vol. 3, *The Church in the Roman Empire* (Chicago: University of Chicago Press, 1986), 172–73.

2. Jerome, *Against Vigilantius*, in Morrison, *Church in the Roman Empire*, 121.

3. Quoted in Peter Brown, *The Cult of the Saints: Its Rise and Function in Latin Christianity* (Chicago: University of Chicago Press, 1981), 7.

4. Diana Webb, *Medieval European Pilgrimage, c. 700–c. 1500* (New York: Palgrave, 2002), 50.

5. Erasmus, *Ten Colloquies*, trans. Craig R. Thompson (Indianapolis: Bobbs-Merrill, 1957), 68, 82; Franco Sacchetti, *Il Trecentonovelle*, ed. Emilio Faccioli (Turin: Einaudi, 1970), 438–41.

6. Sharon Strocchia, "Sisters in Spirit: The Nuns of Sant'Ambrogio and Their Consorority in Early Sixteenth-Century Florence," *Sixteenth Century Journal* 33 (2002): 744; Eve Borsook, "Cults and Imagery at Sant'Ambrogio in Florence," *Mitteilungen des Kunsthistorischen Instituts in Florenz* 25 (1981): 183.

7. Fourth Lateran Council, canon 1, *Decrees of the Ecumenical Councils*, ed. Norman P. Tanner, S.J. (Washington, D.C.: Georgetown University Press, 1990).

8. Jacobus de Voragine, *The Golden Legend: Selection*, trans. Christopher Stace (London: Penguin, 1998), 99–100.

9. Hugh of Lincoln, *Life*, vol. 2, 94, quoted in Miri Rubin, *Corpus Christi: The Eucharist in Late Medieval Culture* (Cambridge: Cambridge University Press, 1991), 122.

10. Miri Rubin, *Gentile Tales: The Narrative Assault on Late Medieval Jews* (New Haven: Yale University Press, 1999).

Chapter Four. The Impact of Architecture

1. In addition to the works in English listed in the suggestions for further reading, I have relied on the following German studies of German churches: Andreas Curtius, "Die Hauskapelle als architektonischer Rahmen der privaten Andacht," in *Spiegel der Seligkeit: Privates Bild und Frömmigkeit im Spätmittelalter*, ed. G. Ulrich Grossmann (Nuremberg: Verlag des Germanischen Nationalmuseums, 2000), 34–48; Antje Grewolls, *Die Kapellen der norddeutschen Kirchen im Mittelalter: Architektur und Funktion* (Kiel: Ludwig, 1999); Klaus Jan Philipp, *Pfarrkirchen: Funktion, Motivation, Architektur: Eine Studie am Beispiel der Pfarrkirchen der schwäbischen Reichsstädte im Spätmittelalter* (Marburg: Jonas, 1987); and Peter Wiek, "Das Strassburger Münster: Untersuchungen über die Mitwirkung des Stadtbürgertums am Bau bisschöflicher Kathedralkirchen im Spätmittelalter," *Zeitschrift für die Geschichte des Oberrheins* 107 (1959): 40–113.

2. Margaret Aston, "Segregation in Church," in *Women in the Church: Papers Read at the 1989 Summer Meeting and the 1990 Winter Meeting of the Ecclesiastical History Society*, ed. W. J. Sheils and Diana Wood, Studies in Church History 27 (Oxford: Blackwell, 1990).

3. Orme, Nicholas. "Church and Chapel in Medieval England." *Transactions of the Royal Historical Society*, ser. 6, vol. 6 (1996): 75–102.

4. Norman P. Tanner, *The Church in Late Medieval Norwich, 1370–1532* (Toronto: Pontifical Institute, 1984).

5. Peter Wiek, "Das Straßburger Münster: Untersuchungen über die Mitwirkung des Stadtbürgertums am Bau bisschöflicher Kathedralkirchen im *Spätmittelalter*," *Zeitschrift für die Geschichte des Oberrheins*, 107 (1959), 40–113.

6. Ronald C. Finucane, "The posthumous miracles of Godric of Finchale," *Durham Archaeological Journal: Transactions of the Architectural and Archaeological Society of Durham and Northumberland*, n.s.3 (1974), 47–50. See also the important forthcoming book of Rachel Koopmans, which reinterprets the miracle accounts from these shrines.

7. Katherine L. French, *The People of the Parish: Community Life in a Late Medieval English Diocese* (Philadelphia: University of Pennsylvania Press, 2001), 1.

8. J. G. Davies, *The Secular Use of Church Buildings* (New York: Seabury, 1968), 59.

9. Ibid., 76.

Chapter Five. Medieval Revivalism

1. Frederick Morgan Davenport, *Primitive Traits in Religious Revivals: A Study of Mental and Social Evolution* (New York: Macmillan, 1905), 42, 184, 217.

2. William James, *The Varieties of Religious Experience* (London: Longman, Green, 1902), 227–28.

3. Norman Zacour, "The Children's Crusade," in *A History of the Crusades*, ed. Kenneth M. Setton (Philadelphia: University of Pennsylvania Press, 1962), 2:325–42, quotation at 328.

4. Emile Durkheim, *The Elementary Forms of the Religious Life*, trans. J. W. Swain (London: Allen & Unwin, 1964), 241.

5. André Vauchez, *Sainthood in the Later Middle Ages*, trans. Jean Birrell (Cambridge: Cambridge University Press, 1997), 245 ("the manifestations of collective enthusiasm of the *devotio*").

6. Translated from Robert of Rheims, *Historia Iherosolimitana*, in *The Crusades: Idea and Reality, 1095–1274*, ed. L. and J. Riley-Smith (London: Edward Arnold, 1981), 44.

7. Translation from the *Chronicon universale anonymi Laudunensis* in *Medieval Popular Religion: A Reader*, ed. J. Shinners (Peterborough, Ont.: Broadview, 1997), 395.

8. Salimbene de Adam, *The Chronicle*, ed. and trans. Joseph L. Baird, Giuseppe Baglivi, and John Robert Kane (Binghamton, N.Y.: Medieval and Renaissance Texts and Studies, 1986), 47.

9. See Salimbene de Adam, *Cronica*, ed. Giuseppe Scalia, new ed. (Bari: G. Laterza, 1966), 1:426–27, 527, 567; 2:675–77.

10. Cited from Jean Lemoine, *Extravagantes communes* (Lyons, 1559), 152, in Gary Dickson, "Revivalism as a Medieval Religious Genre," *Journal of Ecclesiastical History* 51 (2000): 473–96, quotation at 495.

11. Poem by Sacchetti cited in Daniel E. Bornstein, *The Bianchi of 1399: Popular Devotion in Late Medieval Italy* (Ithaca, N.Y.: Cornell University Press, 1993), 117.

12. John Donne, "Holy Sonnets," in *The Penguin Book of English Verse*, ed. John Hayward (Harmondsworth, U.K.: Penguin, 1964), 84–85.

13. *Rodulfus Glaber Opera*: *Historiarum Libri Quinque*, ed. and trans. John France (Oxford: Clarendon, 1989), xixff., 194–97.

14. Revised from B. G. Babington's translation of the Mortemer chronicle in J. F. C. Hecker, *The Epidemics of the Middle Ages*, 3rd ed. (London: Trübner, 1859).

15. Selection from the *Annales S. Iustinae Patavini*, revised from the partial translation of William Heywood, *Palio and Ponte* (London: Methuen, 1904), 18.

16. Translated from the *Cronaca del Graziani* of Perugia by Heywood in *Palio and Ponte*, 154–55.

17. Orderic Vitalis, *Ecclesiastical History*, ed. and trans. Marjorie Chibnall (Oxford: Clarendon, 1973), 4:332–33.

Chapter Six. Clerical Celibacy and the Laity

1. On the early Middle Ages, see Gabriella Rossetti, "Il matrimonio del clero nella società altomedievale," in *Il matromonio nella società altomedievale* (Spoleto: CISAM, 1977), 473–554. On the changes in the eleventh century, see Giuseppe Fornasari, *Celibato sacerdotale e "autocoscienza" ecclesiale: Per la storia della "Nicolaitica haeresis" nell'Occidente medievale* (Udine: Del Bianco, 1981).

2. Gabriel Le Bras, *Institutions ecclésiastiques de la Chrétienté médiévale*, ed. Augustin Fliche and Victor Martin, Histoire de l'Église depuis les origines jusqu'à nos jours 12 (Paris: Bloud & Gay, 1959), 169.

3. Dominique Iogna-Prat, *Ordonner et exclure: Cluny et la société chrétienne face à l'hérésie, au judaïsme et à l'islam, 1000–1150* (Paris: Aubier Montaigne, 1998).

4. Georges Duby, *The Three Orders: Feudal Society Imagined*, trans. Arthur Goldhammer (Chicago: University of Chicago Press, 1980); Jacques Le Goff, *Time, Work, and Culture in the Middle Ages*, trans. Arthur Goldhammer (Chicago: University of Chicago Press, 1980).

5. Giraldus Cambrensis, *Opera omnia*, IV, ed. J. S. Brewer (London: Longman, 1861–1891).

6. Alexander III, *Sane de clericis*, ed. E. Friedberg, *Corpus iuris canonici*, II, c. 457.

7. *De rebus Alsaticis*, in MGH *Scriptores*, 17:232.

8. A. L. Bannister, "Visitation Returns in the Diocese of Hereford in 1397, Part III," *English Historical Review* 45 (1930): 93–94.

9. This has been effectively demonstrated for Tuscany in the cases studied by Daniel Bornstein, "Parish Pzriests in Late Medieval Cortona: The Urban and Rural Clergy," in *Preti nel Medioevo* (Verona: Cierre, 1997), 165–93.

10. Louis Binz, *Vie religieuse et réforme ecclésiastique dans le diocèse Genève (1378–1450)* (Geneva: Jullien, 1973), 366, 407.

11. M. C. Gasnault, "Le clergé dans les paroisses rurales du diocèse de Sens à la fin du Moyen Age," in *L'encadrement religieux des au Moyen Age et jusqu'au Concile de Trente: La paroisse, le clergé, la pastorale, la dévotion* (Paris: CTHS, 1984), 300ff.

12. This treatise has been published by Nicole Grévy-Pons, *Célibat et nature: Une controverse médiévale* (Paris: CNRS, 1975), 135–61.

13. Published in ibid., 165–92, and in E. Du Pin, *Johannis Gersonis opera omnia* (Antwerp, 1706), 2:617–34.

14. See Charles M. de la Roncière, "Dans les campagnes florentines au XIVe siècle: Les communautés chrétiennes et leurs curés," in *Histoire vécue du peuple chrétien*, ed. Jean Delumeau (Toulouse: Privat, 1979), 1:281–314.

15. V. Tabbagh, "Croyances et comportements du clergé paroissial en France du Nord à la fin du Moyen Age," in *Le clergé délinquant en France du XIIIe au XVIe siècle*, ed. Benoît Garnot (Dijon: EUD, 1995), 49–53; Pierrette Paravy, *De la chrétienté romaine à la Réforme en Dauphiné* (Rome: École Française de Rome, 1993), 1:129–33; 2:319–29.

16. Tabbagh, "Croyances et comportements," 57–58.

Chapter Seven. Hearing Women's Sins

1. *Decrees of the Ecumenical Councils*, ed. Norman P. Tanner, S.J. (Washington, D.C.: Georgetown University Press, 1990), 245.

2. Victor Massena, prince d'Essling, *Les livres à figures vénitiens de la fin du XVe et du début du XVIe siècle* (Florence: Olschki; Paris: H. Leclerc, 1907–1914): II/1, 181, num. 712.

3. John Myrc, *Instructions for Parish Priests*, ed. Edward Peacock, rev. F. J. Furnivall, Early English Texts Society 31 (New York: Greenwood, 1969 [1902]), 24, lines 773–76; 25, lines 788–94.

4. J. P. Migne, *Patrilogia Latina* 112:61.

5. Francis J. Fazzalaro, *The Place for the Hearing of Confession: A Historical Synopsis and a Commentary* (Washington, D.C.: Catholic University of America Press, 1950), ch. 1.

6. *Councils and Synods, with Other Documents Relating to the English Church*, ed. F. M. Powicke and C. R. Cheney (Oxford: Clarendon, 1964), II, Cap. XXV; Joannes Dominicus Mansi, *Sacrorum Conciliorum nova et amplissima collectio*, vol. 22, col. 1115.

7. *Le statuts synodaux français di XIIIe siècle*, ed. and trans. Odette Pontal, vol. 1, *Les statuts de Paris et le Synodal de l'Ouest* (Paris: Bibliothèque Nationale, 1971), 62; and vol. 2: *Le statuts de 1230 à 1260* (Paris: CTHS, 1983), 288, 290.

8. Cap. VIII, "De sacramento poenitentiae et confessionis, et eorum attinentiis," in Joannes Dominicus Mansi, *Sacrorum Conciliorum nova et amplissima collectio*, vol. 24, col. 453.

9. Burchard of Worms, *Decretorum liber decimus nonus. De poenitentia*, in PL 149, 949–1018, esp. ch. 58, 997CD (but see also chs. 75, 111, 140, 141, 149, 152, 155, and 156).

10. Robert of Flamborough, *Liber poenitentialis: A Critical Edition with Introduction and Notes*, ed. J. J. Francis Firth (Toronto: Pontifical Institute of Medieval Studies, 1971).

11. Thomas of Chobham, *Summa Confessorum*, ed. F. Broomfield (Louvain: Nauwelaerts, 1968), 296–97, 375–76.

12. Alain de Lille, *Liber poenitentialis*, ed. Jean Longère (Louvain: Nauwelaerts, 1965), 2:29, 34.

13. Beverly Mayne Kienzle, "The Prostitute Preacher: Patterns of Polemic against Medieval Waldensian Women Preachers," in *Women Preachers and Prophets through Two Millennia of Christianity*, ed. Beverly Mayne Kienzle and Pamela J. Walker (Berkeley: University of California Press, 1998), 99–113.

14. Raymond of Penyafort, *Summa on Marriage*, trans. Pierre J. Payer (Toronto: Pontifical Institute of Mediaeval Studies, 2005).

15. S. Raimundus de Pennaforte, *Summa de paenitentia*, ed. Xaverio Ochoa and Aloisio Diez (Rome: Commentarium pro religiosis, 1976), 830–31.

16. Francesco da Barberino, *Reggimento e costumi di donna*, ed. Giuseppe E. Sansone (Turin: Loescher, 1957).

17. Alfonso Martinez de Toledo, *Little Sermons on Sin*, trans. Lesley Byrd Simpson (Berkeley: University of California Press, 1959).

18. THEMA (Thesaurus Exemplorum Medii Aevi), Paris, Bibliothèque Nationale, ms. Lat. 16481, sermo 32.3 and sermo 202.2; http://www.ehess.fr/gahom/thema/index_en.php.

19. *Liber exemplorum ad usum praedicantium saeculo xiii compositus a quodam fratre minore anglico de provincia Hiberniae*, ed. Andrew George Little (Aberdeen: British Society of Franciscan Studies, 1908), 57, num. 100.

20. Frederic C. Tubach, *Index Exemplorum: A Handbook of Medieval Religious Tales* (Helsinki: Suomalainen Tiedeakatemia, 1969), num. 1192 (see also num. 1208).

21. Antonini archiepiscopi Florentini, *Summa theologica in quattuor partes distributa* (Verona: Tipografia del Seminario, 1740), 117 (part 3, tit. 1, cap. XXV).

22. Paolo da Faenza, *Confessione utile et breve per insegnare a disponersi et confessarsi* (Bologna: Giovanni Antonio Benedetti, ca. 1500) (IGI 7187; ISTC if00051600).

23. *Uno bello e utile interrogatorio in vulgare* (Milan: Ulderico Scinzenzeler, 1493) (IGI VI 5187-A; ISTC ic00822900).

24. Anne Jacobson Schutte, *Printed Italian Vernacular Religious Books* (Geneva: Droz, 1983), 141 (copy in the Vatican Library).

25. *Questo sie una breuissima introductione maxime de done che se voleno ben confessare compilata per frate Francisco da Mucianica* (Milan: Alessandro Pelizzoni, 1510) (CNCE 19744; copy in the Vatican Library).

26. Gábor Klaniczay, "The 'Bonfire of Vanities' and the Mendicants," in *Emotions and Material Culture* (Vienna: Verlag des Österreichischen Akademie der Wissenschaften, 2003), 31–57.

27. Emilio Pasquini, "Confessione e penitenza nella novellistica italiana tardo-medievale (secolo XIII–XV): Fra stilizzazione e parodia," in *Dalla penitenza all'ascolto delle confessioni: Il ruolo dei frati Mendicanti* (Spoleto: CISAM, 1996), 175–207.

28. Giovanni Boccacio, *The Decameron*, trans. Mark Musa and Peter Bondanella (New York: New American Library, 1982), 437 (day 7, story 5).

29. Masuccio Salernitano (Tommaso Guardati), *Il Novellino*, novella 3, *The Novellino of Masuccio*, trans. W. G. Waters (London, 1895), 50.

30. On this, see Roberto Cobianchi, "The Practice of Confession and Franciscan Observant Churches: New Architectural Arrangements in Early Renaissance Italy," *Zeitschrift für Kunstgeschichte* 69 (2006).

31. Anastasius van den Wyngaert, "Statuta provincialia Fr. Minorum Observantium Ianuae an. 1487–1521," *Archivum Franciscanum Historicum* 22 (1929): 127.

32. Michael Bihl, "Ordinazioni di capitoli generali degli Osservanti Cismontani (1490-1500) e di capitoli provinciali degli Osservanti veneti (1467–1513)," *Le Venezie Francescane* 32 (1965–1966): 22–23.

33. Geroldus Fussenegger, "Statuta Observantium Provinciae Bohemiae annis. 1471 et 1480 condita," *Archivum Franciscanum Historicum* 47 (1954): 378, 384.

34. Howard Burns, "Progetti di Francesco di Giorgio per i conventi di San Bernardino e Santa Chiara di Urbino," in *Studi Bramanteschi* (Rome: De Luca, 1974), 293–311.

35. *Atti della visita pastorale del vescovo Domenico Bollani alla diocesi di Brescia (1565–1567)*, ed. Paolo Guerrini (Brescia: Edizioni Brixia Sacra, 1915), 1:70.

36. Quoted in Wietse de Boer, "*Ad audiendi non videndi commoditatem*: Note sull'introduzione del confessionale soprattutto in Italia," *Quaderni storici* n.s., 77 (1991): 570, n. 64.

37. *Le costituzioni per il clero (1542) di Gian Matteo Giberti vescovo di Verona*, ed. Roberto Pasquali (Vicenza: Istituto per le ricerche di storia sociale e religiosa, 2000), 436, 438 (tit. VI, cap. XXII).

38. *Instructionum fabricae, et supellectilis ecclesiasticae libri II* (Milan: Pacifico da Ponte, 1577) (CNCE 24376). The text is also available in *Trattati d'arte del Cinquecento*, ed. Paola Barocchi (Bari: Laterza, 1962), 3:63–68.

39. *Rituale Romanum ex veteri ecclesiae vsu restitutum* (Rome: Domenico Basa, 1584) (CNCE 11992 and 11994).

40. *Rituale Romanum Pauli 5. Pont. Max. Iussu editum* (Rome: Stamperia Camerale, 1614).

41. *Instruttione de' sacerdoti* (Venice: Gabriele Giolito de' Ferrari, 1568), 88 (CNCE 13790).

42. Juan Ortega Uhink, *De delicto sollicitationis: Evolutio historica—Documenta—Commentarius* (Washington, D.C.: Catholic University of America Press, 1954), publishes the papal bull on 26–29.

43. Cited in Giovanni Romeo, *Esorcisti, confessori e sessualità femminile nell'Italia della Controriforma* (Florence: Le Lettere, 1998), 176.

Chapter Eight. Heresy and Dissent

1. Durand of Huesca, *Liber Antiheresis*, in *A History of Christianity: Readings in the History of the Church*, vol. 1, *The Early and Medieval Church*, ed. Ray C. Petry (Grand Rapids: Baker Book House, 1981), 352.

2. Walter Map, *De nugis curialium*, in *Heresies of the High Middle Ages: Selected Sources*, trans. Walter L. Wakefield and Arthur P. Evans (New York: Columbia University Press, 1969), 204.

3. Frances Andrews, *The Early Humiliati* (Cambridge: Cambridge University Press, 1999), 39.

4. Translation of *Incumbit nobis* based in part on ibid., 105.

5. *The Chronicle of Salimbene de Adam*, trans. Joseph L. Baird with Giuseppe Baglivi and John Robert Kane (Binghamton, N.Y.: Medieval and Renaissance Texts and Studies, 1986), 249–93. The quotations from Salimbene come from this translation, with some modifications.

Chapter Nine. Jews, Muslims, and Christians

1. Yiktzhak Baer, *A History of the Jews in Christian Spain*, trans. Louis Schoffman (Philadelphia: Jewish Publication Society of America, 1961–1966), I, 24.

2. See Angel Barrios García, ed. *Documentación medieval de la catedral de Avila* (Salamanca: Universidad de Salamanca, 1981), documents 170, 171, and 180, pp. 164–69, 178–79.

3. Teofilo F. Ruiz, *Crisis and Continuity. Land and Town in Late Medieval Castile* (Philadelphia: University of Pennsylvania Press, 1994), 281.

4. David Nirenberg, *Communities of Violence: Persecution of Minorities in the Middle Ages* (Princeton: Princeton University Press, 1996), 127–65.

5. *Las Siete Partidas*, trans. Samuel Parsons Scott, ed. Robert I. Burns (Philadelphia: University of Pennsylvania Press, 2001), 5:1433–34.

6. *Crónica de Juan II*, ed. C. Rosell (Madrid: Biblioteca de autores españoles, 1953), vol. 68, 565.

7. John Edwards, "Reply to 'Religious Faith, Doubt, and Atheism,'" *Past and Present* 128 (1990): 155–61. This is part of a discussion initiated by John Edwards' most suggestive article, "Religious Faith and Doubt in Late Medieval Spain: Soria circa 1450–1500," *Past and Present*, 120 (1988): 3–25.

Chapter Ten. Domestic Religion

1. 1. See Margaret Deanesly, *The Lollard Bible and Other Medieval Biblical Versions* (Cambridge: Cambridge University Press, 1920), 45.

2. Lambert of Ardres, *The History of the Counts of Guines and Lords of Ardres,* trans. and intro. Leah Shopkow (Philadelphia: University of Pennsylvania Press, 2001), ch. 127 at 160–61.

3. Dhuoda, *Handbook for William: A Carolingian Woman's Counsel for Her Son,* trans. and intro. Carol Neel (Lincoln: University of Nebraska Press, 1991), 18–20, 44.

4. Eileen Power, trans., *The Goodman of Paris (Le Ménagier de Paris)* (London: Folio Society, 1992), 38.

5. Ibid., 63.

6. William Caxton, *The Book of the Knight of the Tower,* ed. M. Y. Offord, Supplementary Series 2 (Oxford: Early English Text Society, 1971), 14, 16–17 (language modernized).

7. Ibid., 19–20.

8. Christine de Pisan, *The Treasure of the City of Ladies,* trans. and intro. Sarah Lawson (Harmondsworth, U.K.: Penguin, 1985), pt. 3, ch. 5 at 161; ch. 9 at 168.

9. Ibid., pt. 3, ch. 12 at 176-77.

10. Ibid., pt. 1, ch. 14 at 68.

11. Iris Origo, *The Merchant of Prato* (Harmondsworth, U.K.: Penguin, 1963), 276–78.

12. See Diana Webb, *Saints and Cities in Medieval Italy* (Manchester: Manchester University Press, 2007), 174.

13. Ancrene Wisse translation in *Anchoritic Spirituality: Ancrene Wisse and Associated Works,* trans. and intro. Anne Savage and Nicholas Watson (Mahwah, N.J.: Paulist, 1991), 53.

14. See the translation of Umiliana's *Vita* in Webb, *Saints and Cities,* 97–140.

15. Benvenuta's *Vita* is in *Acta Sanctorum,* Octobris 13, at 152–53. See Diana Webb, *Privacy and Solitude in the Middle Ages* (London: Hambledon, 2007), 122–23.

16. Ambrogio's *Vita* is in *Acta Sanctorum,* Martii 3, at 183; cf. Webb, *Privacy and Solitude,* 126.

17. See Blessed Raymond of Capua, *The Life of St. Catherine of Siena,* trans. George Lamb (London: Harvill, 1960), 42–51.

18. Morelli's ritual is described with extensive quotation by R. C. Trexler in *Public Life in Renaissance Florence* (Ithaca, N.Y.: Cornell University Press, 1980), 176–85.

19. See ibid., 377; cf. Christiane Klapisch-Züber, *Women, Family and Ritual in Renaissance Italy* (Chicago: University of Chicago Press, 1985), 114–15, 310–29.

20. See *Councils and Synods with other Documents relating to the English Church, II, A.D. 1205–1313,* ed. F. M. Powicke and C. R. Cheney, 2 vols. (Oxford: Clarendon, 1964), 2:766, 1003.

21. See Rosalind Hill, ed., *The Rolls and Registers of Bishop Oliver Sutton, 1280–1299* (Lincoln Record Society 48, 1954), 3:l–liii.; cf. Diana Webb, "Domestic Space and Devotion in the Middle Ages," in *Defining the Holy: Sacred Space in Medieval and Early Modern Europe,* ed. Andrew Spicer and Sarah Hamilton (Aldershot, U.K.: Ashgate, 2005), 38–40, for a more extensive discussion.

22. Webb, "Domestic Space," 37.

23. Dale Kent, *Cosimo de' Medici and the Florentine Renaissance* (New Haven: Yale University Press, 2000), 306.

24. See *Wills and Inventories from the Registers of the Commissary of Bury St. Edmunds and the Archdeacon of Sudbury*, ed. Samuel Tymms, Camden First Series 49, 1850. John Baret's will in its entirety occupies 15–44.

25. Agnes Paston, *The Paston Letters*, ed. J. Gairdner, 6 vols. (London: Chatto & Windus, 1904) 2:286.

Chapter Eleven. Parish Life

1. Marion Gibbs and Jane Lang, *Bishops and Reform 1215–1272, with Special Reference to the Lateran Council of 1215*, Oxford Historical Series (Oxford: Oxford University Press, 1932).

2. John Mirk, *Mirk's Festial: A Collection of Homilies*, ed. Theodor Erbe, Early English Text Society, extra series, 96 (1905), 278. All translations are my own.

3. *Dives et Pauper*, ed. Priscilla Heath Barnum, Early English Text Society, original series, 275 (1976), 1:196.

4. "Statutes of Exeter II," in *Councils and Synods II*, part 2, ed. F. M. Powicke and C. R. Cheney (Oxford: Oxford University Press, 1964), 1008, no. 12.

5. Herbert Edward Reynolds, *Wells Cathedral: Its Foundation, Constitutional History and Statutes* (Wells, 1882), 126.

6. Public Record Office C1 520/33.

7. Charles Drew, *Early Parochial Organisation in England: The Origin of the Office of Churchwarden*, St. Anthony's Hall Publications 7 (York: Borthwick Institute of Historical Research, 1954), 6.

8. David Gary Shaw, *Creation of a Community: The City of Wells in the Middle Ages*, Oxford Historical Monographs (Oxford: Clarendon, 1993), 166.

9. Devon Record Office, PW1, ff. 1v., 3, 9, 15; PW2 f. 82.

10. Toulmin Smith, *The Parish* (London: H. Sweet, 1857).

11. Clive Burgess, "Shaping the Parish: St. Mary at Hill, London, in the Fifteenth Century," in *The Cloister and the World: Essays in Medieval History in Honour of Barbara Harvey*, ed. John Blair and Brian Golding (Oxford: Oxford University Press, 1996), 261.

12. Somerset Record Office, DD/CT 77, folders 20, 56.

13. Westminster City Archives, E1 and E2.

14. *The Church Book of St. Ewen's, Bristol: 1454–1485*, ed. Betty Masters and Elizabeth Ralph, Bristol and Gloucestershire Archaeological Society 6 (1967), 74–75.

15. J. C. Cox and W. H. St. John Hope, *Chronicle of the Collegiate Church of All Saints, Derby* (London, 1881), 49.

16. Katherine L. French, "To Free Them from Binding: Women in the Late Medieval English Parish," *Journal of Interdisciplinary History* 27 (1997): 387–412.

17. *The Rhymes of Robyn Hood: An Introduction to the English Outlaw*, ed. R. B. Dobson and J. Taylor (Gloucester: Sutton, 1989), 37.

18. "Church-Wardens' Accounts of Croscombe," in *Church-Wardens' Accounts for Croscombe, Pilton, Yatton, Tintinhull, Morebath and St. Michael's Bath: Ranging from*

1349–1560, ed. Edmund Hobhouse, Somerset Record Society, vol. 4. (1890), 9, 24, 28, 29, et passim.

19. Somerset Record Office D/P/yat 4/1/1, folders 104, 108, 116, et passim.

20. Colin Richmond, "Halesworth Church, Suffolk, and Its Fifteenth-Century Benefactors," in *Recognitions: Essays Presented to Edmund Fryde*, ed. Colin Richmond and Isobel Harvey (Aberystwyth: National Library of Wales, 1996), 259–60; Audrey Douglas, "Salisbury Women and the Pre-Elizabethan Parish," in *Women, Marriage, and Family in Medieval Christendom: Essays in Memory of Michael M. Sheehan*, ed. Constance M. Rousseau and Joel T. Rosenthal, Studies in Medieval Culture 37 (Kalamazoo, Mich.: Medieval Institute Publications, 1998), 101–2; Kathleen Kamerick, *Popular Piety and Art in the Late Middle Ages: Worship and Idolatry in England, 1350–1500*, The New Middle Ages (New York: Palgrave, 2002), 87–91.

21. *Lincoln Wills*, ed. C. W. Foster, Lincoln Record Society 5 (1914): 1:5–7.

22. *Lincoln Wills*, 1:109; *Ancient Deeds Belonging to the Corporation of Bath*, ed. C. W. Shickle (Bath: Bath Record Society, 1921), 90.

23. *Dives and Pauper*, 1:189–90. See Exod. 30:11-16; Mark 12:41-44.

24. Eamon Duffy, "The Parish, Piety, and Patronage in Late Medieval East Anglia: The Evidence of Rood Screens," in *The Parish in English Life: 1400–1600*, ed. Katherine L. French, Gary G. Gibbs, and Beat A. Kümin (Manchester, U.K.: Manchester University Press, 1997), 136.

25. Eamon Duffy, "Holy Maydens, Holy Wyfes: The Cult of Women Saints in Fifteenth- and Sixteenth-Century England," *Studies in Church History* 27 (1990): 175–96; W. W. Williamson, "Saints on Norfolk Rood-Screens and Pulpits," *Norfolk Archaeology* 31, part 3 (1956): 335–36.

26. Somerset Record Office D/P/yat 4/1/1, folder 11. Francis Bond, *Screens and Galleries in the English Church* (London: Henry Froude, 1908), 34.

27. Margaret Aston, "Segregation in Church," *Studies in Church History* 27 (1990): 238–42; Roberta Gilchrist, *Gender and Material Culture: The Archaeology of Religious Women* (London: Routledge, 1994), 133–35.

28. Winifred M. Bowman, "Order of Seating in Asheton Kirk," in *England in Ashton-under-Lyne* (Cheshire: John Sherratt & Sons, 1960), 167–68; Aston, "Segregation in Church," 266.

29. Charles Kerry, *A History of the Municipal Church of St. Lawrence, Reading* (Reading, 1883), 77.

30. British Library Add. Ms. 40729.

31. J. Charles Cox, *Bench-Ends in English Parish Churches* (Oxford: Oxford University Press, 1916), 21.

32. Kerry, *Municipal Church of St. Lawrence*, 77–78.

33. "How the Good Wife Taught Her Daughter," in *The Babees' Book*, ed. F. J. Furnivall, Early English Text Society, original series, 32 (London: N. Trübner, 1868), 37.

34. Cox, *Bench-Ends*, 17.

Chapter Twelve. The Burdens of Purgatory

1. J. D. Mansi, ed., *Sacrorum conciliorum nova et amplissima collectio*, vol. 24 (Graz: Akademische Druck, 1961 [1903]), 70–71.

2. A. N. Galpern, "The Legacy of Late Medieval Religion in Sixteenth-Century Champagne," in *The Pursuit of Holiness in Late Medieval and Renaissance Religion: Papers from the University of Michigan Conference*, ed. C. Trinkaus and H. A. Oberman, Studies in Medieval and Renaissance Thought 10 (Leiden: Brill, 1974), 149. Use of this description is now almost a commonplace.

3. Edmund Dudley, *The Tree of Commonwealth: A Treatise*, ed. D. M. Brodie (Cambridge: Cambridge University Press, 1948), 63.

4. John R. H. Moorman, *The Grey Friars in Cambridge, 1225–1538*, Birkbeck Lectures 1948–49 (Cambridge: Cambridge University Press, 1952), 251.

INDEX